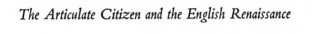

The Articulate Citizen and the English Renaissance

THE ARTICULATE CITIZEN AND THE ENGLISH RENAISSANCE ᔕ ARTHUR B. FERGUSON

ᔕ   ᔕ

ᔕ

DUKE UNIVERSITY PRESS

DURHAM, N. C. 1965

© 1965, Duke University Press

Library of Congress Catalogue Card number 65-19447

Printed in the United States of America by the Seeman Printery, Durham, N. C.

To JANE

ACKNOWLEDGMENTS

When one has worked on a project over a considerable period of time one becomes, in a sense, indebted to that whole segment of the academic world in which one moves. Even if I tried, I could not do justice to everyone who has contributed to the growth of this book, so I shall not attempt to thank individually those many of my colleagues and of the scholarly world beyond Duke University whose minds I have picked and whose ideas I have, consciously or otherwise, absorbed. I have, however, incurred a few obligations of a special sort which require special acknowledgment. I am most indebted to Hans Baron for reading and rereading the manuscript and offering, from the vantage point of roughly parallel interests and vastly more mature scholarship, criticisms and suggestions of the utmost value. I am, as always, in the debt of my brother, Wallace K. Ferguson, whose comprehensive view of the Renaissance has, more often than I perhaps realize, made it possible for me to see my own more limited specialty in perspective, and who, in addition, read my manuscript with critical care. I must, however, take full credit for whatever errors and eccentricities remain. My thanks also go to Dr. Mary Dewar for permitting me to use her work on Sir Thomas Smith while still in proof, to John R. Yost for many miscellaneous, but greatly appreciated scholarly services, and to Linda Yost for preparing the index. Research and writing were facilitated by generous grants from the Duke University Research Council, and the staff of the Duke Press has labored with commendable patience and forbearance over a sometime recalcitrant manuscript. Finally I must thank the editors of *Studies in the Renaissance*, *The Journal of the History of Ideas*, and *The Journal of British Studies* for permission to reproduce substantial portions from articles of mine which have appeared in their publications.

TABLE OF CONTENTS

INTRODUCTION

With remarkable unanimity those citizens of early Tudor England who undertook to comment upon the condition of their society did so in the name of the "very and true commonweal of this realm." In pursuit of the commonwealth ideal, still so redolent of medieval thought, they anatomized the political body (the corporate analogy came as readily to their minds as to their predecessors'), sought out the causes of its ailments, and prescribed remedies. Their endeavors raised few new questions of theory. Their purposes were very practical, and for practical purposes the forms of an inherited culture could for the most part be made to suffice. But in the process of their zealous investiga- tions of cause and of their optimistic application of mind to the dis- cussion of policy, they adopted new attitudes toward the problems of government and citizenship and achieved insights, at times startlingly original, into the workings of what a few of them were coming to recognize as the mechanism of social forces. By the middle of the Tudor century, they may be said to have prepared the way for, in a sense to have actually inaugurated for Englishmen, the modern era of public discussion and to have adumbrated many of the more charac- teristic attitudes of the modern citizen toward the society in which he lives. In other ways, too, they make it possible to trace the growth of a climate congenial to modern thought. Many of them were able to observe the revolutionary changes of their time from the vantage point of the new, historically oriented learning of humanism as well as from the less detached position of the policy-maker. And so their obser- vations possess at times a depth of focus, a quality of perspective, a sense of the relativity of social problems to the conditions of time and place, which is one of the most characteristic achievements of Renais- sance culture.

There are difficulties, however, in dealing with these writers and with this period. They are the difficulties inherent in any attempt to interpret an age of more than ordinarily marked transition, where changes in the circumstances of life have outrun the conceptual apparatus for dealing with them. As one moves from those writings of late medieval England, loosely designated as political, to those of the early Tudor publicists and commentators, one has the distinct feeling of passing from one era to another. But it is not always possible to chart one's progress by means of the usually recognizable landmarks of intellectual history. What A. O. Lovejoy called the "unit ideas" seem in many instances the same. We must look, then, for shifting patterns of emphasis and for implicit assumptions, and for the new attitudes and fresh approaches which those assumptions have made possible.

Failure to pay sufficient attention to these processes taking place just below the literal surface has in fact resulted in a tendency to underestimate the writings of the early Tudor period, especially those of the humanists, and to misinterpret their place in the history of thought. Without some more or less systematic way of looking not only at the lines but between and beneath them, the historian is likely to find these materials baffling rather than illuminating. The picture initially evoked by much of the "commonwealth" literature is confused and contradictory. The spectacle of the new growing within the old, of constructive thought employed in the cause of a static social order, of a mounting awareness of change achieved in the course of an apparently deliberate reaction against it, may seem at first little more than an annoying paradox, hardly worth the effort to explain. Paradox it is, but it is very much worth explaining, for it lies close to the heart of English Renaissance culture. And not the least paradoxical thing about it is that it contains within itself the key to its own explanation. Much, however, depends on the nature of the questions asked.

But before we formulate our questions, let us determine more exactly what the sources are from which answers of any value may be expected, where, that is, we may find reflected the mind of the articulate citizen. It will, I believe, be found, not in any particular category of subject or form (to seek there the criteria of change has as often been the cause of distortion as of understanding), but wherever the citizen, as citizen, becomes articulate, wherever he registers his "griefs," seeks out their causes, and hopefully prescribes some remedy. Taken as a whole, materials of this sort may be described broadly as the literature of public discussion, or, more specifically, as that of diagnosis and prescription. In its most sophisticated form it becomes the literature of social analysis and constructive policy. It has been selected not for the light it casts upon the events and conditions discussed, but rather for what it tells about the character of the discussion, for whatever key it may provide to the thought of its authors. By the same token, it does not include political propaganda, as such, though many items may well have served such purposes.

I have tried to approach this literature from a more or less consistent point of view. I have asked the authors first of all what they believed to be wrong with the English commonweal (note that the emphasis is on what they *believed*, not on what may have been the fact, objectively considered), then what they considered to be the cause of the ills they have discovered in the body politic, and finally what they feel can be done by way of remedy. On the basis of these rather elementary questions, it becomes possible to seek the answer to questions of a more indirect nature and possibly of more far-reaching significance. How, for example, should a commonwealth be ordered? What is the nature of the social organism? What place has the articulate citizen himself in the business of government? What are the qualifications for the effective discharge of such responsibility? What are the possibilities and limitations inherent in the process of social analysis, especially the analysis of causal forces? To what extent is it possible, by the application of mind to policy, to shape a people's environment? These questions cannot, of course, be applied uniformly, nor are the answers uniformly enlightening. But the materials used have been chosen for their ability to return some sort of answer to at least some of them.

I have concentrated largely on the early Tudor period, because I consider it the era of critical importance in the transition from medieval public thought to modern. It was a time of unusually rapid and disturbing change in the circumstances of English life. A revolution in the relations of church and state and in the religious life of the country went along with, and was closely related to, equally revolutionary changes in economic and social life. It was therefore a period more than ordinarily likely to evoke public discussion. More than that, it was a period in which discussion was encouraged as never before. In the thirties and again during the middle years of the sixteenth century, the atmosphere of public life and the conditions of authorship and publication were such as to be unusually conducive to thoughtful discussion. By the end of Edward VI's reign, the first great era in the history of English public discussion had come to an end, but its work had been done, its lasting contribution made.

When, after the Marian hiatus and the troubled early years of Elizabeth, discussion again quickened its pace, it followed pretty much the lines foreshadowed by the pamphleteers of the mid-century. What had been uncommon and, to the historian, extremely noteworthy in the earlier period now becomes too ordinary a part of English public life to warrant study on a comparable scale. The great era of the pamphlet —to which, incidentally, England contributed more than her share— had arrived.

There is one more problem. In order to see the work of the early Tudor commentators in the perspective of time (the problem of transition remains stubbornly in the center of Renaissance historiog- raphy) it is necessary to view them in relation to what went before as well as what came after. This has too often been neglected in favor of a treatment conducted more strictly within the context of the day. In- deed, if we are to consider the Renaissance in England as a period of transition and not merely as a particular cultural configuration, certain aspects of fifteenth-century life and thought must be considered an in- tegral part of its history. I have accordingly devoted a number of chap- ters to what, in deference to customary terminology as well as to certain inescapable facts, is called the medieval background. In this first section I have selected those items from the writings of the fourteenth and fif- fifteenth centuries that help establish characteristics more or less typical of medieval thought and also those in which new problems may be seen eliciting new approaches.

If, then, we examine the early Tudor literature of analysis and prescription, not only in itself and in relation to its own day, but also in relation to analogous expression in the preceding century and a half, certain tendencies become apparent. Most noticeable, and no doubt most important, is what may be called a trend toward reality. It is a tendency not always clearly marked nor consistent in its mani- festations: old habits died hard; the theocentric character of Protestant thought if anything reinforced the penchant of medieval critics to treat society *sub specie aeternitatis* and in relation to the ultimate considerations of man's moral nature and the will of God. But it is pervasive none- theless. It is composed in part of an increasing willingness to see in the concrete and tangible an area of experience susceptible of analysis in terms of its own observable characteristics, without necessary reference to the transcendental factors inherent in the Divine Plan. In part also it is a tendency to recognize in the analysis of fact such stuff as laws are made on, or at least policy. It does not, of course, imply any denial of the basic values of the Christian tradition, nor does it raise embarrassing questions concerning final causes and the purpose of God; the policy toward which it moves is always thought to suffer from the fragility of all temporal designs and from the vanity of human wishes. But as we move into the early Renaissance, especially as the influence of the humanistic learning is brought to bear on the practical issues of public life, we can see the ceiling of moral and theological absolutes perceptibly lifting and the area of temporal visibility gradu-ally broadening.

From this increasing willingness to analyze and to search for constructive policy, certain implications arise. Discussion of this sort implies a growing confidence in the ability of man to apply his intelligence effectively to the problems posed by his changing environ-ment. It implies a sense of duty on the part of the man of learning, experience, and virtue, the man of wisdom in the Renaissance meaning, to contribute to the flow of counsel upon which he believed good government to depend. It implies a progressive ability to distinguish between the public and private spheres, to accept as a fact that society is more than an aggregate of moral entities whose collective problems are governed by the same ethical considerations as are those of its in-dividual components. It implies that there are secondary causal factors situated this side of Providence and the moral nature of man, well within reach of the inventive mind. Seen from this point of view, government becomes more than the simple maintainer of peace and justice, the defender of the community, the establisher of rights and the righter of wrongs. It becomes a potentially constructive agency through whose offices the intelligence of citizens as well as of specially designated advisers may be applied to the practical problems of the national community.

Such a view of government and society depends, in turn, on an understanding of the nature of change itself, an understanding con-siderably more profound than was common in medieval discussion: for the change was not merely from health to disease within the political body or vice versa, but also more or less purposeful, depending in part at least on the application of mind to policy. This growing sense of change found expression in, and was also the product of, that willingness already mentioned—to catechize experience and to analyze the causal forces in society.   And for a few perceptive minds it made possible a new perspective, one in which the relativity of customs, institutions, and positive laws became, virtually for the first time, clearly apparent.   This awareness of the uniqueness of time and place went hand in hand with an ability, equally characteristic of the Renaissance temper, to separate the eternal and absolute from the contingent and changing, to distinguish those things that constitute the unalterable, "natural" circumstances of human life from those that are subject to adjustment by human effort.

Englishmen achieved this new perspective rather late, a fact which helps explain why the systematic attention given by scholars to parallel but earlier developments in Renaissance Italy has not hitherto been extended to the English scene.   But, characteristically, they gave ex/ pression to it in their own way—which suggests that their thought needs systematic attention.   For example, whereas fifteenth/ and six/ teenth/century England produced nothing like the secular, causal analysis of the political world that stemmed from Italy, a very similar attitude of mind gave direction to the discussion by English humanists of social and economic problems.   Although the insularity still very much a part of the Renaissance Englishman's make/up was by no means impermeable, although in fact he shared in all the cultural movements of his day, he was primarily concerned with the problems of his island kingdom, and, to the extent that England's problems differed from those of her Continental neighbors, her articulate citizens were bound to react to them in their own peculiar way.

The plan of the book is dictated both by chronological and ana/ lytical considerations.   After a general survey of the late medieval literature of comment and criticism, calculated to serve as a sort of road map to guide the reader through a sometimes dangerously ill/marked territory, the following chapters begin with a study of social criticism characteristic of the later Middle Ages.   The remainder of Part I is devoted to the emergence of a more realistic attitude toward society, government, and citizenship as seen in discussions of the problem of counsel, of economic life, and of government itself.   Part II, covering the early Tudor period, follows a more or less analytical pattern.   It deals successively with the general conditions of the new age which helped shape the character of public discussion, with the particular point of view of the humanists toward articulate citizenship, with the growth of an ability to analyze the causal forces in society and with the concomitant growth of a willingness not only to debate matters of public policy but to treat them in constructive terms.   In these chapters, however, the contribution of Tudor humanism, a theme of central importance in this part of the work, is considered in three fairly well-marked phases, corresponding to the work of More, Starkey, and Smith.   The humanist pamphlets, together with those of such non-humanist commentators as Armstrong and with the social comment of the English reformers, are of necessity also related to the events and issues which, especially in the 1530's and the 1540's, were changing English life in all its aspects.   The resulting sense of change, itself a dominant theme of the chapters preceding and one of the most fundamental characteristics of Renaissance thought, is in the last chapter related to the Tudor Englishman's favorite concept of the "very and true commonweal."

In the interests of the reader, and in view of the fact that this study is not primarily philological in purposes, I have modernized the spelling of quotations wherever it was possible to do so without destroying a word or warping the meaning.

PART ONE. THE MEDIEVAL BACKGROUND

CHAPTER I. THE LITERATURE OF COMMENT AND COUNSEL

THE MEDIEVAL BACKGROUND, AGAINST WHICH IN THE interests of historical perspective the early Tudor commentators must be placed, is in itself curiously lacking in perspective. It is dominated by a few outstanding figures, whose size and importance seem to have little relation to the distance actually separating them from each other and from the eye of the observer. The effect of a Gothic painting is heightened by the paucity of incidental detail which at times renders the intervening spaces insubstantial and arbitrary. But there is a difference. What makes the work of the medieval artist all the more meaningful makes the historical landscape merely obscure and confusing. Yet here as elsewhere in the intellectual history of late medieval England the scholar must make what use he can of the landmarks that exist. And so it is to these that the succeeding chapters will be devoted. Rather than attempt to survey the whole of the literature of late medieval comment and criticism in uniform detail I shall subject only what I believe to be for the purposes of this study the few really significant documents to anything like a thorough analysis. The reader would, I am sure, appreciate it nonetheless if these works were placed to some extent in context, if, in particular, they might be set against a background of contemporary conditions and events and within the flow of written comment of which they are simply the more outstanding examples. This I shall try to do in the present chapter.

Certain aspects of the medieval scene are especially relevant. Basic of course, was the degree to which the articulate English citizen was able to achieve national consciousness. Modern public discussion was born and nourished within the confines of the national state: the increasing capacity for realistic analysis that marks the Renaissance pamphleteer was gained through the contemplation of problems affecting the national community; the concomitant willingness to entertain practical solutions presupposed at least a centralized government. A prerequisite, then, for the discussion that will permit useful comparison with that of Renaissance England was a feeling for the interests of the national community, a feeling that found expression in an ability to recognize the specifically English character of public grievances and to see in the king's government the only secular means through which remedy could be sought.   By the sixteenth century this degree of national consciousness had largely been achieved and can therefore in most instances be taken for granted.   Such is not to the same extent true with the writings of the late medieval period. Signs of any tendency to discuss popular grievances in relation to specifically English government are consequently worth noticing.

National consciousness helped to redeem much of the late medieval political literature from the stereotype of a universal and increasingly decadent culture, but it did not by itself insure analytical or constructive criticism.   That emerged much more slowly.   It had to rise above the inveterate habit of generalized complaint, a tradition strongly in' fluenced by the pulpit, moral in its roots, universal rather than par' ticular in its scope, and negative rather than constructive in its emphasis. It had also to rise above pure propaganda, a genre already pretty well developed by the fourteenth century.   The point at which the litera' ture of conscious citizenship can be separated from generalized com' plaint on the one hand and the particular concerns of propaganda on the other is by no means easy to determine.   In the long run the literature of analysis and policy becomes clearly enough marked to constitute in itself a category.   But in the later Middle Ages, writings can seldom be so easily classified.   In this respect also it should prove enlightening to see to what extent isolated characteristics of Renaissance public con' sciousness can be seen emerging, and as a result of what factors.

∽ ∽ ∽

In a sense the first important period in the history of English public discussion was that which fell between the Treaty of Bretigny (1360) and the resumption of the war with France by Henry V (1415). Earlier periods had witnessed brisk outbursts of political or ecclesias' tical propaganda.   The thirteenth'century Barons' War is a case in point.   And it is very difficult to generalize about what actually took place on the basis of writings that happen to have been preserved. Much of the comment written during the Middle Ages has obviously been lost.   Unless it bore the stamp of official approval, either that of a political power or of the church, or unless it was very popular in its appeal, it was not likely to survive.   But it seems not until the period of disillusionment and turmoil following the Black Death and the earlier stages of the Hundred Years' War that a significantly large body of more or less critical comment made its appearance.

Conditions and events had conspired to make that a period of more than ordinarily widespread and thoughtful discussion. By then especially, it is possible to recognize a rather well developed national consciousness, a sense of common interest stirring within the framework of a central English government.   By then there could have been no doubt in the mind of the politically alert Englishman but that in the royal court and its related institutions lay the mainspring of government.   Men of substance in shire and town were already familiar, through personal participation, with the machinery of the king's justice and with the ways in which the king's clerks, trained and articulate, took his business directly into the local districts and gave both practical and verbal expression to the relation of king and subject.[1]   By that time, too, Parliament was in the process of becoming the institutional embodiment of the national unity.[2]   More the creature of "monarchical empiricism" than of constitutional principle,[3] it nevertheless constituted an essential bridge between the local community and the national.   If the knight sent to Parliament as a representative of his shire could carry with him, however reluctantly, the interests of the people back home, he could also, and did, carry back some idea of common policy, or more frequently some version of the national interest implanted in his mind by the king and his councilors for home consumption.[4]   Even the idealism of chivalry, which the governing class of medieval Europe accepted as its secular scheme of values, tended in England to be expressed more than ordinarily in a national context.   Edward III was especially successful in focusing the symbolical expression of chivalric idealism on the royal court and

1. G. P. Cuttino, "King's Clerks and the Community of the Realm," *Medieval Representation in Theory and Practice, Speculum*, XXIX, No. 2, Part 2 (April, 1954), 395-409.

2. Helen Cam, "The Legislators of Medieval England," *PBA*, XXXI (1945), 127-150.

3. J. E. A. Joliffe, *The Constitutional History of Medieval England* (London, 1937), p. 331.

4. H. G. Richardson, "The Commons in Medieval Politics," *TRHS*, 4th Series, XXVIII (1946), 21-45.

allowing the knight-errantry of his aristocratic subjects to find political outlet in a war at once dynastic and national.[5]

Other factors were working in the same direction. The peculiar uniformity of economic interests, which in England gathered about the wool trade, tended to bind town and country together in common endeavor and accustomed both landlords and merchants to seek the protection of a central government, itself fiscally dependent on the staple trade. A "wool consciousness," as Eileen Power called it,[6] thus sharpened the sense of community in English affairs and at the same time emphasized the need for common action in external relationships. Foreign competition constituted in itself a powerful stimulus to national consciousness. Distrust of foreign influences at court, antipapal sentiments, and jealousy of merchants and craftsmen did perhaps more than common endeavor to clarify national feelings. When foreign frictions blazed into actual war, popular patriotism lent a deceptively brilliant color to a still imperfect sense of national interests.[7] And, with the opening of the Hundred Years' War, military service became, as never before, clearly the king's service, service by indenture having largely replaced the feudal levy as a means of raising armies.[8]

In the growth of national feeling, the increasing use of the English language obviously played a part. Englishmen could not have felt so keenly the community of interests that held them together during the fourteenth century had it not been increasingly possible for them to communicate in a common tongue. Certainly a general acceptance of the national language was a prerequisite for public discussion in any modern sense. And the fact is that the rising national consciousness

5. The author has undertaken to explore this subject to some extent in *The Indian Summer of English Chivalry* (Durham, N. C., 1960), especially chap. v.

6. Eileen Power, *The Wool Trade in English Medieval History* (Oxford, 1941), p. 18.

7. See, for example, Thomas Wright (ed.), *The Political Songs of England from the Reign of John to that of Edward III*, Camden Society (1839), pp. 19-27, 160-179, 262-263, 212-224; Isabel S. T. Aspin (ed.), *Anglo-Norman Political Songs*, Anglo-Norman Texts Society, XI (Oxford, 1953), 51-53; Thomas Wright (ed.), *Political Poems and Songs Relating to English History . . . from the Accession of Edward III to that of Richard III*, Rolls Series (1861), I, 26-40, 58-94. Some of this material has been reprinted with illuminating annotation by Rossell Hope Robbins in *Historical Poems of the XIVth and XVth Centuries* (New York, 1959); see pp. 30-39 and appropriate notes. Patriotic sentiment was echoed in the pulpit to some extent; G. R. Owst, *Literature and Pulpit in Medieval England* (Cambridge, 1923), pp. 131-132, 216, 225.

8. Barnaby C. Keeney, "Military Service and the Development of Nationalism in England, 1271-1327," *Speculum*, XXII (Oct., 1947), 534-549.

ran parallel to the ever more general use of English from the days when Henry III issued proclamations in English as well as in French to the time when Henry V may be said to have abandoned the use of French for all official purposes. But the increasing use of English was an evidence of national feeling more than a cause, and even then its importance must not be exaggerated. Latin continued to be the language of the "intellectuals," and French, though to a decreasing extent, the language of polite interchange between members of the aristocracy.[9] Yet both groups shared the prevailing sense of Englishry. That very generation which witnessed Chaucer's decisive handling of English as a literary language looked with equal respect on John Gower's ponderous outpourings, set forth as readily in French and Latin as in English. Yet Gower's sense of nationality cannot be denied. His *"O gentle Angleterre, à toi J'écris"* would have sounded no more sincere to his contemporaries if it had been said in English. It is, however, instructive to watch him move through his long and terribly productive career ever closer to the national language. When he died in 1408, England was on the threshold of an era when public discussion would be carried on predominantly in English.

Whatever its roots, national consciousness was by the last half of the fourteenth century deeply ingrained in English thought. It was as yet immature. It must not be confused with the "nationalism" of modern experience. It involved no absolute loyalty to the national state to the exclusion of all other loyalties. Englishmen were also subjects of the popes and loyal, if not always to them, at least to the ideal of a united Christendom. Though to a rapidly decreasing extent, they were also conscious of their membership in and loyalty to their social group. The values of chivalry remained essentially non-national and could be expressed only partially in national terms. And in the mid-fifteenth century personal loyalties, never entirely superseded, undoubtedly reasserted themselves within that "bastard feudalism"[10] which, given the opportunity provided by a chronically weak executive, tended to dissolve the bonds of national life. G. R. Elton

9. V. H. Galbraith cautions against tying nationalism to the use of English in "Nationalism and Language in Medieval England," *TRHS*, 4th Series, XXIII (1941), 113-129. See also Helen Suggett, "The Use of French in England in the Later Middle Ages," *ibid.*, XXVIII (1946), 61-83.

10. K. B. McFarlane, "Bastard Feudalism," *Bulletin of the Institute of Historical Research*, XX (May and Nov., 1945), 161-180.

would also have us believe that, in its structure, English govern/ ment in the late medieval period should be called "royal" rather than "national."[11]

Such subtle distinctions should not, however, be allowed to obscure the fact that the late medieval English citizen was ready to think of public problems in national terms, if only in the sense that he had come to recognize in the government of the English king the only agency from which redress of grievances could ordinarily be expected. This was especially true of secular affairs. But by the last quarter of the century Wyclif was prepared to argue, forcefully if prematurely, that it was also the only agency capable of reforming the church.

The political literature of the period prior to the mid/fourteenth/ century forecasts both the strength and the limitations of this national consciousness. That of the thirteenth century reveals among the governing classes a sense of common interest in things English which found expression in the idea of the "community of the realm."[12] This concept, drawn from the common store of medieval thought, with its emphasis on the organic nature of the political body, was given a local habitation and a name in England by those sophisticated clerks who contributed to the political life of that period its high intellectual tone. In the documents stemming from the era of the Barons' War, medi/ eval culture in England may be said to have reached its maturity, a maturity which in the peculiar circumstances of English history brought with it a lively sense of nationality. In the *Song of Lewes*, especially, ideas common to the political thinking of medieval Christendom were stated within a clearly national setting.[13]

11. See G. R. Elton, *The Tudor Revolution in Government* (New York, 1953), intro/ duction and chap. i for a discussion of this problem. But cf. Penry Williams and G. L. Harriss, "A Revolution in Tudor History," *Past and Present*, No. 25 (July, 1963), 3/58.

12. A good deal of attention has been paid this concept in recent years: see, for example, F. M. Powicke, *Ways of Medieval Life and Thought* (London, 1949), pp. 115/129; the same author's *Henry III and the Lord Edward, the Community of the Realm in the Thirteenth Century* (2 vols.; Oxford, 1947); G. T. Lapsley, *Crown, Community and Parliament in the Later Middle Ages* (Oxford, 1951); the essays by Helen Cam, G. P. Cuttino, Gaines Post published under the general title *Medieval Representation in Theory and Practice, Speculum*, XXIX, No. 2, Part 2 (April, 1954); B. Wilkinson, *Constitutional History of Medieval England* (3 vols.; London, 1958), III.

13. *The Song of Lewes*, ed. C. L. Kingsford (Oxford, 1890). Cf. Powicke, *Henry III and the Lord Edward*, II, 370/471.

This active intellectual approach to the king's government is apparent again in the reigns of the first two Edwards. Those strange documents, the *Mirror of Justices* and the *Modus Tenendi Parliamentum*, to say nothing of the *Tract on the Office of Steward*,[14] though poised uncertainly between party propaganda and the discussion of policy, between fact and fancy, at least indicate that there were men near the center of government capable of subjecting its institutions to a thoughtful, perhaps constructive, appraisal. And at the opening of the reign of Edward III, someone, perhaps Archbishop Simon Islip or the earlier Archbishop Simon Meopham, wrote a "letter" to the king entitled *Speculum Regis Edwardi III*[15] which is remarkable for its sustained treatment of specific administrative problems in the light both of national policy and of the political theory common to all medieval Christendom.

We should, however, be careful not to read too much into these early commentaries on English government. The literature of the Barons' War, especially, should be considered rather the end product of medieval culture than the beginning of anything new.[16] It is still a feudal monarchy that the author of the *Song of Lewes* is talking about—uniquely centralized, it is true, but still feudal. Moreover, remarkable as was his grasp of political principles, he saw government in action largely as a matter of personal relationships rather than of policies. He saw clearly the practical problem involving the king's alien favorites, and he urged, as a master remedy, that the king have about him good and native-born counselors.[7] But this is no more than the standard medieval answer to the problem of good government, the implication being that the king alone is the source of policy and that the critic is bound only to call his attention to the general nature of his duty.

14. *The Mirror of Justices*, ed. and trans. W. J. Whittaker, Selden Soc., VII (1895); *Modus Tenendi Parliamentum*, printed in M. V. Clarke, *Medieval Representation and Consent* (London, 1936); *Tract on the Office of Steward*, printed in L. W. V. Harcourt, *His Grace the Steward and Trial of Peers* (London, 1907), 164-167, tr. 148-151. For a discussion of these tracts and a review of the scholarship pertaining to them, see Wilkinson, *Constitutional History*, III, 90-91, 323-331.

15. J. Moisant, *De Speculo Regis Edwardi III . . . quem . . . conscripsit Simon Islip* (Paris, 1891). J. Tait, in "On the date and authorship of the 'Speculum Regis Edwardi'" *EHR*, LXI (Jan., 1901), 110-115, argues the case for Meopham as author.

16. Powicke, *Henry III and the Lord Edward*, II, 469. Cf. E. F. Jacob, *Studies in the Period of Baronial Reform and Rebellion, 1258-1267* (Oxford, 1925), pp. 276 ff.

17. *Song of Lewes*, ll. 777-783.

Nor was the intellectual promise of this period fulfilled in the more fugitive political literature, presumably more popular in its appeal. Indeed it is possible to see much that is immature, even accidental, in the national sentiment expressed. The popular verse commentators saw things readily enough in their insular setting. From an early date[18] they wrote of English events and of the issues that lay on the surface of English life—of politics and taxes, of battles against the Scots, the Welsh, and the French, and of the failure of justice in the courts— and they commented upon what they saw unencumbered for the most part by the burden of too much thought.[19] But the national tone in this literature is only too often drowned out by the discordant voice of baronial[20] and ecclesiastical complaint,[21] and even at times by the gayer and more irrepressible tones of feudal minstrelsy,[22] reminding us that it was always easy for both the medieval baron and his clerical contemporary to think in terms of his class interests rather than those of his country. And it sometimes blends imperceptibly into the moralism of the typical "Song of the Times"[23] which is concerned chiefly with the standard vices and touches national affairs, if at all, because of the purely coincidental fact that taxation and justice lay obviously within the province of the central government. Occa‐ sionally, indeed, a note of almost calculated reaction can be heard. In a song written by a partisan in praise of Edward I at the time of his coronation, the composer refers to the troubles of the preceding reign and tells how "the degenerate race of the English, which used to serve, inverting the order of things, ruled the king and his children."[24] One of the first poems of the Hundred Years' War, the *Vows of the Heron*,[25] reminds us that, side by side with apparently clear conceptions of

18. A few pieces have survived from the reign of John and that of Henry III prior to the Barons' War. See Wright, *Political Songs*, pp. 6‐18.

19. In addition to those items mentioned in the preceding note, see, especially for examples of comment on domestic politics and related problems, *ibid.*, pp. 121‐124, 133‐136, 149‐152, 155‐160, 224‐230, 237‐240, 244‐245, 251‐252, 325‐345; *Adam Davy's Five Dreams about Edward II*, ed. F. J. Furnivall, E.E.T.S., O.S., No. 69 (1878), 11 ff., Aspin, pp. 62‐63, 69‐73, 108‐111.

20. E.g., Wright, *Political Songs*, pp. 1‐6, 26‐43, 121‐124, 129; Aspin, pp. 62‐63.

21. E.g., Wright, *Political Songs*, pp. 14‐18.

22. E.g., *ibid.*, pp. 59‐63; Wright, *Political Poems*, I, 1‐25.

23. E.g., Wright, *Political Songs*, pp. 27‐35, 46‐50, 51‐55, 133‐136, 237‐240, 251‐252.

24. *Ibid.*, p. 129 (editor's translation).

25. Wright, *Political Poems*, I, 1‐25. See B. J. Whiting, "The Vows of the Heron," *Speculum*, XX (July, 1945), 261‐278.

national interest, there existed chivalric ideals and feudal loyalties which were insidiously non-national in their implications. Moreover, national sentiment, though a prerequisite for modern public discussion, did not necessarily bring with it the kind of analytical approach to public issues which above all characterizes that phenomenon. Crécy and Poitiers could move a balladier like Lawrence Minot to compose battle songs animated by a strident and infectious patriotism.[26] Domestic conditions, the evils of maintenance, for example, could elicit angry protests from those wandering clerks and preachers who took it upon themselves to voice the grievances of those who had no other advocate.[27] But neither the minstrel with his gossipy "new song" nor the preacher-poet with his Jeremiad based on the gloomy refrain, "*Dies mali sunt*," could separate the national interests from the context of personal relationships or see in those relationships problems requiring analysis of a sort that reached beyond questions of moral responsibility.

If we except those ostensibly technical treatises on the institutions of central government mentioned above, which barely fall into the category of diagnosis and remedy, and if we pass over the penetrating *Speculum Regis Edwardi*, there remains little or nothing from the whole period prior to the mid-fourteenth century which we can use as a convenient starting point for a study of articulate citizenship. In fact it was not until the last third of the fourteenth century that the materials for such study became available. The period from the 1370's until about the reign of Henry V is one of considerable importance in the history of English public discussion. Though not a period of rapidly maturing social or political consciousness among those who understood the task of airing the problems common to their society, it is one in which those problems were examined by an unprecedented number of commentators who undertook in a mood of sober public spirit to diagnose the ills of the political body, and to do so, moreover, still within the accepted framework of medieval thought. For these reasons it is the period chosen as the starting point for the more detailed treatment of presumably typical figures in the chapters that follow.

26. Wright, *Political Poems*, I, 58-91. See also Robbins, introduction, pp. 30-39, and appropriate notes. T. F. Tout, *France and England: Their Relations in the Middle Ages and Now* (London, 1922).

27. Wright, *Political Songs*, pp. 149-152, 212, 237-240; Aspin, pp. 109 and 112.

During these years the tone of the comment that has come down to us changes from the buoyant jingoism of the era of military success to a mood of brooding concern for society, even to a sort of national introspection, from the martial spirit of Lawrence Minot and the chivalric romanticism reflected in the *Vows of the Heron* to the over/whelming seriousness of a Gower or a Langland striving to see English society in its totality. It is also worth noticing that the major com/mentators are no longer exclusively clerks. Gower, at least, and perhaps also the anonymous author of those two brilliant fragments of political verse now edited under the title *Mum and the Sothsegger*,[28] were laymen. The minor literature of comment also shows the change. Although the minstrel and his "new song" live on, conditions rather than events stimulate the more thoughtful of the writers who served as the pamphleteers of their generation.

Articulate citizenship fed and grew on problems, and these dec/ades of the late fourteenth and early fifteenth centuries provided prob/lems aplenty. Many of them were old ones, but viewed in conjunction with others, new and old, and seen through eyes more than ever accustomed to discern the outline of national interests, even old prob/lems seemed newly urgent.

The war was in itself a major problem and a chronic one. In the days of victory, it was a source of prestige for Edward III and pride on the part of an increasingly patriotic citizenry. But after the gains registered in the Treaty of Brétigny in 1360, things went badly for the English. Whereas the French found in Charles V and Du Guesclin capable leaders who compensated for the tactical superiority of the English armies and who led an aroused population against the invader, the English suffered from the premature senility of their king and the loss of the able Black Prince. By 1377 only five fortified coastal towns remained of a great continental empire. It had become increasingly difficult for Edward, even in the fullness of his powers, to finance the war. As the costs of victory increased, he found that without more money no victory could be had; yet he found it equally difficult to persuade an English Parliament, one which had been willing enough to finance a successful war, to increase its support without continued victory. Neither he nor his successors were, however, able to abandon

28. *Mum and the Sothsegger*, ed. M. Day and R. Steele, E.E.T.S., O.S., No. 199 (1936).

the war completely without damaging the prestige that clung to foreign conquest even in the days of general disillusionment and without losing the support of magnates who had acquired a personal and quite material interest in the war. It is not surprising therefore to find "the War" a recurring subject for comment in the political literature. It not only helped confirm the rising national sentiment, but also, especially in the years of defeat or stalemate, prompted a more or less realistic appraisal of national interests.

Although English opinion seems to have been more interested in better administration than in peace, most of the writers criticized war and supported the less popular alternative. Perhaps even before the war the author of the *Speculum Regis Edwardi* had cast a suspicious eye upon the king's dynastic policy.[29] In the later century, and in fact down to Henry V's victory at Agincourt in 1415, commentators generally took into account the impact of war on the prosperity and happiness of the English commonalty. Gower, Langland, and Hoccleve all criticize the war and agree that it "bringeth in poverty at his heels."[30] Almost equally significant is the fact that all three refuse, either explicitly, as in the case of Gower, or by implication, to accept the chivalric values which served as the medieval equivalent of chauvinism, and which still did much to justify a foreign policy more dashing than statesmanlike in character. Accordingly, as Gower put it, the thing to do was to "lay to this old sore a new salve."[31]

As a subject likely to lead the literary commentator to a deeper understanding of public life, the war was certainly effective enough, but it seldom if ever led him to follow the subtler sequence of cause and effect which is clear enough to the modern historian. Although it was abundantly evident that the war cost money which the English people had in the long run to pay, it was not so apparent that the war also fostered many of the social and political processes that needed or would soon need governmental attention. Livery and maintenance, to take

29. Moisant, pp. 108, 119-120. On the earlier date of the *Speculum*, see Tait.

30. John Gower, *In Praise of Peace*, in *The Complete Works of John Gower*, ed. G. C. Macaulay (Oxford, 1899-1902), III, 481-495, ll. 109-114 and *passim*; *Piers the Plowman*, ed. W. W. Skeat (2 vols.; London, 1924), C-text, iv, ll. 242-243 and B-text, iii, l. 206; Thomas Hoccleve, *The Regiment of Princes*, in *Hoccleve's Works*, ed. F. J. Furnivall, E.E.T.S., E.S., No. 72 (1897), ll. 5223-5404; see also Wright, *Political Poems*, I, 123-215 and II, 209-221. English opinion concerning the war is also treated in Ferguson, *Indian Summer*, chap. v.

31. Gower, *Praise of Peace*, ll. 120-123.

an example especially upsetting to the public-spirited commentator, had been greatly expanded and its evils intensified by the use of indenture. During the long intervals of time between actual fighting these indentured soldiers found employment as armed retainers in England almost as satisfactory a life as that of a soldier of fortune in France. And the spread of liveried private armies among the English aristocracy was recognized as a very serious problem by most of the writers of the period. Clearly it was becoming difficult for a common citizen to get justice in courts intimidated by armed retainers. Badges, the author of *Mum and the Sothsegger* tells us, "cumbered the land" in the reign of "Richard the Redeles." That ill-counseled monarch had himself taken to maintaining something that was little more than a private army. The same author also saw in this practice a cause of faction and a threat to domestic peace.[32] But the problem of livery and maintenance remained to these men largely a separate one, stemming originally from the failure of the lords to do their duty as protectors of the community and, more immediately, from the failure of the central government to limit the practice.[33]

The still more indirect effects of the war—the impetus given to the formation of new loyalties, to the creation of new economic interests, in general to that greater degree of social mobility which in itself constituted a never-ending source of head-shaking on the part of the social critic—naturally enough were not traced to the war. These were very gradual developments, the full implications of which escaped the medieval observer who was unaccustomed to the analysis of social trends and whose sense of history was undeveloped. Similarly the effect of the war on the position of Parliament did not become a subject for reflection in the literature of extra-parliamentary discussion. It is perfectly plain to the historian today that the war forced Edward at every critical turn to secure the consent of the community of his realm as registered in Parliament for any extraordinary grant of funds, and that this dependence on parliamentary consent had a great deal to do with establishing the precedent on the basis of which that institution achieved its ultimate place in the constitution.[34] Men of

32. *Mum*, R-fragment, ii, ll. 28-80; iii, ll. 310-311; M-fragment, ll. 1565 ff.

33. E.g., Gower, *Mirour de l'Omme*, ll. 23317-23328, in *Complete Works*, I; Wright, *Political Songs*, pp. 237-240.

34. One verse writer at the time of Edward's death likened the ship of state to a war-ship and pictured the "communes" as the ship's mast "that with their cattle and their

the fourteenth century tended, however, to think less of constitutional precedent and more of practical government than we, with our commit/ ment to the principle of representation, are likely always to appreciate.

Parliament, indeed, plays less of a part in this informal discussion than might be expected. It appears frequently enough, but it is not the Parliament of nineteenth/century historiography. By the end of the century its existence tended to be taken for granted by a public still largely innocent of historical insight, its form and function less the object of criticism even on the part of the parliamentary leaders them/ selves than were those of the king's own council.[35] In Gower's *Cronica Tripertita*, Parliament becomes the arena in which the personal, factional politics of the period of Richard II are fought out as a preliminary to the final test of force. It is only incidentally the forum in which were debated the policies allegedly responsible for Richard's failure as a king.[36] On the other hand, in *Mum and the Sothsegger* (referring to the same period), Parliament becomes an essential channel through which good counsel may reach the king and his close ad/ visers. It is the place where the grievances of the people should be, but seldom are, fearlessly reported.[37] In fact Parliament's role is generally seen to be that of redressing grievances. It is an essential element in the machinery of government, the basic function of which is to protect life and property and to maintain the existing order. One writer of minor but at times penetrating verse comment expressed it with a clarity and economy of words unusual in that prolix age:

> When all a kingdom gathered is
> In God's law, by one assent,
> For to amend that was amiss,
> Therefore is ordained a parliament.[38]

For the most part, however, the articulate citizen failed as yet to focus his thought at all sharply on institutions or on the impersonal elements of historical continuity. He considered the process of government to be a matter primarily of personal relationships. These

good / maintained the war both first and last." Wright, *Political Poems*, I, 217. But it is unlikely that he thought of the commonalty in terms of representation.

35. Joliffe, p. 455, and cf. pp. 431/432.

36. Gower, *Complete Works*, IV, 314/343.

37. *Mum*, M/fragment, ll. 1119/1121. See below, chap. iii.

38. *Twenty/six Political and other Poems*, ed. J. Kail, E.E.T.S., O.S., No. 124 (1904), xiii, ll. 1/4.

he could study in the concrete instance as something tangible and immediately understandable. At the same time they permitted him, should he prefer a more reflective approach, to transpose political events into the minor key of moral principle, or, if he felt academically inclined, to interpret them with reference to those scholastically elaborated theories which were the common heritage of Christian Europe and depended in their turn on a profoundly moral inter-pretation of human activity. Government, he felt, will be good only as long as the men who run it are good. More specifically, a king will be a good king if, in addition to being a virtuous man, he seeks out and acts upon the advice of good and wise men.[39] Between this basic principle and the concrete political instance lay the large but poorly marked area of institutions, procedure, and policies which the commentator, not technically trained, saw no reason to explore and the expert seems no longer to have cared to analyze.

Experience in actual politics during the later years of Edward III and the reign of Richard II must certainly have confirmed this attitude. Baronial faction had, somewhat paradoxically, grown up within the most centralized feudal monarchy in Europe. It had for long been the ambition of the barons to have a controlling voice in the king's government. The weakness of Edward II's administration had brought them nearer their objective. The preoccupation of Edward III with the French war gave them just what they wanted. While all went well, king and magnates saw eye to eye, and Edward was glad enough to give them a dominant place in his council and, through Parliament, a controlling voice in taxation. When the war effort flagged, Edward found himself virtually in the hands of the baronial families, some of whom were now connected, through his own marriage policies, with the royal family itself. Unfortunately the baronial families did not constitute a united party. When Edward's hand lost its grip, and later when his grandson, still only a child, ascended the throne, no power remained sufficient to curb the disruptive force of faction. Cursed successively by senility, minority, and fickle absolutism, the crown became for a time the ball in a disastrous game of factional politics.

In circumstances of this sort, the commentator might well ask whence good governance could be had. With his eye on what he

39. See below, chaps. ii and iii.

felt to be essential he asked in particular where the king was to get the good counsel upon which all good government depended. A commonplace in the political thought of the Middle Ages, the idea of good counsel was thus given a specifically English context by the writers of this period. Good counsel became, in fact, the master remedy prescribed for the political ills by virtually all of them and, in *Mum and the Sothsegger*, its implications were explored beyond the king's immediate circle of advisers, in the houses of Parliament and in the uncharted area of extra-governmental discussion.[40]

Discussion of this sort turned in this period to a variety of domestic problems, most of which appear also in the Rolls of Parliament. Among those things which, being amiss, must be amended by governmental action, the maladministration of justice constituted, as might be expected, the most constant item.[41] Although less likely to stimulate discussion of governmental action, the agrarian problem became almost as fruitful a subject for comment. The lot of the peasant was no worse than it had been and was in some respects better, but it was always in need of improvement. To men raised always within earshot of the social gospel, Piers the plowman became at once an object of Christian charity and a symbol of the simple life lived in laborious days free from the contamination of wealth and sophisticated vice, a life more readily equated than other careers in secular society with the ascetic ideal of the medieval church. In either case he became also a convenient rod for the back of the propertied classes. But he had been placed in his position in society by God as part of His universal plan and ought not to envy those above him nor attempt to derange the ordained scheme of things. Thus, despite a profound sympathy with the poor, the commentators of the late fourteenth century were not levellers.[42] Only a few social agitators like the famous John Balle carried the equalitarian implications of the Christian tradition to their logical extreme. Nor did the Peasant's Revolt of 1381, shocking as it was to the conservative sensibilities of contemporaries, seriously interrupt the criticisms of social injustice that flowed as a constant theme from the lips of preachers and poets.[43] For

40. See below, chap. iii.
41. E.g., *Piers Plowman*, B-text, iii-iv and *Mum*, M-fragment, ll. 1607-1625.
42. *Piers Plowman*, B-text, Prol., ll. 118-120; cf. C-text, ix, ll. 340-341.
43. Owst, p. 221.

Langland, concerned with the larger truths of the Christian life rather than with passing events, the revolt by itself seems to have had little immediate meaning.[44]　To Gower, on the other hand, who spoke for the propertied classes as well as for the Christian tradition, it symbolized everything that in his day seemed to be threatening the divinely ordained structure of society.[45]　Like the "commonwealth men" of 1549, he was torn between sympathy for the husbandman and fear of social unrest.　Unlike them, however, he failed to see in re-bellion the result of a complex but analyzable sequence of cause and effect.　Complicated as we know the background of the revolt to have been, it appeared simple enough to Gower.　In his ambitious *Vox Clamantis*, a work that rings with the reverberations of 1381, he traces the trouble simply to the knavery of those concerned, whether peasants or landlords.[46]　One of the political songs, it is true, deals specifically with the tax policy which, in the case of the poll tax of 1380, had added the ultimate strain to the burden of popular grievance.[47] And the orthodox clergy, whose vested interests had been peculiarly open to attack, were quick to see in the preaching of Lollard priests a major cause of subversion.[48]

Lollardy, indeed, became the Jacobinism of fourteenth-century England, the whipping-boy for any entrenched interest.[49]　Unlike its eighteenth-century counterpart, however, it had the advantage of being a domestic product, and it is interesting to notice that, in their contro-versy with the friars, the Lollards were quite capable of recognizing their advantage and making the most of it.　The writer of the apparent-ly popular English ballad, *Jack Upland*, stigmatizes the friars as an anti-national body having no clear place in English public life, a charge his opponent, Friar Daw Topias, stoutly denies.[50]

The controversy that grew up around the thorny personality and

44. Cf. D. C. Fowler, *Piers the Plowman: Literary Relations of the A and B Texts* (Seattle, 1961), pp. 168-169.

45. *Vox Clamantis* may have owed its existence to Gower's shocked reaction to the event.　Certainly it is charged with a sense of horror directly inspired by the rising.　See below, chap. ii.

46. E.g., *Vox Clamantis*, Liber V, ix, ll. 577-601, *Complete Works*, IV.

47. Wright, *Political Poems*, I, 224-225.　Cf. Robbins, pp. 55-57.

48. Wright, *Political Poems*, I, 235.

49. E.g., *ibid.*, II, 128.　See also M. E. Aston, "Lollardy and Sedition, 1381-1431," *Past and Present*, No. 17 (April, 1960), pp. 1-44.

50. Wright, *Political Poems*, II, 17, 43.

radical theology of John Wyclif impinged in many other ways on secular concerns and called attention somewhat peremptorily to the position of the church within the national state. During the reign of Edward III, many English men of property were becoming more concerned than the king himself over the alien authority of the pope. Their patriotism was not entirely free from the shadow of self-interest: they resented especially the right of the pope to provide to benefices which they and their ancestors had controlled for generations. Their indignation received some backing from the anticlericalism endemic in late medieval England. It was becoming increasingly evident that the church, up to its very head, was too immersed in the cares of the world to take the interest it should in the cure of souls. And, for patriotic Englishmen, this feeling was by no means lessened by the fact that the pope had been virtually a captive in the French-dominated city of Avignon during all the earlier stages of the war with France. Wyclif, already a theologian and controversialist of repute, became the propagandist for the anticlerical party in the early 1370's, and soon became also the mouthpiece for the more general discontent with the activities of the clergy. But his zeal outran the requirements of practical politics and even the anticlericalism of popular opinion, and he found himself in a position of increasing isolation. Before long he had argued himself into an antisacerdotal, antipapal heresy. Meanwhile, however, he had evolved a plan for letting the secular authority in the country reform the church by disendowing it, thereby removing it by main force from the worldly entanglements into which it had fallen.

Although he failed in his attempt to reform the church through an appeal to the secular lords, his followers continued to peddle the policy of disendowment, along with the more theological aspects of his teaching, well into the following century. By so doing they kept alive a controversy which on this point at least gave food for social and political reflection. The program of disendowment, vague as it was and unrealistic in the circumstances then prevailing, had the virtue of being ostensibly a constructive policy, calling for legislative action in the national as well as the individual interest. More than that, it was a policy formulated on the basis of some analysis of cause and effect. It was an oversimplified analysis, a naïve combination of statesmanship and moralism, but it represented also an attempt to redress the many particular grievances against the existing clerical order, first by tracing them to a common cause and then by devising a scheme for removing that cause. It can for this reason alone be considered an important, if abortive, lesson in political awareness and social analysis.[51]

Among the factors that helped bring to eventual maturity the articulate citizen's social and political consciousness, and in particular sharpened his analytical insights, economic problems constituted a special category. Many of those issues mentioned in the preceding pages bore implications important to the economic life of the country. The war had brought increased taxes and new fortunes and wider choice of careers; the agrarian problem was as much economic in character as it was social; the church was laboring under the growing burden of its own fiscal system; justice seemed to work in direct ratio to the economic power of the litigant; stable government was already considered by some to depend on the ability of the monarchy to maintain its financial power in the face of an increasingly powerful group of magnates. Even the preacher, preoccupied with moral considerations, could not overlook the economic, if only because it was becoming ever more apparent in those degenerate days that the love of money was indeed the root of all evil.[52] But it was in relation to England's overseas trade that the articulate citizen achieved his most profound insights into the nature of national policy and the extent of the central government's responsibility to guide it. The trade in wool and woolen cloth proved especially thoughtprovoking. In this context local interests could readily be seen reaching beyond the locality and becoming dependent on the broader overseas market. That market was one which could be maintained and expanded only under the protection of a central government. Questions could be seen arising concerning the status of English merchants abroad, of foreign merchants in England, of the rate of exchange and the supply of precious metals, all closely related, all clearly requiring decisions on the part of the government. The king, on the other hand, could be seen making the most of this unity existing in the country's economy

51. See below, chap. v. An interesting example of how ecclesiastical problems could inspire more or less realistic examination of the national interest may be found in Wright, *Political Poems*, I, 323.

52. See Owst, pp. 319 and 352.

for his own purposes. Trade promised customs duties, and Edward III had been quick to recognize the importance of possessing in the Staple an administrative bottleneck through which all the wool sacks must pass and be counted. Thus the facts of English economic life pointed constantly to the king's government as the source of construc-tive policy.

Not that it was easy for the medieval observers to grasp the full significance of these tendencies. It was not so clear then as later that government was in fact moving beyond the protective function which was still customarily assigned to it in the political literature, the function of redressing wrongs, and was becoming the constructive agent in a society of moving forces. It was by no means as clear then as it was to the statesmen and pamphleteers of Tudor England that society was a mechanism of such forces, that causal relationships might be empiri-cally discovered and manipulated by creative policy in order to promote the wealth and power of England. Nor did the fourteenth-century monarchy reveal any marked consistency of purpose in economic matters.[53] Edward III, at one time thought to have been something of a pioneer in mercantilist legislation, seems, on closer observation, to have been a thoroughly medieval king, living from hand to mouth in financial matters, shaping economic measure to suit the needs of the moment (usually those of his own dynastic policy) and generally little given to considering underlying principle. Possibly the shrewd merchants had a deeper understanding than the king and his immedi-ate advisers. Closer to the facts and capable of observing them with minds doubtless freer from competing issues and ideals, the merchants had long been accustomed to watching the train of cause and effect in economic matters, the effect of taxation on prices, for example, which Eileen Power tells us was clearly recognized by the beginning of the fourteenth century, or the effect of the export of bullion on Eng-land's prosperity.[54] Yet even these men, realists as it were by trade,

53. M. M. Postan, "The Economic and Political Relations of England and the Hanse from 1400-1475," in Eileen Power and M. M. Postan (eds.), *Studies in English Trade in the Fifteenth Century* (London, 1953), chap. iii. Cf. G. Unwin (ed.), *Finance and Trade under Edward III* (Manchester, 1918), pp. xiv ff.

54. Power, *Wool Trade*, pp. 74-75. A classic example of discussion in Parliament of bullionist policy may be found in *Rotuli Parliamentorum* (6 vols.; London, 1767-1777), III, 126.

may well have taken a more opportunistic attitude toward economic policy than the words of their petitions to Parliament would imply.

Be this as it may, in economic activity there existed dynamic factors which were actually wrecking medieval society as it had been traditionally conceived and were at the same time forging the structures of something quite new; it would be reasonable to expect that a similar revolution was caused in men's minds. Surely nothing was more calculated to reshape the assumptions of men as they moved toward modern times than the rise (and fall) of fortunes amassed through overseas trade, the growth of individual enterprise in the cloth indus, try, the constant competition of English interests with those of her Continental neighbors, and the increasing fluidity in a society the relationships of which were coming to be based more on contract than on customary status. Indeed, the statutes of the late fourteenth and fifteenth centuries reveal in their wording an increasing tendency to consider economic welfare in national terms.[55] A notion of the "*bien universelle*" of the kingdom brings us one step nearer the "common, wealth" of early Tudor England. We are accordingly prepared to find in the economic discussion outside Parliament a correspondingly realistic acceptance of this acquisitive society and of the nascent mer, cantilistic state.

So it is with the feeling of reaching for a step which is not there that we find the literature of comment, those texts especially in which the mind of the period may be seen presumably at its least "controlled" and most reflective, rather slow to show the effect of economic ex, perience. Not until we reach that remarkable pamphlet, *The Libelle of Englyshe Polycye*,[56] composed sometime between 1436 and 1438, do we find any indication that the lessons of economic policy have been absorbed or any foreshadowing of those Tudor pamphlets which ex, plored so energetically the causal relationships in economic affairs and came so near to identifying government with the functions of economic planning. There is plenty of evidence that the writers of the earlier period understood the problems, especially of the wool trade. John Gower, in his first major work, the French *Miroir de l'Omme*, apos,

55. Power and Postan, pp. 102,103. See n. 15 for examples.

56. *The Libelle of Englishe Polycye*, ed. Sir George Warner (Oxford, 1926). On the date and authorship of the poem and its political,economic background, see G. A. Holmes, "The 'Libel of English Policy,'" *EHR*, LXXVI (April, 1961), 193,216. See below, chap. iv.

trophizes wool, "*des marchantz la deusse*," and maintains with at least poetic justification that she' was born in England.   He then describes some of her problems, but fails to analyze them beyond the obvious or to place them in the context of general policy.[57]   Both here and in his later work his treatment of economic cause and effect goes little beyond the particular grievance and soon becomes lost in moral generalization.[58]

Why is it then that we must wait until the fifteenth-century *Libel* for any handling of English economic affairs in terms of consistent analysis and underlying principle? And why is it that the *Libel* itself resembles more closely the Tudor economic pamphlets than anything in its own day? At the risk of getting ahead of the story let us notice that the merchant class, or the gentry of the counties, either of whom might have produced a writer capable of something approaching the *Libel*, and several decades sooner, were not as yet generally articulate. Those, like Gower, who shared their outlook and were at the same time given to expressing themselves in writing (excessively so, one may sometimes feel) were too firmly committed to the habits of thought still dominant in late medieval culture to be able to bridge effectively that gap between experience and formulated concept which imparts to much of the political literature a curious air of unreality.   That appearance of unreality is nowhere more marked than in discussion of the state as the source of constructive economic policy.   Other problems—justice, taxes, faction, the peasant, even ecclesiastical reform— could be discussed reasonably effectively within the traditional system of values.   It was difficult to follow economic policy very far without ending up in a position the pragmatism of which and the realism, to say nothing of the implied acceptance of change in society, would have done violence to that system.   It was hard to reconcile the motives and methods of the entrepreneur with the doctrine of the just price or the picture of society as an established hierarchy of functioning members. It was equally difficult to maintain a sincere feeling for the unity of Christian peoples while pointing out that, by regulating the flow of bullion, by controlling the activity of foreign merchants, and by maintaining a strong naval position in the channel, England might be made to prosper and grow at the expense of her European neighbors.

౧ ౧ ౧

57. Gower, *Mirour de l'Omme*, 280-281, especially ll. 25369-25452.
58. See below, chap. ii.

With the accession of Henry V there began a new phase in English public discussion. The change was neither sudden nor radical. But the literature of the fifteenth century presents peculiar problems of interpretation. On the whole it is mediocre. Yet it reveals here and there an unprecedented ability on the part of a very few writers to see into the workings of society and the issues of public significance. The reader's first impression (and as far as it goes it is sound) is, however, one of deadly mediocrity. He somehow misses the introspective mood that had colored so much of the literature in the preceding half-century. He notices in particular a decline in the more or less popular literature written in the tradition of the socially minded preacher or of *Piers Plowman*, a literature which, even at its most uninspired, must be given credit for its serious attempt to inform those in authority of the people's grievances. To judge from the examples that have been preserved, the place of this literature is taken in the fifteenth century largely by propaganda pieces. This is especially true of the minor poems and songs. In the earlier period this fugitive literature had done the service of both news and running commentary on conditions. It seldom rose above the level of generalized, even stereotyped complaint, the stock-in-trade of the medieval pulpit. Nevertheless, complaint, prompted as it was primarily by conditions rather than events, could act as a culture in which the germs of analysis might someday grow. Political propaganda, on the other hand, proved less capable of transcending particular events and of reaching the level of issues or principles. It was on conditions rather than events, issues rather than persons, the chronic illness in the body politic rather than *res gestae*, that the articulate citizen nourished his analytical faculties and his creative capabilities. In the fifteenth century, however, it was events and persons rather than conditions and issues that inspired the fugitive literature of comment; its authors tended more and more to be the hacks of one political faction or another.

As for the more ambitious efforts, they seem at first glance to follow the taste for platitude of an increasingly literate, yet intellectually immature governing class, for translated platitude at that, something that bore already on it the stamp of tradition and hence of respectability. Perhaps for our purposes the best example may be found in the vogue of the political treatise composed in the tradition of the *Secreta Secretorum*, that letter of advice on the princely virtues which Aristotle was supposed to have written for the edification of Alexander the Great.[59] In its original form, or in its adaptation by Egidius Romanus in the *De Regimine Principum*, it bore no relation to specifically English government and made a poor vehicle for the discussion of English affairs. It never in fact struck deep roots in English political literature. During the fifteenth century, however, several translations or adaptations appeared. Of those who undertook to write a book of counsel for the king, only the author of *Mum and the Sothsegger* at the beginning of the century and Fortescue toward the end entirely escaped the influence of this imported model.

The problems themselves had changed but little. Domestic issues had perhaps passed a peak of urgency by the turn of the century, but there is little reason to believe that the relations of peasant and landlord were greatly improved or that Lollardy had been silenced. The rising of 1381 had settled nothing and, if we may judge from Pecock's massive one-man counterattack on the "lay party,"[60] Lollard sentiments were by no means dead. As for the evils connected with maintenance and the maladministration of justice, the century of the civil wars would hardly be the time to look for improvement in that quarter. The larger political and strategic issues on the other hand were if anything more pressing than ever. The French War, the plight of the king striving to render effective a government hamstrung by aristocratic faction, the problem of maintaining the wealth and power of England in a Europe of increasingly competitive economic powers, all provided an abundance for the articulate citizen to think and write about.

Perhaps the attention of both politician and citizen was deflected from the critical contemplation of conditions by the glamor of events or the partisan excitement of factional politics. The years that fell between Henry V's renewal of the war with France in 1415 and the siege of Calais in 1436 were dominated by a brilliant, if misguided, foreign adventure. From that point, for almost the whole remainder of the century, the commentator was likely to be preoccupied by factional politics. Yet it was a period in which very large problems faced the men actually responsible for the safety and prosperity of the

59. See below, chap. iii.
60. See especially his *Repressor of Over Much Blaming of the Clergy*, ed. C. Babington, Rolls Series (1860).

realm, and, as the *Libel of English Policy* and Fortescue's writings[61] demonstrate, those problems could stimulate penetrating analysis and constructive comment on the part of men who were able and willing to respond.

There, perhaps, lies the answer. The governing classes, both in county and town, were not as yet in the habit of committing their thoughts on society and government to paper. The Tudor gentleman, conscious of his civic responsibility, grounded in the secular example and precept of classical culture, and confident in his ability to speak as a counselor to his king, has few real counterparts in fifteenth-century England. The clergy, on the other hand, still the most consistently articulate class in the community, had lost some of its sense of public duty. It may be that the measures intended to discourage the heretic commended prudence also to the orthodox. More likely the spiritual fatigue which seems to have characterized much of the religious life of western Europe and was manifested in a certain loss of vitality, a rigidity in the observances and thought of the church, may also have sapped the sense of public responsibility or the emotional appeal of the social gospel or whatever it was that had driven so many clerks in the earlier period to act as monitors alike to the English government and to the English people. Certainly the clergy as a group made a relatively slender contribution to the literature of criticism and counsel in the fifteenth century. Except when, like Lydgate, they wrote as publicists for political interests, or, like Hoccleve, to curry personal favor at court, they seem to have had little to say beyond the particular concerns of their order or a somewhat querulous criticism of private manners and morals.[62]

ဢ ဢ ဢ

The news of Henry V's victory at Agincourt was received in London with extravagant demonstrations of rejoicing. It stirred up a spate of popular ballads. Only a few pieces have survived of what must have been a large total, for they were an exceedingly perishable species, unlikely long to outline the enthusiasm of the event.[63] But

61. See below, chaps. iv and v.
62. Wright, *Political Poems*, II, 114-117, 243-251, 251-254, 258-260. See also Robbins, pp. xxxv-xxxvi.
63. C. L. Kingsford, *English Historical Literature in the 15th Century* (Oxford, 1913), pp. 3 and 240.

they are enough to indicate how quickly the news of victory had dis-pelled the atmosphere of uneasiness which had pervaded the verse comment of the preceding generation.[64]   Before many years, however, the war, now one of scarcely concealed aggression, dragged its slow length along toward ultimate defeat.   In the process it called attention more imperatively than ever before to England's relations with the Continent.   It disturbed English markets, and perhaps had more than anything else to do with the fact that the third quarter of the century was a time of trade depression for England.[65]   The defection of Burgundy from the English cause aroused English opinion and raised in particular the question of the importance of Calais.   The events of 1435-1436, leading to the siege of that city, provoked another flood of popular songs, larger, if we may judge from the number preserved, than the output following Agincourt, and for the most part just as devoid of analysis or constructive comment.[66]   But the occasion also brought forth the most penetrating analysis of England's position as a mercantile and naval power to appear prior to the reign of Henry VIII.

The Libel of English Policy, written shortly after the siege of Calais by a spokesman for the views of the Staplers, the cloth exporters, and the political opposition to the Beaufort faction in the council, con-stituted a well-informed and comprehensive program based on a remarkable mature concept of economic nationalism.[67]   For some time the English business community and those who represented its interests in the central government had been groping their way toward a clearer understanding of the relationship between political and economic power and, more particularly, toward a more realistic picture of England's unique geographical and economic position with reference to the other powers of northwestern Europe.   Now the author of the *Libel* was able to give comprehensive and reasoned ex-pression to what had been hitherto only implied or stated in fragmentary form in official documents.[68]   By doing so he showed how long it

64. See, for example, *Twenty-six Poems*, poem xiii.

65. Power and Postan, pp. 1 and 105.

66. See Holmes, especially p. 213, for a discussion of the literature prompted by the siege.   Examples of the popular balladry may be found in Robbins, pp. 78-89.

67. See also *The Debate of the Horse, Goose, and Sheep*, attributed to John Lydgate and written at about the same time as the *Libel*, in *Minor Poems*, ed. H. N. MacCracken, E.E.T.S., O.S., No. 192 (1934), II, 539.

68. Power and Postan, p. 103.

took for economic realities which had been acted upon more or less unreflectively for generations to be rationalized or even comprehended. He also showed how little the bulk of the political literature stemming from these years reflects the kind of realistic and constructive thought of which some at least of Gloucester's adherents were capable.

The war abroad merged almost imperceptibly into the struggle for power between the aristocratic factions at home. The two were not, of course, unrelated. As a result of his Continental operations, the king had been forced to depend more and more on the support of the magnates who, in turn, seized the opportunity to dominate the machinery of government. Neither the problem of the crown's weak‑ness nor that of the over‑mighty subject was new, but it was allowed to develop disastrous proportions during the long and feeble reign of Henry VI. After 1455, the country was plagued by actual civil war, and there were brief periods when no effective government could be said to have existed. Nor was the partial restoration of statesmanlike administration by the Yorkists able quite to redeem the reputation of English government in the eyes of its own citizenry.

The combined effect of defeat abroad and civil war at home must have had a sobering effect on the public‑spirited citizen. There is significant, if scattered, evidence in the more reflective literature of the period to indicate that this was so. But the propaganda pieces and the minor bits of verse‑comment that still constituted the running commentary on events as they happened remained for the most part quite innocent of reflective criticism. They are devoted to the ex‑ pression of partisan feeling, and, insofar as they reflect any attitude at all toward government, it is as personal as the rotting heads that perpetually adorned London Bridge. They praise heroes and narrate battles, much as the songs of the thirteenth‑century Barons' War had done, but they fail to identify their cause, as did the spokesman for the popular cause in the thirteenth century, with England and her interests. Badges once more take the place of more distinctly national symbols.[69]

Here and there, it is true, one of the anonymous verse writers ex‑ presses what was probably a widespread feeling of disillusionment and

69. Wright, *Political Poems*, II, 232; *Trevelyan Papers*, Camden Society (1857‑1872), I, 53‑60; *Archaeologia*, XXIX (1842), 334‑340; *Percy's Folio MS*, ed. J. W. Hales and F. J. Furnivall (London, 1868), III, 321‑363. Cf. Kingsford, *Historical Literature*, p. 252.

frustration. One, for example, calls attention to the disparity between the number of acts passed by Parliament and the few that are actually put into effect.[70] Another warns of the administrative disorder that is bound to ensue when the public order is entrusted to violent men, linked together by the brittle bargains of a decadent feudalism, and he appeals to the lords not to let happen in England what has happened in France.[71] Still another, in a "warning to King Henry" written just before the outbreak of the Wars of the Roses, put his finger on a point which was coming to be recognized as the key to the political problem at home and which Fortescue in fact emphasized in his classic analysis some twenty years later. He recognized that the crown had been dangerously impoverished by the alienation of its resources to buy support from the magnates, that the king could not rule effectively so long as he had, to use Fortescue's phrase, subjects "equipollent to himself," and that the situation would remain critical unless these grants were resumed.[72]

It remained, however, for Fortescue and, to a lesser extent, Ashby, to develop this theme with some analytical insight and with practical proposals for reform. Both were experienced in the affairs of central government, but both were writing in the capacity not of public officials but of volunteer counselors. They agreed that the first requisite in restoring good government to England was to restore the power of the crown, and they proposed specific policies which would contribute to that end and which, by the way, were very similar to those adopted by Edward IV and Henry VII in their actual efforts to reestablish public order in England. Both Fortescue and Ashby had learned a measure of political realism during the civil war period. It was a period of great uncertainty and confusion, but it was also one rich in the lessons of experience for any student of politics sufficiently sophisticated to profit by them. Out of it should emerge something of the realism and the empiricism which we have learned to associate with Renaissance thought, and a willingness to treat public questions

70. Wright, *Political Poems*, II, 252. Cf. sermon quoted by Owst, p. 340, which voices exactly the same sentiment.

71. Wright, *Political Poems*, II, 235-237.

72. *Ibid.*, II, 229-231. Cf. Sir John Fortescue, *The Governance of England*, ed. C. Plummer (Oxford, 1885), chaps. viii and xiv. See also S. B. Chrimes, *An Introduction to the Administrative History of Medieval England* (New York, 1952), pp. 243-244.

as problems capable of being discussed in terms of practical values and solved through intelligently constructed policy.[73]

Fortescue was not, however, content to secure a strong admin⁄istration.   That he considered a prerequisite to the sort of "governance" he believed Englishmen were entitled to.   But he also recognized that there were principles involved in the English tradition of government. Those principles, vague enough at best in fifteenth⁄century thinking, had doubtless suffered additional obfuscation as a result of the dis⁄torting necessities of partisan conflict.   Like Littleton in the narrower area of land law, Fortescue saw the need for definition.   Accordingly he set out to define the features essential to the English constitutional tradition and at the same time to strengthen the position of the king, both financially and administratively, to the point where, presumably, he would not be tempted to adopt the arbitrary methods of his French neighbor together with the equally foreign law of Rome that sanctioned them.   In the process he revealed an unprecedented ability to discuss principle in terms of English realities and to see those realities in their institutional as well as in their personal and ethical aspects.

Frustration and disillusionment not only suggested a more or less agonized reappraisal of the principles and practices of the nation's government, it also prompted an effort to revive the national spirit by means of a revival of chivalric idealism.   Paradoxical, even quixotic, as such an enterprise might seem, it was nevertheless a natural enough answer for fifteenth⁄century Englishmen to make to the problem of national discipline and morale.   Chivalric idealism had come in England to be centered increasingly in the royal court, and expressed in terms of national honor, its inspiration derived from the heroic deeds of Henry V, Sir John Chandos, and those other true English knights who had helped to frustrate the knavish tricks of the French enemy.   It was with this memory in his mind that in the early 1470's William Worcester issued the *Boke of Noblesse* in its final form.   A similar feeling for the discipline of the English knightly class seems also to have conditioned the thought of Sir Thomas Malory and Willam Caxton.[74]

73. See W. J. Bouwsma, "The Politics of Commynes," *JMH*, XXIII (Dec., 1951), 315⁄328, for a treatment of parallel developments in France.

74. For a discussion of the *Boke of Noblesse*, see Ferguson, *Indian Summer*, pp. 143⁄158. On Malory and Caxton, see *ibid.*, chaps. i and ii.

Viewed in relation to the magnitude of the problems that beset England in the later Middle Ages, the literature of comment and counsel seems curiously inadequate. Not that it was in short supply. Considering the number of items preserved and the odds against survival, there was probably enough of it to serve as a running commentary on events and conditions. No doubt it served more than we are now ready to believe as a medium for the transmission of information and opinion between government and that part of the English people which at any given time constituted an effective public and between that public and the source of governmental policy. But, despite its quantity, it somehow fails to foreshadow at all clearly the public discussion of more modern times, or even that of Renaissance England. Only here and there are we permitted to catch a glimpse of what by the mid-sixteenth century had become a settled trend, namely the conscious effort of learned laymen, acting as self-appointed citizen-counselors, to analyze the causal factors conspiring to create the ills of the commonwealth, and on the basis of that analysis to devise constructive policies for remedial action. Yet the problems of that period were those of a society already in the process of radical change—not yet revolutionary change, as in the early Tudor era, but profoundly disturbing to contemporaries just the same and, one would suppose, thought-provoking. Why, then, did the learned and articulate citizen of those days fail to foreshadow more clearly the analytical and constructive approach of the early Tudor pamphleteers? The succeeding chapters will, I hope, help to answer this question. Here, however, are some general considerations to be kept in mind.

Habits of thought no doubt tend always to lag behind the changing circumstances of life, and men are always likely to adjust themselves informally to such circumstances before they are able to change their formal frame of reference. These tendencies are, however, especially apparent in late medieval thought. We see, for example, Englishmen acting upon the assumption that England is the center of their world before we find them expressing a conscious nationalism. We see the merchant proceeding on the assumption that profit is legitimate and that government is capable of adjusting economic causes to produce effects desirable for the common welfare long before he is willing to question canonist notions of price or to justify usury or is able to speak the language of mercantilist policy. English society is becoming worldly in its approach to the practical problem of life, the center of political action clearly established in a laicized government, but the modern note of secularism or the accent of political realism creep but slowly into the formal expression of the period. If, as Professor Wilkinson tells us,[75] the growth of political institutions in the thirteenth and fourteenth centuries reflects a high degree of creative thought on the part of the English politician, it is a long time before creativity becomes an admitted and consciously desired element in the life of the community. The late medieval knight was capable of acting like a gentleman farmer, a Renaissance courtier, or even a *condottiere* long before he was able to see how far his actions were removed from the values of chivalry to which he still gave unquestioning loyalty.

If we recognize the inveterate character of traditional habits of thought in late medieval England we shall find it much easier to understand the limitations within which the articulate citizen operated when he set out at all seriously to air his views on the state of the commonwealth. It was still, for example, easier for men of that day to think in terms either of the universal order or the local instance than of the national entity. They tended, almost instinctively, to treat social problems either in terms of class divisions characteristic of all Christendom or (what was pretty much the same thing) the individ- ual's failure to act as his position in the body politic would require. They accordingly traced the ills of that body to their ultimate source in the moral nature of man and found a remedy in a return to virtue on the part of those whose sinful action had been the cause of the trouble in the first place.

As a result, much of their comment, on social problems especially, appears to be less immediately inspired by strictly English consider- ations than was actually the fact. The conflict between good and evil upon which the common welfare depended seems to be carried on in the breast of Everyman rather than of every Englishman. But as time goes on even the traditional themes of complaint arising out of the inequities that chronically afflicted medieval society tend to be expressed more and more within a specifically English context.[76]

75. B. Wilkinson, "English Politics and Politicians of the Thirteenth and Fourteenth Centuries," *Speculum*, XXX (Jan., 1955), 37-48.

76. Cf. John Peter, *Complaint and Satire in Early English Literature* (Oxford, 1956), pp. 58-59, 67.

Even so, government remained for most of the commentators of this period personal rather than institutional—personal, that is, in the sense that it depended on the moral nature of the men running it, not in the sense, more typical of Renaissance thought, that it depended on the dynamic personality of the artist in politics. They found it consequently hard to discern the mechanism of social forces, of impersonal causes, to the modern eye more susceptible of manipulation by legislation or by administrative policy. These men were so conscious of the final and all-embracing purpose of God that they could see no other moving force in society. There seemed, therefore, little reason for exploring the more immediate factors. Nor did it seem necessary to suggest specific remedies. That was what governments existed to provide. All that was required of the social critic was to criticize, and the remedy could be considered to lie implicit in the criticism.

It could, that is, if society was assumed to be static in its basic structure, be subject to change only to the extent that the whole universe had been infected with the sin of Adam and that there lay implicit in the providential plan the possibility of a millenial perfection. What more than anything else stood between these men of the fourteenth and fifteenth centuries and a modern approach toward the problem of government was their inability to think in terms of change and development as normal attributes of human society. The concept of the static social organism was so deeply ingrained that it prevented them from seeing that government could be more than a remedial agency, that through the creative intellect of its leaders it could fabricate policy which might shape the course of social development as well as relieve more immediate pressures. It prevented them from searching for calculable and tangible causes operating within the limitations established for all time by the will of God and manifested in the law of nature. It also prevented them from recognizing the necessity for some clearly defined sovereign authority from which the active policy essential to the modern state, situated as it already was in a competitive world order, must in the final analysis emanate.

◊   ◊   ◊

Not that medieval Englishmen were at all likely to think in terms of sovereignty as the modern mind understands the term. More accustomed than many of their neighbors to the fact of centralized government, capable in practice of considerable innovation during the constitutionally critical era of the thirteenth and fourteenth centuries, they remained more interested in good government than in theories regarding the nature and location of authority within the realm, more apt to make new law than to admit that they had actually done so, and in any case deeply committed to an ideal of monarchy limited by law which left little room for anything resembling a modern concept of sovereignty.[77]　Yet it is worth noticing that those theorists, mainly Continental, who were forced by circumstances to concern themselves with such questions had their political vision limited by the fixed horizons of their social theory.[78]　The plenitude of power envisioned by the publicists of the fourteenth century who argued the respective cases of the papal and secular authorities remained a power to be exercised within the ordained structure of the social organism and devoted rather to preserving it in peace and tranquility than to directing its growth or altering its form, to maintaining the just relationship be-tween its members rather than augmenting the power of the sovereign part.　Modern ideas of sovereignty differ from medieval ones not so much in the completeness of the jurisdiction they envision as in the opportunity provided in social theory for the exercise of that authority. Not until it became possible to assume a society of moving forces could it become possible also to conceive of a government capable of di-recting or harnessing those forces in the interests not merely of justice and peace but of wealth and power, not merely of remedy but of the sort of reform that necessitates change.

The concept of a static social organism of course bore little relation to the facts.　The later Middle Ages witnessed a great deal of social mobility.　Yet those disturbances on the surfaces of society, stormy as they were, did not greatly affect the basic preconceptions that lay in the dark calm of the deeper waters.　Conversely, an awareness of the dynamic nature of government and society did not have to wait for the appearance of a formulated doctrine of progress.　For practical

77. S. B. Chrimes, *English Constitutional Ideas of the XV Century* (Cambridge, 1936), pp. 69, 301.　Cf. G. L. Harriss, "Medieval Government and Statecraft," *Past and Present*, No. 25 (July, 1963), pp. 8-39.　See also B. Wilkinson, "The Political Revolution of the Thirteenth and Fourteenth Centuries in England," *Speculum*, XXIV (Oct., 1949), 502-509.

78. See Michael Wilks, *The Problem of Sovereignty in the Later Middle Ages* (Cambridge, 1963).

purposes it was enough that the middle deeps be stirred, that the socially conscious and politically alert observer gain a sense of history, that he become aware of the dynamic forces at work in society in the more immediate past and the foreseeable future and of the possibility of channelling or curbing those forces, that government be seen as the source of constructive policy, ultimately of law itself. All of this could take place, and did, within a system of formal ideas in which nature and its law stood still, subject only to the epochal structure and apocalyptic promise of the divine drama.

The momentum of inherited ideas and habits of thought explains a great deal, more in fact than the historian, instinctively on the look-out for signs of new growth, is often willing to admit. But it does not explain everything. Any force can be stopped or diverted by another of sufficient strength. If a society has the choice between two systems of values it will eventually choose that which more nearly meets its needs. But did the governing class of fifteenth-century England really have such a choice, and how long is "eventually"? A new source of inspiration had in a sense been available for more than a hundred years before it helped Englishmen to rethink the values guiding them in their secular activities. By the 1430's, at a time when the English author of the *Libel of English Policy* could count on nothing more than a native shrewdness to sharpen his perception of England's economic position, Italian humanists were already applying the re-sults of their scholarly reinterpretation of classical antiquity to the task of understanding their own society and were in the process of acquiring a new sense of citizenship and a new historical perspective. Especially in Florence, where a tradition of civic freedom together with the efforts necessary to protect it from external aggression had created an atmosphere unusually congenial to its growth, a peculiarly civic humanism was already flourishing. It was secular in its emphasis, sensitive to the passage of time, devoted to the adaptation of classical precept and example to the demands of active citizenship, and con-fident in the ability of the properly informed mind to cope with the issues of civil society.[79]

Nor were Englishmen entirely ignorant of this new learning, however slow they might be to recognize its applicability to the affairs of the commonwealth. Ever since Duke Humphrey of Gloucester

79. See Hans Baron, *The Crisis of the Early Italian Renaissance* (Princeton, 1955).

had led the way to Italy a few scholars had picked up the same path.[80] Moreover, when they returned they could expect a certain amount of encouragement from the court.   For prestige purposes, if for no other reason, it was important for any monarch who would cut a figure in the new Europe of competing states to keep a stable of scholars sufficiently versed at least in the new rhetoric to deliver an oration in the fashionable Ciceronian style.   There is also evidence that, in the latter part of the century, the gentry and merchants of England were beginning to take some small notice of the new classicism.

The seriousness of purpose that marks much of the writing of England in the wake of the disasters in France and in the midst of the chronic disaster of the civil wars found expression both in a revival of chivalric idealism and in a tentative and hesitant sampling of the classical tradition of citizenship.   These two tendencies were not so far apart as they might seem.   The English governing class of the fifteenth century tended to see in the ideals of chivalry the only guide available to them for their secular activities, and, since their secular duties involved administrative and judicial as well as military service, they tended also to see in chivalry the inspiration for a new dedication to citizenship.[81]   But there is also evidence that a few of those whose experience had been relatively broad were beginning to seek a similar inspiration in the tradition of Roman citizenship.   At the behest of his patrons, William Caxton saw fit to interrupt a program of publishing, generally traditional in character, long enough to print two of Cicero's orations meant specifically for the special edification of those "noble, wise, and great lords, gentlemen and merchants that have seen and daily be occupied in matters touching the public weal."[82]   And John Tiptoft translated Buonaccorso da Montemagno's *Controversia de Nobilitate*, one of the earliest products of Florentine humanism to be disseminated beyond Italy.[83]   The English version, it is true, treats the central problem—whether true nobility comes from birth and riches

80. On pre-Tudor humanism, see Roberto Weiss, *Humanism in England during the Fifteenth Century* (Oxford, 1941).

81. Ferguson, *Indian Summer*; see especially chaps. ii and iv.

82. W. J. B. Crotch, *The Prologues and Epilogues of William Caxton*, E.E.T.S., O.S., No. 167 (London, 1928), p. 43.

83. *The Declamacion of Noblesse*, ed. R. J. Mitchell, in that author's *John Tiptoft* (London, 1938), Appendix I. For a discussion of the character and influence of this work, see Baron, *Crisis*, pp. 364-366, 625-628.

or from virtue and learning employed in the service of the common-wealth—very gingerly, leaving the decision up to the reader. And, in the play, *Fulgens and Lucres* (ca. 1497), which Henry Medwall made out of the same theme, the decision in favor of the man of learned attainments and civic virtue is also introduced very cautiously, no doubt in deference to the sensibilities of an audience to whom such an idea still seemed subversive.[84] But the important thing is that the question, basic to the new citizenship, had been raised.

These harbingers of a new age do not, however, alter the fact that the new age had not yet arrived. Nor should they blind us to the fact that the governing class of fifteenth-century England remained to the end of the period, and beyond, almost pathetically faithful to the values of an increasingly anachronistic chivalry, or that outside the court the imported techniques of scholarship were employed rather in the in-terests of the older discipline of scholasticism than as the basis for a new concept of citizenship, or that the books Caxton provided for the gentry and merchants who constituted his patrons and public were predominantly chivalric and devotional in character.

Why, then did it take humanism so long to strike roots in England's soil? The answer is not simple. It would be comforting to be able to say that the wealthy merchant class, the rough counterpart of the men who had made contemporaneous Florence the cradle of civic human-ism, were not yet confident enough to demand or influential enough to get a culture more suited to their way of life than that of chivalry. To some extent this would be true. But the nobility and gentry had also passed beyond the point where chivalric values bore much real relation to their increasingly non-military, administrative functions. Nor were they any more confident in their ability to find anything better. There was, in fact, less cultural difference between the land-owning aristocracy and the more well-to-do merchants in England than elsewhere in Europe outside Italy. The gentry and burgesses shared with the lords the responsibilities of government, sat together in Parliament, and were in many instances bound together by ties of blood and economic interest. They shared a common culture, too. Caxton, in whose list of publications the interests and tastes of his gen-eration are mirrored, enjoyed the patronage of nobles and gentlemen

84. *Fulgens and Lucres. A Fifteenth-Century Secular Play*, ed. F. S. Boas and A. W. Reed (Oxford, 1926). Baron, *Crisis*, p. 627.

and merchants, and it was for the edification of them all that he chose the works to be printed.[85]   The English Renaissance was not to be exclusively, or even primarily, an urban movement.

It would also be easy—and also true up to a point—to say that new ideas could not flourish in an era of political confusion such as that of the Wars of the Roses, or in one of uneven economic prosperity such as was a good deal of the fifteenth century, or in the shadow of the anti-Lollard repression, or in the decadent universities.   These conditions were obviously not in the interests of a new scholarship or a new citizenship.   But the fifteenth century was for England an age of paradox. The wars seem not to have seriously disturbed the life of the country as a whole, however much they may have deranged the government;[86] and insofar as they created political and administrative confusion, they helped create among more thoughtful observers a heightened sense of public responsibility.   If England's trade fluctuated and large fortunes were not in the making, it was a period of unprecedented opportunity for the men of lesser means and more limited ambitions.[87] Inhibiting as were the efforts to police the country against heresy, they did not prevent Reginald Pecock from undertaking a bold but premature experiment in the public discussion of religious issues.[88] Finally, a new reading public—and it is not to be taken lightly—was being educated probably more in the new grammar schools and the Inns of Court than in the universities.

The answer must therefore be sought, in part at least, in the history of humanism itself.   No doubt, as Hans Baron maintains, "before humanism could mean more to late medieval England, the growth of humanism in Italy had to reach the stage where the classicists' enthusiasm for ancient literature and art was balanced by renewed thoughts of religion, and by endeavors to reconcile the classical legacy with the Christian tradition."[89]   That work was accomplished to a large

85. Nellie Aurner, *Caxton, Mirror of Fifteenth-Century Letters* (Boston, 1926).   See also Ferguson, *Indian Summer*, chap. ii; H. S. Bennett, *English Books and their Readers, 1475-1557* (Cambridge, 1952).

86. C. L. Kingsford, *Prejudice and Promise in XV Century England* (Oxford, 1925), chap. iii.

87. M. M. Postan, "The Fifteenth Century," *EcHR*, IX (1939), 160-167; "Some Social Consequences of the Hundred Years' War," *ibid.*, XII (1942), 1-12.

88. Pecock, *Repressor*. See also E. H. Emerson, "Reginald Pecock: Christian Rationalist," *Speculum*, XXI (April, 1956), 235-242.

89. Hans Baron, "Fifteenth-Century Civilisation and the Renaissance," in *The New*

extent by the Florentine school of Neoplatonic philosophy that flourished under the guidance of Marsilio Ficino and Pico della Mirandola. The humanism that finally took deep enough root in England to flourish was, it is true, a distinctly Christian humanism— "Christian," that is, not in contrast to any putative paganism in the earlier Italian tradition, but in the sense that it appealed to men eager to remake their society in soul as in body. It appealed in particular to the generation of Colet and More who succeeded for the first time in domesticating humanism in England. But the leading spirit among that generation was Erasmus, and, despite the deep impression the Italy of Pico and Ficino had made on him and on his English friends, his vision of a society reformed in accordance with both Christian ethics and the rational example of classical antiquity arose more immediately from the socially oriented and spiritually sensitive humanism of the north. It was this vision that was transmitted to the next generation of English humanists who developed both its spiritual and social implications and who, in the secular writings of the 1530's and 1540's achieved a truly "civic" humanism.[90]

It must, however, be borne in mind that humanism did not by itself create the public consciousness of early Tudor England, not even if we grant that it enjoyed in the court of Henry VIII unusual encouragement or found in the revolutionary events of the first half of the century object lessons in social process of a sort most likely to cultivate the sense of change. The Tudor commentators were also able to draw upon an indigenous tradition of realism. The English fifteenth century was a period of decadent culture but vital individuals. To judge the capabilities of the citizen of that period by the fugitive political literature or those works written on the pattern of the *Secreta Secretorum* would be to miss the important fact, namely the realism that enabled a few gifted men to see through the film of stereotype and to achieve insights of some originality. Their originality lay not in any formulation of new theory but in the freshness of their approach

---

Cambridge Modern History (Cambridge, 1957), I, 55. See also W. K. Ferguson, *Europe in Transition, 1300–1520* (Boston, 1962), pp. 531 ff.

90. Cf. Roberto Weiss, "Learning and Education in Western Europe from 1470 to 1520," in *The New Cambridge Modern History*, I, 126. Weiss's contention that the Reformation was "both the culmination and the ruin of humanism" and that the "end of religious unity in western Europe was also the end of humanism," is not borne out by the "applied" humanism of the 1530's and 1540's. See below, chaps. vii–xiii.

to public issues. The *Libel of English Policy* seems more closely related to the economic pamphlets of the mid-sixteenth century than to the generally superficial comment inspired by the later stages of the Hundred Years' War. The problem of efficient government received surprisingly slender reference in the civil war period, yet it prompted Fortescue to the most thoroughgoing analysis and the most practical proposals for reform to be made before the reign of Henry VIII. And George Ashby was able to use the model of the *Secreta* merely as the inert framework for some penetrating comments on English government,[91] at times not unworthy of comparison to Fortescue's. Even the author of *The Boke of Noblesse* could not keep to the conventional categories of chivalric thought, but instead turned what purported to be just another manual of knighthood into an analysis, wrong-headed but original, of foreign policy and military organization.[92]

There is, then, in the fifteenth-century literature of comment and criticism a new realism, sporadic and uneven in its manifestations, but ready to blend effectively with a civic-minded humanism. Stated more specifically it amounts to a tendency to treat public issues in the restricted context of tangible reality rather than in the broader pattern of a universal morality or of a providential history. This rising realism is undoctrinaire, no doubt unconscious. It arose in answer to no new intellectual inspiration, no outside influence. Rather it grew out of the substratum of practical common-sense attitudes, of utilitarian values, of downright materialism if you will, that underlay the idealism still characteristic of the more orthodox thought of the period.

The world was very much with these men of fifteenth-century England, despite their unquestioning adherence to the ideal values of a Christian tradition that had lost much of its vitality or of a chivalry no longer in more than formal touch with the actual affairs of society. Men of modest property and position in particular, those who made up the solid core of the politically conscious public, could seldom in that upset age afford the luxury of contemplation or pure scholarship. They valued education more and more, but for such necessarily practical purposes as training in the law of tenures or perhaps for the

91. George Ashby, *The Active Policy of a Prince*, in *The Poems of George Ashby*, ed. Mary Bateson, E.E.T.S., E.S., No. 76 (1899). See below, chap. iii.

92. *The Boke of Noblesse*, ed. J. G. Nichols (London, 1860). For a discussion of this curious work, see Ferguson, *Indian Summer*, chap. v.

promise of preferment at court. They wanted books, but, like their Victorian counterparts, they expected their reading matter to be useful, or at any rate improving. They even took their romances of chivalry a touch more seriously than their French contemporaries, and liked to keep them within sight of common experience.[93]

This trend toward the practical, toward reality in the narrow sense, was not in itself likely to give rise to new ideas. It does, however, reflect a fresh approach to the discussion of public issues and one which by the end of the fifteenth century had already done much to place the thought of the articulate citizen on the same working level as that of the king's official counselors. To that extent it was all the easier for the early Tudor pamphleteers to act in their largely self-appointed capacity as citizen-counselors and to express themselves in the language of a newer citizenship as well as in the more familiar accents of popular complaint.

93. Ferguson, *Indian Summer*, pp. 42 ff.

CHAPTER II. THE MORAL CRITIC
AND THE SOCIAL ORDER

IN THE PRECEDING PAGES WE HAVE WATCHED, AS FROM A distance, the articulate citizen of late medieval England in his efforts to cope with the problems of an imperfect and changing society. With a few important exceptions, the impression he conveys is that of a man who wants very much to understand what is going wrong and is eager to set things right, yet somehow misses on both accounts. Not that he himself was conscious of any greater degree of failure than the social critic must always feel when faced with the intransigent stuff of reality, nor does he give the impression of having sought without finding. His failure is rather a relative one, apparent mainly when considered in the context of the history of thought. He failed, that is, to think as his successors of early Tudor England were beginning to do. He failed in particular to follow up his realistic observation of social evils with a consistent attempt to discover their social causes and to devise constructive policies for dealing with them. If, then, we are to estimate with any degree of accuracy the distance that separated him from his Renaissance counterpart, if also we are to give due credit to the occasional bold step he made in the new direction, we must reconstruct those habits of thought which prevented him from seeing beyond the customary boundaries of his culture.

This, however, presents certain difficulties. It is not easy to find materials in the political literature of medieval England sufficiently parallel in purpose and mode of expression to the work of the Tudor pamphleteers to make possible any very enlightening comparison. Fortunately, however, the literature of the late fourteenth century, that first significant era in the history of English public discussion, provides us with much that can be made to serve, if only for lack of anything better. The work of John Gower and William Langland is especially suitable. In their voluminous writings it is possible to find a mirror broad enough to reflect the entire configuration of their thought. They intended their writings to be *summae*, both of man's worldly state and of his spiritual life. Comprehensive as was their aim and only incidentally concerned with the affairs of the national community as such, they provide us in passing with comment of a consistency unique among contemporaneous English documents. Quite un⁄ parallel in their personalities and abilities, perhaps also in their ex⁄ perience, their minds nevertheless converged on essentials, and where they remained divergent they make possible enlightening comparisons.

The author of *Piers Plowman*[1] remains to us what he seems to have been to most of his contemporaries, a voice and little more. Except that he was almost certainly a member of the clergy, it is hard to find anything concrete about him. Perhaps he may have been, after all, a figment of the modern scholarly imagination. If so, if the successive versions of the poem were, in fact, the product of different pens, the consistency of thought that pervades them becomes for the historian all the more significant. In contrast, we have reasonably certain, if un⁄ exciting, knowledge of Gower:[2] a prosperous layman whose interests and sympathies lay with the Kentish gentry and the business commu⁄ nity of London, a man of some literary repute, patronized by the royal court, learned in the largely second⁄hand, predigested lore of his day. Never one to seek anonymity in life, in death he lay in an elaborately fashioned tomb on which his effigy appears, solid and consequential, its head pillowed on three massive volumes, bearing the titles of his three major works, *Mirour de l'Omme*, *Vox Clamantis*, and *Confessio Amantis*.

Neither Gower nor Langland seem at first glance at all comparable to the modern, or even the early Tudor commentators. Though both have much to say in passing about the temporal condition of man, their ultimate concern was for his soul. And even when commenting upon his temporal life their preoccupation is with moral rather than impersonal factors and their outlook remains rather universal than national. But it would be dangerous, and very easy, to overestimate these distinctions. At most they represent a conflict of emphasis to be

1. This is not the place to review the complex problem of the authorship of *Piers Plowman*. Anyone wishing to follow the paths of scholarship through this much written⁄ about topic will be able to make at least a good start from the following works: M. W. Bloomfield, "Present State of *Piers Plowman* Studies," ~~*Journal of Medieval Studies*~~, XIV (April, 1939), 215⁄232; E. Talbot Donaldson, *Piers Plowman, the C⁄text and its Poet* (New Haven, 1949); D. C. Fowler, *Piers the Plowman, Literary Relations of the A and B Texts* (Seattle, 1961).

Speculum

2. For biographical data see John H. Fisher, *John Gower, Moral Philosopher and Friend of Chaucer* (New York, 1964), chaps. ii and iii; Macaulay in Gower, *Complete Works*, IV, introduction.

expected in a day when national considerations were only beginning to emerge within a culture universal in its scheme of values. And anyway, they are distinctions that mean more to the modern mind than they would ever have to the medieval. Englishmen were also Chris tians, and England but a part of a theoretically unified Christendom. And the ethical problems uppermost in the mind of the medieval commentator were pertinent alike to the spiritual welfare of man and to the temporal welfare of his society.

Gower, it is true, seems to have been aware of these distinctions, but did not let them deter him from serving as both universal moralist and commentator on English society.³ Although he no doubt con sidered himself first of all a critic of society in its universal aspects—the original copies of *Vox Clamantis* bore a miniature of the author shooting arrows at a *mappa mundi* and an inscription which ran, in part, "*Ad mundum mitto mea iacula*"—and although he laments the passing of unity among Christian peoples,⁴ it was English society that presented the immediate target for his arrows. "I love," he wrote in *Vox Clamantis*, "all the kingdoms which the Lord has established for himself through out the world and which bear standards in Christ's name. But above all I love my own land, in which my family took its origin. . . . I am almost overwhelmed by the weight of her adversities. If she stands firm, I stand firm; if she falls, I fall."⁵

As for Langland, he presents difficulties which might well dis courage anyone from trying to find in his poem any reflection of the mind of the politically and socially conscious English citizen. When Gower speaks of English problems, of wool, the Lombards, or the peasants, the "great city," or the "war," one is justified in assuming that he is referring to historical reality. In a day when the literal sense was seldom left to bear the entire weight of meaning, Gower was unusually literal minded. The same cannot be said of Langland. On the

---

3. For discussion of Gower as a public moralist, see Fisher, chap. iv. I regret that I did not have this book available while writing the present chapter, but recommend it to anyone who would delve further into Gower's thought. See also G. R. Coffman, "John Gower in His Most Significant Role," *Elizabethan Studies and other Essays in Honor of George F. Reynolds, University of Colorado Studies*, Series B., II, No. 4 (1945), 52-61; Maria Wickert, *Studien zu John Gower* (Köln, 1953).

4. *Confessio Amantis*, in *Works*, II-III, Prologue, ll. 849 ff.

5. *Vox Clamantis*, in *Works*, IV, Liber VII, chap. xxiv, ll. 1289-1300. I am using the translation by E. W. Stockton, *The Major Latin Works of John Gower* (Seattle, 1962).

contrary, so intertwined is the literal in his poem with the allegorical, and perhaps also with the anagogical, and the tropological, so subtle are the overtones of symbolism in every reference to mundane life,[6] that the historian would do well to use any such reference only with the greatest care. *Piers Plowman* is, after all, a religious work, one steeped in the rich residue of scriptural and patristic learning. Yet our immediate need is great. However hesitantly, we must use it wherever possible for comparison with Gower's more direct comments.

For the first section of *Piers Plowman*, the *Visio*, does in fact make extensive use of the English scene. Though a dream poem, and as such part of the long tradition of mythical expression, Langland's vision is unusual in dealing less with heaven than with earth, and with English earth at that.[7] "Never," writes Coghill, "was a professed dreamer more practical."[8] Perhaps Jusserand exaggerated when he suggested that *Piers Plowman* seems at times almost a commentary on the *Rolls of Parliament* and the *Liber Albus* of the city of London.[9] Certainly efforts to trace political allusions in it have served little purpose other than to keep scholars from even less rewarding endeavors. Public issues lay nevertheless close to the surface of the poet's mind. They determined much of the literal sense of the *Visio* and many inci-dental references throughout the rest of the work. Moreover, it should be remembered that the literal interpretation had to be meaningful in itself, at least to contemporaries, if it was to serve as an effective vehicle for any transcendent meaning.

It would have been strange indeed if events had not in some way affected the outlook of these men whose minds were as sensitive to the external life of their time as to its spiritual condition. While it is possi-ble to see in the last major revision of Langland's poem a more cautious handling of social problems, perhaps a less radical wording of political pronouncements, perhaps a greater preoccupation with political problems, it is difficult to detect any considerable change in his point

6. See D. W. Robertson and B. F. Huppé, *Piers Plowman and Scriptural Interpretation* (Princeton, 1951). Cf. R. W. Frank, *Piers Plowman and the Scheme of Salvation* (New Haven, 1957), p. 8.

7. Donaldson, p. 121.

8. N. H. K. Coghill, "The Pardon of Piers Plowman," *PBA*, XXX (1944), 303-357 309.

9. J. J. Jusserand, *Piers Plowman, a Contribution to the History of English Mysticism* (New York, 1894), pp. 113-114.

of view.[10] The changes represent for the most part an amplification of ideas already expressed and a confirmation of attitudes already characteristic. Gower's political experience seems, on the other hand, to have ripened his political consciousness. With each succeeding work he became just a bit more willing to treat public issues directly, as matters in themselves worth specific treatment, and to consider the national bearing even of universal conditions.[11]

He may be seen passing in the course of his industrious career from medieval religious verse with political overtones to political comment, with religious overtones; from discussion conducted almost entirely through moral generalities to concrete treatment of political events. In the process, the government of England gradually took a more specific place in his scheme of things and assumed a clearer outline. There is little doubt that national issues looked larger and more distinct to the aged poet who could write critically of foreign policy than to the young-er moralist who could only lecture the king on the sin of pride.

꙳ ꙳ ꙳

If, in the process of casting a critical eye on the society of Christen-dom and exploring the moral nature of man, Gower and Langland came at times to deal with the immediate issues of specifically English life and government, neither man was able to place those issues con-

10. On the conservatism of the C-text, see Donaldson, chap. iv. Some of the changes may have been prompted by the unauthorized and possibly irresponsible use made of the Piers Plowman theme by the agitators of 1381. A. H. Bright, *New Light on Piers Plowman* (Oxford, 1928), pp. 76 ff. Of perhaps greater significance is the fact that a noticeably large number of the additions made to the C-text embodied political or social statements. E.g., iii, 243-248, iv, 317-408 (especially 381-385), vi, 65-81, 183-189, ix, 88-90. All references are to W. W. Skeat (ed.), (2 vols.; London, 1924). As to whether and to what extent the poet was influenced by the Revolt of 1381, much depends on what date is assigned to the B-text. On that subject, see B. Huppé, "The Date of the B-text of *Piers Plowman*," SP, XXXVIII (Jan., 1941), 34-44; J. A. W. Bennett, "The Date of the B-text of *Piers Plowman*," *Medium Aevum*, XII (1943), 55-64; Fowler, pp. 167-169.

11. The contrast in this respect between his early and late writings can, of course, be exaggerated. In the *Mirour de l'Omme*, his first major work, he veiled many comments in conventional generalities which contemporaries would have recognized as references to specific events. See Gardiner Stillwell, "John Gower and the Last Years of Edward III," SP, XLV (July, 1948), 454-471. And Fisher argues persuasively for a conscious, unity of purpose, even a certain simultaneity in the composition of the three major works. But there seems no doubt that Gower was drawn more directly into political controversy in the later years of Richard II's reign.

sistently within the context of constructive policy. Unlike some at least of the Tudor writers, they remained for the most part negative rather than positive in their comment, content to register popular complaint in the hope that the king and his lords, with the aid of Parliament, would adopt what regulatory measures were needed. Nor do they, in their analysis of cause, proceed much beyond the moral responsibility of men living and exercising their social functions in a society of hierarchical status. It is in this latter respect, as I hope to demonstrate in the remaining pages of this chapter, that the key may be found to the medieval citizen's conception of government and of his own position as a citizen.[12]

Of those problems which might be expected to fall in one way or another within the province of the central government the most pressing had naturally enough to do with the church and its reform, the administration of justice, the life of trade and commerce, the manorial relationships, the "over-mighty subject" and the related evils of maintenance, and, finally, the king's foreign policy. The royal administration, of course, constituted in itself a major problem and one which was involved in all other public issues.

Gower and Langland shared the opinion common to most social critics of the day concerning the luxurious lives and temporal entanglements of the clergy.[13] A fiscally preoccupied, politically oriented papacy had become a scandal in the eyes of Christian Europe, and the English branches of the church clearly were suffering from the same diseases that affected the roots. Both writers took it as a matter of course that the failure of the clergy to discharge their appointed duty in society constituted a menace to the commonwealth in its secular as well as in its spiritual aspects—not that they made any clear distinction between the two, so completely was the daily life of man interpenetrated by religious considerations. Gower, in particular, gave explicit expression to an opinion generally taken for granted when he stated that if bad

12. On this subject of the estates, see Ruth Mohl, *The Three Estates in Medieval and Renaissance Literature* (New York, 1933); for Gower's attitude, see especially pp. 27-31, 105-107. Systematic attention has been given the social aspects of Langland's work in D. Chadwick, *Social Life in the Days of Piers Plowman* (Cambridge, 1922) and Wiehe, *Piers Plowman und die socialen Fragen seiner Zeit* (Einsdellen, 1935). Less has been done on Gower, but there is useful information in Coffman's article cited above.

13. E.g., *Piers Plowman*, B, Prol., 87-98 and the many examples cited by Chadwick, chap. i; *Mirour*, 18421-21780; *Vox Clamantis*, III, ix.

times come, if, that is, the kingdom as a whole comes to grief, the clergy must bear their share of the blame, since the body is nothing without the spirit[14]—and before we dismiss this as the stock formula of the conventional critic, let us recall that Gower was here using the very language of those practical men of affairs who deliberated in Parlia ment. In 1376, for example, one of the petitions presented there argued quite seriously that wars, pestilence, hunger, murrains, and other calamities resulted from the failure of the church to perform its spiritual duties.[15]

Thus the matter of ecclesiastical discipline fell logically within the area over which civil government had jurisdiction as the agency re sponsible for the general welfare. So also, for Gower at least, did heresy: we find him in a late poem urging Richard II to take action against the Lollards,[16] but he suggests no specific measure. Neither writer, indeed, was willing to explore the relationship of church and state at all specifically. Langland, it is true, went considerably further than Gower in suggesting one thing that the secular authority could do about conditions in the clerical community. Since the root of the trouble lay in the temporal possessions of the clergy, he, the orthodox if unconventional poet, proposed the Wycliffite policy of disendowment. "Take their lands, ye lords . and let them live by dimes [tithes]."[17] Langland may also have recognized more clearly than Gower the political implications of papal power. A few passing references in dicate that he, like the English Parliament of his day, saw the pope as an alien potentate whose claims and practices at times ran counter to English interests. He complains specifically of appeals to Rome, of the papal claim to provisors, and of the tendency of "Rome runners" to carry "silver over sea that sign of king showeth."[18] But it was the spiritual decadence of the papacy that constituted for both him and Gower the real danger. The political issue, if separable at all, merely provided additional evidence of a condition prejudicial to the health of all Christendom.

Both writers trace the agrarian unrest endemic in their generation to

14. *Vox Clamantis*, IV, xxiv, 1215 1224.
15. *Rotuli Parliamentorum*, II, 337 ff.
16. *Carmen super multiplici viciorum pestilencia*, *Complete Works*, IV, ll. 90 93.
17. *Piers Plowman*, C, xviii, 225 228. Cf. B, xv, 524 526.
18. *Ibid.*, B, ii, 168 ff., iv, 128 133; C, iii, 182, 243 248, v, 125 129. Cf. B, xix, 413 417, 439 442; C, xxii, 418 431, 443 448.

the perversity of all concerned, or, more specifically, to the failure of either laborers or landlords to discharge the duties assigned to them in the social hierarchy. Gower, probably himself a landlord, held the peasants mostly to blame.[19] The revolt of 1381, which seems to have been a really traumatic experience for him, resulted, he felt, from their wanton and violent attempt to break the natural order of things. In the idiom of nightmare he describes men changed into the lowest beasts which, breaking their natural bonds, attack their superiors in the animal kingdom.[20] Langland was more sympathetic to the plight of the poor, if only because his deep hatred of injustice led him to brood over the sufferings of a class on whose ordinarily patient shoulders fell the residual injustices of a society unjust in all its orders.[21] But this did not prevent him from condemning the laborers for being lazy, greedy, and irresponsible.[22] Nor did the equalitarianism that has always clung with an embarrassingly simple logic to the social gospel of Christianity and to which Langland pays passing respect[23] seriously affect his feeling for the sacredness of the social order.[24] Such equality as he recognizes is rather the equality of the Dance of Death,[25] the democracy of the charnel house,[26] than of civil society. Inequality, he suggests, is in fact but a corollary of man's first sin: "No beggar nor boy among us . but of sin it make."[27]

Both Gower and Langland thus wrote of agrarian unrest in the spirit of the Statutes of Laborers, the purpose of which had been to solve the wage problem by fiat. Like their literary contemporaries, the "practical" men of Parliament misunderstood or ignored the processes of social change, seeing in them simply the willful and vicious strivings of inordinate men. Neither Gower nor Langland, however, appear to

19. *Mirour*, 26530·26533, 26437·26442, 26449·26453; *Vox Clamantis*, V, ix, 577·582.

20. *Vox Clamantis*, I, especially ll. 2092 ff. See also Wickert, chap. ii.

21. He felt especially keenly for the pathetic victims of the disordered times who ". . . be abashed for to beg . and will not admit / What they need at their neigh·bors. . . ." *Piers Plowman*, C, x, 86·87.

22. *Ibid.*, C, ix, 340·341; cf. B, vi, 317·319. See also B, iv, and C, ix, *passim*.

23. *Ibid.*, B, xi, 192·193; cf. C, xiii, 108·111.

24. For a discussion of this apparent ambivalence in Langland's social outlook, see Donaldson, pp. 83·86.

25. *Piers Plowman*, B, xx, 99·104; C, xxiii, 111·115. Cf. Gower, *Vox Clamantis*, VI, xiii, VII, ix.

26. *Piers Plowman*, B, vi, 50·51; C, ix, 45·46.

27. *Ibid.*, C, xiii, 111; cf. B, xi, 197.

have placed much faith in legislation as a remedy for such social ills. Langland, no doubt had the Statutes in mind when he described the activites of a government which "for profit of all the people . plough men ordained / To till and travail . as true life asketh."[28] And he gives us a glimpse of the actual administrative machinery in the efforts of the knight, acting obviously in his capacity as justice of the peace, to bring the sanction of the law to bear on Waster, the irresponsible laborer.[29] Gower, on the other hand, simply asserts that, if a laborer refuses to labor or becomes otherwise unco-operative, he must be forced,[30] leaving the administrative problem without comment. Both men, however, prefer to go beyond government to the moral nature of man in their search for both the cause of social unrest and for its remedy. Perhaps the example of the Statute and its subsequent reissuings was such as to discourage them from exploring the possibilities inherent in governmental policy. Certainly they were at best a crude weapon against social change, reflecting no willingness on the part of their authors to investigate secondary causes which might be affected by constructive policy, and, since the conditions they were intended to correct continued, they were patently ineffective.

Langland, in fact, makes it quite clear that laws by themselves will not solve the problem of putting Waster to work. He places somewhat greater emphasis on the natural sanction of hunger. His practical insight, coupled with his sense of social order, led him to take an almost Malthusian attitude toward the labor problem. But, he admits, even hunger is effective in keeping the agricultural laborer working at his appointed task and at a moderate wage only as long as it actually gnaws at his vitals. Give him a full stomach and his memory of hard times grows very dim.[31] So in the final analysis it is again a moral problem to which coercion, whether natural or legislative, can offer but a partial answer. And, since Langland, like Gower, conceives of government primarily as a coercive agency rather than as the source of constructive policy, the role of government in the social ferment remains limited.

The life of trade and commerce presented a somewhat different

28. *Ibid.*, B, Prol., 118-120; cf. C, ix, 340-341.
29. *Piers Plowman*, B, vi, 161-168; C, ix, 156-163.
30. *Vox Clamantis*, V, ix, 621-628, x, 651-654.
31. *Piers Plowman*, B, vi, 309-321; C, ix, 331-343.

problem to the social critic. Agrarian unrest seemed simple enough—deceptively so: get the laborer to work and at the old wage, admittedly a difficult task, but not, as conceived, a complex one. The commercial world, on the contrary, presented, even to the casual observer in fourteenth-century England, a complicated picture indeed, and one he found it hard to reconcile with his traditional picture of the social order. Anyone in a position to watch the life of London in particular could hardly fail to appreciate the interaction of interests within the national economy. The "great city" constituted a microcosm in which the affairs of the national macrocosm might be seen in epitome. Both Langland and Gower enjoyed this opportunity, but Gower appears to have been especially familiar with the commercial community. His comment on its problems far exceeds in concreteness anything he had to say on the agrarian problem and, in fact, goes well beyond the treatment given them by Langland.[32]

Basically the commercial issues are, to Gower as to Langland, still moral ones. Fraud and usury[33] represented the particular expression in economic life of the primary sin of avarice, and achieved social importance because they furthered the individual's interest at the expense of those of the community. Accordingly, the only final answer was also a moral one, namely return to virtuous behavior on the part of the men of commerce. "*Triche*" stands self-condemned. Both writers leave in the air the administrative problem of combatting it.

But it is worth noticing that Gower had grasped certain economic realities, especially the supreme importance of the wool trade, in England's economy. And his discussion of the wool trade led him into the broader realm of foreign trade in which the national government had a necessary and obvious place. "You are," he says, in his famous apostrophe to wool, "the goddess of merchants... You are cherished throughout the world, and the land where you were born may do great things by reason of you.... You were born in England . . . ." He alludes feelingly to the difficulties of Staple administration: "it is said on all sides how badly you are managed, for Trickery, who is made of money, has become director of your staple and takes it into

32. E.g., *Mirour*, 25225-25452; *Vox Clamantis*, V, xii-xv.

33. E.g., *Mirour*, 25225 ff.; *Vox Clamantis*, V, xii-xiv; *Tractatus de Lucis Scrutinio*, in *Works*, IV, 355-357, ll. 63-72. See Chadwick, pp. 63-70 for detailed references to Langland's treatment of these subjects.

a foreign country if it please him."[34]   From wool it is only a step to the problem of foreign merchants who seem to have been a perpetual cause of suspicion and jealousy on the part of Englishmen of the commer-cial class.[35] If, at times, Gower seems to confuse the interests of London with those of the entire country and to nourish a sense of citizenship more akin to that of the city-state than to that of the nation-state,[36] he merely reflects the ambivalence of this period during which the economy was in the process of changing from a town-centered to a nation-centered system.

Both Gower and Langland came as near as they did anywhere to a clear statement of the function of government in the nation's life when they dealt with the administration of justice. This was natural enough. Other problems, ecclesiastical reform, agrarian unrest, and the many ramifications of the wool-trade, might or might not suggest to the observing citizen legislation of a strictly remedial sort.   In the law courts that citizen could watch, if he would, the constant and immediate workings of government in the province he considered peculiarly and characteristically its own, namely, the declaring of rights and the pun-ishing of wrongs, the protection, that is, of the individual and his in-terests within his legal status.   Accordingly the judicial system had for generations been a favorite topic for the social reformer.

Both writers reveal an intimate knowledge of the judicial system. Both make criticisms any reader of contemporaneous literature will recognize at once. For the most part they boil down to a general charge of venality against lawyers and judges.[37]   And, of course, they trace venality to the sin of avarice.   Gower, especially, develops his charges against the legal profession with the air of one who knows it well.   The power of money begins with the lawyers' education at Westminster,[38] and leads them not only to sell justice to the highest bidder, but to make the law intentionally obscure.[39]   He even suggests a practical solution by advising the king to tax the ill-gotten gains of

34. *Mirour*, 25369-25428.
35. *Ibid.*, 25429-25452. Cf. *Vox Clamantis*, V, xv, 835-839.
36. *Vox Clamantis*, V, xv-xvi.
37. *Piers Plowman*, B, Prol., 210-215; cf. C, i, 159-164. *Mirour*, 24193-24204. Cf. *Tractatus*, ll. 55-62.
38. *Mirour*, 24350 ff.
39. *Ibid.*, 24601-24607.

lawyers and apply the proceeds to his wars, if he must wage them.[40]

Gower recognized, perhaps more clearly than Langland, that the administration of justice was something which affected the common good as well as that of the individual suitor. At any rate, some of the remarks he made on the subject in passing deserve to be noticed, for they indicate that Gower could see the connection between private discontent and public disorder. It is here, indeed, rather than in his treatment of the labor problem, that he demonstrates some awareness of the complexity of social relationships. Faulty justice, he declares, endangers the unity and safety of the entire state, for it leads to civil discord.[41] In this context, too, he places the problems of maintenance, though, like Langland, he emphasizes its impact on the private rather than the public interests[42]—if, indeed, either was willing or even able to make such distinctions. Justice, in itself a primary objective of good government, thus leads to domestic peace, another primary objective, the importance of which was more than ordinarily evident as the end of the century brought a weakening of royal power and a resurgence of baronial faction. It is to ensure justice and by so doing to promote peace—the "king's peace," not necessarily peace between states—that the king and his lords have the power of the secular sword.

> It is bidden that a brandished sword always be held, in order
> that judgment may strike wrongdoers more promptly. . . .
> Let he who wishes to rule protect justice with blood. Arms
> bring peace; arms curb the rapacious. A worthy king should
> bear arms so that the guilty man may fear them.[43]

In this period, as in the days of the early Tudor rebellions, the threat to the political organism posed by popular uprising did much to focus attention on the underlying discontents and undoubtedly helped promote a greater willingness to explore the injustices that caused them.

No less desirable than domestic tranquility was peace between countries. Gower's appeal to the sword, quoted above, has nothing necessarily to do with England's external relations. In that area, though by no means a believer in peace without honor, Gower con-

40. *Ibid.*, 24346-24348.
41. *Vox Clamantis*, VI, vii, 483-490 (Stockton trans.).
42. *Mirour*, 23317-23328. Cf. *Piers Plowman*, A, iv, 34-48.
43. *Vox Clamantis*, VI, ix, 709-714 (Stockton trans.); cf. VI, ix, 690 ff., VII, l. 1305.

sistently advocated a policy of peace.[44] In this attitude he was joined by Langland. Both spoke for the Christian tradition which had throughout the Middle Ages inspired efforts, largely futile it is true, to mitigate the bellicosity of the feudal baronage; and both wrote at a time when the first of the great international wars had done much to demonstrate the cost and futility of such a struggle as an instrument of national policy.

This was apparently a subject close to the heart of the aging Gower. Whereas Langland is content to treat it satirically, leaving the cause of the war to the hypocritical pleading of Lady Mede who charges that Conscience in cowardly fashion counsels the king to abandon his "heritage of France" to his enemy,[45] Gower attacks the problem directly and at some length. Although he had touched on the war in each of his three major works,[46] it was in the English poem *In Praise of Peace*, written just after the accession of Henry IV, that he turned his attention exclusively to it. To be sure, much of the tract is made up of the standard medieval sentiments concerning war: Gower, for example, is quite willing to justify a war engaged in by the king "To claim and ask his rightful heritage / In all places where it is witheld," but asserts that otherwise "Peace is the best above all earthly things."[47] Never theless it is *the* war he is concerned with and his concern is heightened, if not actually caused, by its effects on the country's economy.[48]

In this poem the indications that Gower in his later years had matured greatly in his understanding of social and political forces are especially apparent. Not only was he able so see the social and eco nomic results of the war, he could also discern something at least of its social and psychological origins. One particularly curious thing about the poem is its apparently deliberate criticism of the chivalric ideal of military enterprise. It must have occurred to the old moralist, as it has to modern historians, that the chronic war with France

44. Cf. Stockton, p. 447, n. 6, in which he asserts that the above quoted passage (n. 43) indicates that Gower was no pacifist despite his statements on peace in *Praise of Peace*.

45. *Piers Plowman*, C, iv, 242-243; B, iii, 206; cf. C, iv, 265. Note the divergent interpretations on this point in B. F. Huppé, "The A-text of *Piers Plowman* and the Norman Wars," *PMLA*, LIV (March, 1939), 37-64, and Donaldson, p. 112, n. 9. I tend to agree with Donaldson.

46. *Mirour*, 24337 ff.; *Vox Clamantis*, III, vii; VI, xiii, 971 ff.; VII, iv, 269 ff.; xxiv, 1305-1306; *Confessio Amantis*, Prol., ll. 160 ff.

47. Ll. 56-63. Cf. *Vox Clamantis*, VI, xiii.

48. Ll. 109-123.

had not been started or maintained solely for ponderable reasons of state. There had been an element of chivalric romanticism, of irresponsible knight-errantry, involved in Edward III's participation. And Gower may now have feared that a similarly chivalric chauvinism might prove just one more motive for renewing hostilities. He had hitherto always spoken respectfully of the chivalric ideals and had criticized the knightly order only for its failure to live up to them.[49] Now he seems to have felt that the king should be reminded that there are other values pertinent to a knight than those of military renown; and he counsels him

> After reason yet temper thy courage
> For like to peace there is no advantage.[50]

∽ ∽ ∽

Having seen something of the approach made by Langland and Gower to the concrete issues affecting the national life, we are, I believe, in a better position to understand their attitude toward society and toward the problem of government. Neither man was trained in the theory of government, if, indeed, there can be said to have been any such theory in late fourteenth-century England apart from the political philosophy common to all Western Christendom. They were interested in good government, or, as a contemporary writer put it, in "how good governance graciously endeth."[51] And they were very much concerned with the reasons for its failure. But they were not constitutionally minded in any modern sense. It is therefore unwise to lay too much weight on the references they made in passing to such matters as the relation of the crown to the law, the nature of Parliament and its relation to the king's council. Such references must be interpreted in the light of the author's general approach to government as a functioning agency—as, indeed, the only agency capable of applying regulative or corrective measures to the problems besetting the community.

As we have seen, neither Langland nor Gower offered much in the way of specific suggestions for such measures. Nor did they advocate anything at all of what a modern person would recognize

49. *Mirour*, 23593-24180; *Vox Clamantis*, V, i.
50. For a fuller discussion, see Ferguson, *Indian Summer*, chap. v.
51. *Mum and the Sothsegger*, M-fragment, l. 377.

as constructive policy, nothing, that is, of policy devised as a long-term measure with the object of manipulating the causal forces in society toward ends favorable to the national interest. Like his Tudor successors, Gower recognized that a diagnosis, to be worth anything, must lay bare the cause of the complaint—"*nam nichil in terra contingens fit sine causa*"—[52] and that a remedy, to be more than a palliative, must remove that cause. But both his and Langland's analysis of cause led immediately to the moral nature of man which conditions all his actions, both public and private. For the most part both writers passed over the complex of secondary causes which are for practical purposes the object of legislation.

Many people, Gower tells us, seek the cause of England's current loss of glory and prosperity, both of which had at one time surpassed all other nations.[53] They blame the times: with one voice they cry "*Le siecle est mal, le siecle est mal.*"[54] They call on Fortune (Gower uses the term to include any forces, fate, planetary influences etc., not divine but beyond the range of man's will)[55] and ask that fickle lady why she has forsaken them. No one will admit his own fault. Man, whom God made rational and placed over all living creatures, and to whom he gave the freedom to seek either good or evil, is alone responsible for his plight—and, we are permitted to add, Englishmen are solely responsible for their own peculiar tribulations. Gower, indeed, oversimplifies the enigma of evil to the extent of asserting, with characteristic rigidity, that fortune follows virtue: good behavior will bring prosperity; vice will bring bad times. He assumes that God prospers, in every sense, those who obey his commandments and brings misfortune to all sinners.[56] Even the elements work for the righteous man and against the evil, for man is a microcosm, and as he does well or ill the macrocosm functions smoothly or discordantly.[57] Man is a creature of freedom and dignity—not in the relatively modern sense made famous by the Renaissance humanists, but in the sense that he

---

52. *Vox Clamantis*, II, l. 41.
53. *Ibid.*, ll. 17-50.
54. *Mirour*, 26590-26591.
55. Wickert, pp. 144-145.
56. *Mirour*, 26581-26926; *Vox Clamantis*, II, i-ix, VII, xxiv-xxv. Cf. Wickert, pp. 149 ff. and 153 ff.
57. *Mirour*, 26929-27120; *Vox Clamantis*, VII, viii; *Confessio Amantis*, Prol., ll. 954-958.

alone of God's creatures is free and able to seek virtue and avoid vice.[58] Thus he holds in his hand the key not only to his own salvation but to the welfare of society and of nature itself in a universe built exclusively on moral principles, reflecting at every level of being the purpose of God.

If sin is the cause of bad times in England as in the rest of the world, the remedy follows naturally. Repent and turn to God.[59] In particular, Gower exhorts men to flee *luxuria* and avarice. These he believed were the two principal sources of trouble in the world.[60] *Luxuria*, leading as it does to sloth, prevents men from doing what they should, from performing their appointed tasks. Avarice, in contrast, is the positive force driving men to evil. From it stem the aggressions, the discord, the active injustice that plagues society.

Though less ponderous in his moralizing, Langland was thoroughly in accord with this analysis of cause and with the radical remedy proposed by Gower. Again to quote Coghill, "As always with Langland the answer to a practical problem is a practicing change of heart."[61] If men would but labor in their appointed place with love and according to the dictates of reason and conscience, all would be well. Even more than Gower, Langland was aware of the vicious influence of avarice. Mede, who stands for the power of the purse or the search for monetary reward, has corrupted all classes and perverted government and the courts. She is, therefore, the principle enemy of the commonwealth.

This preoccupation with moral factors provides the key also to the general picture of society which existed in the minds of Langland and Gower. Both considered the conduct of man to be the only source of social change that lies within the scope of man's understanding. It is, we gather, through man's conduct, determined by his moral choice, that Providence, the ultimate cause, operates. It is also and unquestionably the only source of change over which man himself has any control. If men acted as they should, society would operate smoothly as a hierarchy of estates and functional groups, each perform-

58. On Gower's emphasis on nature and human responsibility, see Coffman's article. A sense of man's dignity as a rational creature doubtless prompted him to make extravagant use of the beast allegory in the first book of *Vox Clamantis*.

59. *Vox Clamantis*, XXIV-XXV.

60. *Ibid.*, VII, i; cf. *Carmen*, ll. 225 ff.

61. Coghill, p. 312.

ing its appointed task for the welfare of the whole, each working as limbs or organs of the body politic, none seeking to usurp the place or prerogative of the others. In his criticism of the estates, Gower makes it quite clear that it is not the estate itself that he castigates, but those individuals in it who fail in their appointed duty.[62] But man's tendency to sin is inveterate and transgressors are always to be found. Hence change is likely to take the form of deterioration within this rigidly ordained social structure. Indeed change could hardly take place in any other way, unless virtuous action would restore the balance of things presumed to have existed at some point in the past.[63]

Gower's nostalgia for a lost perfection is in direct proportion to his consciousness of deterioration in the society of his own day. At times he looks back to specifically English conditions within his own memory. In his disappointment over the course of events in the reign of Richard II, he idealizes the days when Edward III and the Black Prince brought glory and prosperity to England beyond anything enjoyed by other countries.[64] This was also the time before the lower class had in their beastly unreason striven to upset the social order. The entire first book of *Vox Clamantis* is colored by the shock of that most unnatural of events and by an implied nostalgia for the *status quo ante*. Otherwise, however, Gower's Golden Age seems not much more than an intellectual convenience, much as the state of nature was to a later generation, a starting point adopted for the simple reason that one has to start somewhere. Set in the indefinitely distant past, it served to emphasize the general deterioration observable in society and had the virtue of fitting nicely into the scriptural account of world history. These, he tells us, are the latter days foretold by Christ, the final era of deterioration, the fourth monarchy of Nebuchadnezzar's dream.[65] In any case, the practical affairs of government, like all man's activities, he set in the context of a social order static in structure but declining in moral quality and hence in prosperity. Thus Gower was able to see little hope for improvement. Despite his belief in the

62. *Vox Clamantis*, III, Prol., 25-26.

63. J. Peter, *Complaint and Satire in Early English Literature* (Oxford, 1956), pp. 68-71. See especially, reference to *Confessio Amantis*, Prol., 93 ff., 1002-1011, V, 333 ff.

64. See especially, *Vox Clamantis*, VI, xiii, cf. II, i-ii. See also *Confessio Amantis*, Prol., 93 ff.

65. *Confessio Amantis*, Prol., 93 ff., 663-1088, V, 333 ff.; *Vox Clamantis*, VII, i and xii; cf. VI, xix-xxi.

possibility of individual improvement through repentances, he seems to have believed that both virtue and vice were present in society in fairly constant proportion: "*Les bons sont bons, les mals sont mals.*"[66] But they were not in stable equilibrium, for the bad seem to have had more potentiality for affecting the health of the microcosm than the good.

The Christian view of history as providential and redemptive could, of course, also be made to include social amelioration. Indeed, in more recent centuries, millenialist interpretations no doubt helped prepare the way for a concept of progress.[67] Although this was not the version popular in the Middle Ages, it remained a possible one, and Langland may well have looked forward to the attainment of a perfect society on earth as the penultimate act in the drama of man's salvation.[68] Certainly in the dramatic structure of his poem he left room for man's search for social as well as spiritual perfection through a progressive conquest of sin.

But the problem of history in this sense, the problem of *Heilsgeschichte*, is not immediately relevant. It has little bearing on the attitude of either Langland or Gower toward society as it exists or on their conception of government's part in it. Whether the perfect society lay in the past or in the future, it was only a better society, not a different one. Much as it might hope for social improvement through the expanding beneficence of justice and peace, the medieval mind could see little that was manageable in its environment, nor could it conceive of history as the autonomous province of human endeavor.

The fact of immediate importance is that Langland shared Gower's vision of a hierarchical society, an organism static in form but subject to fluctuation in its general health. In that society some had for their sins been ordained to serve others,[69] but all were supposed to perform some function for the good of the whole community and to labor patiently in the status to which they were born. Much of the trouble in the society of his own day had, he felt, come about because this

66. *Mirour*, 25225. See also Macaulay, in *Complete Works*, I, liii.

67. See E. L. Tuveson, *Millenium and Utopia* (Berkeley, 1949). G. B. Ladner explores this and related ideas in the patristic period; *The Idea of Reform* (Cambridge, Mass., 1959).

68. M. W. Bloomfield, *Piers Plowman as a Fourteenth-century Apocalypse* (New Brunswick, 1962); see especially chap. iv. Cf. Fowler, chaps. iii-v.

69. *Piers Plowman*, C, xiii, 108 ff.

hereditary system had been deranged through the inordinate ambitions of all classes.

> Bondsmen and bastards . and beggars' children,
> Thus belongeth to labor . and lord's kin to serve
> Both God and good men . as their degree asketh;
> Some to sing masses . others sit and write,
> Read and receive . whatever reason ought spend;
> But since bondsmen's bairns . have been made bishops,
> And bastard children . have been archdeacons,
> And soap-sellers and their sons . for silver have been knights,
> And lord's sons their laborers . . . .
> Holyness of life and love . have been long hence,
> And will, till it be worn out . or otherwise changed.[70]

It is this sense of social order, rather than any class feeling or any political conviction, that accounts for the paradoxical conservatism which made Langland, the prophet of hard work, the poet of the plowman, the acidulous critic of society in all its branches, at the same time the stout defender of things as they are. It was the purification of the social order he wanted, never change as such, restoration, not revolution.

Without being fully aware that in fact he was living in an age of profound social change in which the old order was not merely deteriorating but altering in structure, Langland nevertheless seems at times to have sensed the forces of change. He was much too keen an interpreter of his times not to have noticed the encroachment of the cash-nexus upon the immemorial custom of the manor and the many other ways in which a little "silver" could be made to bridge the barriers between class and class. In his preoccupation with Mede and his treatment of her marriage and trial there are indications of a deeper understanding of social forces than Gower was able to achieve—though it is no accident that Gower saw in the multifarious manifestations of the sin of avarice the most disturbing, because the most dynamic, influence in the society of his day.[71] But in the last analysis the forces Langland personified in Lady Mede also originated in the moral nature of man. They were by no means the impersonal factors familiar to the modern analyst. The economic man had not yet been invented

70. *Ibid.*, C, VI, 65-81.
71. *Vox Clamantis*, VII, i-ii.

nor was his nature foreseen, even as a few of the Tudor pamphleteers were able to foresee it.

These basic assumptions concerning the moral and social order determined the attitude of both men toward the actual workings of government. Gower thought of it as acting within what a modern mind would consider a very limited province. Its task is to protect society from its enemies—to keep the peace, and to see that justice is done—to remove, that is, the physical obstacles to the achievement of man's main purpose in this world, a virtuous and God-serving life.[72] Gower was not greatly concerned with defense against outside enemies: England was not in serious danger of invasion and Gower interpreted the French war correctly enough as one largely of dynastic aggrandize-ment. He was chiefly concerned therefore with the maintenance of justice and order in England itself.

Law for Gower, as for most of his contemporaries, was at once the foundation upon which all government must be built, the chief object of its care, and the structure within which it must do its work. Laws are made to deal with transgressors and assure to each his own.[73] They are essential to a community. "What," he asks, "is a people without law?"[74]

> Do law away, what is a king?
> Where is the right of any thing,
> If that there be no law in land?[75]

No king can flout the laws and still hope to keep his kingdom legiti-mately.[76] Gower recognized that the king must have the means with which to rule and a certain discretionary power in dealing with the laws. In some respect his power "stands above the law"; but "things which are excessive /Against the law, he shall not do."[77] Although at one point Gower says to the king "*Tu supra es jura*," he adds in the same metrical breath, "*iustus set vive sub illis*."[78] The king is head of

72. *Ibid.*, V, xvi, 993-994, VII, vi and xxiv, 1303-1308; *Confessio Amantis*, Prol., 499 ff.; *Cronica*, p. 314.
73. *Vox Clamantis*, VI, 369-370.
74. *Ibid.*, 481.
75. *Confessio Amantis*, VII, 375-377.
76. *Ibid.*, 373-374.
77. *Ibid.*, 2709-2724; *Vox Clamantis*, VII, 1007-1008.
78. *Vox Clamantis*, VI, 613.

the political body, but he must respect that body.[79]   He has duties to the community which nicely balance his kingly rights.[80]   He remains, however, ultimately responsible to God who can chastise a king "where that none other may suffice."[81]

Government was thus to Gower primarily a protective agency, the definer of rights, the righter of wrongs.   It is not primarily creative: its task is not to shape social forces, and for the simple reason that in a society of fixed structure the processes of change all related in one way or another to the inordinate nature of man himself.   For that reason, too, Gower failed to think in terms of institutions, much less of constitutions.   He has, for example, a good deal to say in his *Cronica Tripertita* about Parliament, yet, so far from being the pioneer legislative body dear to Victorian scholars, it turns out to be simply the arena within which a political battle is fought to decide what persons would command the ear of the king.   The question was simply whether the king would have good or bad counselors, and hence be able to render good or bad governance.

In a government of this sort the responsibility devolves upon the king considered as a mortal man rather than as a never-dying office symbolized by the crown. (The latter notion, though widely enough held on the Continent, made slow headway in England.)[82]   Gower certainly spoke to and about a particular king.   No other poet, "devoted himself so consistently to the single theme of the responsibility of a particular ruler for the welfare, morals, and integrity of his country."[83]   But it is to the king as a moral individual that he speaks, not to the office.   His is an ethical function, and, conversely, the people suffer for his sins.[84]   Gower felt strongly on this point.   Though an anti-Lollard, he argued himself close to the Wycliffite doctrine of dominion.   "*Est qui peccator, non esse potest dominator*," he declares at the close of his indictment of Richard II.[85]   The king must learn to govern himself if

79. *Confessio Amantis*, Prol., 151-156. Cf. *O Deus immense*, ll. 85-86.

80. *Vox Clamantis*, VI, viii, *passim*.

81. *Confessio Amantis*, VII, 2728-2736. Cf. *Vox Clamantis*, VI, 592-600.

82. E. H. Kantorowicz, *The King's Two Bodies* (Princeton, 1957), p. 147.

83. G. R. Coffman, "John Gower, Mentor for Royalty: Richard II," *PMLA*, LXIX (Sept., 1954), 954-964, 953.

84. *Vox Clamantis*, VI, vii, 501; VII, 927.   See also Wickert, 122.

85. *Vox Clamantis*, end of Liber IV; *Cronica*, iii, 486; Coffman, "Gower in His Most Significant Role," p. 56.   On Gower's attitude toward the Lollards, see *Carmen*, ll. 13-93; *Confessio Amantis*, Prol., 346 ff.

he is to govern his people rightly.[86] The moral responsibility of government is, however, by no means confined to the king, but extends to the ruling class from whom the king must draw his chief advisers. On these men, the "natural" counselors of kings, rested the duty of providing the king with good counsel, and good counsel was the essential ingredient of good governance.

Good counsel was not, however, to be confined entirely to those immediately surrounding the king or even to the governing class, considered as men actually engaged in the work of government. It was, as we shall see in the next chapter, a function in which men like Gower himself might and should share. His task is to see that the king and his aristocratic advisers are kept truthfully and consistently informed concerning the evils that need their attention. His is not the duty of prescribing specific remedies—that is the function of the king's appointed advisers—but rather that of pointing out to all and sundry their shortcomings and to act as the voice of a distressed people.

ဟ   ဟ   ဟ

The picture of government that emerges from the pages of *Piers Plowman* is, like Gower's, determined less by critical observation of the functioning parts than by basic assumptions concerning the nature of man and society. It is with the stability of the social order and with man's moral responsibility for maintaining it, rather than with government as such, that Langland, no less than Gower, is primarily concerned. Government is merely the agency by means of which the hierarchical social structure ordained by God may be kept in repair, the body politic preserved in health—provided, that is, the men who run it follow the ways of virtue. Health in the political body derives from peace and justice: taken together they ensure order and stability and consequently make possible the life of virtue which is the end of human society. What characterizes good government, then, is less the capacity for invention, for the construction of policy or the making of law, than simply a sense of right and a willingness to listen to and act upon good counsel. It is protective rather than creative.

A closer look at Langland's obiter dicta on the subject will, I think, bear out this interpretation. It must be remembered that it is the quality of government that interested Langland rather than its formal

86. *Vox Clamantis*, VI, viii, especially ll. 605606.

structure. He had a clear enough idea of what it should do, but he was no more given than Gower to debating constitutional questions. He thought in terms either of persons and specific grievances or moral generalities, but seldom in those of institutions or powers. He was not concerned, for example, with the relative status of crown, council, and Parliament. He refers to the king's council,[87] but to him the council means the men who are appointed to advise the king, not an institution with clear legal structure and specific relationship to the other parts of the central government. While it is true that the coun-cil was in Langland's own day being examined critically and more or less constructively by the men who took the lead in Parliament,[88] its institutional character remained indistinct to the more distantly placed observer.

Langland also refers to Parliament, as, for example, in the passage where Peace comes into Parliament and presents a bill against Wrong.[89] But in this instance it is Parliament acting in its primitive, petitioning, quasi-judicial capacity rather than the legislative, deliberative, and policy-moderating body it had already in some degree become. (Here, as so frequently in medieval writing, we see how slowly reflective thought followed that of the men of affairs.) Langland was apparently personally acquainted with the activity of Parliament. Whether the allegorical reference he makes to Parliament in the B prologue is to be read straight or as "sardonic fancy,"[90] it was undoubtedly inspired by the actual events of 1376-1377. But there is in the fable of the rats and their plan to bell the cat of the court nothing that reflects on the con-stitutional position of Parliament: the little fellows merely "come to counsel . for their common profit."[91]

Nor should the modern reader be misled by Langland's use of the term "commons" (the "comune" or "comunes"). It is a term he used very frequently, but in almost no instance did he use it in an institu-

87. E.g., *Piers Plowman*, B, Prol., 143-145.

88. Joliffe, p. 462; S. B. Chrimes, *An Introduction to the Administrative History of Medieval England* (New York, 1952), p. 245; *Rotuli Parliamentorum*, II, 322, III, 221 and 585.

89. *Piers Plowman*, B, 47 ff.

90. Coghill, p. 331; cf. Bennett, "Date of B-text"; Donaldson, p. 115; and B. F. Huppé, "The Authorship of the A and B Texts of *Piers Plowman*," *Speculum*, XXII (Oct., 1947), 578-620.

91. *Piers Plowman*, B, Prol., 148.

tional sense.[92]   Rather, he seems to have meant by it pretty much what the legal minds of the preceding century had meant by the "community of the realm." Perhaps the term "commonwealth" might be a more satisfactory translation.   But he also used the "comune(s)" to mean sometimes the common people, sometimes the people in general.   In no instance is it absolutely clear that he had anything so specific in mind as the representatives of the third estate assembled in Parliament.   Read in this light, the famous lines,

> Then came there a king . knighthood him led,
> Might of the commons [comunes] . made him to reign,[93]

lose a great deal of their controversial color, but gain considerably in sense.   Langland is here merely saying that the king cannot rule without the support of his people.   It implies no democratic idealism, no premature constitutionalism.

To Langland the king is clearly the center of government.   It is a co-operative affair, but the king retains clearly the final responsibility. He alone can see that justice is maintained and that peace and tranquility prevail.   To do so he must have the means, and, in fact, he has a legal right to take what he needs.   In addition to funds, he can expect from his people military support and counsel.[94]   It is therefore to his advantage to cherish the good will of the community.[95]   Few would have quarrelled with this concept of government.   It was an old principle in English political thought that the king is under no man.   But the other half of that maxim is that he is under God and the law.   And that for which he is responsible is the welfare of the community.   The people have a right, vested in law, to the royal protection, to the king's justice and his solicitude.[96]   There are limits to what the king can take from his subjects.   If he rules within reason and in truth he may have what he needs, but "*Omnia tua sunt ad defendendum, set non ad devredandum.*"[97]   He is "head of law," but not above it:

92. Donaldson, pp. 94 ff.
93. *Piers Plowman*, B, Prol., 112-114.
94. *Ibid.*, B, xix, 462-473 and C, xxii, 467-478; see also B, Prol., 112-122, C, IV, 377-385, xviii, 289-291.
95. *Ibid.*, B, v, 49 ff.; cf. C, VI, 181-182.
96. *Ibid.*, C, iv, 381-385.
97. *Ibid.*, B, xix, 474-477; cf. C, xxii, 479-482.

Spiritus iusticie . spareth not to spill
Them that be guilty . and for to correct
The king, if the king fall . in any thing guilty.[98]

It is, moreover, practically impossible for the king to get anything done "but the comune will consent."[99] Again these are sentiments with which few, if any, would have disagreed in Langland's day.

When, however, the advice and consent of the community had been secured, the resulting acts derived their final authority from the king and were binding on all.[100] Langland gives small comfort to those who would take popular action to bring the king and his chosen advisers to account. As the sage and experienced mouse in the fable points out, the cat of the court, though a grievance to all mice and rats, remains a social necessity, because without him property would no longer be safe and the rats would be unable to protect themselves.[101] Langland repeatedly counseled the people, the common people especially, to obey those in authority.[102]

The conservatism that shines through passages like these derives, however, not from vested interest, but from the author's profound assumption of an ordained social order. He may, as Fowler suggests, have been a member of the higher clergy, in close touch with the aristocracy.[103] His point of view may therefore have been not far removed from Gower's. But he was no enemy to reform, if by reform we mean the removal of injustice and the consequent restoration of the social order to its divinely prescribed equilibrium. To him govern‑ ment was the regulating factor in a society of functioning groups, each performing its appointed task for the good of the community. He could not have conceived of a government as an agency separable from that community, possessed of its own interests, its own "reasons." Thus in his most complete, and certainly best known, passage on

98. *Ibid.*, C, xxii, 303‑305; cf. B, xix, 298‑300. It is probable that "of law" in the phrase "head of law" is meant to be read in an adverbial rather than in a genetive sense; Wickert, p. 125.

99. *Piers Plowman*, B, iv, 182‑184; C, v, 176‑178.

100. Assuming that Langland was not indulging in some subtle form of irony, as is quite possible, this may account for the enigmatic cry of the "comune" (which, by the way was not repeated in the C‑text—"construe who‑so would"): *"Praecepta Regis sunt nobis vincula legis."* B, Prol., 143‑145.

101. *Ibid.*, B, Prol., 197‑201.

102. *Ibid.*, C, ix, 88‑89; B, vi, 82‑83; cf. C, ix, 84.

103. Fowler, chap. vii.

government, the king becomes the head of a social system rather than of a state.

> Then came there a king . knighthood him led,
> Might of the comunes . made him to reign,
> And then came kind wit . and clerks he made,
> For to counsel the king . and the comune save.
> The king and knighthood . and clergy both
> Cast [contrived] that the comune . should
>   themselves find [provide for].
> The comune contrived . of kind wit's crafts,
> And for profit of all the people . plowmen ordained,
> To till and toil . as true life asketh.
> The king and the comune . and kind wit the third
> Shaped law and loyalty . each man to know his own.[104]

It is a society of status and degree, based on labor and service and the holding of property. In this still feudal society the king must "stand as a stake . that sticketh in the mire / Between two lands . for a true mark."[105] He is the establisher and maintainer of the reciprocal rights and duties that hold it together. (Langland may well have felt that it was too much preoccupied with the protection of property, its political leaders consequently dedicated too exclusively to the preservation of things temporal,[106] but he presents these as the facts of a world made imperfect in all its parts by Adam's fall.) In this society the king's estate is barely distinguishable in kind from any other property interest.[107] In such a society the typically modern questions regarding the locus of power become irrelevant: the purpose of government is not the exercise of power, except it be for the protection of the community and the preservation of the social order.

In a government thus meant to protect the rightful interests of the community rather than to expand or enhance them, the most important element is not power but counsel. And the kind of counsel likely to make for good governance is that which transcends the merely temporal, which can see beyond the myopic calculations of

104. *Piers Plowman*, B, Prol., 112-122; cf. C, i, 139-147.
105. *Ibid.*, C, iv, 384-385.
106. Robertson and Huppé, pp. 17-35.
107. S. B. Chrimes, *English Constitutional Ideas in the Fifteenth Century* (Cambridge, 1936), pp. 34-35.

the worldling.   Too often counsel is prompted simply by "kind⁄wit,"
the natural faculty by which men adjust to the practical exigencies of life
in this world.   But it will only be really good counsel if it is directed
by conscience, reason, and truth and is not subverted, as man's un⁄
aided intellect too often is, by falsehood, flattery, and greed.   Counsel
is thus essentially a moral issue, occupying the same relation to govern⁄
ment as conscience to the individual citizen.   But more of this in the
following chapter.

ᔕ   ᔕ   ᔕ

It is in their picture of the social order rather than in any particular
pronouncements regarding government itself that we must look for
whatever passed for political theory in the work of Gower and Lang⁄
land.   In this respect they were neither unique nor especially retarded
—not that they laid claim, of course, to philosophical or legal expertise.
Throughout most of the Renaissance period English political thought
remained conditioned by, one might almost say determined by, social
rather than strictly political considerations.   What distinguishes them
from their successors of the sixteenth century was rather their more
consistent tendency to interpret the social order in terms of private
morality, especially to seek for the causes of disease in the political
body, not in such tangible factors as might be susceptible to adjustment
by governmental policy, but in the moral failure they saw at the bottom
of all problems affecting the commonwealth.   Perhaps they failed to
recognize the former; more likely they held such an approach to be
futile in the face of the fundamental and overriding fact of man's per⁄
versity.   They concentrated their critical attention especially upon the
aggrandizement and indulgence of self which made men restless and
acquisitive and generally unwilling to labor patiently at their appointed
tasks within the social hierarchy.

The remedy followed logically from the diagnosis.   Just as both
men in their analysis of its ailments passed lightly over the causal
relationships in their society, so in their discussion of remedy they dwelt
much less than would a modern observer on the role of government.
They by no means ignored it: on the contrary, the judicial system, the
king himself, and his counselors are always in the background in any
reference to the common welfare.   But they failed for the most part
to contemplate constructive policy or even specific legislative or ad⁄

ministrative action of more than a piecemeal sort, meant merely to redress a particular wrong. Government they saw as a primarily protective, coercive agency, operating within an ordained social organism. Its task was to restore that organism as nearly as possible to an ideal state of health from which it had supposedly deteriorated through the sinful actions of the men who made up its parts.

This limited, essentially negative concept of government was thus a corollary of the view of society as an organism, static in form, and subject to such change in its health as might require the remedial ministrations of government only because of the inveterate tendencies of man to sin. Accordingly, whatever visions the authors may have nourished of an apocalyptic regeneration of man's earthly existence (and in Gower's work, at least, there is little evidence of any such hope), their immediate prognosis for society was pessimistic. The king and his council, with the help of the community represented in Parliament, could do much to right specific wrongs—the remedy was, indeed, supposed to be obvious, but they could do no more than the moralist to get at the basic cause.

Moral exhortation and a true reporting of grievances rather than discussion of policy thus became the articulate citizen's public duty. This, in turn, constituted an essential part of the larger problem of good counsel upon which all good government depended. In the next chapter we shall take a closer look at this fundamental question.

CHAPTER III. THE PROBLEM OF COUNSEL

"WHAT," ASKED GOWER, "IS A KING UNLESS HE HAVE GOOD counsel? What counsel unless the king heed it?"[1] To him, the problem of counsel was the crux of the problem of government.   And to that extent he spoke for all of his contemporaries who yearned over the sad state of society and who saw in the relationship existing between the prince and his advisers the only hope of remedial action.   The character of that relationship in turn depended on the moral qualities of the men involved, and so it was a faint hope at best.   But the critic must not be discouraged merely because he is fighting against odds; he must therefore labor as best he can to solve the problem of counsel, and in that task endure to the end.

The idea of counsel, so pervasive in medieval thought, is a hard one for the modern scholar to pin down.   It was clear then, as now, that good government depended on the ability of the governor to get the best advice available.   To us, however, this is a truism which must be expressed in terms of a highly institutionalized society in order to have much meaning.   To the medieval thinker, even when his mind was conditioned by the increasingly complex circumstances of life, it remained a satisfying statement of a great fact.   The modern scholar must always be careful not to overestimate the degree of sophistication in the political consciousness of that period.   He must remember especially that, even when precedents were being made which have come to be recognized as milestones of constitutional development, their full significance often escaped the contemporary observer who continued to think of government as an essentially personal thing, ethical in character as in purpose.   A good king will seek good counsel; good men will give good counsel.   And that, more often than not, is that. Literary commonplace, almost as much as moral generality, obscures the problem of counsel.   "Work all things by counsel" is a constantly recurring theme in medieval literature, applicable alike to public and

1. *Vox Clamantis*, VI, vii, 529-532. Cf. *Confessio Amantis*, Prol., 151-156.

private affairs,[2] and the "mirror of princes" formula deflected a good deal of thought on the subject into highly conventional channels having little or nothing to do with specifically English conditions. There are, fortunately, two or three documents in which the problem is given a refreshingly original treatment within the specific context of English public life. It is accordingly with these that the present chapter will be chiefly concerned. We shall, however, be able to evaluate the ideas they contain more accurately if we understand what may be considered the standard approach of the medieval commentator toward this problem of counsel. And that, I think, can be found at its most eloquent in the works examined in the preceding chapter.

∽ ∽ ∽

Gower, as we have seen, recognized in the king the mainspring of all government. Its bearing on the community would depend on the degree to which the king took his responsibility seriously and discharged it honestly. But it is not enough for the king himself to be wise and well-meaning. He must have the information upon which to act and he must be able to tap the pooled wisdom of his subjects.

> Although a man be wise himself
> Yet is the wisdom more of twelve.[3]

It was in this respect that Gower found the administration of Richard II especially deficient. The young king had about him counselors who were either young and vicious, his own appointees, or old and cynical, flattering the king for personal gain.[4] To Gower counsel was the channel through which for political purposes flowed the moral and rational currents essential to all human relationships. Nor did he see any dichotomy here. In the medieval tradition right reason involved not merely the mechanical operation of the intellect but also the knowledge of what is right and good. It all added up to right thinking, which in political affairs meant not inventive or creative thinking but only a capacity for judicial perception and sound judgment.[5]

2. C. F. Bühler, " 'Wirk alle thyng by conseil,' " *Speculum*, XXIV (July, 1949), 410-412.

3. *Confessio Amantis*, Prol., 157-158.

4. *Vox Clamantis*, VI, vii-viii. See especially vii, 555 ff.

5. On the history of the idea of right reason see Robert Hoopes, *Right Reason in the English Renaissance* (Cambridge, Mass., 1962), chaps. i-v. See also Gower, *O Deus immense*, ll. 95-96.

The measures by means of which the king's government fulfils its essentially negative, protective function in a society of fixed degrees are relatively simple. They require no complex analysis of cause and effect. They look to no shaping of the social order. They should, therefore, be obvious to any honest king if he is truthfully informed of the trouble to be remedied. Accordingly it is of the utmost importance that such information get to the king and his immediate advisers as fully and as fearlessly as possible. Here is where Gower, the writer, makes his own contribution. He is able to discharge the duty he shares with all true subjects to serve their king by reporting grievances and recalling all men to their social duty.[6] Gower is at pains to disclaim any professional expertise in this respect. He is, he said at one point, not the physician, but merely the one who summons him and provides him with the materials he must use.[7] He can provide the king and his council with the truth, with, that is, an accurate description of what ails the body politic, and he can offer moral regeneration as a panacea. Any more specific treatment is up to those in actual charge of government.

Gower took pains also to disclaim any originality in the counsel he, as a citizen, might tender. It was, he insisted again and again, simply the voice of the people that he was relaying to those in authority.[8]

> I am not speaking of these things on my own part; rather, the voice of the people has reported them to me, and it complains of their adverse fate at every hand. I speak as the masses speak, and even as I write I lament over what I say, namely, that no estate is pious as in days gone by.[9]

Nor is it always the English people for whom he speaks. At times he fancies himself speaking for humanity at large, for the people "of every land."[10] At times he equates in traditional fashion the voice of

6. *Vox Clamantis*, VI, vii-viii, especially 581-588; *Confessio Amantis*, Prol., 41-53.

7. *Carmen super multiplici viciorum pestilencia*, in *Works*, IV, 346: "Unde ego, non medicus set medicine procurator, . . . vt inde medicos pro salute interpellam, consequenter declare propono."

8. See Wickert, pp. 72-79, for an analysis of the many examples to be found in Gower's work.

9. *Vox Clamantis*, III, Prol., 11-14.

10. E.g., *Confessio Amantis*, Prol., 123.

the people with the voice of God.[11] For the most part, however, *clamor populi* is the cry of the English, and he uses it to strengthen the counsel he tenders to the English king.[12] In any case he exhorts kings to give ear to what the people say.[13]

Langland's attitude toward this problem is subtler than Gower's, more profound, yet more difficult to determine with any degree of assurance. To him also, the key to the problem of government lies in counsel, and the key to good counsel in the moral and spiritual caliber of the governing class. Counsel is the human variable in the equation of government. The results will be good or bad according to the quality of counsel upon which governmental action is based.[14] In its ordinary, minimal form it is the Kind Wit of the familiar lines:

> The king and the comune . and Kind Wit the third
> Shaped law and loyalty . each man to know his own.[15]

It is the natural wisdom, the common sense of man by means of which he makes the practical adjustments necessary to civil society. Since those adjustments involved primarily the establishing and enforcing of rights, the maintenance rather than the creation of law, Kind Wit was not expected to be an inventive faculty. It was enough for it to be just and honest. But there precisely lay the difficulty. Left to itself, man's natural wisdom is fallible and corruptible. Unless it is informed by a higher authority, an absolute sense of right, its vision is limited to the exigencies of the immediate situation. Though normal in structure, the government described in the Prologue, that in which Kind Wit is the third element, is, indeed, far from perfect in its effects. It is in practice too often served by Wit and Wisdom, those very human faculties that are inclined to compromise with the corrupting influence of material reward personified by Mede, who, in turn, is supported in her trial before the king by Falsehood and Flattery.[16] They represent the worldly cleverness, the devotion to expediency displayed by clerks

11. E.g., *Vox Clamantis*, III, 1267-1268.
12. See especially *ibid.*, VI, 545, 577-580.
13. *O Deus immense*, ll. 53-54.
14. See Robertson and Huppé, pp. 27 ff. Cf. R. Quirk, "Langland's Use of Kind Wit and Inwit," *JEGP*, LII (April, 1953), 182-188.
15. *Piers Plowman*, B, Prol., 121-122.
16. *Ibid.*, B, iii.

and lawyers who construe a clause "for the king's profit, / But not for the comfort of the comune   .   nor for the king's soul."[17]

Kind Wit must therefore be aided by a higher authority, one whose judgments are not made in relation to the contingencies of the moment but are based on the certain knowledge of right and wrong and on a higher wisdom.   In the trial of Lady Mede, Kind Wit is accordingly helped out by Conscience and Reason.   Together they labor in the service of Truth who stands at the right hand of God. Together they personify that quality of counsel which is the essence of good government.   And in the end they convince the king.   He accordingly declares against Mede and Wrong, and commands Reason to stay with him as a permanent member of his council.

As Langland viewed it, good counsel thus involved two things. It required true and fearless reporting of grievances—the kind of thing that made Peace come "into parliament   .   and put forth a bill" stating injuries at the hand of Wrong.[18]   This to Langland was still the commons' way of providing the necessary and sufficient infor' mation upon which a government, considered primarily as a protective agency, could act.   But Peace's petition would be useless if those in authority could not or would not distinguish clearly between right and wrong, truth and falsehood.   So there remained another essential, the ability and willingness of the king and his advisers to recognize and abide by the dictates of right reason and conscience.   Those faculties, nearly identical in medieval tradition, were both profoundly ethical in their bearing.

This implied the need for some supplementary source of counsel beyond the formal offices of government.   There is, of course, no reason why the forces of reason and conscience could not work through the king's official advisers: the king in Langland's allegory finally summons Reason to his side to serve as a member of his council.   But in practice it is too much to expect that the kind of right thinking personified in Reason and Conscience can ordinarily be found in the men of affairs who actually serve the king.   More can be expected from the clergy.   It is their function in the social system to provide moral inspiration of this sort which goes beyond the merely practical or expedient, and Langland makes it clear that they shared with the secular

17. *Ibid.*, B, iii, 151-152; Huppé, "Authorship of the A and B Texts," pp. 583-584.
18. *Ibid*, B, iv, 47 ff.

governing class the responsibility of government. In the B-text Kind Wit makes clerks "to counsel the king," and in the C-text he again creates clerks, but Conscience is substituted for the estate of the clergy as the third member of the ruling group.[19]

It would, I believe, be not too farfetched to consider Conscience, whenever that personification appears in a political context, to stand ideally for the counseling function of the clergy, however much the clergy as a group might fail in practice to live up to this high purpose. We are thus left with the implied conclusion that much depends on the volunteer work of preachers and poets, men like Langland himself, "poetic homilists who had been harping for generations upon the same general themes."[20]

∽ ∽ ∽

What Gower said in scattered obiter dicta and Langland in allegorical and often cryptic form, the author of *Mum and the Sothsegger*[21] stated with relative clarity and consistency. More than that, he placed the idea of counsel in a specific context of English institutions, and he made especially clear the position of the articulate citizen with reference to those institutions.

The two verse fragments that apparently constituted parts of his longer poem have already proved useful to the historian of ideas and institutions.[22] *Mum and the Sothsegger* remains, however, a curiously neglected text. And one reason is that it has not been studied for what the author undoubtedly intended it to be, namely a substantial (if not very closely knit) and only partially satirical commentary on

19. *Ibid.*, B, Prol., 114-115; C, i, 141-142; cf. C, vi, 68-69.

20. Owst, *Literature and Pulpit*, p. 228.

21. *Mum and the Sothsegger*, ed. M. Day and R. Steele, E.E.T.S., O.S., No. 199 (London, 1936). The first of the two fragments edited under the above title was known for some time and edited by Thomas Wright under the title *Richard The Redeless* in *Political Poems and Songs*, Rolls Series (1858), I, 368 ff.

22. In 1939, Helen M. Cam made very good use of them to illustrate the relation of English members of Parliament to their constituencies. "The Relation of English Members of Parliament to their Constituencies in the Fourteenth Century: A Neglected Text," originally in *L'organisation corporative du Moyen Age à la fin de l'Ancien Régime* (Louvain, 1939), III, and reprinted in *Liberties and Communites in Medieval England* (Cambridge, 1944). More recently Ruth Mohl placed them in relation to the more formal aspects of medieval political thought; "Theories of Monarchy in *Mum and the Sothsegger*," *PMLA*, LXV (March, 1944), 26-44. Miss Mohl follows the editors in considering the fragments part of a single poem. Miss Cam expresses doubts on this point.

the problem of counsel. It might almost be called a treatise on counsel except for the fact that the author is concerned less with the technicalities of government than with the general problem of truth-telling in public life. There is, however, no doubt that he was preoccupied with the problem of counsel. The picture he has left of Parliament and the law courts is vivid largely because he sought to bring that problem, so often discussed by his contemporaries in universal terms, down to the level of events and into contact with the actual conditions of English life. His willingness to work close to the data of experience occasionally makes it possible to examine such academic concepts as those of law and kingship. But it must be remembered that he was not a man trained in the subtleties of medieval philosophy. He was a practical man, probably a member of the lesser gentry, perhaps one who had actually served in Parliament as a knight of the shire; his purpose was practical, despite the conventional trappings of dream allegory and personification in which he clothed his argument.

He appears to have set out to do two things: first, to analyze the failure of the English monarchy under Richard II to provide the desired "abundant governance," a failure he traced to lack of good counsel, and, second, to explore the general problem of counsel in the immediate context of English life. In the process he managed to produce a work which, even though it survives in fragmentary form, occupies a unique position in the considerable literature of counsel written in England during the late fourteenth and early fifteenth centuries. The author of *Mum and the Sothsegger* alone marked off that issue as one capable of being treated by itself and worth considering separately. More than any of his contemporaries he used in his discussion of counsel the facts which he had either observed personally or had derived from a critical study of recent history. He approached his task in a spirit of realism quite unusual in the political literature of his day. And he was the first English writer we know of to explore at all fully the function of written discussion in public life. These tendencies point toward a new era, toward the Tudor pamphleteers in particular. They are matters of emphasis, to be sure, rather than of formulated ideas, for the author shared most of the habits of thought peculiar to an age still recognizably medieval, but they are indications not to be overlooked by the student of the transition from medieval to modern thought.

Those politically critical years that witnessed the deposition of Richard II and the uncertainties of the early Lancastrian rule (the parts of *Mum* were written somewhere between 1399 and 1406) were a time unusually conducive to a discussion of the problem of counsel. In fact, the problem of providing the king with adequate and trust/ worthy counsel appears to have impressed men of the governing class more deeply than any question regarding the nature and powers of Parliament.[23] The medieval Englishman thought of government in personal rather than institutional terms, and it was to the persons immediately surrounding the king that he looked with most concern, and with not a little suspicion. Parliament, of course, was itself one of the essential institutions through which counsel reached the king. That had long been recognized as its primary function. Its task was essentially that of providing the data upon which legislative action could be taken and policy built. It was, moreover, a task which was generally understood, its importance freely admitted. The same could not be said of the other major institution in the process of counsel, the king's chosen council, and most of the constitutional controversy during the period under review centered upon it. Throughout the period, therefore, efforts were constantly being made to define the form and function of the council. By the early part of the following century, it is apparent from their petitions that the keener minds among the commons had begun to see the need for a new technique of counsel. They were by no means interested in limiting the prerogative of the king, which they took pretty much for granted, or in controlling his council. On the contrary, an improved system of counsel was in/ tended to strengthen the executive and to make of it the instrument of that "abundant" government which they considered the essential characteristic of all good rule.[24] As S. B. Chrimes tells us, "a great part of the constitutional history of England in the medieval period might be said . . . to be a commentary, not upon *Magna Carta*, but upon the simple fact of the king's crying need for counsel and ever more counsel."[25]

23. Joliffe, p. 455.
24. *Ibid.*, pp. 455/485. This book contains what is still the best treatment of the council in the period under review; see also Chrimes, *Introduction to the Administrative History of Medieval England*, p. 245. For the text of such petitions, see, for example, *Rotuli Parliamentorum*, II, 322, III, 221, 585.
25. Chrimes, *English Constitutional Ideas in the Fifteenth Century*, p. 39.

The same problems of national life that had impressed the rep‑ resentatives of the commons with the need for an improved technique of counsel, as we have seen, stimulated also an unprecedented literature of comment and criticism in the world beyond Parliament. Curi‑ ously enough this literature does not reflect the concern of the commons in Parliament for a more clearly defined council. It treats the prob‑ lem of counsel in terms of the moral basis underlying all human relationships. The political context is clearly English, but the prob‑ lem remains a universal one. It is not until Sir John Fortescue wrote his *Governance of England*[26] (1471‑1476) that council reform received specific treatment in a political pamphlet. Even the author of *Mum and the Sothsegger*, though somewhat more realistic in his handling of political issues than other writers of his generation, appears to have taken the position of the council for granted, preferring no doubt to emphasize the role of the representatives of the commons and the possibilities to be found in extra‑parliamentary discussion.

ꙅ ꙅ ꙅ

The relationship between the two fragments of *Mum and the Sothsegger* (referred to by the editors as fragments R and M) is not entirely clear. The editors are undoubtedly correct in assuming that both are by the same author. Certainly they are closely related in substance. Taken together they constitute quite logically two parts of what may well have been a considerable volume built around the idea of good counsel and applied to the contemporary scene.[27] In Fragment R, hitherto known, aptly enough, as *Richard the Redeless*, the author undertakes to explain what had gone wrong in the reign of Richard II. The result is a remarkably sustained and penetrating analysis of the effects of bad counsel. He tells sadly of how the young king made the initial mistake of choosing young men for his council. As he put it in his characteristically homely speech, it is as fitting for young men to act as counselors "as becometh a cow to hop in a cage."[28]

26. George Ashby also recognized the problem and about the same time, but treated it in much less specific terms in his *Active Policy of a Prince*. On both, see below, chapter v.

27. The parts do not appear, however, to have been written at the same time. The first written before the death of Richard, the second certainly some time thereafter. It is quite possible that they were composed and circulated in separate form. But they reflect a fundamental unity of thought and singleness of purpose on the part of the author.

28. *Mum*, R, iii, 260‑262.

The author's essentially puritan soul recoiled at the spectacle of foppish extravagance these youngsters "of twenty-four years" presented. But he was much more concerned with the indirect effects of Richard's perverse choice of advisers, in particular the way in which it aggravated the problem of the over-mighty subject. Furthermore, the folly of Richard and the selfishness of his advisers had undermined the royal finances.[29]

Fragment R, then, gives a picture, perhaps a trifle colored, of a kingdom in which things have gone badly awry and where, especially, the rights of subjects have been overstepped by a badly advised and impoverished crown. Fragment M may be considered a semi-allegorical discussion of the remedy. It tells of the conflict of Truth-teller (Sothsegger) with Mum. The latter apparently represents either the way of least resistance in public life, the way of those who keep the truth from the king out of a misplaced sense of prudence, or the actively iniquitous way of those who pervert the truth into flattering counsel for their own private ends.[30] Truth-teller stands for the tougher moral fiber that causes a man to speak out even when the truth is disagreeable or dangerous. "In man's heart his housing is."[31]

A truth-teller is the most necessary of all officers in a king's household, or for that matter in the retinue of any other lay lord.[32] For the lack of his services Richard lost his kingdom, and, the author hints, there is danger that even the comparatively well-ordered household of Henry IV may suffer from his absence.[33] Yet there is a general feeling that to tell the truth to the king is unwise and dangerous, and Mum prospers mightily the while.[34] Here, then, is a problem that weighs heavily on the poet's mind. He seeks everywhere for some clarification. He goes to the ancient authorities and to the "Seven Sciences" at the universities, but none of them can help him. They tell only of how "good governance graciously endeth,"[35] not of the means by which that end may be attained. This problem of good counsel they suggest

29. *Ibid.*, R, iv, *passim*.
30. *Ibid.*, M, 232-276.
31. *Ibid.*, M, 1224. Cf. 1247-1248.
32. *Ibid.*, M, 29-41.
33. *Ibid.*, M, 206-231.
34. *Ibid.*, M, 125-128, 232-276.
35. *Ibid.*, M, 377; cf. 313.

(perhaps significantly?) is a newfangled notion.[36] He goes to the clerical orders, but again fails to find his answer and in the process is propelled into a lengthy diatribe against the venality and general unworthiness of these men who were supposed to be the intellectual and moral leaders of the community. In fact, society in all its branches appears to be tied by self-interest to Mum and can therefore give but a biased answer.

Finally, weary of his search, he resorts to the standard device of the medieval poet with something on his mind and falls asleep to dream the answer he was unable to obtain while awake. In his vision a bee-keeper (apparently something of an authority on society because of his long years of experience with those most social and exemplary of insects) tells him what he knew already, namely that Mum was the source of most of the evils of the land. He goes on, however, to say that Truth-teller may be found in the hearts of men, presumably men of good will. He may be found in the author's own heart, and, in fact, the bee-keeper suggests that the author do some truth-telling himself, that he exercise a truly articulate citizenship. This he proposes to do and at once proceeds to plan out a series of "books" of advice to the king and the lords.[37]

☙ ☙ ☙

Such is the plan discernible in these remarkable fragments. In the course of his argument the author reveals several things about the idea of counsel, of articulate citizenship in particular, and also about his general approach toward government. To him the king is very much the center of government, the source of justice. He must, however, rule by reason and "rightful dooms," the purpose of which is to protect the life and property of the subject.[38] Government is thus primarily protective in function, limited by law and considerations of the public welfare. But, even after the deposition of Richard II, the author seems not to have considered any constitutional check on the king. That event had come about chiefly because of the folly and

36. *Ibid.*, M, 375; cf. 311.
37. *Ibid.*, M, 854-1351.
38. *Ibid.*, R, i, 9-19, iii, 267; M, 1036-1037. On the political theory in the poem see the article cited above, n. 22, by Mohl. It should be remembered, however, that the author of *Mum* did not speak the formal language of medieval thought. He appears to have been very familiar with the legal machinery, but more from a practical than from a theoretical point of view.

misrule of the king and his council which finally impoverished the crown and alienated those elements (the commons, for one) who might otherwise have been a source of strength. The author indicates no possible recourse had Richard maintained a powerful and efficient tyranny.

Among the most important of the king's responsibilities—the one indeed, underlying all others—is the duty to seek out and listen to good counsel. Richard's evil advisers were the immediate cause of his downfall, but he was himself responsible for having them around him in the first place.[39] The author has little to say about the council as an institution. He seems to have taken the executive branch of government for granted and to have concentrated on the problem of getting honest complaints, what "the commune [commonalty] talketh," fearlessly reported. He can only assume that the king will have sufficient good will and self-interest to act upon this information and to "amend that were amiss into more ease."[40]

It is knowledge of what the "comune talketh" that is the essence of good counsel, and it should normally reach the king through Parliament,

> When knights for the comune been come for that deed,
> And assembled forto show the sores of the realm
> And spare no speech though they spill [die] should, . . .[41]

Indeed, there is little indication in the poem that the author considered Parliament to have any other function than that of airing grievances and protecting the property rights of the subjects. The members are delegates paid to lay before the king the problem of their constituents and "pass no farther," and especially not to grant away their money except in case of war.[42] Now consent to taxation inevitably involved some consideration of the purpose for which extra grants were asked, for to the medieval citizen taxation could only be justified by some dire emergency, and so the commons in Parliament could hardly avoid some discussion of national policy. But our author sees their function primarily as that of a petitioning body which grants taxes in return for the amending of "griefs." His attitude in this respect is probably

39. *Mum*, R, i, 80-81.
40. *Ibid.*, M, 133-138.
41. *Ibid.*, M, 1119-1121.
42. *Ibid.*, R, iv, 44-52, 80-90.

quite representative, for it is substantially the same as that reflected in the parliamentary records.[43]

Unfortunately the knights of the shire (our author has nothing to say about the borough representatives) do not always speak up boldly, as it was their duty to do. Experience, apparently personal, with the Shrewsbury Parliament of 1398, where under pressure from the king's own retainers the commons had made him the unprecedented grant of the duties on wool and leather for the remainder of his life, had left the author with a low opinion of the average member's courage and integrity. The picture he paints of the bickering, the time-serving, the lethargy, and the loose-jointed debates that characterized that assembly, though probably not too far from the historical fact,[44] is certainly far from his ideal. In the face of such a striking triumph for "Mum," the responsible citizen himself must speak up.

ഗ ഗ ഗ

Thus, in his disillusionment with institutional channels through which counsel should normally flow, the author is driven to explore the possibilities of extra-parliamentary discussion. There is nothing new about this part of the intelligent citizen's duty. (Like his contemporaries in Parliament, he was capable of investing quite fresh ideas with the sanction of immemorial custom.) It is, in fact, part of his ancient duty to his lord.

> And as my body and my beast ought to be my leige's;
> So rightfully by reason my rede [counsel] should also,
> For to counsel, if I could my king and the lords; . . .[45]

Nor is this duty merely theoretical. Reason commands

> . . . if God have granted thee grace for to know
> Any maner mischief that might be amended,
> Show that to they sovereign to shield him from harms; . . .[46]

It must be done tactfully, for it is as personal a matter, we gather, as if the advice were tendered a fellow subject.[47] But it must also be done

---

43. H. G. Richardson, "The Commons in Medieval Politics," p. 32; *Rotuli Parliamentorum*, II, 336, III, 420.

44. Richardson, p. 44.

45. *Mum*, R, Prol., 47-49.

46. *Ibid.*, R, ii, 72-74.

47. *Ibid.*, R, ii, 69-71; M, 1270-1272.

courageously. He who sees a scandalous thing and does not denounce it "shall be deemed doer of the same deed."[48]

This duty does not fall equally on all subjects. It is chiefly the task of the responsible classes, the knights of the shire for example, and the clergy and other learned men. The laborer he exempts. He cannot think of

> A kindly [natural] cause why the comune should
> Counter the king's will nor construe [criticize] his works.
> I carp not of knights that cometh for the shires,
> That the king clepeth [summons] to counsel with other;
> But it longeth to no laborer the law is against them.[49]

Rumor flies among these common people swiftly and dangerously,[50] so that they think they know more than the king's council and become accordingly unco-operative in their response to the laws.[51] The poet shared with most writers of his time, especially those who followed in the *Piers Plowman* tradition, a deep concern for the poor.[52] But the memory of 1381 was doubtless too fresh in the minds of propertied men to let them look upon popular agitation with equanimity. The laborer should be seen to, but not heard.

It is to men of letters and preachers that the author looks for this extra-parliamentary, informed counsel. The clergy, he suggests, have the greatest responsibility because of their learning and their position in society as guardians of the morality upon which all human relation-ship depends. For that reason he feels they are the more culpable for their refusal to criticize abuses fearlessly.[53] Men like himself, however, responsible members of the lay community able at the same time to present their ideas to the king and the ruling class in written form, have also an important function.

There is no doubt whatever that this poet interpreted his duty both literally and literarily. He was familiar with books and preoccupied with the idea of "book-making." Richard's misrule had made him consider frequently "For to write him a writ to wissen him better."[54] So

48. *Ibid.*, M, 745-750.
49. *Ibid.*, M, 1457-1462.
50. *Ibid.*, M, 1388 ff.
51. *Ibid.*, M, 1408-1412.
52. *Ibid.*, M, 135, 1489-1497.
53. *Ibid.*, M, 759-762, 1233 ff.
54. *Ibid.*, R, Prol., 30-31.

he determined to begin a treatise of admonition and advice. In his vision, the bee-keeper who tells him how to find Truth-teller also requests him to write down what he has heard, and to

> . . . let no faint heart
> Abate thy blessed business of the book-making
> Till it be complete to clasping . . .[55]

This book, fully bound, must be presented at once to the king for whom it is specially meant. Afterward let anyone also see and copy it who will. Inspired by the vision, the poet plans out a series of books which he may actually have intended to elaborate later.

> Now for to counsel the king unknit I a bag
> Where many a privy poesy is printed within
> In books unbreded [opened?] in ballad-wise made,
> Of vice and of virtue full to the margin.[56]

These lines tell us a great deal. They show the author taking his writing seriously, conscious that it is comment of a special kind. There is the moral preoccupation which he shared with almost all commentators of his day. There, too, is the determination, also characteristic of the time, to write in verse. The poet will write in verse not as a literary tour de force, but as a readable essay meant for a practical purpose in a day when verse was believed to lend dignity and memorability to any argument.

What were these books of advice to contain? Like Gower and Langland he would treat society in its organic unity, and human life as a seamless web. He would touch on most of the evils of the day. His books would range from abuse of the law courts to the immorality of the clergy, from royal finance to the tendency of some people to put faith in old prophecies.[57] He assumes that the king and his council are as responsible for one of these evils as they are for another. Since the body politic can only be healthy when its various members are sound, it follows that whatever agency has responsibility for the larger unit must watch for any sign of vice in the various parts. A vicious or lazy clergy, for example, lies within the province of the

55. *Ibid.*, M, 1280-1282.
56. *Ibid.*, M, 1342-1346 cf. Gower, *Confessio Amantis*, Prol., 41-53.
57. *Ibid.*, M, 1343 to end.

royal administration for the simple reason that it constitutes a weakness in one of the most important organs of the social body.

Our author thought of his duty as a real one and of his contribution as tangible. He modestly begs the king to read his poem, and if there is anything wrong in it, to let that be corrected while still unpublished.[58] Moreover, he leaves little doubt as to the persons for whom he intended the work. It is primarily, of course, for the king. But he also had in mind the governing class as a whole. He mentions specifically "my king and the lords,"[59] and he had a special, if apparently forlorn, hope for the "young lords . . . that never read good rule nor reason's books."[60]

∽ ∽ ∽

Although the author of *Mum and the Sothsegger* explored the subject more fully than any of his contemporaries, there are signs that he was by no means alone among the writers of the early fifteenth century in his concern for the true and fearless reporting of grievances. Another anonymous poet, a man apparently experienced in the deliberations of Parliament, echoes much of the *Mum* author's thought.[61] To him, also, the central problem of government was to provide the king and the lords with accurate and dependable information on whatever needed reform in English society. Government is a constant struggle between Truth and Falsehood.[62] And he insists that the wisest wits, whether or not in the formal employ of the government, be permitted to offer their advice to the king.[63]

In this respect he specifically designates preachers and poets.[64] They bear apparently a special responsibility for the kind of extra-parliamentary discussion upon which Parliament itself, to say nothing of "the king and the lords," seem to depend. The idea appears to have been a popular one. Another poet of the reign of Henry IV

58. *Ibid.*, R, Prol., 57-63.
58. *Ibid.*, R, Prol., 49.
60. *Ibid.*, R, iii, 113-119.
61. *Twenty-six Political and other Poems*, ed. J. Kail, E.E.T.S., O.S., No. 124 (1904); see also Introduction, p. ix.
62. See especially *ibid.*, poem XII.
63. *Ibid.*, poem XIII, ll. 133-136. The author of *Wynnere and Wastoure* (*ca.* 1352) laments that poets are no longer favored as once they were by the lords. J. Spiers, *Medieval English Poetry* (London, 1957), pp. 272-273.
64. *Twenty-six Poems*, poem IV, ll. 81-84.

dramatizes it by having a "clerk" come forward in Parliament and proffer his counsel directly to the king.[65] Though part of a typical dream sequence, this scene was no doubt meant to symbolize just this duty on the part of the typical literate man to serve as the voice of the people. It is not a duty easy or even always safe to discharge. The author of *Mum* suggests that Mum's own power over men responsible for the public welfare stems from fear of reprisals.[66] And another poet warns that a country is in a bad way "when prelate is forbad to preach," for then "no true man truth dare teach."[67] But it is a duty nonetheless, and it lies at the very heart of the problem of counsel.

Something even more like the attitude of the *Mum* author reappears in that landmark of fifteenth-century mercantile thought, the *Libel of English Policy*.[68] Like his predecessor this writer had great faith in written discussion. Like him he apparently recognized the duty of the lettered man, the articulate citizen, to express himself in writing: "My soul discharge I by this present letter."[69] Like him, too, he planned other treatises. Indeed he refers to others that he has already written.

> And if ye will more of Calais hear and know,
> I cast to write within a little scroll,
> Like as I have done before bye and bye
> In other parts of our policy.[70]

He proposes another "little book" on the subject of Ireland.[71] (Not the least remarkable characteristic of this unusual man is his willingness to write another pamphlet rather than digress too flagrantly in the one in hand.) Finally, the *Libel* recalls the devoted people who, according to *Mum*, discharge their public duty by telling the truth about things as they are. Though no doubt situated much closer to the heart of government than the earlier writer, perhaps a person of some consequence, accustomed to speaking not merely the language of complaint but also of policy, he at times adopts the same tone as the "Sothsegger." Of his analysis of the importance of Calais he writes,

65. *The Crowned King*, in Robbins, pp. 227-232.
66. *Mum*, M, 156 ff., 1136.
67. *Twenty-six Poems*, poem XVI, ll. 67-70.
68. See below, chapter iv for discussion of this treatise.
69. *Libel*, l. 851.
70. *Ibid.*, ll. 834-837.
71. *Ibid.*, ll. 752-755.

See well thereto and hear the great complaint
That true men tell, that will no lies paint,
And as ye know that writing cometh from thence.[72]

∾ ∾ ∾

The only other treatises of the fifteenth century that carry forward
the notion of counsel are those of Ashby and Fortescue, both the product of the years of Yorkist supremacy. The intervening period was,
as we have noticed, one of strangely isolated landmarks in the history
of thought. But the paucity of such outstanding examples must not
be construed to mean that there were no other books on counsel.
There were, in fact, several. The trouble was that they followed the
stereotype form of the "mirror of princes," the treatise "*de regimine
principum*," a form strongly influenced by that hardy perennial of medieval political literature, the *Secreta Secretorum*.[73] It was a form hard to
adapt to English conditions, never, indeed, thoroughly domesticated
in England,[74] and quite ill-suited to realistic analysis or the discussion of
policy. But it did possess the hallmark of antique tradition, and the
cautious Aristotelian morality it relayed no doubt commended itself to
medieval readers.[75]

The image of an Aristotle advising an Alexander was not entirely
incompatible with that which the author of *Mum*, for example,
envisaged of the man of wit and wisdom, capable of setting forth his
counsel in written form and offering it voluntarily as a public-spirited
private citizen for the use of his king. But the advice which medieval
adapters like Aegidius Romanus put into Aristotle's mouth had so
little bearing on any specific situation that it led its several fifteenth-
century English translators and adapters[76] away from the practical issues

72. *Ibid.*, ll. 820-822.
73. On the mirror of princes tradition, see Robert Steele (ed.), *Secrees of old Philosoffres*,
E.E.T.S., E.S., No. 66 (1894), introduction; A. H. Gilbert, "Notes on the Influence of
the *Secretum Secretorum*," *Speculum*, III (Jan., 1928), 84-98, and the same author's *Machiavelli's Prince and its Forerunners* (Durham, N. C., 1938); W. Kleineke, *Englische Fürstenspiegel vom Policraticus Johanns von Salisbury bis zum Basilikon Doron König Jakobs I*
(Halle, 1937); W. Berges, *Die Fürstenspiegel des hohen und späten Mittelalters* (Leipzig, 1938).
74. Gilbert, *Machiavelli's Prince and its Forerunners*, p. 231.
75. George Cary, *The Medieval Alexander* (Cambridge, 1956), p. 250. See also above,
chap. i.
76. With the exception of one English translation that dates apparently from the late
fourteenth century, all the direct translations of the *Secreta* are of the fifteenth. Steele (ed.),
Secrees, p. xiii. Two of those remaining merely translate French or Latin texts and nothing

of English life and toward generalities. More than that, it led toward the kind of moral generality to which medieval English comment was always prone and toward a concept of government centered to an unrealistic degree upon the person of the king.

As E. M. W. Tillyard has pointed out, the men of the fifteenth century "felt terribly dependent on the character that their ruler hap-pened to possess, and they believed that the ruler's character might really be influenced by the example of virtue and vice met in literature."[77] They felt the same way about the ruling class as a whole, for whom the "mirror of princes" literature was also meant. Viewed in this light the efforts of the translators and adapters of fifteenth-century England to set before both king and ruling class such books of un-questioned wisdom as those of the "mirror of princes" tradition or the standard tales of chivalric deeds, full as they were of improving ex-ample,[78] become more understandable. It remains a wonder, how-ever, that those authors who undertook to write or translate the con-ventional treatise *de regimine principum* were ever able to say anything worthwhile about English problems.

Thomas Hoccleve's *Regement of Princes* (1411-1412) is a case in point. For the most part it is a series of excerpts adapted freely from Aegidius and arranged so as to teach the prince how to rule: he should keep his coronation oaths and be true to his word at all times; he should do justice to all and be especially solicitous of the poor; he should observe the laws; his conduct should be guided by pity, mercy, patience, chastity, magnanimity, liberality, and prudence; he should seek peace; and, of course, he should seek out good counselors and beware of flatterers. So far it is the standard handbook of the prince considered

---

more. A third, written by James Young and dedicated to the Earl of Ormonde in 1420, makes use of contemporaneous Irish history to point up the advice in the original treatise: *Three Prose Versions of the Secreta Secretorum*, ed. R. Steele, E.E.T.S., E.S., No. 74 (1898). Hoccleve in his *Regiment of Princes*, in Hoccleve's *Works*, ed. F. J. Furnivall, E.E.T.S., E.S., No. 72 (1897), applies the borrowed precepts more immediately to England. Lydgate and Burgh, about 1450, simply added one more verse translation without any attempt to apply it to existing conditions; Steele (ed.)., *Secrees*. Finally Ashby succeeded in freeing his mind almost completely from the *Secreta* in his comment on English affairs and owes only the tone of his *Active Policy of a Prince* and the form of his *Dicta et Opiniones Diversorum Philosophorum*, ed. Mary Bateson, E.E.T.S., E.S., No. 76 (1899), to the tradi-tional type.

77. E. M. W. Tillyard, *The English Renaissance: Fact or Fiction* (Baltimore, 1952), p. 68.
78. Ferguson, *Indian Summer*, chap. ii.

primarily as a Christian man. Into these uncontested generalities Hoccleve managed, however, to inject a few remarks on specifically English problems. Such lapses into originality occur chiefly on the subject of public finance, the administration of justice, and the prob' lem of peace,[79] and indicate that Hoccleve, hack'writer and time' server that he was, could observe realistically and interpret the function of unsolicited written counsel to some extent in a practical light.

George Ashby, writing about 1470, alone of those who adhered to the *Secreta* tradition, managed to free his mind almost completely from its narrower limitations and owes only the tone of his *Active Policy of a Prince* and the form of his *Dicta Philosophorum* to the arche' type. The former is, indeed, a remarkably penetrating commentary on English public life. In many ways it foreshadows the work of the humanist pamphleteers who commented both critically and con' structively on the English scene in the 1530's and 1540's. Ashby himself resembles in some respects that category of intelligent and more or less literary men whom the early Tudors drew into public life from the middle classes, men free from commitments to noble factions, de' voted rather to the orderly administration of government than to the fortunes of political parties, and above all practical rather than doctri' naire on matters of policy. Although he wrote the *Active Policy* to' ward the close of a long career in the king's service—probably as clerk of the signet—he spoke as a citizen rather than a professional public servant, and, as we shall see in the next chapter, he distilled the accu' mulated wisdom of his life in recommendations not unlike those actually put into effect by a reformed and revitalized monarchy.

Toward that same end Sir John Fortescue also labored—likewise at the end of a long career in active public life, yet also in the capacity of a citizen conscious of having something of importance to tell. Like Ashby he wrote ostensibly to instruct the young Prince Edward of Lancaster. But, unlike those who followed in the tradition of the *Secreta*, he spoke directly and consistently to the issues immediately facing English government. Having served for many years as Chief Justice of the Court of King's Bench, Fortescue felt no need to justify his efforts; and, as far as the problem of counsel is concerned, he ad' dressed himself specifically to conciliar reform rather than, like the author of *Mum and the Sothsegger*, to the question of extra'governmental

79. Hoccleve, *Regiment*, ll. 2791'2803, 4425'4431, 4831'4834, 5523'5236, 5335'5404.

discussion or of truth-telling in the abstract.   But his analysis and proposals also belong to the next chapter.

∽   ∽   ∽

When next we meet the problem of counsel it is in a new setting.
The citizen-counselor of early Tudor England has for his frame of
reference that civic-minded, strongly utilitarian brand of humanism,
that "applied" humanism which became so characteristic a feature of
early Tudor thought.   He still has much in common with the author
of *Mum and the Sothsegger*—more perhaps than the tone of his remarks
would always lead us to recognize.   In certain fundamental respects
he is still medieval.   But in adopting as his source of inspiration the
culture of ancient Greece and Rome, reinterpreted with reference to
the realities of early Tudor England, he managed nevertheless to take
a decisive step in the direction of modern thought.

CHAPTER IV. EMERGING REALISM: ECONOMIC DISCUSSION

IN THE PRECEDING CHAPTERS THE POLITICALLY ALERT and articulate Englishman of the later Middle Ages has appeared in the strictly conventional garb of medieval culture. Despite his keen interest in the issues of his day and even his sense of public duty as a spokesman for the common good, despite his consistent Englishry and his unswerving patriotism, his view of public life remained limited by the fixed horizons of a prescribed moral order and a providential history. He found it consequently difficult to proceed from complaint to analysis and from moral exhortation to the discussion of constructive policy. This remains a general tendency throughout the literature of the fifteenth century. But there were exceptions, and the exceptions are, in that age of sharp contrasts and eccentric personalities, often as important as the rules. To use Kingford's now classic generalization, "morally, intellectually and materially it was an age not of stagnation but of ferment."[1] And nowhere is that ferment more apparent than in the literature of public discussion.

Sporadically there emerges in that literature a new realism. It is a very different kind of realism from that which characterizes much of late medieval English literature, from that of Gower for instance, or Langland. Like the artist, the critic of late medieval society was often able to see with microscopic clarity the individual instance and to depict what he saw with an often startling exactness. Scattered through *Piers Plowman* are a rich and varied assortment of vignettes in which the courts, the life of the peasants, even Parliament stand out as in the miniatures and marginal drawings of a master illuminator. And if Gower's treatment of similar subjects fails to achieve quite the same degree of clarity it is only because his reportorial ability was of a lesser order. At least he tried. Nor were Langland and Gower either unable or unwilling to generalize or to develop a systematic argument. They simply examined society from a different point of view from that of the modern observer. Accurate as was their eye, it was directed by

1. Kingsford, *Prejudice and Promise*, p. 66.

the mind of the moralist. The unity that holds together their examination of the particular (and in which the particular, even the particular
instance we should consider secular, finds its meaning) is the unity of
man's spiritual predicament. What these men could not do, or rather
saw no reason for doing, was to examine particular conditions in their
temporal relationship and to recognize in them some system or process
or to achieve a synthetic view of the whole—something like a monocu-
lar perspective, perhaps—that was as realistic as their view of its parts.
However co-ordinated their picture of English society might be, indeed
by virtue of the very fact that it possessed what the medieval mind considered the higher unity of moral truth, it failed to reveal those immediate
causal connections between one fact and another upon which the constructive intelligence of the policy-maker might work.

That a more comprehensive realism appears so late in the literature
of discussion was not, of course, owing to a general defect of vision.
Men of statesmanlike quality were able to speak the language of policy
long before they acquired the habit of committing themselves to
writing. The articulate citizen of medieval England tended to be the
public moralist rather than the man of affairs, his mind conditioned by
the values, if not the training as well, of the clergy. Even when, like
Gower, he was a layman with business interests, he was still prone to
follow the habits of thought and expression (they are not easily separated) typical of his clerical contemporaries. Otherwise he kept silent
or reserved his counsel for the council chamber. It becomes therefore
a fact of some significance that in the fifteenth century a few men of
affairs undertook to express themselves on matters of national and
secular concern and with a new realism, the realism of analysis and
policy rather than that of complaint and moral criticism.

ഗ ഗ ഗ

Two areas of fifteenth-century English life seem to have provided
especially fertile soil for the new realism: first, the area of economic
relationships, in particular those involving the wealth and power of
the realm, those that provided the greatest opportunity for the exercise
of constructive policy by the national government and which, when
more fully understood, came to be comprehended in a more or less
consistent theory of mercantilism; and second, the area of government

itself, that to which the upsetting experience of the civil wars called attention with peculiar insistence.

It should not be surprising that economic problems were the earliest and most fruitful subject for realistic analysis. In them could be observed more readily than in any other category of the national life the impersonal causal forces that move the social mechanism. In contrast to the moral factors with which the medieval commentator was preoccupied, these were subject to intelligent manipulation by the government. They lay well within the limits set by human nature, with its inveterate and inordinate tendencies, and by the providential pattern of history. That is to say, they lay within practicable reach of human ingenuity.

Economic relationships, moreover, raised questions which became increasingly difficult to answer within the traditional framework of Christian thought. True, the schoolmen themselves labored ingeniously, and not without effect, to expand that framework so as to comprehend the problems of the rapidly changing economic life of late medieval Christendom. Even the canonist hostility toward purely financial transactions was modified in an increasingly flexible treatment of usury.[2] But the tendency of economic life was ineluctably secular. Its problems continued (as indeed they still do) to bear moral implications of the most profound significance, and as such they continued with good reason to provide material for the preacher and the moralistic writer. But for practical purposes they could be, in a sense had to be, and to an increasing extent in fact became, the object of analysis in and for themselves, not necessarily related to the transcendent issues of the moral and spiritual life.

For practical purposes Englishmen had for a long time been forced to examine the economic mechanism, and, owing to the remarkably early development of central government in England, and the peculiar position in English affairs of the wool trade as the national staple, they had at an early date been required to project their examination on a national scale. Eileen Power tells us, for example, that experience with the wool tax soon made the fourteenth-century Englishman, wool-grower as well as wool-merchant, aware of the effect it had on prices. Toward the close of the century the abbot of the great wool-

2. T. P. McLaughlin, "The Teaching of the Canonists on Usury," *Medieval Studies*, I (1939), 81-147, II (1940), 1-22.

growing abbey of Meaux traced the decline in the price of English wool directly to the tax: "And so it is those who own the wool who pay this tax to the king, and not the merchants who appear to make the grant to him; for wools are sold at a lesser price the greater the tax payable to the king for them."[3]

The problem of money, too, came at an early date to be recognized, if only dimly, as part of a complex mechanism of cause and effect and one that fell within the province of the king's government.   Early examples of such analysis are rare, a fact which accounts for the following instance being frequently quoted.   It seems that in 1381 an inquest was held into the lack of money in the realm.   One Richard Aylesbury replied in terms of what seems to be a clear theory of the balance of trade, one indeed that went well beyond the simple bullionist principles that actually governed English monetary policy for a century and a half thereafter.   "If," he is reported to have said, "the merchandise which goes out of England be well and rightly governed, the money that is in England will remain and great plenty of money will come from beyond the sea, that is to say, let not more strange merchandise come within the realm than to the value of the denezin merchandise which passes out of the realm."[4]   This, it must be remembered, was not the analysis of a theorist, however realistic, but the commonsense reaction of a practical man faced with a specific problem.   It reveals nevertheless the kind of attitude that was conducive to, indeed prerequisite to, the rise of a more conscious, intellectually sophisticated realism.

It is the attitude which no doubt inspired much of the protomercantilist legislation of Edward III's reign.   Without going into the controversial question as to how consciously or consistently that legislation expressed a national economic policy,[5] it is apparent that, in undertaking to foster the native cloth industry the government was applying itself inventively to the task of adjusting tangible economic forces in the interests of national prosperity.   The men responsible were probably not aware of being especially inventive or of doing anything really new.   But they were apparently quite capable of thinking in

3. Quoted in Power, *Wool Trade*, pp. 73-74.

4. *Rotuli Parliamentorum*, III, 126-127.   Reprinted in A. E. Bland, P. A. Brown, and R. H. Tawney, *English Economic History, Select Documents* (London, 1915), p. 222

5. On this subject, see, for example, Unwin (ed.), pp. xiv ff.; E. Lipson, *The Economic History of England* (3 vols.; London, 1956), I, 455-456; Power and Postan, p. 102.

terms of England's material needs.   Attention to the national interest
continued throughout the following century to characterize at least the
stated aims of economic legislation.   And, as M. M. Postan has reminded us, the wording of preambles to statutes, though usually
rationalizations of one sort or another, express for that very reason the
ideas and attitudes their authors consider most important.   The
emphasis of the Tudor pamphleteers on the common "wealth" has its
medieval counterpart in the notion of the *"bien universelle"* of the realm.[6]

As the French war moved into its more disastrous stages after the
death of Henry V, especially after the siege of Calais had brought home
to all those capable of profiting by the knowledge the significance of
England's relations with the Continent, a new dimension was added
to English economic thought.   To the desideratum of wealth was
added that of power, and questions of national power came necessarily
to be interpreted, in that island community, largely in terms of economic
competition, and economic competition to some extent in terms of
moving forces.

Thus the problems of economic life required that some attention
be given to the dynamic elements operating in late medieval society.
If their nature was not yet fully understood, if indeed they were not
ordinarily recognized as such, they could hardly be overlooked by the
observer whose mind remained at all consistently on the level of the
practical.   It was out of prolonged contemplation of those forces that
the new realism arose.   Out of such study was eventually to come
that awareness of the interrelation of the parts of the social system, that
sense of process which is so basic a part of modern thought.

Considering the fact that practical men were constantly being
forced to analyze the economic phenomena of their day, however *ad hoc*
and inaccurate their analyses might be, considering also the fact that
such analyses made it possible for them to think in terms of policies
that went far beyond the mere piecemeal remedy of that which is amiss,
it is surprising to find these facts reflected at such a late date and,
withal, so seldom, in the medieval literature of comment and counsel.
Gower and Langland and the preachers of their day whose outlook
they shared had commented freely and frequently upon particular
economic problems.[7]   Gower, as we have seen, spoke out of a more

6. Power and Postan, pp. 102-103.   See especially, n. 15.
7. See above, chap. ii.

than ordinarily intimate knowledge of the world of trade. Nor do they appear to have had any difficulty seeing economic issues in their specifically English context—this despite the universality of the moral order which provided the broader context of their thought, and, in Gower's case, despite his special concern for the prosperity of the "great city." Yet theirs remained essentially the point of view of the moralist rather than the man of secular affairs or the objective analyst, and what held their piecemeal complaints together was the relevance of those complaints to the moral order, not their relation to each other.

Wyclif and his Lollard followers had also reason, a very special reason, to investigate economic relationships. Having traced the ills of the church in England to the worldly entanglements connected with property holding, and having come to the conclusion that reform could only be brought about by disentangling the clergy from its prop/ erty, they found themselves examining with a more than canonical eye the place of clerical endowments, to say nothing of the church's fiscal system, in the life of the national community. And, be it noticed, their analysis had issue in a policy which, however futile in the existing circumstances, was certainly meant to be practical. "Let it be resolved," he wrote somewhat late in his career,

> that, upon the death of a bishop or abbot or anyone notably endowed in England, his temporalities should fall into the king's hands and that no election be held until a license is obtained from the king, and that the alienated lordships of the kingdom shall not be held by the person elected unless the king once again gives his approval. Let the king therefore restrain himself from renewing the great laxity of his progenitors, and in a short time the realm will be purged of the stagnant amor/ tisment of temporal possessions which are now in mortmain.[8]

If spiritual in their fruits, endowments remained firmly rooted in the secular soil of England. Clearly—and these were considerations of more than academic significance in the Lollard campaign of prop/ aganda—they could not be removed without all sorts of social reper/ cussions. Wyclif thus found himself explaining the place and func/ tion of "clerks possessioners" in society in an effort to demonstrate what effect removing them from their possessions would have, not only on

8. John Wyclif, *Trialogus*, ed. G. V. Lechler (Oxford, 1869), p. 313.

England's religious life, but on her temporal fortunes. The endowed clergy, for example, destroy knighthood by having "great lordships amortized to them," by which "knights should be sustained to govern the people."[9] These "secular lordships" should be "given wisely by the king and witty lords to poor gentlemen that would justly govern the people, and maintain the land against enemies." In this way "many thousand men of arms [more] than now is" might be main-tained "without any cost of lords or tallage of poor commons."[10] We are permitted to wonder how he thought resumed lands would go to "poor gentlemen" rather than to the great magnates whose ancestors had been mainly responsible for the original grants. And he had a rather limited notion of the social function of such wealth. Unlike the Tudor preachers and pamphleteers who in many other respects shared his views, he seems not to have seen the other social uses, education for instance, to which church wealth could be put. But it is still an interesting fact that he recognized as realistically as he did the economic and military effects of disendowment.

The effects of disendowment would, in fact, be felt in many di-rections. If there were no endowments to lure greedy churchmen from their spiritual duties, the government would no longer need to be wary of those "Caesarean" clergy who served two masters to the undoing of both.[11] From the proceeds derived from church property the king might pay lay officers.[12] The increasing and unnecessary number of clerks would be reduced, thus relieving the country of an improverishing burden.[13] "Clerks possessioners" Wyclif blames in-directly for the peasant uprisings for which his Lollard preachers were

9. *The English Works of Wyclif Hitherto Unprinted*, ed. F. D. Matthew, E.E.T.S., O.S., No. 74 (1880), pp. 116-117.

10. *Select English Works of John Wyclif*, ed. T. Arnold (3 vols.; Oxford, 1869-71), III, 216-217; cf. Wyclif, *Opera Minora*, ed. J. Loserth (London, 1913), p. 174. See also petition to Parliament, 1382, in Thomas Walsingham, *Historia Anglicana*, ed. H. T. Riley, Rolls Series (2 vols.; 1863-1864), II, 51-52.

11. *De Civili Dominio*, ed. R. L. Poole and J. Loserth (4 vols.; London, 1885-1904), II, 239. Cf. *De Simonia*, ed. Dr. Herzberg-Fränkel and M. H. Dziewicki (London, 1898), p. 8.

12. *Opera Minora*, p. 51; cf. *De Officio Regis*, ed. A. W. Pollard and C. Sayle (London, 1887), p. 52.

13. *De Officio Regis*, p. 158; *Opera Minora*, p. 293. Cf. *Select English Works*, III, 346-347.

also sometimes blamed.[14]   With endowments would go pluralism and absenteeism and all their train of local ills.

> O how happy would our country be, and how productive if every parish there had, as formerly, its rector, if every estate in the land had a just owner living there with his family; then there would be no lack of corn and cattle, and there would be plenty of servants, farm laborers and artizans.   But now there are only tenants bearing the rule of the clergy hardly; they care not for tillage of the grounds, as it is not theirs; they live by theft, as there is nobody to look after them, and in their wantonness they disturb the kingdom.   The clergy, overburdened with worldly goods, seek to equal the splendour of the laity, or to surpass it. . . .   How different would all that be were those temporalities in the possession of poor owners; more homes would be founded, the population, and with it the state would grow, but the priests could devote themselves to an edifying life, as becomes them.[15]

It must, however, be remembered that Wyclif came to economic analysis by way of religious conviction and scholastic argument.   He drew the line between secular interests and religious no more clearly than did any other of his contemporaries.   Like Gower or Langland, he assumed that, since the church was to be the body politic as the conscience was to the body natural, what caused the clergy to err would exaggerate the all too marked tendency of the rest of society to stray from the paths of virtue.   And sin brought divine retribution: Wyclif never tired of quoting Ecclesiastes to the effect that a kingdom shall be translated from one people to another for unrighteousness. When the Parliament of 1376 solemnly declared that the evils of the church were "the cause of all the plagues, murrain, famine, and poverty of the realm,"[16] they were speaking in terms Wyclif and his con-temporaries would have applauded and in which they would have noticed nothing odd.

ᡈ   ᡈ   ᡈ

14. *De Civili Dominio*, II, 14⁄15; *Select English Works*, p. 236; *De Blasphemia*, ed. M. H. Dziewicki (London, 1893), pp. 188⁄203.

15. *De Civili Dominio*, II, 14⁄15.   I have used Loserth's free translation of this excerpt printed in *ibid.*, IV, xi.   Cf. *Opera Minora*, p. 82.

16. *Rotuli Parliamentorum*, II, 337 ff.   See also H. B. Workman, *John Wyclif* (2 vols.; Oxford, 1926), I, 96.

The author of the *Libel of English Policy*,[17] whoever he was, made no such indirect approach to the secular affairs of his day. True, he viewed economic affairs from the outside, from the vantage point of politics. But his was a secular point of view, and it served to set the problems of English economic life in a single, secular perspective. The occasion of his writing was the curious situation that followed the siege of Calais by the Duke of Burgundy in 1436. In the preceding year Burgundy and France had reconciled their differences in the Treaty of Arras. Refusing to come to terms with either power, England found herself without allies, isolated in her attempt to maintain her conquests in France. Philip the Good, Duke of Burgundy, undertook to hasten the English withdrawal by laying siege to Calais, thereby calling attention in the most dramatic way possible to the value of that port city not only to England's military position but to her economic prosperity. Fortunately for both, Philip failed to press the siege and the English were permitted to celebrate their deliverance as if they had gained a great victory. Among the several comments elicited by these events,[18] the *Libel* stands out in towering isolation, its jingoism redeemed by a seriously proposed policy. The author spoke for the Duke of Gloucester, the merchants of the Staple, and the cloth exporters, all of whom were opposed to the policy being followed by the dominant Beaufort faction in the council. Committed to reinforcement of the army in France and saving the king's position in Normandy, the council had decided to spend as little as possible on naval defense and on Calais, and to court instead the favor of foreign merchants. The latter were, in the circumstances, more likely than heir English competitors to be a source of profit to the royal exchequer.[19] Thus it was a complex situation the author of the *Libel* set out to analyze, a situation in which political and dynastic factors, complicated enough in themselves, were overshadowed by economic and strategic, or, if you will, geopolitical considerations.

The argument of the *Libel* is, however, simple enough—too simple, in fact; yet therein lies its uniqueness. Its author was able to contemplate the complex situation in northwestern Europe in something

17. On the authorship of the *Libel*, as well as for a summary of the scholarship concerning it, see Holmes, pp. 193-216.

18. See above, chap. i.

19. On all the above, see Holmes.

approaching its totality. By recognizing the relationship of its parts
he was able to achieve a synthetic view and by so doing to arrive at a
uniquely comprehensive, if crudely oversimplified policy. What he
calls the "true process of English policy" is epitomized in the couplet

> Cherish merchandise, keep the admiralty,
> That we be masters of the narrow sea.[20]

The argument of the poem proceeds with only a few minor digressions
from this initial statement. England's welfare depends on her ability
to control the home waters, especially the "narrow sea," which in turn
depends on the preservation of Calais. For then England would be
able to control all commerce to and from Flanders. And, since "the
little land of Flanders is / But a staple to other lands,"[21] the trade of all
western Europe, from Spain and Italy in the south to the Hanseatic
towns in the north, would be at the mercy of England's sea power.

Not only can England, if she will only look to her naval power,
control the bottleneck of western trade in her own interests, but she can
bring direct pressure to bear on the key marts of the Netherlands. For
she has, so our author insists, what they cannot long do without. Despite the fact that the Duke of Burgundy was even then trying to impose
an embargo on English trade, with the somewhat frantic support of the
Flemings who viewed with alarm the growing competition of English cloth, he maintained with good reason that English wool was
essential to the cloth trade of the low countries.[22] Its superior quality
made it always in demand on the Continent. Even the good Spanish
wool does not measure up to standard unless it is "mixed well /
Amongst English wool the greater deal."[23] If England would with-
hold her wool then "this foloweth in certain / Flanders of need must
with us have peace."[24]

This emphasis on peace is characteristic of the author of the *Libel*.
At first glance it seems oddly at variance with the tough-minded
realism of his central thesis. The last section is devoted entirely to the
"unity" (meaning harmony between states) which will result from
"our keeping of the sea." It contains so pious a statement of the

20. *The Libelle of Englyshe Polycye*, ll. 6-7.
21. *Ibid.*, ll. 116-117.
22. See Holmes's treatment of this subject.
23. *Libelle*, ll. 100-101.
24. *Ibid.*, ll. 93-95; cf. ll. 1084-1085.

Christian ideal of peace, so well and, for this writer, so unwontedly documented from the Scriptures, that it seems hardly to come from the same pen as wrote the body of the poem. Perhaps, indeed, it did not.[25] Yet the ideal of peace and tranquility it preaches merely echoes statements made in the first and eighth chapters. And even the Christian sentiment in the last chapter comes mixed with strategic realism. The full heading of the chapter is "Of unity, showing our keeping of the sea, with one final process of peace by authority." Peace by authority indeed! Harmony forced upon unwilling neighbors by means of a favorable geographical, economic, and, in general, strategic position. If England would but command the narrow seas "we should of our cruel enemies / Make our friends for fear of merchandise."[26] Peace of this sort with a Flanders in danger of economic strangulation would also bring peace with Spain,

> For Spain and Flanders is as each other brother,
> And neither may well live withouten other.[27]

This author sees trade as an instrument of policy, to be used for the purposes of power as well as plenty. "Power," he declares bluntly, "causes peace finally."[28] He recognizes that England is in deadly competition with other powers and that in such a struggle political and economic considerations are inseparable. If the seas are kept, he says, "many lands would seek here peace of need," and their "ambassadors/ Would been here soon to treat for their succours."[29] What he has in mind is a sort of *pax Britannica* in miniature, the harsh realities of its policy, to be sure, somewhat veiled by the medieval ideal of Christian unity, just as those of its mature nineteenth-century counterpart were decently clothed with the garments of liberalism.

Cherishing merchandise meant also controlling the domestic market. The prosperity, and indirectly the power of England depended not only on naval command of the straits and domination of foreign markets but on protecting England's own markets and her own industry from exploitation by foreigners. By a searching analysis of apparently quite accurate data concerning the import trade he argues

25. Holmes, p. 215.
26. *Libelle*, ll. 576-579.
27. *Ibid.*, ll. 86-87.
28. *Ibid.*, l. 1091.
29. *Ibid.*, ll. 1082-1087.

that English policy should be highly selective. Whereas, for example, the Genoese carracks bring in desirable and useful commodities, gold, silk, pepper, woad, cotton, alum, even "wool-oil" and "wood ashes,"[30] the Venetians and Florentines bring luxuries, "things of complacence,"

> Apes, and japes, and marmosets tailed,
> Nifles, trifles, that little have availed,

"things not enduring," wines and exotic medicinal herbs that are soon wasted.[31] In addition the Venetians and Florentines are guilty of sharp practice. They buy wool on credit in the Cotswolds and in Calais, ship it to Venice for cash, transfer the money back to Flanders, then use it to cash bills of exchange for English merchants trading with Flanders and are ready to repay their debts to the English, having made up to three shillings on the pound on the transaction.[32] By this sort of practice they "wipe our nose with our own sleeve." Meanwhile they carry away England's staple products, cloth, wool, and tin, and drain the land of its gold.[33]

This is by no means all the author of the *Libel* has to say, but it should suffice to show the man's peculiar cast of mind. It shows, for one thing, his marked preference for the tangible, his willingness to find in concrete facts the proper materials for analysis, the stuff of which policy is made. He seems to have looked quite consciously to ex-perience as a guide.

> He that trusts not to my saying and sentence,
> Let him better search experience.[34]

His argument is based not on the moral nature of man (he takes the deceit of foreign merchants into account simply as a matter of fact), but rather on a wealth of specific, largely impersonal data, most of it apparently accurate,[35] much of it gained by personal investigation.[36] When he goes beyond what is observable in his own day it is to the

30. *Ibid.*, chap. vi.
31. *Ibid.*, chap. vii.
32. Holmes, p. 201.
33. *Libelle*, ll. 375-379, 396-397.
34. *Ibid.*, ll. 370-371.
35. Holmes.
36. See, for example, his information concerning the existence of gold and silver deposits in Ireland which he claims to have gotten from a London jeweler who had tested the ore and found it good. *Libelle*, ll. 692-695.

experience stored up in history rather than to the authority of the ancients, the Fathers, or even of the Scriptures: "thus conclude I by authority / Of chronicle . . ."[37] and, with the exception of an excursion into the earlier history of England in the days of King Edgar, it is in the chronicles of the immediately preceding hundred years that he finds his most useful materials.[38] In general he appears to have been rather proud of his analytical ability and of the methods he used. Of his main argument he says

> . . . this process hath proved by and by,
> All by reason and expert policy,
> And by stories which proved well this part.[39]

Still more significantly, his argument reveals his quite unprecedent-ed ability to reduce the complexities of external trade to manageable proportions, to recognize the relationship between trade and foreign policy, and on the basis of his analysis to arrive at a comprehensive economic-strategic, distinctly national policy. That his analysis was oversimplified and his policy, however practical in intention, was in the circumstances unworkable should be pretty obvious. Though given special significance by recent events, Flanders was not the only focal point of English trade, as Englishmen were to find out later in the century in their unfortunate dealings with the Hanseatic League.[40] To have controlled the channel as the author proposed would have taken a larger navy than Henry V or any other of his historical heroes had maintained or in those days could ever have been maintained. And merely to discourage foreign merchants was not sufficient to encourage those of England.[41] But perhaps the important thing—certainly so in the context of this study—is that, if the author was wrong, his mistakes were recognizably modern. When he concentrates the weight of his argument on Flanders as the bottleneck through which all the trade of western Europe must pass, we are reminded of another bottleneck a group of analysts found in the ball-bearing industry of Germany during World War II. Was he, with perhaps less data to go on, any more

37. *Ibid.*, ll. 944-945.
38. See especially, *ibid.*, chap. xi.
39. *Ibid.*, ll. 1078-1080.
40. Power and Postan, chap. iii.
41. E. F. Jacob, *The Fifteenth Century, 1399-1485* (Oxford, 1961), pp. 348-349.

in error than they? Certainly his methods, if not quite so sophisticated, were not dissimilar.

It is not as a pioneer treatise in mercantilist theory that the *Libel* is important. Indeed, although it deals with many of the problems later to preoccupy mercantilists—the flow of gold, the regulation of trade, of luxury imports in particular, the relation of economic prosperity to national power—he makes no attempt to work them into a consistent theory and, in his failure, may well have reflected the essentially cutandfit approach to national economic policy actually made by English government up to that time. What sets him apart from his predecessors and foreshadows most clearly such mercantilist pamphlets of the midsixteenth century as the *Discourse of the Commonweal* is his sense of economic process, his awareness, that is, of the secondary causes governing economic relationships, the impersonal forces at work in human society which can be understood by rational investigation and to some extent controlled by intelligent policy.

ৎ ৎ ৎ

Though far and away the most significant piece of economic discussion remaining from the late medieval period, the *Libel of English Policy* is not alone. Not that it is easy, or for present purposes necessary, to discover any direct influence stemming from it. The raw materials of mercantilist policy were already common property. It does, however, appear that the pamphlet marks the beginning of a new era in economic discussion. It was itself reissued soon in slightly altered form, and it was apparently copied from time to time during the rest of the century.[42] More important, its ideas, or at any rate similar ideas, found their way into other writings.

At about the middle of the century a little Yorkist pamphlet complained of three things: that gold and silver "goeth in to divers realms and countries," that "the wools and fell hath course and passage out of the realm, wherefore all strangers take but little reward to buy our English cloth, but make it them self," that alien merchants are allowed to "abide so long within the land, and to utter their good at their own lust."[43] Legislation is suggested to remedy each grievance. At about

42. Warner (ed.), *Libelle*, p. xlvii. See also F. Taylor, "Some Manuscripts of the *Lybelle of Englyshe Polycye*," *Bulletin of the John Rylands Library*, XXIV (1940), 376418.
43. Printed in Kingsford, *English Historical Literature*, Appendix XI, pp. 362363.

the same time a tract entitled *The Commodytes of England* echoed the
Libel's factual data concerning English trade and also its economic patriotism without, however, reflecting in any way the earlier author's
grasp of overall policy.[44]

On the other hand, an English poem of about 1470 not only repeats the main argument of the *Libel*, but adds to it an important message of its own. Like the *Libel*, it begins with the theme of national
power through economic supremacy. The Latin line, evidently
intended as a descriptive title, epitomizes this policy: "*Anglia, propter
tuas naves et lanas, omnia regna te salutare deberent.*"[45] Every land, the poet
continues, needs three essentials, food, drink, and cloth. Now England, "by God's ordinance," has enough of each for her own sustenance.
But of cloth and its makings she has surplus and that is something
other lands lack; so with this surplus "We might rule and govern all
Christian kings." Accordingly he proposes that great care be taken
to see that English wool and cloth be sold for a good price and especially that wool be kept at home so that "the commons of this land may
work at the full"—adding that, if any wool be sold out of the country,
let it be of the poorest quality.

Even more interesting than this shrewd statement of policy with
regard to external trade is the author's discussion of domestic industry.
This was a subject the *Libel* largely ignored in favor of the strategically
more critical problem of foreign commerce. Beginning with the policy
of regulating the wool trade so that English workers could be kept
busy, he devotes the latter half of the poem almost entirely to the subject of industrial regulation. He would, for example, see to it by
"ordinance" that the cloth workers be paid in money and not half in
goods. He is convinced, moreover, that prosperity in one aspect of
the country's industry, the mining and coining of silver, for instance,
will in the long run profit the whole community. These positive proposals for regulating home industry are the first of their kind in the
literature of discussion. Legislation had occasionally been hinted at,
if not directly proposed, in connection with external trade where the
role of the central government was clear and plain for all to see. Prob-

44. Printed in *The Works of Sir John Fortescue*, ed. Lord Clairmont (London, 1869),
pp. 449-454. Its ascription to Fortescue has always been doubtful. Comparison with
Fortescue's known work and with the *Libel* would point to an author of lesser intellectual
caliber than either.
45. Wright, *Political Poems*, II, 282-287.

lems of industrial organization, on the other hand, had hitherto elicited for the most part the familiar negative complaint.

The English workers appear, in fact, to be this writer's chief concern. The larger policy of sea power is important primarily because it ensures full employment at a decent wage. This is what led the author to explore the causal relationships within the economic system with fully as realistic an eye as the author of the *Libel*, if with less circumstantial detail; and it is what gives consistency to his argument.

∽ ∽ ∽

In the fifteenthcentury literature of economic discussion, it is possible to see foreshadowed those Tudor pamphleteers who argued the problems of English economic life with an increasing consciousness of the causal forces operating therein and with a growing confidence that those forces could be manipulated by intelligent policy. These preTudor writers remind us that the approach to modern thought is gradual, not sudden. They are well on their way, but have still a long distance to travel. In their work the national interest appears with especial clarity and with marked consistency. Mercantilist policy is adumbrated here and there but without any such consistency. These men were aware of the mechanism of economic relationships, but, like the blind sages who examined the elephant, they interpret the whole in terms of the part with which they came first into contact. They no doubt represent an even more widespread interest in such analysis and in the possibility of legislative remedy on the part of the business community. They simply felt called upon to express in written form what a governing class, as yet unused to public discussion of this sort, was striving to express in Parliament. The *Rolls of Parliament* bear witness to the practical efforts being made to regulate economic life in the interests of national wealth and power, but seemingly with no greater consistency of policy than the writers demonstrated. Yet these writers, and doubtless many of the inarticulate citizenry for whom they spoke, were nonetheless trying to achieve a realistic point of view; and this apparently conscious effort is more significant than their only partial success.

CHAPTER V. EMERGING REALISM: THE PROBLEM OF GOVERNMENT

IT WAS PROBABLY A GOOD DEAL EASIER FOR THE CITIZEN of medieval England to focus on the structure of government than on the mechanism of economic relationships. Since the middle of the thirteenth century the king's government had been the object of comment and criticism. *The Song of Lewes* is not alone in bearing witness to the sophistication with which it was possible for a few clerks, well grounded in the legal traditions of medieval Christendom and moved by the requirements of practical politics, to discuss the problems of the central government in the days before the nation and its monarchy were alike subjected to the testing processes of foreign and civil war. Pressures foreign and domestic, political and economic, factors inherent in the history of the English monarchy and contingent upon the accidents of hereditary succession combined in the fifteenth century to make the problem of good and politic governance one of peculiar urgency. And, if there were then few observers as capable as those of the thirteenth and early fourteenth centuries of examining it in the light of legal and scholastic thought, there were some who were better equipped to see in it an autonomous issue, calling for realistic analysis and reform, and to re-cut the threadbare garments of medieval theory to fit after a fashion the ungainly form of a disturbed and changing England.

Two writers in particular are cases in point, namely, George Ashby and Sir John Fortescue. Both wrote about English government at the time when the Wars of the Roses bade fair to undermine all effective administration. Both spoke from the experience of a long career close to the heart of government; but both wrote in the capacity of a private citizen, volunteering his advice to his prince—the same young Lancastrian prince, by the way. Both anticipated many of the reforms actually put into effect by Edward IV and Henry VII. Both interpreted the problem of counsel in terms of English realities. Beyond these not unimportant similarities, the two men had little enough in common. Fortescue was the better-known figure in the affairs of his day and by far the more significant in the history of English thought.

He had served as Chief Justice and was at one point the official spokes/
man for the Lancastrian cause. Ashby was for many years Clerk of
the Signet, a responsible but obscure post. Fortescue was educated
at the Inns of Court in the non/clerical tradition of the Common Law.
Ashby, though also a layman, carried with him the more conventional
baggage of medieval culture. He wrote in English verse, admittedly
under the influence of Gower, Chaucer, and Lydgate (in that order),[1]
rather than in the more direct form of Latin and English prose used by
Fortescue with such practical effect. And, unlike his greater con/
temporary, whose vision was as little hampered as Commines' or
Machiavelli's by traditional forms of expression, he struggled with only
partial success to free himself from the inhibiting heritage of the
"mirror of princes."[2] His obiter dicta on English government are
nevertheless worth noticing. Although Fortescue is the more reveal/
ing and significant writer and will therefore be the principal object of
our attention in this chapter, Ashby will serve to remind us that he was
not the only Englishman in the later fifteenth century capable of dis/
cussing the condition of government in realistic terms and also that
realistic analysis did not necessarily lead to uniform conclusions.

ᔕ ᔕ ᔕ

It is not always easy to recognize the originality of Ashby's com/
ments on English government, veiled as they are by a dense curtain of
literary and didactic conventions. Nearly eighty when he wrote the
Active Policy of a Prince, he can be forgiven for casting it in the familiar
mold of the treatise *de regimine principum*—especially when the tradi/
tional forms still retained for most English readers something very like
their face value as intellectual currency. But his adherence to traditional
forms exacted its toll just the same. It gave his discussion of con/
temporary English affairs an oddly archaic setting, one to be sure more
confusing to the modern reader than to those of his own generation,
but still no suitable vehicle for realistic analysis. It led him, despite
his obviously intimate knowledge of the already complex institutional
character of English government, to concentrate his attention upon the
prince. What is more, it led him to treat the prince as a man, and to
ignore the distinction, by no means unknown to medieval thought,

1. *Active Policy,* l. 1.
2. See above, chap. iii.

between the king in his public and private capacities.[3] Thus the implication still arises from his pages that if the prince would only choose his servants carefully, pay his debts, keep within his income, hear counsel patiently, be resolute, moderate, pious, and honest, in short cultivate the virtues ordinarily pertaining to private life, the result would be good and abundant governance. To this extent government is still, for Ashby, fundamentally a matter of moral character rather than intelligent or "active" policy. The fifteenth-century poet, accustomed to transposing all issues into moral terms and given, a little like Bunthorne, to uttering platitudes in stained-glass attitudes, seems to have stood very much in the way of the experienced civil servant.

What nevertheless separates Ashby from his predecessors in the "mirror of princes" tradition is his tacit admission that it is not enough to have a virtuous prince. The prince must also see that active policy is used in an effort to solve the problems of the realm. Nor is he willing to see in good counsel an adequate supplement to the virtuous intentions of the prince. Or, more accurately, he saw that the broader problem of counsel, including his own share in it as an informed citizen, must go beyond the honesty and general integrity of individual counselors. Accordingly, Ashby devoted a much greater proportion of his treatise that even the relatively practical Hoccleve had done in his *Regement of Princes* (a work in the same literary tradition) to a discussion of specific issues and specific remedies.[4]

His long experience at the hub of English government in that time of troubles had impressed upon him the need for strong, efficient administration on the part of a ruling house secure in its succession and free from the paralyzing drain of foreign war and from the distractions of internal faction. So he advocates a systematic campaign against conspiracy and rebellion. The chronicles, he says, will supply the needed data on hereditary disloyalty.[5] The king must guard against pretenders.[6] He must take care not to let any class or persons gain too much power. He must not make too many lords.[7] Make knights, squires, and gentlemen rich, he says, and the poor commons prosperous,

3. Chrimes, *English Constitutional Ideas*, pp. 34-35. See also Kantorowicz, *The King's Two Bodies*.

4. See above, chap. iii.

5. *Active Policy*, ll. 387-393.

6. *Ibid.*, ll. 415-421.

7. *Ibid.*, ll. 632-635.

> But to your richness make never man like
> If ye will stand in peace and be set by.[8]

The advice is similar to Fortescue's admonition to the king that he allow no subject to be "equipolent to himself."[9] Both men had wit‑ nessed the failure of the Lancastrian regime to rise above the conflict of rival nobles, and they saw that this sort of thing must above all be pre‑ vented from ever happening again.

Ashby also suggests something like the Tudor policy of employing men of low estate in the royal administration in preference to those of the aristocracy.

> . . . let never temporal lord
> Be your treasurer, nor your receiver,
> For a mean person will thereto accord
> More mete and a better solicitor,
> More available in active succour.
> For a lord's reward is infinite,
> A mean person may be content with little.[10]

The king must be dependent as little as possible on forces beyond his personal control.

Nor should he look for popular support. Ashby had the pro‑ fessional administrative officer's distrust of the people. They are "ever wavering in variance." He should trust rather in "good faithful‑ ness and equity, / In plain truth, justice and good governance."[11] In other words, the commonalty needs only to be kept content, not rallied in support of the king's cause. And the best way of doing that is to see that they are prosperous. To that end Ashby advocates laws calcu‑ lated to revive the cloth trade.[12] At the same time he suggests that sumptuary laws be passed, not only to keep the working class from extravagance but to maintain order and degree.[13] The prosperity that Ashby is striving to achieve is that of stability within a fixed social order, not that of individual opportunity. But he recognized that stability required more than prosperity. Temptation to riot must be

8. *Ibid.*, ll. 639‑642.
9. *The Governance of England*, ed. C. Plummer (Oxford, 1885), p. 130.
10. *Active Policy*, ll. 807‑813.
11. *Ibid.*, ll. 870‑873.
12. *Ibid.*, ll. 527‑529.
13. *Ibid.*, ll. 534‑540.

removed by removing the means: the commonalty should be prevented by law from bearing arms, and livery and maintenance, that
inveterate enemy of civil order, must cease.[14] Yet, he also advocated
a law making archery compulsory and providing for the erection of
practice butts in every town for the use of "every creature," as a measure
"for all our defence."[15]

Taken together, Ashby's positive proposals add up to a co-ordinated
legislative programme. As such they are unique in the political
literature of medieval England.

Ashby was, however, concerned primarily with the practical
business of government rather than with broad national policies. He
understood the importance of England's staple trade and the virtues of
peace,[16] but he held the problem of effective government to be the most
immediately pressing. To this end he proposed a variety of statutes
without, however, commenting on the legislative machinery by which
they were to become law. For him, and, as we shall see, for Fortescue,
it was the king's council, not Parliament, that was on trial. Well
manned with the right kind of advisers and managed with political
common sense,[17] it could become, as it did in fact become under
Tudor rule, the source of policy and an informal but effective administration—always, of course, under the watchful eye of the well-
trained and well-disposed prince. In Ashby we are all but conscious
of the creative personality in political life, the prince who can by intelligent policy shape his own fortunes, perhaps even be said to make law
rather than merely to guarantee the determination and protection of
what were generally held to be customary rights. The distance
separating him from those who wrote in the spirit of medieval thought
is narrow indeed compared to that which stretched between him and,
say, Machiavelli. But it is significant that he has apparently undertaken the journey.[18]

ဢ   ဢ   ဢ

Fortescue came nearer than Ashby to the outskirts of modern
thought, but he traveled a more circuitous route. Ashby's road seems

14. *Ibid.*, ll. 541-547, 548-552.
15. *Ibid.*, ll. 569-575.
16. *Ibid.*, ll. 674-680.
17. E.g., *ibid.*, ll. 618-624, 716-722.
18. Cf. Kleineke, p. 137.

to lead to the Cromwellian version of the Machiavellian prince; Fortescue's seems to be weaving its way among the familiar landmarks of medieval constitutionalism. The difference is, however, more apparent than real. What the modern mind finds familiar in both is a quality of realism, an awareness of the nature of political and social life not only as it is but also to some extent as it may be made to be. In Ashby this insight is brought to bear on the immediate problem of effective government; in Fortescue it encompasses the broader implications of that problem, the need for ideological definition, the relationship between government and society, the bearing of past events on the present. Although Ashby adumbrates many novel aspects of Tudor administration, Fortescue was concerned for the continuity of English political values in an age of profound social change. He was not fully conscious of the nature of that change, nor even able always to follow up the insights he was able to achieve by sheer intuition; yet it is those insights more than anything in his political theory, formally considered, that establish his affinity with Renaissance thought. It will therefore be our purpose in the following pages to place Fortescue in the broader context of the history of ideas rather than in the more specialized one of legal studies or political theory. The latter cannot, of course, be ignored, and, indeed, I hope that the following analysis may shed some light on Fortescue's theory of government. But it is rather to the attitudes that conditioned his ideas that I would direct the reader's attention than to the ideas themselves.[19]

Fortescue's mind labored in a curiously deceptive light shed on the one hand from the traditions of scholastic thought and on the other from the rapidly maturing realities of Renaissance life. It was a time when, for the best of practical reasons, men of insight were making new approaches to these realities while still working with the theoretical apparatus inherited from their ancestors. To concentrate on either is, therefore, to run the risk of misinterpretation.

Misinterpretation has, indeed, dogged Fortescue's steps ever since the constitutional struggle of seventeenth-century England led partisans of both king and Parliament to seek justification in his writings and to find respectively in the regal and political side of the balanced con-

19. The following treatment of Fortescue is taken with a few alterations from the author's paper, "Fortescue and the Renaissance: a Study in Transition," *Studies in the Renaissance*, VI (1959), 175-194.

stitution that he seemed to be describing precedent for a theory of sovereign power such as he himself would have found totally in-comprehensible. Subsequent students of English constitutional his-tory, raised in the tradition of parliamentary supremacy, have until relatively recently argued that Fortescue, in adapting medieval theory to a type of government for which Thomas Aquinas recognized no exact precedent, was developing a theory of parliamentary, con-stitutional monarchy to fit the unique character of English government. Having shaped Sir John in their own image, they thought very highly of him.[20]   More recent scholarship has cast upon him a more critical, and, in general, a more discerning eye.   C. H. McIlwain interpreted him in the light, not of modern constitutional thought, but of a thoroughly medieval notion of dominion in which sovereignty and the ideas related to it could have no place whatever.   It has even been argued that Fortescue, so far from being an original or profound the-orist or even an accurate observer of contemporaneous events, was thoroughly traditional in theory and often quite romantic in his assessment of fact.[21]

Yet, if Fortescue's stature has been diminished in the eyes of con-stitutional historians, he remains a very large toad in relation to the not so very large puddle that is fifteenth-century England.   If only

20. See, for example, C. Plummer's introduction to his edition of Fortescue's *The Governance of England* and Lord Clairmont's introduction to his edition of *The Works of Sir John Fortescue* (London, 1869). R. W. K. Hinton has just recently undertaken to defend Plummer's interpretation against Chrimes and McIlwain (see n. 21 below), "English Constitutional Theories from Sir John Fortescue to Sir John Eliot," *EHR*, LXXV (July, 1960), 410-425. The most recent investigation of Fortescue's debt to Aquinas is in Felix Gilbert's "Sir John Fortescue's *Dominium Regale et Politicum*," *Medi-evalia et Humanistica*, II (Jan., 1944), 88-97; but cf. Jacob, *The Fifteenth Century*, pp. 314-316.

21. C. H. McIlwain, *The Growth of Political Thought in the West* (New York, 1932), pp. 354-363. See also his *Constitutionalism, Ancient and Modern* (Ithaca, 1947). Most famous of the evaluations unfavorable to Fortescue as an interpreter of fact is A. F. Pollard's: "The constitutional ideal which Sir John Fortescue depicted at the close of the middle ages had little more relevance to the practice of his day than More's *Utopia* had to the government of Cardinal Wolsey." *The Evolution of Parliament* (London, 1934), p. 133. See also C. A. J. Skeel, "The Influence of the Writings of Sir John Fortescue," *TRHS*, 3rd Series, X (1916), 77-114; S. B. Chrimes, "Sir John Fortescue and his Theory of Dominion," *TRHS*, 4th Series, XVII (1934), 117-147, and his edition of Fortescue's *De Laudibus Legum Augliae* (Cambridge, 1942), p.c.; R. W. and A. L. Carlyle *A History of Medieval Political Theory in the West* (8 vols; Cambridge, 1936), VI, 175-179, 192-226.

for this reason, if only because he is unique as an interpreter of that era of radical and confusing transition, he continues to demand and to receive critical attention. One has, indeed, at times the feeling that he is in some odd way more than the sum of his parts. By no means trained in the subtleties of scholastic thought, not in fact a philosophi‑cal mind, perhaps not even very well educated beyond the labyrinthine intricacies of the Common Law, he seems to have sensed more clearly than any of his English contemporaries the need for defining English institutions and clarifying the values they embodied. By no means an accurate reporter of fact—his most famous writings were composed at a relatively advanced age and are colored by the romantic hindsight of the elderly and patriotic exile—he nonetheless achieved an intuitive grasp of social and political reality which, if it fell short of modern realism, fell only a little short. Less of a legal mind than his con‑temporary Littleton, or at any rate inferior in his contribution to the study of substantive law, he became a pioneer in the investigation of comparative law and was unique in his awareness of the close relation‑ship between law and the society it served.

Let us, then, examine Fortescue as a pamphleteer, a commentator, an articulate citizen, rather than exclusively as a theorist. Let us in‑quire what he believes to be wrong with English government and especially where he looks for the causes of the trouble. Let us see whether he looks for those causes in the constant factor of man's sin‑ful nature or in those factors that lie within reach of man's ingenuity. Let us see whether he considered government as the source of con‑structive policy or as a basically protective agency. Finally, let us notice the extent to which he was able to appreciate the implications of social change and how that appreciation helped determine his con‑ception of the role of government.

ᔆ ᔆ ᔆ

Any student of the period knows that Fortescue's reputation derives in large part from the fact that he interpreted the standard elements of medieval political theory in terms of the realities of contemporary life, or what he conceived them to be. It is not, however, so generally recognized that his reputation for realism depends less upon his grasp of those realities than upon his appreciation of the ideological conflict they implied. What was Fortescue's purpose in writing? It seems reasonably certain that practical considerations directed Fortescue's pen to a very large, indeed to an ever increasing extent. Even his first major work, the *De Natura Legis Naturae*, highly theoretical and abstract as it seems, he began in answer to the specific need of the Lancastrian cause for propagandist support.[22] The *De Laudibus Legum Angliae* he began ostensibly as a means of grounding his pupil, the young Prince Edward, in the law of England. And in the last of his major works, *The Governance of England*, he undertook the strictly practical task of outlining a program of much needed administrative reform.[23] Yet it would be wrong to stop at the circumstances that elicited and perhaps conditioned each work. There runs through all three writings, especially the last two, a consistency of thought that cannot be explained merely by immediate circumstance, nor can it be laid to a more or less academic interest in law and government for which England provided simply a particularly interesting case study. It suggests, rather, that Fortescue was thinking in response to more far-reaching developments in the life of his day.

England in Fortescue's day was passing through an era of administrative confusion. At its best, as Professor Joliffe has pointed out,[24] Lancastrian government had advanced in practice without the formation of adequate constitutional theory to direct and maintain it. Now, in the third quarter of the century, in circumstances of civil war and a concomitant deterioration within the organs of government, it was possible for the principles underlying the English tradition to become so weakened that the virtues they embodied might also be lost. Demands for efficiency could lead to a government that recognized no other criterion than its own ability to govern. While in exile after the defeat of the Lancastrian party, Fortescue had become very much aware of what had happened in France in circumstances not too different from those that had affected England. He saw that King Louis had

22. *De Natura Legis Naturae*, in *Life and Works of Sir John Fortescue*, ed. Lord Clermont (London, 1869). Felix Gilbert has called attention to the impact of practical considerations on this seemingly so theoretical work in "Sir John Fortescue's *Dominium Regale et Politicum*." In this same article he stresses also the progressive impact of events on Fortescue's thought, especially the events of his exile.

23. *Governance of England*, reprinted in W. H. Dunham and S. Pargellis, *Complaint and Reform in England* (New York, 1938), pp. 51-82. Unless otherwise specified, references will be made to this convenient version, done in modern spelling.

24. Joliffe, p. 430.

strengthened his control over his realm, but only at the expense of the traditional limitations inherent in customary representative institutions and in feudal law. The French king, he tells us, had not always ruled despotically and taxed his subjects at will. He had been induced to do so under stress of the late war with England.[25] Despite a robust faith in the stability as well as in the excellence of the English tradition of mixed or limited government, the *dominium politicum et regale*, Fortescue seems to have felt that similar forces were impelling the English king to follow the lead of his neighbor across the water. He recognized the necessity for any monarch to act arbitrarily in cases of emergency;[26] and he repeatedly states that the civil law (which, by the way, he virtually identifies with the rival system of government, the *dominium regale*) had, through its maxim *quod principi placuit legis habet vigorem*, already made a strong appeal to certain English kings and to certain of their advisers.[27] It could, in short, happen in England.

Now it would not, I am sure, be too fantastic to see in this, the basic problem of fifteenth-century government, the source of Fortescue's preoccupation with constitutional principle. Despite the academic paraphernalia he borrowed, probably at secondhand, from the non-national culture of the medieval schools, it was English government he was concerned with, and the task he had ever before him was that of clarifying the principles that underlay the limited monarchy he believed England to be.[28] Clearly also his concern was with the limited monarchy in operation. Its test, like that of its rival, is its fruits, and its fruits are found, with more patriotic enthusiasm than objectivity, to be not only good in themselves but good in comparison to those of the despotic monarchy of France. The English people live well, make good soldiers, and can be ruled safely only with their consent: the French live poorly, and have neither the strength to fight nor

25. *Governance*, chap. iii.

26. *De Natura*, chap. xxv.

27. *De Laudibus*, chap. xxxv (p. 84, ll. 34-35); chap. xxxvi (p. 88, ll. 11-13); chaps. xxxiii and xxxiv.

28. *De Laudibus*, chaps. xxv and xxxvi *Governance*, chap. iii. On Fortescue' *Essays in History and Political Theory in honor of Charles Howard McIlwain* (Cambridge, Mass., 1936), pp. 295-296, Max A. Shepard called attention to Fortescue's background of the moderately well-to-do country gentry as an explanation of his interest in the Lancastrian tradition. I am not at all sure that either factional affiliations or social background were likely to affect the general approach of a fifteenth-century Englishman to the principles of government.

the will to rebel. Essentially Fortescue is comparing a government, the virtue of which lies in its administrative efficiency, with one in which the rights of the subject, and hence his welfare, are protected by law.[29] From this comparative and highly pragmatic view of the two rival systems—the one based on and for practical purposes identical with the law of Rome, the other equally closely related to the English Common Law[30]—there follow logically such reform measures as Fortescue has to offer. *The Governance of England* embodies a specific plan for the reform of the royal administration which is intended to

29. *De Laudibus*, chaps. xxxv and xxxvi; *Governance*, chap. iii. On Fortescue's accuracy, see Chrimes (ed.), *De Laudibus*, pp. 181-183 (re chap. xxv); cf. R. W. and A. J. Carlyle, *A History of Medieval Political Theory in the West*, VI, 175-179, 192-226; C. Petit-Dutaillis in E. Lavisse, *Histoire de France* (Paris, 1911), IV, Pt. 2, 207ff., 251-252, 299-400; P. S. Lewis, "The Failure of the French Medieval Estates," *Past and Present*, No. 23 (Nov., 1962), 3-24. See also J. Russell Major, *Representative Institutions in Renaissance France 1421-1559* (Madison, 1960), chaps. i-iii.

30. The general outlines of Fortescue's ideas may be found in *De Natura*, Pt. I, chaps. xvi, xxii-xxvi; *De Laudibus*, chaps. ix, xiii, xiv, xviii, xix, xxxv-xxxvi; *Governance*, chaps. i-iii. Fortescue's tendency to identify law and constitution is fundamental in his thought. The mixed government of England had its foundation in the Common Law, which in turn was the particular expression for English needs of the higher law of nature. Hence he was able to write the *De Laudibus Legum Angliae* primarily in an effort to justify what we should call the English constitution. In his zeal for the "mixed" monarchy, Fortescue all but identified despotism with tyranny. Having enshrined the rights of private property in the absolute law of nature rather than in the mutable *ius gentium* as the practice had been among medieval theorists (Shepard, pp. 300-301), and having set up respect for property as a fundamental criterion of good government, he made it very difficult for a despotic monarch to reap any benefit from a power unlimited by positive law without being guilty of tyranny; because, if he took property without the consent and advice of the subjects, it implied that he could not get it with their consent, that he was therefore acting in violation of the law of nature, ruling for his own convenience, in short, becoming a tyrant (*De Natura*, Pt. I, chap. xxviii). But Fortescue treated the civil law with great deference and followed biblical and philosophical authority in declaring that a despotism is good when at its best (*De Laudibus*, chap. xxv; cf. *ibid.*, chap. xxxv, *De Natura*, Pt. I, chaps. xi, xii, xvi-xviii), and moreover, he was careful to point out that in practice a despotic regime does not necessarily become tyrannical (*De Laudibus*, chap. ix; *Governance*, chap. iii). He merely tended to take it for granted that all good government must be, in its effects, like that of England (when the latter was functioning properly) no matter what its legal powers might be. What he distrusted was not the rule of a benevolent despot, but the entire lack of any limitation other than the *digna vox* within the breast of the king to prevent him from degenerating into a tyrant. "Therefore [he said] clap your hands, ye subjects of a king ruling royally, under a good sovereign, when such a one there is, because ye must needs mourn when an insolent or grasping king rules over you. And you, ye subjects of a king presiding royally and politickly over his kingdom, console yourselves in this respect, that, if your king be equally arrogant, he hath not a loose rein for it, like the other." (*De Natura*, Pt. I, chap. xv, p. 87).

strengthen the position of the king and his council.[31] Curious as this proposal may seem from one who is supposedly interested in protecting the rights of the subject from a too strong monarchy, it was meant to remedy that very lack of governance of which he and several of his comtemporaries most bitterly complained,[32] and which he conceived to be the worst threat to the English way of life.

Fortescue saw a threat to the English tradition on the one hand in an administration pressed beyond caring for the legal rights and welfare of its subjects by the necessity of maintaining itself, and on the other hand in ignorance of the principles upon which the limited monarchy rested. Unlike his contemporary, Ashby, he could not be content merely to contemplate the techniques by which strong government might be achieved. He seems, in fact, to have been keenly aware of this tendency to seek good government in techniques rather than in properly implemented principles and to have found it dangerous.

If we examine his writings in the light of this implied ideological conflict, a conflict which, by the way, Fortescue seems to have been alone among Englishmen in sensing, several things about him become clearer. We can the more readily appreciate why he turned the first book of his treatise on the law of nature, undertaken initially as propaganda for the Lancastrian succession, into a vindication of the English tradition of government; why, when he undertook to write a book of instruction for young Prince Edward, he abandoned the inveterate habit of medieval tutors and, instead of writing generally *de regimine principum*,[33] he wrote in commendation of the laws of England, and did so, moreover, at a time when to commend anything in England was rare, but to praise the judicial system was certainly unique; why, also, in *The Governance of England* he set himself to analyze the causes of that lack of governance which seemed to point to a system of government better adapted than the English for coping with disorder, and to suggest specific alternatives. This preoccupation of his also helps explain why Fortescue, though a professional lawyer, onetime Chief Justice, set forth the results of his investigations and thinking in his last two works in semipopular form rather than in formal treatises, stiff with

31. *Governance*, chaps. x, xi, xv, xvii, xviii.
32. *Ibid.*, chaps. ivix. See also Chrimes, *Introduction to the Administrative History of Medieval England*, pp. 243246.
33. See above, ch. iii.

scholarly apparatus.[34]   Like another contemporary, Reginald Pecock,[35] he was interested in placing the conclusions of his professional thought before the educated public.   Similarly, if our hypothesis is correct, it becomes clearer why he, alone of fifteenth-century English-men, brought the political philosophy of Western Christendom into contact with what he believed to be actual English conditions, and recognized both the essential sturdiness of English institutions and the need for defining their principles.

Fortescue may thus be said to have been conservative in his purpose. He hoped, by clarifying the principles upon which English govern-ment had, he thought, from time immemorial rested, and by present-ing a program of specific reforms which would remove from English kings the temptation to rule despotically, to shore up a venerable edifice.   By virtue of his precedent-regarding lawyer's training, per-haps also by temperament, he tended to look to the past; nor was his mind to any appreciable extent diverted by that newer antiquarianism already filtering into English scholarly circles from Renaissance Italy.

But if conservatism gave substance to his thought, realism dictated its form.   In his attitude toward the issues he recognized as most urgent in English public life, he demonstrated an ability to translate even the most abstract principles into concrete terms and to keep his mind, even when exploring theory, at the level of observable conditions.   If his observations became at times distorted by the romanticism of the aging and exiled patriot, if they do not always tally with what historians have discovered to be the fact, they constituted nonetheless the groundwork for his thought.   Fortescue's realism has little enough to do with factual accuracy.   It is part rather of his grasp of the underlying tendencies which remain discernible despite the existence of contrary instances.   His picture of French and English societies may have as little resemblance to the facts as Hogarth's graphic comments two and a half centuries later.   But, like Hogarth, Fortescue had seized upon

34. Some modern scholars have hesitated to credit Fortescue with a truly scholarly or profound treatment of his subject.   Skeel, pp. 79-80; McIlwain, *The Growth of Political Thought in the West*, p. 354.   Chrimes allows that Fortescue's comparisons of English and Roman law "may not be very profound," but emphasizes the fact that mark the beginning of a less insular outlook on the part of the common lawyer and foreshadow the comparative study of law. *De Laudibus*, Preface, p. c.

35. Pecock, *Reule of Crysten Religioun*, ed. W. C. Greet, E.E.T.S., O.S., No. 171 (1926), pp. 17-19; *The Repressor of Over Much Blaming of the Clergy*, ed. C. Babington, Rolls Series (1860), I, 46-47.

certain essential differences which went a long way toward justifying such exaggeration as he was guilty of. If he had little else in common with the social scientist of modern times, he had a preoccupation with the problems of actual life and a willingness to let observation take precedence over authority. Especially in the baldly practical chapters of the *Governance*, the philosophers and even the Scriptures recede into the background. Of the standard sources of authority, history alone, the record of accumulated experience, occupies a really prominent position, reinforcing the findings of more immediate experience.[36]

∽ ∽ ∽

Both the extent and the limitations of Fortescue's realism will become more apparent if we inquire where he looked for the cause of the evils he hoped to remedy, for the factors which must be removed if a remedy is to be more than a palliative. Perhaps the freshest, the most "modern" characteristic of his thought is his ability to take for granted the conditions of the Divine Drama, to accept the limits set upon human choice by Providence and by the sinful propensities of man, and to seek more immediate causes which might be comprehended by men of intelligence and used by them as the basis of public policy.

Now Fortescue, though dealing with the problem of government where impersonal forces were less apparent than in the economic affairs explored by the author of the *Libel of English Policy*, was nevertheless quite able to concentrate his analytical attention upon institutional, historical, even what would now be called sociological considerations—not that he was amoral after the manner of Machiavelli or so cynical in his treatment of human motives as his contemporary Commines—with whom, incidentally, he had much else in common.[37] His was a kindly, optimistic nature, through which ran a strong current of piety and orthodox belief. He accepted the Christian cosmology, the authority of the Scriptures, the primacy of the pope, and the moral underpinning of all society.[38] Government, in particular, was to him primarily ethical in purpose, the necessary means

36. E.g., *Governance*, chap. ix.
37. On this subject, see the article by Bouwsma, pp. 315328.
38. G. L. Mosse, "Sir John Fortescue and the Problem of Papal Power," *Medievalia et Humanistica*, VII (1952), 8994; E. F. Jacob, *Essays in the Conciliar Epoch* (Manchester, 1943), ch. vi, especially p. 119; H. D. Hazeltine, introduction to Chrimes (ed.), *De Laudibus*, p. iii. Cf. Kleineke, pp. 174179.

to the attainment of the good life which he defined in terms of happiness, attained through virtue and justice.[39]   He recognized the importance of personal factors in a government of men by men.   But he
chose to limit the personal element by so reforming institutions as to
leave the individual the least possible room, and, more important, the
minimum of incentive, for selfish or vicious action.   He knew that a
prince would do anything he felt he had to in order to maintain his
power.   So, just as Clement Armstrong in a later generation sought
to increase Tudor husbandry by making sheepraising unprofitable
through policies regulating the Staple,[40] so Fortescue sought, by increasing the endowment of the crown, to make it unnecessary and less
attractive for the king to seek "exquisite means of getting of good . . .
to the perversion of justice and perturbation of the peace and
quiet of the realm."[41]   He knew that, in circumstances of disorder
then prevalent, the king's councilors were likely to be selfish, so he
recommended a balancing of interests within a reformed council in
such a way as to check the special interests of any one person or clique.[42]
Even more interesting is the fact that, in his awareness of impersonal
causes and his preference for institutional remedies, he avoided not only
the helplessness of the Christian moralist, painfully aware that only
spiritual regeneration could affect lasting reform, but also that glorification of the princely personality which marks the work of Machiavelli,
and to a much lesser extent Fortescue's compatriot, George Ashby.

Worth noticing also is the fact that Fortescue, while accepting the
medieval commonplace that good government depends on good counsel, embodied that commonplace in a specific recommendation for reform of the actual group of councilors surrounding the king.   Good
counsel might well be, as the author of *Mum and the Sothsegger* saw it at
the opening of the century, a function of the fundamental conflict of
truth with falsehood within the human soul.[43]   But to Fortescue the

39. *De Laudibus*, chap. iv; *De Natura*, Pt. I, chap. xlvi, p. 113.

40. *A treatise concerninge the Staple*, in R. H. Tawney and Eileen Power (eds.), *Tudor
Economic Documents* (London, 1924), III, 90114.

41. *Governance*, chap. v; see also chaps. viiixiv.

42. *Ibid.*, chaps. v, ix, and xv.

43. See above chap. iii. See also *Governance*, chap. xvi, and the related fragment
entitled *Example what good counsayle helpith and advantageth and of the contrary what folowith*,
printed by Plummer in *Governance*, Appendix A. A "new technique of counsel" was
an increasingly recognized issue in late medieval government; Chrimes, *Introduction to
Administrative History of Medieval England*, p. 246.

practical question is how to arrange things so as to curb, as far as possible, the vicious propensities of men by intelligently constructed institutions.

His willingness to think in terms of impersonal forces made it possible for Fortescue to anticipate other typically modern points of view. As S. B. Chrimes has pointed out, Fortescue was "the first Englishman, so far as we know," to perceive "that the causes of national differences in legal and constitutional institutions must be sought in underlying differences of economic and social conditions, and in so doing he anticipated the outlook of Bodin and Montesquieu."[44] Eng-lish institutions, he argued, owed certain of their distinctive charac-teristics and virtues in part at least to the prosperity of the country and the existence of a large group of middling people prosperous enough and with sufficient leisure and freedom of mind to take part in com-munity affairs. This was why the jury system, which Fortescue felt to be an essential element in the English legal structure, could work in England and could not in France, where, he says, there is scarcely a single village where one man can be found with enough means to serve on a jury. He even sees an important causal factor in the pre-dominance of pasture in England, for, he argues, sheep farming as practiced in England within well-enclosed fields and subject to a minimum of depredation from wild animals leaves much more time of leisure than the constant tilling of the soil practiced in other lands. Hence Englishmen "are more apt and disposed to investigate causes which require searching examination than men who, immersed in agricultural work, have contracted a rusticity of mind from familiarity with the soil."[45]

In like manner Fortescue traces the strength of English arms to the prosperity of the English yeoman farmer and insists on the close relation-ship between poverty and rebellion: "For nothing may make [a king's] people to arise but lack of goods or lack of justice. But yet certainly when they lack goods they will arise, saying that they lack justice."[46] In other words, the English system of law and government was suited to the people of England just as that of France was what the people of France deserved.

44. *De Laudibus*, introduction, p. cii.
45. *Ibid.*, chap. xxix.
46. *Governance*, chap. xii.

Yet Fortescue also sees it the other way. He recognizes that a sys-tem of law and government will affect the social and economic conditions within the realm. The prosperity of England is simply one "fruit" by which may be known the *jus politicum et regale*, just as the poverty of Frenchmen stems from the *jus regale* under which they have come to live. These two forms of government are in turn conditioned by their respective historical backgrounds—the one resulting from an agreement between governor and governed, the other from the exercise of force by the king.

Fortescue has, indeed, a noteworthy, if rudimentary, sense of history. If the past he examines is only too often beclouded in mythology (he accepts, with no more questions than any other Eng-lishman of his day, the legend of Brutus, the first king of England), it is still important that he, like Ashby, felt it possible and useful to examine the past as recorded not only in the classical authors and the Scriptures but in the chronicles of England and France, above all, the chronicles of recent events.[47] It is in those events that Fortescue sees the more immediate cause of the difference between the French and English forms of government. In a sense his comparative study of law rests upon the assumption of historical contingency. Perhaps, had he been able to draw inspiration from humanist scholarship as well as from experience and from medieval theory, he might well have inaugurated a tradition of historical interpretation in the study of law which came late in England, long after the lawyers of sixteenth-century France had already brought history to the aid of law and made it pos-sible for legal studies to illuminate history.[48]

Particularly interesting is Fortescue's awareness, however dim it may be, of social development. Social history commanded much less attention in the fifteenth century than political. Yet Fortescue, as

47. E.g., *ibid.*, chap. iii. See also chap. ix. His reference to the Brutus legend is in chap. ii. It is worth noticing that Fortescue's historical approach to the government of his day anticipates that of Sir Thomas Smith in *De Republica Anglorum*, ed. L. Alston (Cambridge, 1906), Book I, chap. xv. Ashby demonstrates in the first part of his *Active Policy* a practical appreciation of the uses of history. He tells young Prince Edward of the general lessons to be learned from the chronicles (ll. 148-168). Then there is the more immediate experiences of the civil wars. Ashby does not, however, attempt to analyze them historically except to ascribe them to covetousness (ll. 169-203). Finally, the prince should think of his own reputation, as future chronicles will pass judgment on it (ll. 232-238).

48. J. G. A. Pocock, *The Ancient Constitution and the Feudal Law* (Cambridge, 1957).

we have seen, manages to find in social and economic considerations conditioning factors of real significance. He assumes that there took place in the far distant past a gradual maturing of society. The mystical body of the state developed like an embryo into the body natural. Men originally were under kings who ruled arbitrarily, but as they became more civilized they were able to insist on a government in which laws could be passed and taxation imposed only by their consent.[49] Fanciful as it was, this notion of social evolution was at least as discerning as the myth of the state of nature, so dear to the hearts of later theorists. Considering more recent times, Fortescue traced, as we have seen, many of the peculiar virtues of English law to the peculiarities of the English economy. And at one point he offers a most ingenious explanation for the continuing use of French and Latin in a largely English-speaking England.[50]

ᔕ ᔕ ᔕ

It would, however, be easy to exaggerate the historicism of Fortescue's thought as well as his awareness of social cause. Indeed, it is the rudimentariness of his historical sense that impresses itself upon us almost as much as the fact that he possessed it. Like most English lawyers for generations after his day, he assumed that the custom upon which the Common Law rested was of immemorial antiquity.[51] And in his explanation of the divergence between English and French government he falls back only too readily on such questionable factors as the inherent sturdiness of the English temper as contrasted with the cowardice of the French.[52]

It is hard, indeed, to avoid the impression that Fortescue retained an essentially static view of society. He accepted the possibility of change, but only up to a point. Sooner rather than later he is pulled up short by a sense of the unalterable nature of things, a feeling considerably more deep-seated than his sense of historical development. When he undertakes to describe the origin of a state, he reverts with the sureness of instinct to the popular analogy of the natural body, with all that it implied of ordained organic structure. The analogy provided

49. *Governance*, chap. ii; *De Laudibus*, chap. xiii.
50. *De Laudibus*, chap. xlviii.
51. *Ibid.*, chap. xviii. Chrimes notices this in his introduction, p. xlvi. See also, on general subject the immemorial antiquity of the law, Pecock, *passim*.
52. *Governance*, chaps. xii-xiii.

for change, it is true, but it is change determined by the nature of the organism, the growth of the body politic from infancy to maturity.[53]

Perhaps, also, it is his inability to conceive of society as a moving thing that prevented him from assigning to government a function broader in scope or more primitive in character than that which a Langland or a Gower had envisaged almost a century earlier.[54] Even in this respect Fortescue impresses us above all by the apparent realism of his observations. Unlike the "moral" Gower who was constantly op′ pressed by the vastness of the reformer's task in a society where sin itself is the enemy, Sir John could see the possibility of reform through governmental policy. Indeed, his awareness of the need for regulation of foreign trade—he specified, for example, that his reformed council would be responsible for just such bullionist measures as Edward IV and Henry VII were actually adopting—seems to place him just next to the author of the *Libel of English Policy* as a prophet of mercantilism.[55] But it is equally clear that his practical proposals were meant to restore to proper working order a government still essentially protective in function rather than to establish it as an agency from which constructive policy might emanate. "Good and politic governance" meant, to him as to most fifteenth′century Englishmen, the maintenance of justice and the preservation of peace. A king's office, he tells us in the *Governance*, amplifying a statement made years earlier in the *De Natura*, "stands in two things, one to defend his realm against their enemies without by the sword; another that he defend his people against wrong doers within by justice"—and cites the first book of Kings as his authority.[56] And we should do well to interpret this statement literally. Much mis′ interpretation of medieval English political thought has crept into history books by way of the modern historian's unwillingness to believe that such utterances, the constant refrain of political expression from fugitive verses on the times to speeches recorded in the *Rotuli Parlia*′

53. *De Laudibus*, chap. xiii. As Jacob reminds us, Fortescue is here echoing John of Salisbury; *The Fifteenth Century*, pp. 315′316. See fuller discussion in Chrimes, "Sir John Fortescue and his Theory of Dominion," pp. 119, 134′136. See n. 49 above.

54. See above chap. ii. Hinton, though committed to the idea that Fortescue was talking about a truly parliamentary monarchy, finds it necessary to point out (p. 417) that he "of course did not believe in progress, and therefore did not conceive that the function of parliament was to be continually inventing better laws. He thought that laws were made to remedy abuses rather than to initiate improvements."

55. *Governance*, chap. xv. See above chap. iv.

56. *Governance*, chap. iv. Cf. *De Natura*, Pt. II, chap. viii.

mentorum, were more than rhetorical commonplaces.[57] Although the king is very much the source of government, Fortescue did not see in him or in his counselors the source of that ingenious statecraft which Machiavelli and his humanist forerunners recognized in Italian politics.[58] It is society, as ordained by God, that Fortescue is concerned with, not statecraft; it is welfare, the proper working of the political body, that he seeks as the true end of government, not power.[59]

Close as he came to the threshold of modern thought, Fortescue was never quite able to appreciate the dynamic implications of Renaissance society, even as a few choice minds of early Tudor England were able, however imperfectly, to do. He seems not to have recognized that government, in a rapidly changing society and in a world of competing powers, must have the ability to set up something positive where nothing before existed. Indeed it is his devotion to the ideal of a society in which stability is the desired norm and of a government whose function is simply that of maintaining justice and peace, that made it difficult for those who came after him to understand fully the constitutional theory he helped to clarify for his own contemporaries. It was especially difficult for those who came to think of government in terms of sovereign power. It is still not easy, for example, to understand why Fortescue sought to protect the rights of subjects in a limited monarchy by strengthening the executive. Nor is it clear what, if any, positive check he would place on the actions of a king.[60] No doubt

57. Examples may be found in many earlier and contemporaneous texts; see, for excellent examples, *Rotuli Parliamentorum,* III, 336, and V, 622. For discussion of this concept of kingly duty, see Chrimes, *Constitutional Ideas,* pp. 14-17, 197; and Wilks, pp. 114-115.

58. F. Gilbert, "The Humanist Concept of the Prince and the *Prince* of Machiavelli," *JMH,* XI (Dec., 1939), 449-483.

59. G. L. Mosse notices that Fortescue spoke of the "good publique," but failed to rationalize it into an idea of "reason of state"; *The Struggle for Sovereignty in England* (East Lansing, 1950), p. 50.

60. Fortescue undoubtedly sensed the need for some more adequate guarantees for English freedom than the intangible forces of custom, of a law devoid of coercive sanctions, or of the royal conscience, the latter too likely to fall discreetly silent before the ultimata of brute facts. (Cf. Chrimes, *Constitutional Ideas,* p. 322.) How he conceived the problem, and what he proposed to do by way of solving it are much more difficult questions to answer. He never confronted the problem as men of a later day did because, unlike them, he could not see it as one involving positive, institutional controls within a monarchy that was constitutional in a distinctly modern sense (McIlwain, *The Growth of Political Thought in the West,* pp. 358). In the *De Natura* he admitted that divine vengeance alone could be counted on to punish a king who ruled tyrannically (Pt. I,

he considered the reformed council an effective guardian of English liberties rather than as a tool of the crown, for it was supposed to pro-vide the king with that sage and politic counsel from which alone good governance could flow.[61]   It was to be the servant of the king, but strictly in his capacity as servant of the people.   In fact, however, it was not a strong administration that he feared—that could to his way of thinking lead only to better government—but a despotic one, that is, one that recognized no limitation of human law.   Conversely, it was a limited monarchy he valued, limited, that is, by law, not a controlled one.   His ideally balanced *dominium politicum et regale* encompassed all he felt to be necessary to the government of man: its "political" side gave legal protection to the rights of the subject; its "regal" side provid-ed the king with all he required to carry out his duty of providing the active means of protection both from external aggressors and from domestic transgressors.

He seems to have had no clear idea of the creation of new law, in the sense of establishing principles that had no precedent, or of imple-menting policies calculated to shape as well as to reform society.[62] Hence he has much less to say about Parliament than we of a later age, accustomed still to consider the development of parliamentary govern-ment a *leitmotif* of English history, are likely to expect.   He grants Parliament unique legislative authority, as far as that concept had meaning for him, and the principle of assent, as expressed by the estates of the realm in Parliament, is fundamental to his thought.[63]   Yet the legislation he has in mind is apparently confined either to the granting of subsidies and therefore related to his idea that property rights are vested in the law of nature and cannot legitimately be overridden without consent expressed in Parliament, or else measures of a remedial sort, still closely related to the judicial activity of the "high court."   In

chap. xxvii).   The only practical alternative, as he implies in the *Governance*, is rebellion (chaps. x and xii; cf. chap. xiii), but that is a desperate remedy, good enough for French-men who have not a good law to rely on, but likely to cause almost as much trouble to respectable Englishmen as tyranny itself.

61. *De Natura*, Pt. I, chap. xxiii; *Governance*, chap. viii.   On the early sixteenth-century theory, in which the council was considered as much a check against tyranny as a tool of irresponsible government, see F. L. Baumer, *The Early Tudor Theory of Kingship* (New Haven, 1939), pp. 180 ff.   Cf. Chrimes, *Constitutional Ideas*, p. 322, in which a contrary view of Fortescue's conception of the function of the council is expressed.

62. Chrimes, *Constitutional Ideas*, p. 203.   Cf. Hinton.

63. *Governance*, chaps. xv and xix; *De Laudibus*, chaps. xviii and xxvi.

either case, legislation was declaratory of the law of nature, not supple-mentary to it.[64]   Parliament may well have appeared to Fortescue, as to the author of *Mum and the Sothsegger* at the beginning of the Lan-castrian era, to have derived its importance less from its legislative or judicial functions than from its part in providing the information and advice, the counsel of the many, without which the king could not be said to rule "politically" at all.[65]   And that function, it should be not-ed, could be performed more effectively by that permanent, that "con-tinual" body of picked men who would make up Fortescue's reformed council.   Almost a century later, Sir Thomas Smith was to add to Fortescue's picture of the English constitution the single feature of a truly legislative Parliament.   The resulting difference measures, in one way at least, the distance between medieval and Renaissance attitudes toward government.[66]

Fortescue could hardly have foreseen a conflict, such as that which later took place, between the king and his council on the one hand and Parliament and the courts on the other.   Conflict would occur only when and if the king overstepped his legal limitations and tres-passed upon the properties of his people, and that, in circumstances Fortescue considered normal, there was little reason for him to do. Only with the utmost use of the historical imagination can those who have been raised in the era of sovereign power appreciate with what complacency, and withal how logically, given the assumption of a static social order, the fifteenth-century Englishman could expect good government to flow from an administration purged of faction, wealthy enough to live of its own, and thus made capable of preserving peace and maintaining justice.   The utopian enthusiasm that illuminates the penultimate chapter of the *Governance* is a tribute less to Fortescue's buoyant faith in the virtues of English government than to his extremely limited view of the scope and nature of all government.

His grasp of political reality had, in fact, outrun the conceptual equipment he had inherited.   This, I think, goes a long way toward explaining the oddly ambivalent character of his thought, the quality that has made it possible for later generations to read into his analysis

64. Chrimes, *Constitutional Ideas*, pp. 201-202.
65. *De Natura*, Pt. I, chap. xxiii.
66. *De Republica Anglorum*, Book II, chap. i.   See also G. L. Mosse, "Change and Continuity in the Tudor Constitution," *Speculum*, XXII (Jan., 1947), 18-28.

widely divergent meanings. Unusual among his English contemporaries in his understanding of the conditions affecting human
action, possessed of a simple but lively sense of history, he could not
quite surmount the restricting assumption of a static social order.
Hence he saw no need to control the king and undertook merely to
re-emphasize his legal limitations. Nor, despite a quite specific recognition of the role of policy in directing the economic and military
affairs of the kingdom, does he seem to have envisaged in government
an agency responsible for more than the traditional maintenance of
justice and order, or possessed of the creative attributes of sovereignty
in the modern sense of the term. Yet Fortescue's limitations, no less
than his insights, enhance his usefulness to anyone who would chart
the transition from medieval to modern England; nor should they
obscure the fact that he came to the very threshold of modern thought.

PART TWO. THE EARLY RENAISSANCE

CHAPTER VI. THE ARTICULATE CITIZEN AND THE NEW AGE

AMONG THE MANY CHANGES THAT MAKE THE EARLY Tudor period one of crucial significance in English history, the rapid growth of public discussion should occupy a prominent place. That it has not always been given such prominence is largely because discussion has ordinarily—and understandably—been treated in connection with the subjects discussed rather than as a phenomenon in itself. Yet, apart from the substantive issues, the pamphlet literature of that period reflects a new sense of citizenship and new attitudes toward society and government, in particular a new willingness on the part of the educated, experienced, and potentially articulate citizen to explore the problems of public concern analytically as well as critically, and even to volunteer positive suggestions for constructive policy. True, much of what is new is often obscured by older habits of thought and expression. But it we examine the work of the more penetrating minds we shall, I think, see taking recognizable shape many of the attitudes which, often more clearly than formally expressed concepts, distinguish the new era from the old. These are the developments to which the succeeding chapters will be devoted.

In the present chapter I intend first of all to sketch, in the briefest form possible, the conditions of the Tudor age that encouraged the citizen to take part in the discussion of policy, and then to examine in greater detail evidences of a new awareness of the possibilities and responsibilities—and also the limitations—of articulate citizenship.

This part of our investigation involves the period of the earlier Tudors, but it does not begin promptly with the accession of Henry VII. The year 1485 has little more than dynastic significance in this connection—or in any other for that matter. The Tudor monarchy came nevertheless to preside over one of the most critical periods in the history of English culture as well as in the history of English political life, and in the changes that made the period so important it served both as catalyst and active agent. So it is still largely in terms of the new monarchy that we must analyze the factors making for increased public discussion. Not, however, until the middle of the reign of the second Tudor do those factors actually culminate in the kind of revolutionary situation most likely to stimulate discussion.

Most of them had been at work in English life for a long time: economic individualism and the agrarian unrest, the increasing social mobility and the freedom of contract that went with it, a national consciousness, only recently sobered if not deepened by the fiasco of the French wars and the ensuing confusion of civil conflict, anti-clerical sentiment, a constant theme of late medieval criticism, now newly stimulated by the failure of the church to satisfy the spiritual needs of an increasingly restless public, a native tradition of heretical thought, not in itself very vigorous, but ready to combine effectively with the more durable variety filtering in from Germany, and, finally a new learning, slow to take root in the not altogether congenial soil of England, but destined to bear fruit essential for the nourishment of a new intellectual generation. Less a dynamic force in itself than a condition prerequisite to the revolutionary events and movements to come, there was also the steadily growing reading public, laymen of diverse social origins, the product of the increasing number of grammar schools, by the end of the fifteenth century already accustomed to look to the printing press for their reading matter.

Together these currents had already seriously eroded the foundations of feudal society and weakened the structure of values inherent in the Christian tradition as it had been interpreted by the schoolmen and in the more or less Christianized and nationalized ideals of chivalry, still, if only *faute de mieux*, the secular guide for the life of the governing class. Together they would eventually have changed England beyond recognition, for they represented powerful forces by no means peculiar to England. As it happened, however, the monarchy, for reasons of its own, did much to create the circumstances within which these forces were actually to operate. The Royal Supremacy, the dissolution of the monasteries and the subsequent dispersal of the abbey lands, the administration of Thomas Cromwell on lines of national sovereignty, secular control, and bureaucratic paternalism, and his use of the new learning in the interests of royal policies, all conspired to make the fourth decade of the century one of revolutionary significance not only in government but, indirectly, in the life and thought of Englishmen.

That decade will, then, serve well enough for the purposes of this study as the beginning of a new age. Yet the history of thought is not so easily pinned down by the more readily dateable data of conventional history. We shall have to leave room for many apparent anomalies in chronology. Thomas More, for example, anticipated some of the most penetrating social analysis of the revolutionary thirties by almost a generation. And at the mid-century mark Robert Crowley was still able to survey English society in terms the "moral" Gower would have found thoroughly familiar. For the time being, however, our concern is primarily with the fact of increased discussion and with the related conditions conducive to the emergence of a new sense of citizen-ship.

When Henry VIII undertook to become his own master as well in matters ecclesiastical as in things secular, he raised issues which made the resulting Reformation the first event of national importance in England to be debated before the bar of public opinion through the medium of the printing press. By that time he could count on a public ready as never before to have an opinion and to make it felt in the affairs of state. Those who constituted this "public" were, to be sure, still a minority—how large or small we shall doubtless never know for sure—and concentrated geographically in that part of the kingdom most accessible to the influence of the "great city." But the growth of lay literacy, of the book trade, and of Parliament itself had already made it possible to reach the mind of the provinces to a greater extent than ever before.

Within the embryonic public, moreover, the small but self-conscious and increasingly influential group of humanist scholars and publicists formed an exceedingly fertile nucleus. The new studies, reflecting not only the civic humanism of the Italian Quattrocento but also the utilitarian and reforming tendencies of northern humanism, made it possible for discussion of public issues to be carried on within a context of examples and values which, though derived from a fresh, more or less historical interpretation of classical antiquity, nevertheless proved much more suitable to the life of sixteenth-century Englishmen than the values and models inherited from medieval culture. These studies provided fresh matter for a comparative study of society and government and hence a fresh incentive to explore life in contemporary England. Of even greater importance at the time was the fact that the humanists, by virtue of their mastery of the still new and highly fashionable arts of persuasion, commended themselves to a govern/ ment more concerned than ever before to influence opinion.

Although we are not here primarily concerned with propaganda as such, nor as such with the nebulous problem of public opinion, it is important to recognize how the crises of the thirties and forties stimulated discussion of all sorts. Henry VIII and Thomas Crom/ well nowhere demonstrated to better advantage their political genius than when they recognized that the success of their unprecedented policies depended upon leadership and persuasion rather than upon fiat. Lacking a military force of his own, Henry could, of course, hardly have done much to enforce an arbitrary and unpopular decree. No great statesmanship was needed to appreciate that fact. But it is re/ markable that a government with little experience in courting public opinion beyond Parliament should have recognized with such speed and clarity the need for appealing to the increasingly broad reading public by means of printed pamphlets.

Beginning with the divorce question, every climax in the stormy public life of the 1530's was accompanied by a spate of government/ sponsored propaganda aimed at all levels of society.[1] Bishops Gard/ iner, Sampson, and Fox lent the weight of their dignity—and of their controversial style—to the king's cause. Their Latin works were apparently meant for the academically expert, both in England and on the Continent.[2] Cromwell himself is credited with organizing for home consumption a more varied and probably a more effective group of propagandists. He was especially astute in appreciating the unique value of those English humanists who had gathered in Padua

1. *Letters and Papers, Foreign and Domestic, of the Reign of Henry VIII*, ed. J. S. Brewer and James Gardiner, (21 vols.; London, 1862/1910), V, 1/9, in which about twenty/five treatises are listed on the divorce question alone. The fullest study of the Henrician propaganda is an unpublished doctoral dissertation by Julius King, Jr., "The Official Propaganda of the Reign of Henry VIII," Cornell University, 1955. F. L. Baumer deals with the subject from the point of view of the history of political thought in his valuable book *The Early Tudor Theory of Kingship*. See especially pp. 38/45, 49/56, 216. See also Pierre Janelle, *L' Angleterre Catholique à la veille du Schisme* (Paris, 1935), especially pp. 309/319.

2. Stephen Gardiner, *De Vera Obedientia Oratio*, ed. P. Janelle in *Obedience in Church and State* (Cambridge, 1930); Richard Sampson, *Oratio quae docet hortatur admonet omnes potissimum Anglos regiae dignitati cum primis ut obediant*, etc. (London, 1533); Edward Fox, *Opus eximium, de vera differentia regiae potestatis et ecclesiasticae* (London, 1534). See also Janelle, pp. xxv ff.

under the patronage of Reginald Pole and who had there absorbed much of the stimulus of the already mature and civic-minded human-ism of the Italian city-states. These men—Thomas Starkey and Richard Morison are the best known—willingly enough entered the service of their prince and contributed to the elucidation of his policy both a persuasive vernacular style and a sophistication of outlook derived from an intellectual tradition still new to most Englishmen.[3] On a lower level, but perhaps no less effective, Cromwell appears to have employed a motley assortment of ballad-mongers and playwrights, among whose often ribald and usually scurrilous offerings the plays of Bishop Bale ("bilious Bale," Fuller called him) stand out in very uncanonical eminence.[4]

Propaganda was, to be sure, a double-edged weapon. Opinion, once aroused, tended to become articulate in some form or other. Henry was accordingly soon at as great pains to control it as he was to instruct it.[5]   Spoken and written words were made treason by statute in 1534, and a later statute singled out for suspicion unauthorized "printed books, printed plays, rymes, songs, and other fantasies."[6] The Privy Council seems to have been kept fairly busy dealing with individual instances of seditious expression,[7] ranging from published writings of considerable weight to highly fugitive utterances induced by the conviviality of the local tavern.[8]   And Cromwell has been charged with maintaining a spy system and of creating through its offices an atmosphere of terror.   Considerably better evidence supports the less dramatic thesis that he encouraged an informal but effective network of informers.[9]   Whether or not even this latter charge is deserved, it should come as no surprise: liberal principles had little place in Renaissance society.   Insofar as he deliberately set up a spy

---

3. W. G. Zeeveld, *Foundations of Tudor Policy* (London, 1948).

4. *The Dramatic Writings of John Bale*, ed. J. S. Farmer (London, 1907).   Thomas Fuller, *History of the Worthies of England* (London, 1652), p. 61, calls him "Biliosus Balaeus."

5. F. S. Siebert, *Freedom of the Press in England, 1476-1776* (Urbana, 1952), chaps. i-ii.

6. 26 Henry VIII, c. 13; 34 and 35 Henry VIII, c. 1.

7. See *LP*, XIII, *passim*.

8. E.g., *ibid.*, Pt. I, Nos. 93-95.

9. A good deal of fresh light, modifying the more extreme charges and clarifying the problem, has been provided in a master's thesis by W. A. Moffett, "The Long Arm of Thomas Cromwell: Problems in Controlling English Opinion, 1537-1540," (Duke, 1959).

system, Cromwell was doing no more than William Forrest, one of the most idealistic and critical of the mid-century pamphleteers, urged in his *Pleasaunt Poesye of Princelie Practise* where he devoted a whole chapter to the problem of "how a king ought to be much desirous to know the opinion of his commons toward him by the exploration of some secret servant whom he doth best credit."[10]   At any rate, the action taken by the government in an effort to stem and control public discussion indicates how deeply ingrained the habit of discussing affairs of common concern was becoming during this decade of the thirties.

Matters of common concern did not, of course, end with the great affairs of state. The latter seem, in fact, only to have headed a long list. Stimulating as the politico-ecclesiastical controversies unquestionably were, significant also as the patronage of pamphleteers by the government may well have been, the fact remains that much of the pamphlet literature of the 1530's, and perhaps the bulk of it in the 1540's bore only indirectly on those events. They dealt rather with those chronic ailments of English society which had for long been the stock-in-trade of the commentator: enclosures and rack-renting, high prices and usury, wool growing and the cloth trade. Or, if they touched upon political and religious events, it was very often to explore their social and economic consequences. The dissolution of the monasteries, for instance, they quickly recognized as an event of very far-reaching importance, impinging ultimately upon every aspect of contemporaneous life. Some of the official propaganda tends also in the direction of social analysis. Such tracts as those written by Morison and Cheke in the wake of the risings of 1536 and 1549 and in the interests of obedience in church and state reveal the ability and willingness of those men to explore the economic roots of rebellion and to examine its social repercussions.[11]

∽ ∽ ∽

The patronage of Cromwell coincided with, if it did not actually create, the first significant growth of public discussion. The vigorous, but high-handed administration of Thomas Wolsey in the period preceding had provoked a fugitive literature of criticism, largely

10. S. J. Herrtage (ed.), in *England in the Reign of Henry VIII: Starkey's Life and Letters*. E.E.T.S., E.S., No. 32 (1878), appendix.
    11. See below, chaps. viii-x.

aimed at the great man himself.[12]   And the religious controversy that came to England with the smuggled Lutheran books no doubt did a good deal to stimulate native discussion.   More's *Utopia* remains, however, the only work prior to the thirties in which the author makes any attempt to examine English society as a whole.

Cromwell's fall from the royal grace was followed by a relatively barren period.   The extent to which this blight can be explained by the fall of the Vicar General himself depends, of course, upon the amount of credit he deserves for stimulating discussion in the years of his ascendancy.   The fact remains that, after Cromwell's fall, Henry's conservative tendencies in religion were accompanied by a repressive attitude toward the discussion of such matters.   The resulting atmosphere at court must have been discouraging also to the discussion of other issues as well.   And, in the country as a whole, the potentially articulate citizen could have found little encouragement in the ominous shadow of the Henrician law of treason and the act "abolishing diversity in opinions."[13]   Certainly the humanists as a group were not much in evidence as official spokesmen after Cromwell's fall.   And many of the best minds of the period—Stephen Gardiner is a case in point—were no doubt diverted, by command or inclination, from criticism of secular society to the more immediately pressing business of government or to the troublesome questions of political and confessional controversy.

The accession of Edward VI was followed by a second and, from the point of view of the historian of ideas, an even more significant outburst of public discussion.   Whether this second and more concerted expression of articulate citizenship was the result of the growing gravity of social and economic issues (such were, as a matter of fact, the chief subject of pamphlet discussion in that reign—outside, that is, of the constant flow of religious writings) or whether it reflected a newly

12. See, for example, *The Poetical Works of John Skelton*, ed. A. Dyce (London, 1843), especially "Magnificence," "Why come ye not to courte?" "Speke Parrot," and "Colyn Clout"; W. Roy and J. Barlow, *Rede me and be nott wrothe*, ed. Edward Arber (London, 1871).

13. 26 Henry VIII, c. 13 and 31 and Henry VIII, c. 14.   The severity of the latter act was mitigated by leniency in application and by subsequent acts: 32 Henry VIII, c. 10 and 35 Henry VIII, c. 5.   See Isabel Thornley, "The Treason Legislation of Henry VIII, 1531-1534," *TRHS*, 3rd Series, XI (1917), 87-123.   See also L. B. Smith, "English Treason Trials and Confessions in the Sixteenth Century," *JHI*, XV (Oct., 1954), 471-498.

encouraging official attitude toward discussion is difficult to say with any certainty. It would, however, appear that the restrictions of the preceding reign were relaxed and men of ideas were once more en' couraged to comment on issues of national concern.

It is more than likely that, as in the thirties, such encouragement was in large part the work of one man. But, whereas Cromwell valued his pamphleteers primarily as propagandists, the Protector Somerset looked to them as consultants. Although little direct evi' dence remains regarding his intellectual life and the influences that shaped it, and although at least one author complained that men of learning were not given the preferment that was their due,[14] Somerset's policies and his choice of men to implement them would indicate that he was profoundly influenced by the civic ideal of humanism. He apparently sought the aid and counsel of laymen like Hales and church' men who, like Latimer, coupled a somewhat antihumanist taste for confessional controversy with an Erasmian enthusiasm for social re' form; the idealism, sincere if too often misplaced or misdirected, that animated his own program of social reform indicates that he was deeply committed to the ideal of the "very and true commonweal."

Somerset, however, did more than merely listen to the social re' formers and incorporate their intellectual formulas in his official papers. By repealing the treason laws which Henry VIII had used to enforce the Royal Supremacy, he undoubtedly helped to create an atmosphere more conducive to free discussion. In the preamble to the Act of Repeal[15] it was argued that, whereas stringent laws were necessary in a time of turmoil and crisis in order to prevent rebellion and the undoing of good governance, such extreme measures were no longer necessary in a time of greater peace and stability—such as the era of regency adminis' tration was hopefully believed to be. Accordingly that part of Henry's legislation which made it treason to speak or preach, as well as to write, in denial of the king's supremacy was mitigated to the extent that spoken words no longer, by themselves, constituted high treason. It remained dangerous to question the supreme authority of the king in written or printed form, and seditious words could still be punished by loss of goods and by imprisonment. Free speech was never

14. *Discourse of the Common Weal of this Realm of England*, ed. Elizabeth Lamond (Cambridge, 1893), pp. 28'29.

15. 1 Edward VI, c. 12.

in Renaissance society the nearly absolute principle, nor even the generally acclaimed desideratum, it later became in the liberal tradition. Nevertheless, the new law marked a deliberate break with the repressive policies of Henry VIII. And, what is more, its spirit outdistanced its letter. To the dismay of more conservative minds, Somerset also relaxed restrictions on the printing press, a fact which in itself does a good deal to explain the vigorous renewal of public discussion under his administration.[16] And the opportunity his brief term of office gave for some of the best English minds to express themselves in a more consistently realistic analysis of their society than had ever before been attempted goes a long way toward redeeming that strange interlude from the charge of utter futility.

For futile it was in only too many of its efforts. Somerset's own career presents a painful example of the reformer whose far-sighted vision of a better society prevented him from focusing with any clarity upon the actualities that lay between him and his promised land. Even his encouragement of discussion, if he may be credited with such, stimulating as it unquestionably was to public thought, overreached the values of his own society. Many, possibly most, of the governing class would no doubt have agreed with John Mason when he declared, in retrospect, that "the worst act that ever was done in our time was the general abolishing of the Act of Words by the Duke of Somerset."[17]

But Englishmen never forgot the lesson they had learned in these revolutionary decades of the sixteenth century. Despite periods of confusion and discouragement, of silence officially enforced, Renaissance England became, in its period of cultural maturity, "the classical home of the pamphlet."[18] Englishmen never lost that sense of intellectual participation in the work of governing which, however illusory it may often have been, made them ready to speak their mind on a multitude of issues, confident that they would be heard for their much speaking.

∽ ∽ ∽

The culture of early Tudor England reveals at best a confusing mixture of things old and new. The difficulty of distinguishing

16. A. F. Pollard, *England under Protector Somerset* (London, 1900), p. 323; Siebert, pp. 51-53.
17. Quoted by Pollard, p. 58.
18. J. A. Schumpeter, *History of Economic Analysis* (New York, 1954), p. 160.

clearly between the elements of change and those of continuity is, however, made greater by the fact that fresh attitudes are often masked by
conventional language. Much of the written discussion of the period,
especially that still couched in verse form, sounds oddly like the medieval literature of good counsel. And the sermon literature maintains
the strongest of ties with the medieval past. In a sense all the pamphleteers who hastened to offer their advice to the Tudor monarchy
were simply bringing up to date the classic problem of good counsel.[19]
They were, of course, doing much more, even if they were not always
ready to recognize the degree to which they had expanded the function
of their kind. If these men who faced the new, or newly intensified,
problems of the sixteenth century felt really as the early fifteenth-century
author of *Mum and the Sothsegger* that the duty of the wise and literate
man is primarily that of reporting to the king and his lords whatever
he sees that is amiss in the society around him, that his place in the
scheme of "good and abundant governance" is merely to supplement
the accurate information the king is supposed to get through his council
and his Parliament, that Parliament itself serves primarily the purpose
of setting the truth before the king in order that he, in his paternal
wisdom, would act upon it, if, in short, they continued to look upon
government as essentially a protective agency depending on all responsible men for complaint and petition, we could be sure that, however
revolutionary the external changes in English society might be, Englishmen were indeed still medieval in their thought. During the second
quarter of the Tudor century, however, it was becoming increasingly
clear to most intelligent observers that government must perform a more
positive function than that envisaged by the author of *Mum*. Counsel
must now include constructive policy in addition to the simple truth-
telling, the honest, courageous, unflattering counsel the poet of a century and a half earlier hoped would flow from "man's heart" to quicken
the roots of justice.

But there is just enough of the old attitude still apparent to remind
us that ideas as well as their linguistic formulas change slowly—in
times of rapid social change more slowly than conditions. Robert
Crowley, the preacher-printer who combined in himself the tradition
of moralistic comment with the newer techniques of mass appeal and
something also of the new ideal of the "very and true commonweal,"

19. See above chap. iii.

would probably have seen little in the ideas or language of *Mum* to criticize. There is in his pamphlet entitled *An Information and Petition against the Oppressors of the Poor Commons of this Realm* (1548) a strong resemblance, especially, to the *Mum* author's attitude toward Parliament.[20] In it he undertakes to provide the "godly minded men" in Parliament with the ammunition needed in their fight against the evils of the times, so that they "may hereat take occasion to speak more in the matter than the author was able to speak." In other words, government, to be good, depends on information, and the literate man must supplement the normal, parliamentary channel by which such intelligence reaches the king and his council. In words reminiscent of those in which John Gower expressed his role as public moralist— *"non medicus sed medicinae procurator"*—Crowley says in another pamphlet that he must do what he can, namely "hold the candle to them that have wherewith, and will settle lustily to it."[21]

In similar vein the early Tudor preachers thundered against those who subverted the right order of the commonwealth, and their spoken words re-echoed again and again in printed editions. Like the medieval preacher and the poet who shared his point of view, John Hooper believed he was in duty bound, indeed "commanded," to "speak against the faults of all degrees without exception."[22] Perhaps the Tudor preachers saw the national implications of their social criticism more clearly than those of the preceding period, though the latter were, as we have seen, ready enough to recognize that, as the voice of the people, it was the English people for whom, first of all, they had to speak. A newly intense tone of patriotism becomes audible in Hooper's words: "The love I bear unto this commonwealth of England compelleth me to speak."[23] The preachers of the reign of Edward VI in fact took a prominent place in the movement for social reform associated with the newly vitalized concept of the commonwealth. Hugh Latimer, in particular, undertook to lead the agitation for both social and religious reform from his episcopal pulpit.

20. In *Select Works*, ed. J. M. Cowper, E.E.T.S., E.S., No. 15 (1872). See also *Vox Populi Vox Dei* [1547-1548] in *Ballads from Manuscripts*, ed. F. J. Furnivall, Ballad Society (2 vols., 1868-1872), I, 124-146.
21. *The Way to Wealth* [1550], in *Select Works*, p. 131. For reference to Gower, see above, chap. iii.
22. *Early Writings*, ed. S. Carr, Parker Society (Cambridge, 1852), p. 451.
23. *Ibid.*, p. 468.

Yet the great Tudor preachers remained essentially traditional in their attitude toward public discussion. Despite occasionally keen insights into the causes of England's ills, they for the most part maintained the attitude of the medieval critic, traced social dislocation and national disaster to sin, and left specific remedies to those "that have wherewith and will settle lustily to it." Their duty was to exhort their countrymen to righteous living. The national state they considered a kind of theocracy to whose people a stern but longsuffering God issues warnings of impending punishment through the mouth of His preachers, just as in days gone by He spoke through His prophets.[24] But the actual business of governing was still the responsibility of the king and the lords. In correcting transgression, the temporal sword remained distinct from the spiritual.[25] The clergy are, like Jonah, enjoined to preach, "not to take the regiment of governance of the commonwealth."[26] Yet both preachers and secular governors could be said to be laboring toward the same ends once discussion had been translated into terms of the moral and religious meaning underlying all human endeavors.

∽ ∽ ∽

Certainly a medieval Rip van Winkle who awoke in England during the second quarter of the sixteenth century would have found much that was familiar in the discussion taking place around him. If he happened to be in or around London at the time he would surely have been surprised by the sheer amount of publication, but, if he did not read too critically, the words, even to a large extent the subject matter, would have had a familiar ring. He would in particular have found the idea that the virtuous and responsible citizen of whatever order should speak out on matters of common concern a familiar one. But if he listened and read more carefully he would have detected a new tone of urgency, a more specific sense of purpose. He would have been amazed, I think, to hear Crowley, who embodied perhaps

24. E.g., *ibid.*, p. 450.

25. Hugh Latimer, *Works*, ed. G. E. Corrie (2 vols.; Parker Society, 18441845), I, 8587.

26. Hooper, *Early Writings*, pp. 506507; cf. Thomas Lever, *A Sermon preached at Paules crosse the xiii daie of December, . . . 1550*, epistle, in *Three fruitful Sermons made by Thomas Lever, . . . 1550* (London, 1572) *STC* 15551, and Edwin Sandys, *Sermons*, ed. J. Ayre, Parker Society (1841), introductory epistle (to 1585 ed.).

more than most of the more prominent Tudor publicists the still strong links with the past, speaking nevertheless with a strange intensity of the duty of articulate citizenship: "It shall be every true Englishman's duty forthwith to employ his whole study to the removing of so great an evil [sedition] out of so noble a realm and commonwealth; . . . Give ear therefore (Oh my countrymen) give ear! And do not disdain to hear the advice of one of the least of your brethren, for the matter requireth every man's counsel."[27]   Perhaps he would have found even stranger the words of Thomas Becon, the exceedingly voluble proponent of religious reform, in which he expressed what he conceived to be his duty, as one "trained . . . in the court of Lady Mnemosyne and her daughters, and exercised in the wrestling-place of Apollo," to "bring forth some literal lucubrations [in this instance on the current threat of war], which, being diligently read and followed of my countrymen should not be altogether unfruitful to our common country."[28]   If, as is conceivable, he had read any of the several fifteenth-century English versions of the *Secreta Secretorum* (or, as is even more likely, he had fallen into his long sleep over one of them), he might have been surprised to find William Forrest bringing even this traditional treatise *de regimine principum*, in which the idea of counsel had received an especially stereotyped form, into actual contact with the realities of sixteenth-century life and projected in the interests of constructive reform.[29]   And he would have found in Elyot's *Governor* a work that had all but left the traditional "mirror of princes" behind.

There was, however, more to the new citizenship than a tone of patriotic urgency. If our hypothetical sleeper had read very far in the pamphlet literature of this world of his new awakening, if especially, he had made the acquaintance of the humanists who were now turning their attention ever more intently and systematically to the analysis of the common weal, he would have found the idea expressed in terms almost wholly strange to him. Take, for example, the matter-of-fact, yet remarkably far reaching statements with which the author of the

27. *Way to Wealth*, pp. 131-132.

28. Thomas Becon, *The Policy of War* [1543], in *Early Works*, ed. J. Ayre, Parker Society (1843), pp. 230-261, 236; see also pp. 232-235 for an especially fervent expression of patriotic sentiment.

29. *Pleasaunt Poesye of Princelie Practise*, ed. S. J. Herrtage, E.E.T.S., E.S., No. 32 (1878). See above chap. iii.

Discourse of the Common Weal of this Realm of England (1549?)[30] prefaced
his brilliant discussion of England's economy:

> Albeit I am not of the King's council, to whom the reformation
> and consideration [of the commonwealth] . . . chiefly be-
> longs, yet knowing myself to be a member of the same common
> weal, and called to be one of the house, where such things
> ought to be treated, I can not reckon myself a mere stranger in
> the matter; no more than a man that were in a ship, which were
> in danger of wreck, might say, that because he is not (perchance)
> the master or pilot of the same, the danger thereof did nothing
> pertain to him.[31]

Although he recognizes the inequality of capacity among the citizenry,
he is more impressed by the variety of their skills and experience.
Accordingly he urges, if not the broadest discussion of high policy,
certainly a pooling of expertise.

> Therefore I would not only have learned men (whose judgments
> I would wish to be chiefly esteemed) herein, but also merchant
> men, husbandmen, and artificers (which in their calling are
> taken most wise) freely suffered yea and provoked to tell their
> advices in this matter; for some points in their feats they may
> disclose that the wisest in a Realm could not again [say].[32]

With that in mind he had assembled for his "discourse" a knight, a
merchant, a doctor, a husbandman, and a craftsman.

The humanist scholar had more than the average concern for the
public discussion of issues important to the national welfare. He
sincerely believed that the man trained in *literae humaniores*, the heritor
of classical precept and example, skilled in the arts of persuasion, could
and should offer his services to the state, either directly as a counselor
of the prince or indirectly through written comment. In either case
he was confident that, no matter how far the prince might actually have
been from the Platonic ideal of the philosopher-king, the defect might
be at least partially corrected if only he would listen to the advice of
philosophers. Thus More and Starkey, though writing almost a
generation apart, explore with philosophical care this same problem

30. *A Discourse of the Common Weal of this Realm of England*, ed. Elizabeth Lamond
(Cambridge, 1893). See below n. 45 on question of authorship.
31. *Ibid.*, pp. 10-11.
32. *Ibid.* Cf. Becon, *Policy of War*, p. 235.

as they saw it in the specific context of the Tudor monarchy. The dilemma they faced is crucial to an understanding of humanist thought and must be dealt with in more detail in another chapter.[33]   For the moment, however, it is worth pausing to notice that the humanists raised the problem of counsel from the level of mere truth-telling to that of intelligent citizenship and there considered it in relation to practical considerations, antique example, and moral philosophy.

These men became newly aware of the importance of public discussion.   Assuming, as they did, the rational nature of man and to some extent the positive role of government, they sometimes argued for free discussion of public issues with the hopeful logic of a Victorian liberal.   Thomas Starkey argued that the free exchange of opinion on the part of good and experienced men would strengthen the commonwealth, for it would allow the wise man to compare one point of view with another and so make it possible for him to arrive at what is best for all concerned.[34]   Roger Ascham approached the same problem, if not so philosophically, yet from a point of view very typical of the later humanists.   In his *Report and Discourse . . . of the Affairs and State of Germany,* in the course of a most judicious analysis of the background and peculiarities of contemporaneous Germany, he draws for English use the lesson that wise and good men ought to be allowed to speak out more freely than they do.[35]   Both Ascham and Starkey are quick, however, to add to their plea for freedom of the press the equally characteristic proviso that irresponsible speech should not be tolerated.   It is always easy to underestimate the conservatism of these scholars who were progressive only in relation to their still more conservative contemporaries.

Humanism not only reinforced the tendency to interpret counsel in terms of articulate citizenship, but made written discussion a respectable, almost an obligatory endeavor for the qualified member of the governing class.   There were still those among the gentry of early Tudor England who maintained that learning should be left to clerks. But the chivalric tradition, which in its purer form prescribed for the knight a primarily, indeed almost exclusively military function, had

33. See below, chap. vii.
34. W. G. Zeeveld, *Foundations of Tudor Policy* (London, 1948), p. 91.
35. *Report*, pp. 158-165, in *English Works*, ed. W. A. Wright (Cambridge, 1904). The *Report* was written in 1553 but not printed until ca. 1570.   See also L. V. Ryan, *Roger Ascham* (Palo Alto, 1963), especially chap. viii.

long been giving way before the pressure of increasingly varied duties devolving upon the aristocracy and the gentry.[36]   Not, however, until the advent of the new, classically inspired education was a new source of precept and precedent available, one sufficiently pertinent to the life of the sixteenth-century English governing class to serve it as the basis for a new secular ideal.   Within the expanding horizons of the new age, knights and gentlemen of the type of Sir Thomas Elyot or John Hales or Sir Thomas Smith, men whose experience in the actual offices of local and central government was considerable and whose learning was commensurate with their experience, could reasonably feel that the informed pen was a more effective weapon against the enemies of society in their fast-moving age than the now somewhat rusty sword of the knight.   As Elyot wrote on one occasion, in answer to those who criticized him for writing about spiritual matters which "doth not pertain to a knight, much less to a sheriff,"

> A knight hath received that honor not only to defend with the sword Christ's faith and his proper country . . . but also, and that most chiefly, by the mean of his dignity . . . he should more effectively with his learning and wit assail vice and error, . . . having thereunto for his sword and spear his tongue and pen.[37]

All the more was he fitted to speak his mind on secular affairs.

ᔕ ᔕ ᔕ

Another tendency that emerges in early Tudor discussion is to think of counsel in an institutional rather than a personal context.   To the medieval observer, to Gower, for instance, or the author of *Mum and the Sothsegger*, government still seemed relatively simple, its processes explainable in personal terms.   The historian knows that it was, in fact, anything but simple, that its institutions were, during the fourteenth century, rapidly taking recognizable shape—recognizable, that is, to him—and that constitutional precedents of far reaching importance were being established.   To the contemporary observer, especially if his point of observation lay outside the actual machinery of government or if, as was usually the case, it was situated on the lofty terrain of

36. On this subject see Ferguson, *Indian Summer of English Chivalry*, chaps. iv and vi. See also below, chap. vii.

37. *A Preservative agaynste Deth* (London, 1545), *STC* 7674, sigs. Aii-Aiii.

moral judgment and first principle, it depended entirely on the character of the men involved in it. It depended in particular on the willingness of all concerned to see and speak the truth and for those in positions of final authority to listen to true and unflattering advice. Observed from this point of view the institutions of government remain shadowy. Parliament becomes mainly the clearinghouse for petitions, the place where grievances, conceived essentially as private, could be aired. Now, in the surcharged atmosphere of Tudor England, in the glare of (quite literally) burning issues, the institutional machinery of government stood out with unprecedented clarity. Again, of course, contemporary observers did not, could not indeed, recognize in Cromwell's administration the revolution in government which a modern scholar is able to trace.[38] Yet he could undoubtedly see much more clearly than his medieval prototype the necessary relationship between public discussion and the institutions which alone could transform counsel into policy and, if need be, legislation. In the fifteenth century, Fortescue, almost alone among those who wrote about government, was similarly able to see beyond persons and private rights to institutions and the impersonal issues of national life.[39] In the second quarter of the century following, such an ability, if not usual, is no longer rare.

Parliament seems to have been the favorite institution of the independent commentator. This is especially true in the case of those who were not very close to the personalities in the royal administration or who could not, as More and Starkey could, contemplate the possibility of acting as actual advisers to the king. But it is nonetheless interesting. Parliament had received less attention in fifteenth-century writings than the modern reader, accustomed to think of English history in terms of parliamentary supremacy, is likely to expect. Fortescue, though he paid his respects to its legislative function in passing, largely ignored it in favor of the council which he rightly recognized to be the source of policy as well as of administration. On the other hand, those who made of the late fourteenth century and the early years of the fifteenth the first significant period in the history of political comment and social criticism looked to Parliament as the place where wrongs could be righted and counsel heard. But again it

38. G. R. Elton, *The Tudor Revolution in Government: Administrative Changes in the Reign of Henry VIII* (Cambridge, 1953).
39. See above, chap. v.

must be remembered that this view of Parliament is really a function of the personal and private approach toward governments as a whole.[40] The Tudor pamphleteer, on the contrary, is beginning to see Parlia, ment as the source of legislation conceived on a broader, national scale—still largely remedial, but at times reaching beyond the simple protection of rights to encompass the collective, potentially dynamic concerns of the whole commonwealth.

He talks about "bills"; but they are rather suggestions for legislation than petitions for redress. The anonymous author of a tract bearing the familiar sounding title, *Pyers Plowmans Exhortation unto the Lordes, Knightes and Burgoysses of the Parlyamenthouse* (1550)[41] turns out to be speaking the language of practical politics rather than of the Piers Plowman tradition of moral analysis: "And for these purposes I have drawn forth certain rude bills to be exhibited to you of the Parliament, house, trusting that by your wisdoms, learning and knowledge, said of the same rude bills may be reduced unto due form of good statutes." Although his role is strictly that of the volunteer amateur, he is writing about very real problems and has actual legislative remedies in mind.

Henry Brinkelow, who also followed a traditional pattern in the form of his *Complaynt of Roderyck Mors* (*ca.* 1542), likewise directs his analysis of specific issues and his occasional practical recom, mendations for reform toward Parliament. For, he says somewhat hyperbolically, Parliament is the "head council of all realms," its laws, with the consent of the king, binding on all.[42] It is a place where "godly,minded" men can "devise ways" to cope with the knottiest problems—the distribution of the confiscated abbey lands, for example. It is a place where ingenuity can and should be exercised. Yet its several heads are not so wise that they cannot profit by the advice of such as himself.[43] And so, "seeing so many cruel laws and heavy yokes upon the shoulders of the people of my native country . . . I can but reckon myself bound to open and disclose unto the said council of Parliament, part of the foresaid yokes."[44]

As might be expected from a person so experienced in the actual

40. See above, chaps. ii and iii.
41. *STC*, 19905.
42. Ed. J. M. Cowper, E.E.T.S., E.S., No. 22 (1874), pp. 5,6.
43. *Ibid.*, pp. 50,51.
44. *Ibid.*, p. 6. Cf. Crowley, *Informacion and Peticion*, p. 153, where he makes the point that Parliament is simply the place where grievances are debated and redressed.

affairs of government, Sir Thomas Smith has a broader, and no doubt a more accurate appreciation of the way in which discussion can be translated into policy and legislation. The Doctor in his *Discourse of the Common Weal* (I am assuming that he was the author)[45] with cautious modesty hesitates to discuss detailed remedies for the dislocation of the coinage on the ground that such "would be devised by the great wise heads of the council, or of the parliament, or of some picked number of learned and wise men, chosen of them and put together to consult of this matter a great space." The Knight, however, urges him to proceed, for "I may hear some sensible reason, that, when I come to parliament (whereof I am unworthy), I may declare there, which might enter into some mens ears, that might do good herein; and therefore tell your device."[46] A little later he presses him again to tell his remedy for the particular evil of enclosures, for, he says, "I have heard this matter of long time and oft reasoned upon, as well in parliament as in council, and yet small remedy found therefor that took effect.[47] It is this emphasis on "devices" and "remedies" rather than simply on "truth" and the fearless reporting of grievances that distinguishes the most mature Tudor discussion from that of the late fourteenth century. And it is noteworthy that Smith recognizes a variety of possible channels through which such devices might receive official consideration.

Much of the advice offered by volunteer counselors was still, of course, addressed to particular persons nearer to the seat of government. Parliament they knew was the place where policy was translated into law (it was the genius of Tudor government to do everything of a radical nature in full accord with constitutional tradition), but they also knew that it was among the more intimate advisers of the king that policy was usually made. And so we find many of the most penetrating analyses of conditions and some of the most constructive

---

45. Since Miss Lamond attributed the *Discourse* to John Hales (see her introduction to the *Discourse*), doubts have gradually been accumulating, and there has been an increasing tendency to attribute it to Sir Thomas Smith. See E. Hughes, "The Authorship of the *Discourse of the Common Weal*," *Bulletin of the John Rylands Library*, XXI (1937), 167-175, and Jean-Yves le Branchu, *Ecrits notables sur la monnaie* (Paris, 1934), I, pp. lvii-xciv. Dr. Mary Dewar has recently subjected the problem to its most thorough scrutiny to date and is convinced that Smith was the author. *Sir Thomas Smith: A Tudor Intellectual in Office* (London, 1964), pp. 53-55. More detailed proof must await her forthcoming critical edition of Smith's writings.

46. *Discourse*, pp. 110-111.

47. *Ibid.*, p. 120.

suggestions for reform addressed to the king, no doubt in the knowl-edge that it would be processed by some responsible member of the council, or to some person near the king who might be influential in securing a hearing. So, for example, we find John Hales writing to Sir Anthony Browne, Master of the Horse, in the hope that he might show to the king a "rude" oration of his in which he undertakes to defend the Common Law against incursions from either the civil or canon laws.[48] Or, again, Thomas Starkey addresses a letter directly to the king in which he subjects such matters of high policy as the distribution of the abbey lands to constructive criticism.[49] Both Hales and Starkey were not unknown in government circles. One John Bayker, on the contrary, was apparently an itinerant craftsman, yet he also felt impelled to write a letter of advice to the king, in this instance concerning a cause of poverty.[50]

Although Tudor government was in the process of achieving a permanent bureaucratic machinery commensurate with the more broadly national function it was being called upon to perform, it still remained simple enough to permit a good deal of personal contact with the private citizen. To this extent there remained in it a personal quality which encouraged the public-spirited citizen to express him-self directly. Yet the assumption in these direct expressions of citizen-ship is that they might influence the mind of government rather than that they might serve to recall the persons concerned to the conscienti-ous discharge of their duties.

John Hales provides us with an interesting comment on the way in which the opinion of particular interests could be brought infor-mally to the attention of the council through the literary skill of a man like himself who, though holding no official post, is recognized as a man of experience and wisdom. In 1559 he wrote a letter to Sir William Cecil, secretary to the newly crowned queen, pointing out the disadvantages of a new imposition on cloth.[51] He had done so, he tells, at the request of the merchants of London. They had approached

48. *LP*, XVII (1542), Appendix 1.

49. S. J. Herrtage, *England in the Reign of Henry VIII: Starkey's Life and Letters*, E.E.T.S., E.S. No. 32 (1878), pp. xlvii-lxiii.

50. *Tudor Economic Documents*, ed R. H. Tawney and Eileen Power (3 vols.; London, 1924), II, 302-305. This same collection contains several other interesting examples of letters from merchants and craftsmen.

51. Tawney and Power, II, 223-226.

him as men "that be extremely sick commonly, when they cannot get the best physician, they be contented with every one that seemeth to have any skill in physic, and if no such can be found, yet do they think themselves much eased, when they may have to whom they may utter their griefs, albeit he can do them no good." He was doubtless being elaborately deferential and self-deprecating in all this, as was the custom, for he then proceeds to set forth an extremely able analysis of the cloth trade in relation to the prevailing mercantilist concepts, and we may be permitted to question how futile he really believed his efforts to be. But it is interesting to notice just the same how he justifies such an expression of opinion for its psychologically purgative effect.

The curious career of Clement Armstrong[52] provides perhaps the most useful illustration of the kind of relationship that existed between the council and the public-spirited citizen, at least during the administration of Thomas Cromwell. He was a London merchant, born of a mercantile family. Originally connected with the grocers, he later developed a somewhat off-beat and doubtless lucrative business as a provider of building materials and a garnisher of ceilings—a sort of decorating contractor—and had even had a hand in gilding that diplomatic extravaganza, the Field of the Cloth of Gold. He does not, however, appear to have been especially prominent politically, and his only apparent connection with the court was through his friend John Rastell, the printer and propagandist, whom Cromwell had enlisted in his service. Nor was he especially well educated. His style would indicate a formal training not at all beyond that which could in those days be expected of the more prosperous London families. In the ordinary dimensions of his life, he was, in fact, a very average sort of man—which fact makes him for present purposes all the more valuable.

A glance at his pamphlets (he wrote three that have survived, dealing with the economic problems of England) reveals the kind of restless, inquiring mind that could only be considered average if, as there is some reason to do, we were to hold that restlessness and an analytical kind of curiosity was in itself typical of a large number of alert citizens. A keen observer, and himself an entrepreneur of more than ordinary ingenuity, he knew a great deal about the economic problems of the country and thought he knew even more. He really

52. See S. T. Bindoff, "Clement Armstrong and his Treatises of the Commonweal," *EcHR*, XIV (1944), 64-83.

believed that he had something to say which would save the government from mistakes and contribute to the common weal. Of special
significance was the fact that he, like so many others of the "commonwealths," was able and willing to proceed from factual analysis to constructive remedy, and, if his analysis was not always correct and his
remedy sometimes questionable, that is less important than that he attempted both and had the utmost confidence in them. Accordingly,
perhaps with the help of Rastell, he later in his career submitted the
fruits of his experience to Cromwell. The following excerpts from a
letter, written probably in 1536, are, I think, revealing.[53]

> Please it your Mastership to consider where I have been your
> servant in my mind this three years taking time labor and pain
> to help set forth the knowledge of the right order of common
> weal of all people in the realm, to the intent that ye should help
> the king to set it up to be ministered in exemplum to all other
> realms.

He calls Cromwell's attention to a particular plan for solving the problem of poor relief by setting to work those capable of working. And
he reminds him of two other books he has recently sent containing
"somewhat of the destruction of the common weal of the realm and
somewhat of the remedy." He even had the temerity to suggest that
he could be of still more service to Cromwell if he were given a place
in his household with a secretary to help him elaborate his counsel—
and perhaps to render it into a more readable style—for he has much
more to say "pertaining to the right order of common weal which we
yet know not."

What, if anything, Cromwell did about Armstrong's pamphlets
we do not know. He may never have read them at all—his secretary
seems not to have known from whom they came, or at any rate did not
recognize the name of the author. And Armstrong died shortly
thereafter. But there is a fair likelihood that Cromwell paid some
attention to this sort of thing. We know he encouraged more literate
advisers to come to court. Indeed his actual patronage gave a certain
meaning, in terms of actual political life, to the emerging ideal of the
citizen-counselor. As for poor, shrewd, garrulous, and conceited old
Armstrong, even if he remains in the limbo of unread writers, he

53. R. Pauli, *Drei volkswirthschaftliche Denkschriften aus der Zeit Heinrichs VIII. von
England* (Göttingen, 1878), pp. 49-51.

deserves to be remembered, for, as S. T. Bindoff wrote of him, "it might with some justice be claimed that in him Everyman was made ungracefully, yet sincerely articulate."[54]

∽ ∽ ∽

It is important to understand how firmly this notion of citizenship was founded upon a regard for the written—and published—word. Today we take written discussion for granted.   And in a more or less limited degree it had no doubt existed since the invention of writing. But in this early Renaissance period, when the techniques of modern public discussion were still in the experimental stage, and when the printing press was for the first time being tested in the heat of revolutionary controversy, such confidence rested on faith rather than experience. Perhaps more than we are likely to think, the articulate citizen of early Tudor England was prepared to take part in a battle of books. "I desire," wrote an anonymous pamphleteer in a paper dated 1549, ".   .   .   that they which make any objection to the contrary hereof, may entitle their objection in a piece of paper.   And I doubt not but [I shall] answer it sufficiently.   And thus I make an end of this little book."[55]

The words here remind us of the author of *Mum*, with his "bookmaking," but the context is that of Renaissance discussion in which writing and publishing were becoming a normal aspect of public life and one, moreover, in the process of rapid expansion through the allied offices of the press and the book trade.   It is the context of those "exhortations," and "supplications," of those hastily printed and highly topical sermons, those "bills," those pessimistic "lamentations" and optimistic "remedies" which encrust the pages of the *ShortTitle Catalogue*.   In it we find emerging the articulate citizen, eager to make himself heard in the only way possible before the era of editorial journalism.   Edwin Sandys even found it necessary to explain away the somewhat discouraging scriptural text concerning the making of many books, but in the process composed a stout little manifesto for the printed word.   Such warnings apply, he says, only to idle stuff, not to "the writing of necessary and needful works, which, to the singular

54. Bindoff, p. 83.

55. *Policies to Reduce this Realme of Englande vnto a Prosperous Wealthe and Estate*, in Tawney and Power, III, 311345, 345.

advancement of kingdoms and commonweals, . . . have been printed and published notwithstanding." Writing, moreover, lasts longer than mere speaking and carries more weight.[56] In this same picture there appears also the figure of the printer-propagandist, the scholar, like William Marshall or John Rastell, or the preacher like Robert Crowley, who turn their technical vocation to the task of ful- filling their largely self-imposed duty as citizens. Looking back from the momentous but unsettled year of 1558 over the previous thirty years or so, the author of a tract entitled *The Lamentacion of England*[57] was able to discern a continuous process of written discussion in which such names as Simon Fish and Henry Brinkelow appear as examples of some importance, but by no means unique. By that date discussion had arrived at the point where it could be recognized by a contemporary as a force in public life with a history of its own, a history, moreover, worth reviewing at a time when, so the author apparently felt, it had entered upon a depressing and critical period.

ഗ ഗ ഗ

These Tudor writers would not have been men of their age had they not set limits to the scope of public discussion. Naturally enough the government itself was interested in limiting discussion which it had, in a sense, invited by its own propaganda campaign. It was well and good to cultivate by persuasion and cajolery the opinion without which no broad national policy could succeed in a country such as England. But when popular agitation could lead to rebellion, as it did in 1536 and again in 1549, the full force of officially sponsored persuasion had to be turned against those who, in their inordinate nature, dared to challenge the policies of the king and his council.

Richard Morison, who had been called from his studies in Italy to plead the case for the royal policy, was given the special task of mounting a literary offensive against the rebels during the Pilgrimage of Grace. The burden of that offensive was the ideal of obedience. But to the doctrine of obedience the corollary was silence. "It is no part of the people's play," he wrote in the *Remedy for Sedition*, "to discuss acts made in parliament."[58] Again, in his *Lamentation, in which is*

56. *Sermons*, ed. J. Ayre, Parker Society (1841), epistle to 1585 ed.
57. *STC*, 10015.
58. Ed. E. M. Cox (London, 1933), p. 21. See below, chap. viii for a more extended discussion of Morison's work.

showed what Ruin and Destruction cometh of Seditious Rebellion: "It far passeth Cobbler's craft [a punning reference to a rebel leader] to dis‑ cuss, what lords, what bishops, what councilors, what acts and statutes and laws are most meet for a commonwealth, and whose judgment should be best or worst concerning matters of religion."[59] In 1549, John Cheke did similar service and made a similar point with regard to popular discussion. In *The Hurt of Sedition* he argued that the king intended reform before the rising of that year, but he did not intend "that every subject should busily intermeddle with it of their own head, but only those whom his council thought most meet men for such an honest purpose."[60]

These official warnings run oddly counter to the more frequently reiterated emphasis on the duty of the citizen, especially the wise and experienced citizen, to profer his counsel in the interests of the common weal. They also run counter to the actual examples of the several merchants, men such as Armstrong, who wrote letters or booklets of advice to the king's council on such economic problems as came within the scope of national government.[61] If policy were indeed so strictly the preserve of professional councilors or of those specially tapped for the purpose by the king himself, or if the Tudor citizen took such a limitation seriously, the age would not have been so important as it is in the history of public discussion. The English humanists, of whom Morison and Cheke were prominent examples, would have had to modify their faith in the illuminating efficacy of their studies and in the practical results to be had from free and rational discussion.

It must be remembered, however, that this faith was always tem‑ pered by a deep sense of the public interest in an age of aristocratic and authoritarian government. It is true that the official propaganda quoted above was prompted by temporary conditions. It reflects the plight of a government, still very vulnerable to popular uprising, and the alarm of even the most liberal of those in a position of responsibility in a day when religious reform tended almost inevitably to foster among the ignorant and less favored of the population a certain amount of social radicalism. But it is also true that the English humanists did

59. *STC*, 15185, sig. Aiii.
60. *STC*, 5110, sig. Fiii. See below, chap. ix. See also Crowley, *The Voyce of the Laste Trumpet*, in *Select Works*, ll. 345‑352, in which Crowley maintains that it is not up to yeomen to discuss what the king's taxes are for, but just to pay them.
61. See n. 50 above, and below, chap. viii.

not ordinarily look upon public discussion as something arising spontaneously and beneficently from the rational nature of man. They held a high enough opinion of man's reason. But, except for such extreme statements as that in which the author of the *Discourse of the Common Weal* said he would have men of all degrees urged to take part in the discussion of affairs—a statement not unlike that in which Erasmus some years earlier spoke of his hope that even the plowman might be able to read the Scriptures, and as consistent with the huma-nist concept of man—the humanists tend to follow a more conservative course, admitting that government is for those born to it and trained for it. It is in a sense a vocation requiring, as Sir Thomas Elyot maintained in his *Governor*, and Starkey in his *Dialogue*, a broad and humane education.[62]

It will be recalled that both Starkey and Ascham qualified their advocacy of free speech by saying that, of course, irresponsible publi-cations should be censored. Ascham specified "railing bills . . . taunting songs, or else some scoffing common play,"[63] all the kind of thing which might be written by the semi-educated or the ill-disposed for the purpose of rabble-rousing. Not that Ascham or Starkey or anyone else would have tolerated for a moment writings of a down-right treasonous or even heretical ring, no matter how learned their author or sophisticated their form. Even the essentially tolerant mind of Thomas More, the More of the *Utopia* and its all but absolute free-dom of speech, seems to have narrowed alarmingly in the face of actual controversy over what were to him vital issues.

There appears, however, to have been a strong predisposition in favor of allowing at least the highly educated and/or experienced man to speak out. The humanist movement had by the second quarter of the century far outgrown the academic confines of its earlier years and was finding its way into the councils of "practical" men. It was accordingly becoming easier to assume that the man well seen in classical studies and, preferably, also experienced in the world of affairs possessed the keys to a wisdom which was equated with virtue and hence could not be wrong when applied to the councils of state. The result was an ideal of citizenship approximating the Platonic ideal of an aristocratic society, ruled by an elite of education, ex-

62. See below, chap. vii.
63. *Report*, p. 159.

perience, and virtue rather than of birth or status—an ideal applied by Elyot to English society[64]—more nearly than the modern democratic faith in the native ability of the average man to cast an intelligent vote. And there is in it just the first faint signs of that characteristically modern confidence in the expertise of the specialist. Smith might have the Knight in his *Discourse* pick the mind of the Doctor on the most complicated of economic problems, and with deferential eagerness. Yet Thomas Wilson, in his *Discourse upon Usury* (1569), appears to agree with his speaker who asserts that merchants "must not thus be overthwarted by preachers and others, that can not skill of their doings."[65] Wilson, to be sure, had in mind the kind of moralistic badgering the early generation of English Puritans directed against the fast-growing system of Renaissance finance rather than the broad and humane learning of Smith's Doctor. It is the Doctor, however, who remains the ideal type of the wise man, capable of contributing— informally and indirectly, if not officially—to the store of good counsel without which governance could be neither "good" nor "politic" nor "abundant."

Yet even the "doctors" of that day had to proceed with caution. The government was quite capable of applying an official, if not very systematic or institutionalized form of censorship. Even where Cromwell's long arm did not reach, however, there were persons in a position of sufficient influence to exercise an unofficial, yet dangerously effective control on the expression of opinion. Writers occasionally complained of such pressure. Elyot admitted concern over "the malignity of this present time all disposed to malicious detraction" and the machinations of those "that fail not to rent and deface the renown of writers."[66] And William Marshall, in the dedicatory preface he attached to his translation of an important contemporary treatise on poor relief, begs the queen to persuade the king to protect his book from those who decry all books of reform, yet will not write any themselves.[67]

64. See below, chap. vii.
65. Ed. R. H. Tawney (London, 1925), p. 250. This tract was written in 1569, but not published until 1572.
66. *The Boke named the Governour* [1531], ed. H. H. S. Croft (2 vols.; London, 1883), Proheme, p. cxciv.
67. *The Forme and Maner of Subvention or Helping for Pore People, Devysed and Practysed i*

The Doctor in the *Discourse of the Common Weal* seems to have been just a bit nervous about speaking out so boldy on as sensitive an issue as the coinage. No doubt reflecting Smith's own uneasiness over Somerset's increasing sensitivity to any criticism of his policies, he says "It is dangerous to meddle in the king's matters, and specially if it may have any likelihood to minish his profit."[68] He wants the Knight to assure him that their conversation is truly private;[69] and, when he wishes to reveal some of the subtler implications of the king's policy of debasement, he excludes the husbandman, the craftsman, and even the merchant and whispers into the ear of the Knight whom he considers a man of breeding and, apparently for that reason, one of discretion.[70] But his duty as a learned citizen is stronger than his fear of offending. "I am a subject, and I owe him [the king] not only obeisance but also the obsequy I can, either in deed or device; and therefore I will put the case thus."[71]

For the most part volunteer counselors covered themselves with excessive care by disclaiming any specialized knowledge of government or the kind of ability which supposedly could be found only among those actually in the king's council or, perhaps, in Parliament. As Pole states in Starkey's *Dialogue*, it is "two things . . . to correct and amend errors in deed, and to show the manner and mean how they should be reformed and amended. For as the one is full of hardness and difficulty and, by the providence of God, put only in the power of princes of the world, so the other is facile and easy, and open to every prudent man and politic."[72] This is simply a more elaborate way of rendering Crowley's "hold the candle to them that have wherewith and will settle lustily to it."[73] All these men claimed for themselves was wisdom. With that curiously inverted modesty not infrequently found in the academic mind, they disclaimed any skill in administration.

ഗ   ഗ   ഗ

the *Cytie of Hypres in Flanders* [1535], in *Some Early Tracts on Poor Relief*, ed. F. R. Salter (London, 1926).

68. *Discourse*, p. 111; cf. p. 110. See Dewar, p. 55.

69. *Ibid.*, p. 36.

70. *Ibid.*, p. 45.

71. *Ibid.*, p. 111.

72. *A Dialogue Between Cardinal Pole and Thomas Lupset*, ed. K. M. Burton (London, 1948), p. 127.

73. See also *Vox Populi*, extract in Tawney and Power, III, 30.

It is to the problem of the reforming intellectual, represented in Tudor England by the humanist or the articulate citizen whose inspiration derived from humanism, that we must now turn attention. Although by no means all the writers we have to deal with fall strictly into that category, although the edge of their comment was always tempered in the heat of experience and whetted on the hard surface of reality, the humanist tradition nevertheless provided the new intellectual framework within which they all developed their ideal of citizenship. The humanists were able, through their classical studies as well as from experience, to achieve that vision of a rational and virtuous society in which learning would make possible a life of virtue expressed in the active service of the national community. The following chapter will be devoted to clarifying, as far as is relevant to the present study, the nature of this frame of reference within which the humanist reinterpreted the problem of counsel and within which he came to understand the function of constructive citizenship.

CHAPTER VII. THE INTELLECTUAL AND THE PROBLEM OF COUNSEL

AMONG THE HUMANISTS OF TUDOR ENGLAND THERE appeared a new figure, new, at least to England. He was the intel-lectual, the man, now more often than not a layman, widely read in the secular culture of the antique world, and confident in the broad-ening beneficence of such studies in the actual ordering of the common-wealth. In him the intelligent citizen becomes fully articulate. No doubt, in the crises of a society in transition, he would eventually have found his voice without the inspiration of classical studies. But, in fact, it was to the ancient Greek and Roman culture that he turned for example and precept more pertinent to the secular life of his day than were those of medieval Christendom. Not that he renounced or even ignored his medieval heritage. On the contrary, he accepted, perhaps to a greater degree than we have been accustomed to think, the world picture and the story of man that had been the common property of his ancestors. Like them he sought a life of virtue. But there the similarity ends. For his was not a cloistered or speculative virtue, but virtue informed by experience as well as by philosophy, ordered by reason, and expressed in action. In him the traditional dichotomy of the *vita contemplativa* and the *vita activa* tends to disappear, the antithesis resolved in favor of a life of active citizenship in which the mind, quickened by those studies he held most worthy of man, is devoted to the service of the commonwealth.

The terms "humanism" and "humanist" have been used and misused for so long and in relation to so many different situations that they need to be redefined almost every time they are used. If, that is, they are used at all—and I, for one, would be perfectly happy not to use either but for the fact that some equally problematical terms would then have to be invented to take their place. Here I intend to use the word "humanism" to indicate the conscious reinterpretation of the literature and history of Greece and Rome, of *literae humaniores*, to use the Renaissance scholar's own self-conscious terminology, made within the specific historical context of a society in the process of transition from a medieval to a modern form. And, in dealing with the early

Tudor literature of diagnosis and remedy, it is with the application of these studies to that historical context that I am especially concerned. The pamphlets we shall be examining are examples of what might therefore more strictly be called "applied humanism." In them, humanism appears not so much as the actual study of antique culture, although that plays its part, but as a state of mind, a set of attitudes toward society and the affairs of the national community initially made possible by, and conditioned by, such study.

By the same token (for those readers who prefer not to think of humanism at all but only of humanists) a humanist appears in the ensuing pages not simply as a grammarian[1]—that would merely make the semantic difficulty more manageable by reducing it in size—but as one whose mind has been shaped by study of this reinterpreted antiquity and who has in consequence become able to make a char-acteristically fresh approach to the problems of public life. Many of the men we shall be meeting will be humanists in the narrower sense, like Thomas Starkey, scholars by training, or like Roger Ascham, or John Cheke who "taught Cambridge and King Edward Greek," truly grammarians. But these men went far beyond their purely scholarly pursuits in search of the "very and true commonweal." And there will be some, Sir Thomas More, for example, or John Hales, or, in a sense, Sir Thomas Smith, who were first of all concerned with their own society and sought in classical learning primarily the means toward a better understanding of it. If this dual role of the English humanists is recognized it should in some measure reconcile the rather dramatically divergent evaluations placed upon their work. The literary scholar, understandably alienated by the complacency, the air of superiority to medieval authors, the general priggishness of these men when dealing with *bonae literae*, have at times conceived a very low opinion of them.[2] It is similarly easy to criticize them for their failure to work out a new philosophy or to take a properly modern interest in

1. P. O. Kristeller, *The Classics and Renaissance Thought* (Cambridge, Mass., 1955), pp. 8-11. See also Denys Hay, *The Italian Renaissance in its Historical Background* (Cam-bridge, 1961), pp. 8 and 135. Cf. Kristeller's more recent statement, "Studies on Renaissance Humanism during the last Twenty Years," *Studies in the Renaissance*, IX (1962), 7-30.

2. C. S. Lewis, *English Literature in the Sixteenth Century* (Oxford, 1954), introduction. For a more balanced view, also from a literary scholar, see H. A. Mason, *Humanism and Poetry in the Early Tudor Period* (New York, 1959), p. 49.

science. All of these criticisms, though justified as far as they go, miss the main point. For they fail to take into account the strongly utilitar/ ian character of English humanism and therefore pass over the essential facts concerning these Tudor humanists, namely, that their most con/ sistent concern was the "common weal of this realm of England" and that their best and most characteristic contribution was in the analysis of their society and their willingness, on the basis of such analysis, to profer their counsel on matters of policy.

ᔕ ᔕ ᔕ

Traditional as the humanist's world picture tended to be, when it became a question of adjustment to the actual conditions of life in civil society he diverged more or less abruptly from his predecessors. He found it especially difficult to accept the antithesis, deeply ingrained in medieval thought, between the life of action and that of contemplation. The medieval mind had been plagued with polarities inherent in the radically dualistic character of early Christian thought. Man, himself an unstable conjunction of soul and body, his loyalties divided by a dual citizenship in the City of God and the Terrestrial City, could do little more than deplore the resulting discrepancy between the life of the spirit and the life of daily existence spent within the contaminating confines of the world and the flesh. The medieval thinker tended to accept the discrepancy as inevitable, just as he accepted with varying proportions of sorrow and resignation the more comprehensive divergence between the ideal and the actual.

As a matter of fact the antithesis represented by the active and con/ templative lives was by the early Renaissance becoming increasingly artificial. The clergy were fast losing their once virtually complete monopoly of learning—a monopoly which had had the ironical effect of drawing men whose ideal remained that of study and meditation into the affairs of secular government for lack of others sufficiently trained in the laws or in fiscal administration. At the same time government was coming to depend more and more on the services of educated laymen. And it became consequently more and more difficult to square the life of the governing class with the narrowly military ideal of the knight as the protector of the community, the sword/arm of the body politic. That class, wide and varied, but responsible almost exclusively for the local government of England, was necessarily groping toward a system of values more nearly suited than the chivalric to their actual social function.[3]   To serve its purpose, the new idealism would have to take into account the fact that service to the national community required training far beyond that which had been considered adequate for the knight.   It would have to remove the prejudice, still common in the early sixteenth century among the more conservative of the gentry, against book-learning as fit only for clerks.   It would, in short, have to reconcile, if only by way of a practical compromise, the differences between the active life and that of contemplative study.

It was the peculiar genius of Renaissance thought, and of the reform-minded humanism of Tudor England in particular, to strive constantly to bring the life of the mind into a working relationship with the life of wordly affairs, and to discover a source of idealistic inspiration which would be relevant to the needs of the governing class in their increasingly demanding secular capacities.   The humanist scholar tended also to be a reformer, not only in matters of religion, where he strove, after the Erasmian pattern, to bring together the best of the classical and Christian traditions and to make religion itself a vital, undoctrinaire, primarily ethical force in actual life, but also in the secular affairs of the community.   As best he could, he turned his learning to the task of anatomizing the political body in an effort to find out what made it behave in a way that was in accord neither with Christian precept nor classical example, which was, in short, unreasonable and unnatural as well as sinful.   And he hoped by his efforts to contribute to some practical remedy.   That he was a bit naïve about it all, that his confidence in a life ordered by reason in the light of classical and Christian experience was not entirely borne out by events, is less important than that, for a couple of generations, he and his fellow travelers (if the term can still be used in a non-specific sense) recognized in the contrast between the ideal and the actual in the life around them a demand upon their duty as citizens and a challenge to their intelligence.

This ideal of active citizenship, of "applied" humanism, this ideal of the lay intellectual, grew up in part as a response to the practical needs of a society to which the older ideals had little to say.   It was also rooted deeply in classical thought.[4]   It owed much to the Platonic

---

3. Ferguson, *The Indian Summer of English Chivalry*, treats this problem in some detail.
4. On the origins and nature of this ideal, see Fritz Caspari, *Humanism and the Social*

vision of a good and just state governed by an elite of guardians and philosophers, and to the related idea that knowledge will lead to right thinking expressed in virtuous action. It also owed a good deal to the notion, of Aristotelian origin, that man is a social and political creature, not only because of his natural, physical needs, but because he can never realize the potentialities of his inborn nature unless he assumes the responsibility appropriate to his status in the life of his community or country.

It thus involved a strong tendency toward the *vita activa*. It represented a tendency away from an emphasis on the purely intellectual virtues to a preference for the active moral virtues and to a concern for their mobilization in the battle against the forces of folly and ignorance in the actual life of man. In learning, it meant a preference for moral philosophy over theology or metaphysics, for the tools of the rhetorician over those of the logician, for the persuasive application of learning over its painstaking elaboration. In time, as I shall try to develop in more detail below, it also involved a growing willingness to analyze the forces that were in fact shaping the life of the national community, and confidence in the possibility of intelligent and constructive reform.

It was a secular tendency, too, although to stress that aspect to the detriment of the traditional element in humanist thought would be grossly inaccurate. The English humanists were slow indeed to challenge the basic principles of medieval thought. Even a man like Elyot, who did perhaps more than anyone else to popularize among the governing class the ideal of informed and active citizenship, fell back on traditional forms when he undertook to define the "knowledge that maketh a wise man."[5] The new thought differed from the old rather in emphasis than in mutually exclusive values, and it was secular in effect rather than intent. Secular attitudes, consciously assumed, are rare in early Tudor England. There is no question, however, but that the drift even of this distinctly conservative humanism was secular in comparison with the ideals accepted by medieval society. It was secular in the sense that the problems of vital importance were held

---

Order in Tudor England (Chicago, 1954), especially chap. i; Hans Baron, "Secularization of Wisdom and Political Humanism in the Renaissance," *JHI*, XXI (Jan.-March, 1960), 131-150, and "Moot Problems of Renaissance Interpretation: An Answer to Wallace K. Ferguson," *ibid.*, XIX (Jan., 1958), 26-34; E. F. Rice, Jr., *The Renaissance Idea of Wisdom* (Cambridge, Mass., 1958).

5. Rice, pp. 85-89.

to be ethical rather than theological, that they were set within the frame/
work of man's terrestrial life, and made subject to the power of his
reason working where practicable through the institutions of civil
government.   It was secular also in the sense that the humanist in/
tellectual found his principles in the moral philosophy of the ancients,
tempered of course by Christian tradition, and his data in history and in
the direct observation of society.

The new scholarship had to justify itself in the eyes of its practi/
tioners by means of an improved approach to education, essentially an
education for citizenship, shaped to fit the particular needs of the
governing class.   It was at this point that the contemplative ideal
became most satisfactorily combined with the requirements of the active,
especially the political life.   Since, according to the Socratic/Platonic
tradition, the man who knows what is right will always act in accord/
ance with his knowledge, learning could be identified with virtue,
and virtue expressed in the life of active citizenship.   Moreover, to
educate the governing class was in itself to contribute, perhaps a bit
indirectly but very significantly nonetheless, to the practical business of
achieving the ideal of a just and harmonious commonwealth.

The intellectual had still to make a choice between the active and
contemplative ideals.   That was what gave point to the classic argu/
ments concerning the problem of counsel as they appear in More's
Utopia and in Starkey's *Dialogue between Pole and Lupset*.   But the al/
ternatives are no longer so far apart as they once had been.   Although
in theory there remained the alternative of ascetic withdrawal, the
choice was now not between the life of pure meditation and that of
purely worldly activity—to the humanist, thought without reference to
action was as difficult to imagine, and would have been as reprehensible
if it had existed, as was action uninformed by thought—but rather
between the life of the scholar whose learning is potentially useful, but
must be applied in order to realize its potentiality, and that of the
learned man who is willing to apply it in the service of the state.   The
problem of counsel tends now to center upon the dilemma of the
"unattached intellectual," the man, wise in the ways of the world as
well as in the knowledge that comes from scholarship, the scholar not
necessarily remote from the actual life of the community, but still in/
sulated from the more corrosive effects that come from emersion in
practical politics.   Should he abandon this relatively free position in

the hope that he may be able to affect the decisions of the prince—at best a frustrating prospect, and at worst one fraught with real peril—or should he remain unattached and risk falling into utter ineffectuality? Should he wait to be asked, and run the risk of remaining in a position of impotent obscurity, or should he remain outside it all, free if he felt strongly enough to sow his ideas broadcast in the hope that the return would be manifold? These were difficult choices; and they brought the age-old problem of counsel up to date in a peculiarly compelling form.

ᔕ ᔕ ᔕ

Humanism came late to England.[6] But that was probably fortu-nate. For the result was that in one generation the English governing class was able to draw inspiration from a humanism already mature, sensitive to the fact of social change, eager to reform society in its secular as well as its religious life, and confident in the ability of men versed in the new learning to achieve such reform. Yet the process of domestication still took time. Despite the brilliance of More and the fructifying influence of Erasmus, it was Sir Thomas Elyot who, in the 1530's became the truly effective apostle of humanism to the English governing class.[7] In More's early days, the period of *Utopia*, when he enjoyed the immediate influence of Erasmus, the movement was still confined to a coterie. However serious their purposes may have been, these earlier humanists spoke for the most part to each other and in Latin. Elyot set out deliberately to bring the new studies to the broad and literate group of laymen who bore the responsibility of government.[8] And it was in the thirties that Thomas Starkey and Richard Morison brought England once more into direct contact with Italy as a result of their experience in Padua as protégés of Reginald Pole.

The humanists saw the national community in the clear—perhaps deceptively clear—light shed from the freshly interpreted store of classical example. With equal clarity they saw that it was their

6. The problem of the late arrival of humanism is discussed at the end of chap. i above.
7. Caspari, p. 79.
8. Sir Thomas Elyot, *Governor*, proheme, p. cxcii. Useful biographical material on Elyot may be found in S. E. Lehmberg, *Thomas Elyot, Tudor Humanist* (Austin, 1960). J. M. Major, *Sir Thomas Elyot and Renaissance Humanism* (Lincoln, 1964) undertake as more comprehensive interpretation of Elyot's writings, with special references to their sources. This work appeared too late to be used in the present study.

duty, as Elyot put it, "to profit thereby to my natural country; where-unto according to the sentence of Tully we be most specially bound-en."[9] As we have seen, it was a commonplace of the early Tudor pamphleteer that the man of experience should place the fruits of that experience at the disposal of his king. All the more was it a duty encumbent upon the man of learning as well as of experience to turn his talents toward that same end.

But what, exactly, did the humanist, as such, expect to contribute to the counsel of princes? He held his mission to be essentially that of promoting right thinking, and conversely, of uprooting "evil opinions and naughty persuasions." This he believed he could do by disseminating sound knowledge, thoroughly digested, of the sort that would lead to virtuous living, which, in turn, was both the end of civil society and the means of attaining it. For he held, with Plato, that virtue and knowledge are identical and that, if a man has really clear knowledge of what is right, he will always act in accordance with it.[10] As Elyot put it, virtue, as far as "governance" is concerned, is to be found in counsel. And good counsel is "the end of all doc-trine and study."[11]

This importance Elyot attaches to mind in public life is for present purposes the most remarkable aspect of his thought. Like most men of his generation, he is more convincing when he is not dealing in formal definitions. Wisdom in the abstract he defined in various ways, combining the classical and the Christian points of view. At one point he defines it as the knowledge of divine things, especially those related to the second person of the Trinity.[12] At another he gives the standard classical definition, taken from Cicero: "Sapience is the science of things divine and human."[13] It is something that comes rather from experience than from revelation.[14] It is clearly related to the virtue of prudence, which is the virtue that leads to success in government and the life of worldly activity.[15] (Had Elyot gone

9. Sir Thomas Elyot, *Of the Knowledge which Maketh a Wise Man*, ed. E. J. Howard (Oxford, Ohio, 1946), proheme.
10. *Ibid., passim.* Cf. Elyot, *Governor*, II, 378ff.
11. *Governor*, II, 433-435.
12. *Of the Knowledge*, proheme, p. 13. See also Rice, pp. 85-89 and *passim*.
13. *Governor*, II, 351.
14. *Ibid.*, II, 383, 402-403.
15. *Ibid.*, II, 354-355.

farther and identified wisdom and prudence he would have antici/
pated a tendency more typical of later Renaissance thought.)[16] Above
all, wisdom is a virtue that finds expression in counsel and, finally, in
"perfect operation."[17] For practical purposes, wisdom is something
that is essential to the welfare of man both as an individual and in his
collective capacity. In either case, it must be applied. It is in coun/
sel that the wisdom pertinent to the individual and that which is
essential to the *respublica* become one. Elyot ends the *Governor* with
a discussion of the problem of counsel, presumably as the highest
expression of that active citizenship in the principles of which he has
undertaken to instruct the prospective bearer of public responsibility.
And his final word on the subject of counsel is that it is "the last part
of moral sapience, and the beginning of sapience politic."[18]

It is important to understand just how practical Elyot's purposes
were. He was always striving to reconcile the old and the new, the ab/
stract and the concrete, the ideal and the actual. He sought to draw
upon all that was best in both the classical and the Christian tradi/
tions, and in his scheme of education for the "governor" he tried to
combine all that was still relevant in the traditional chivalric training
with the newer learning. Above all, he was concerned with the
application of wisdom in the governance of the "weal public"—not
just any "weal public," but that of England. The purpose of the
education he prescribed for the gentry was to make it possible for
them to be of use to their country. Equipped with it, "they shall
always be able to serve honorably their prince, and the public weal of
their country, principally if they confer all their doctrines to the most
noble study of moral philosophy which teacheth both virtues, manners,
and civil policy: whereby at the last we should have in this realm
sufficient of worshipful lawyers, and also a public weal equivalent to
the Greeks or Romans."[19]

This is his ideal, to make England as great as the ancient states. It
is an ideal for the realization of which, one gathers, learning and
virtue must combine in a positive way. It is not enough merely to
know what is right and act virtuously—if that had been all there was

16. Rice, especially chaps. vii/viii.
17. *Governor*, II, 358, 447. See also Caspari, p. 98.
18. *Governor*, II, 447.
19. *Ibid.*, I, 161/162; Caspari, pp. 94/95.

to it, the problem of counsel as Elyot envisaged it would have differed little from the same problem as seen by Gower or the author of *Mum and the Sothsegger*. Somehow the public weal must be not only main- tained but furthered: "where the governors of realms and cities be founden adorned with virtues, and do employ their study and mind to the public weal, as well to the augmentation thereof as to the estab- lishing and long continuance of the same: there a public weal must needs be both honorable and wealthy."[20]

            ॐ   ॐ   ॐ

The reasoning underlying this emphasis on the well-conditioned mind in public life may be seen most clearly in Starkey's *Dialogue*.[21] Elyot was by far the more influential apostle of humanism. Starkey never published his *Dialogue*—no doubt for the very good reason that he followed the logic of his argument beyond the limits acceptable in Henrician England. That does not, however, mean that it is irrelevant to the intellectual history of the period. On the contrary, the very same vigor and originality that no doubt made the manuscript un- acceptable for publication at the time makes it possible for us to see how far the most penetrating mind among the humanists of his generation was able to proceed from his classically inspired premises toward the realization of a modern concept of citizenship. It must also be remembered that Starkey was in a position to exert a great deal of personal influence among the others of that intimate group of intellectuals that was encouraged to gather about the court during the 1530's, and his thought, in turn, unquestionably reflected much that was current in that group.

In the *Dialogue*, Starkey has his interlocutors, Reginald Pole and Thomas Lupset, discuss the entire problem of civil society and govern- ment, both in its ideal form and with reference to the actualities of English life. Their primary purpose is to find the cause of England's shortcomings and, by doing so, to point the way to practical rem- edies.[22] But basic to the entire colloquium is the problem of counsel.

---

20. *Governor*, I, 28. See below, chap. xiii.

21. On Starkey's career, see S. J. Herrtage, *England in the Reign of Henry VIII: Starkey's Life and Letters*, E.E.T.S., E.S., No. 32 (1878); and Zeeveld.

22. See below, chap. viii. The biographers of Pole and Lupset generally agree that Starkey did not seriously distort the opinions he ascribed to these men. J. A. Gee, *The Life and Work of Thomas Lupset* (New Haven, 1928), p. 155; Wilhelm Schenk,

Pole, the character who gives most of the answers and through whose lips Starkey himself seems usually to have been speaking, lays the philosophical foundation, relying heavily on the identification of virtue and learning. "For," says he, "This I judge to be of sure truth: that if men knew certainly what is the true common weal, they would not so little regard it as they do. . . . For now as every man speaketh of it and hath it oft in his mouth, so few there be that esteem it . . ., which plainly cometh as (after the mind of the most wise philosopher Socrates) all other ill doth—of vain, false and corrupt opinion. For no man wittingly and willingly will do himself hurt."[23] Lupset questions whether, in fact, ignorance is the "ground of all vice"; for all know they should follow virtue but do not do so. Pole admits that the matter needs clarification, that the term "ignorance" as used by Plato and Socrates needs to be defined in relation to the more qualified wording of Aristotle.

At first glance the great philosophers seem to be at variance. According to Aristotle,

> . . . the mind of man first of itself is as a clean and pure table, wherein is nothing painted or carved, but of itself apt and indifferent to receive all manner of pictures and image. So man's mind hath first no knowledge of truth, nor first hath no manner of will whereby it is more drawn to good than to ill. But after, as opinion and sure persuasion of good and of ill groweth in by experience and learning, so ever the will conformeth and frameth himself to the knowledge before gotten; insomuch that if it be persuaded that good is ill, and ill good, then ever the will chooseth the ill and leaveth the good, according as she by opinion is instructed. And if the opinion be strong and confirmed with right reason and with right judgment, then she followeth ever that which is good; like as, contrary, when the opinion is wavering and not groundly set, then she, overcome and blinded by pleasure or some other inordinate affect [appetite], followeth the ill. So that other out of sure and certain knowledge or light and wavering opinion all the incli-

---

Reginald Pole: Cardinal of England (London, 1950), p. 36. It seems more likely, however, that Starkey placed in the mouths of his *personae* arguments by means of which he was trying to clarify his own thought.

23. *Dialogue*, p. 41.

nation of will taketh his root, which ever is framed according to the knowledge.[24]

Socrates and Plato, on the other hand, called this "light and wavering opinion," easily blinded by appetite, "plain ignorance." That is all. Between the philosophers there was a difference of words, not of meaning. The important thing is that "if man had certain and sure knowledge of the good, he would never leave it and follow the ill." For, as Aristotle held, "after the common opinion of every man," even a wavering knowledge of the good, once received, will arouse the mind to an awareness of it, so that if a man act contrary to it he will feel "a grudge in conscience." Furthermore, man's will is free to follow the good. Still, "if the reason and will be customably blinded with any persuasion, hard it is to resist thereto." Accordingly, some say man's will is not really free at all, but subject to "strong opinion" and "persuasion." This, however, is for Starkey-Pole the crux of the whole matter. For "undoubtedly diligent instruction and wise counsel may at last in long time restore the will out of such captivity, and bring it again to the old liberty."[25] And so he and Lupset put their minds to the task of circumventing ignorance and the evil that stems from it by inquiring what is the "true common weal," by searching out the shortcomings of the English commonwealth, by inquiring into the causes thereof, and devising remedies. In such a manner they hope to make their own peculiar contribution to the store of wisdom which is the essence of good counsel.

Thus the truly learned, and hence virtuous, man occupies a place of key importance in society. His position will become clearer if we examine some of the other supports upon which Starkey built the edifice of his thought, especially his concept of man's nature and his definition of civil life. The latter he defined as follows: "a politic order of a multitude conspiring together in virtue and honesty, to the which man by his nature is ordained."[26] What he meant by this "conspiring together in virtue and honesty," especially as far as the wise man is concerned, Starkey had already indicated in an earlier passage.

For hither tendeth all prudence and policy; to bring the whole country to quietness and civility, that every man, and so the

24. *Ibid.*, p. 42.
25. *Ibid.*, pp. 42-44.
26. *Ibid.*, pp. 35-36.

whole, may at the last attain to such perfection as by nature is to
the dignity of man due, which as it seemeth resteth in the communing of all such virtues as to the dignity of man are convenient,
to the profit of other, living together in civil life and politic; yea,
and, as it were, in the forming of other to their natural perfection.
For like as the body of man is then most perfect in his nature
when it hath power to gender another like thereunto, so is the
mind then most perfect when it communeth and spreadeth his
virtues abroad to the instruction of other.   Then it is most
like unto the nature of God, Whose infinite virtue is therein most
perceived, that He communeth His goodness to all creatures: to
some more, to some less, according to their nature and dignity.[27]

Civil life depends on mind, on right thinking and on sound
knowledge and the virtue that stems from it.   It is co-operative, and
its purpose is to allow man to develop his nature to its highest potential.   Man has in him a Promethean quality, a spark of the divine
creativity.   And he has the freedom of will to seek the good and flee
the bad, to strive, that is, to attain to that perfection which God has
deemed appropriate to his nature.   Human nature is therefore something that can only be expressed in terms of striving, of becoming, of
potentiality.   It is neither static nor, as in the more pessimistic statements of the Christian story, necessarily degenerative.   What is true
of man as an individual is true also of man in the "multitude."   Starkey, like More and most other English thinkers of the day, while
clearly distinguishing between the public and private capacities in
which man was required to act, made no qualitative distinction between his public and private life.   What separated him from the
medieval preoccupation with man as a moral creature was his emphasis also on man's mind and his recognition of man's constructive
potential.   As Pole declares at one point "the perfection of man
resteth in the mind and in the chief and purest part thereof, which is
reason and intelligence."[28]

It is here that the function of the learned man emerges with what to
Starkey must have been an intoxicating clarity.   The task of all men

27. *Ibid.*, p. 26.
28. *Ibid.*, p. 23. Rice illustrates a somewhat similar tendency among Continental writers
of the period to think in terms of the potentiality of the human mind: pp. 117-123.   Interesting light is cast upon the notion of "right reason" in Renaissance thought, though
unfortunately with little reference to the early Tudor humanists, in Hoopes.

in civil society is to work together for the common profit, each accord⁄
ing to his endowment. It is the special task of the intellectual to
apply his intelligence to the ordering of society after "the example of
Plato, Lycurgus, . . . [and] of Solon, by whose wisdom and
policy divers cities, countries and nations were brought to civil order
and politic life."[29]   And one judges that it is about the most sophisti⁄
cated function that man is called upon to perform.   Human nature,
moreover, and therefore society, is susceptible to constructive intel⁄
lectual leadership of this sort.   The mind of man is hindered by no
inborn obstacle from profiting by the "policy" of the philosopher.   As
we have seen in a passage already quoted, Starkey's Pole points out
that, "after the sentence of Aristotle, the mind of man first of itself is as
a clean and pure table, wherein is nothing painted or carved, but of
itself apt and indifferent to receive all manner of pictures and image."[30]
(True, he also has an inborn conscience which reacts like a Geiger
counter to impulses from that which is evil or good.   But then even
John Locke found in the mind certain natural tendencies which left
the natal *tabula* not quite *rasa*.)   Whether or not he was aware of all it
implied, Starkey had in this assumption regarding the mind of man
the key to much of modern thought.   And, indeed, the subsequent
course of the *Dialogue* would indicate that he had to some extent di⁄
gested the idea that man is what his environment makes him.   He
develops by "experience and learning."   Although he had made no
sharp distinction between the two, it is learning with which, as a scholar,
he was especially concerned—not simply "bare knowledge and learn⁄
ing without application of it to any use or profit of other," but "the
communing of high wisdom to the use of other, in which standeth
man's felicity."[31]   If it is good learning a man will be good, and so
will a society made up of his like.   If it is "pestilent," so also will be
the commonwealth.

Few characteristics separate more sharply the thought of the early
Renaissance from that of medieval England than this shifting of the
responsibility for man's welfare from the unaided, unqualified moral
nature of man to his intellectual potentialities—or, more accurately, to
the fusion of the two in the synthesis of virtue and knowledge, the

29. *Dialogue*, pp. 21⁄22.
30. *Ibid.*, p. 42.
31. *Ibid.*, p. 26.

identification of vice and "ill education."[32]   This, together with Starkey's borrowed psychology of the *"tabula rasa,"* points ahead toward the
age of the Enlightenment when philosophers again sallied forth with
new confidence to do battle with the same old dragons of ignorance
and, assuming victory, to remake man by remaking his environment.

Yet, optimistic as he was for the most part, Starkey was not un-
aware of those aspects of human nature which were antirational,
antisocial, and hence likely always to counteract the effectiveness of
even the best counsel.   He recognized that man is a natural creature,
not only by virtue of his mental processes, but also of his corporeal
make-up.   He was therefore always subject to the animal drives.
He was, indeed, free to realize the beast in him, just as he was also
free to allow that spark of the divine, which was also in him, to lead
him toward the angelic.   Starkey hoped that good learning and good
counsel would curb this appetitive side of man's nature.   But any discussion of the commonwealth which was to have any pretense to
practicality must take into account "the nature of man as it is, which
is more commonly ruled by affects [appetite or passions] than by
reason."[33]   And the intellectual who would counsel princes must also
take into consideration the realities of time and place.   These are not
always conducive to effective counsel.   But they must neither be
ignored nor taken as an excuse for silence.[34]

ഗ ഗ ഗ

Although his chronological place is with an older generation,
Thomas More really belongs with this generation of Starkey and Elyot
who shared his interests and spoke his language and undoubtedly
profited by his example.   Certainly he had already in *Utopia* given
classic expression to the humanist belief in the potential power of the
informed mind employed in the service of princes—and its limitations.
The *persona* More of the dialogue of counsel utters these familiar words:

> For whereas your Plato judgeth that weal publics shall by this
> means attain perfect felicity, either if philosophers be kings, or
> else if kings give themselves to the study of philosophy, how far
> I pray you, shall common wealths then be from this felicity,

32. *Ibid.*, p. 32.
33. *Ibid.*, p. 168.
34. *Ibid.*, p. 38.

if philosophers will vouchsafe to instruct kings with their good counsel?[35]

This, of course, is only one side of the argument. To the other we shall have to return in a moment. But it is the classic attitude of the Christian humanist as he faces the duty of his citizenship, as he contemplates his public function as an intellectual and (the two go together in his thought) as a "good man." It is his duty to "pluck out of . . . [the prince's] mind the pernicious original causes of vice and naughtiness."[36] But his is not the function simply of the moral critic or preacher. It is rather that of a man who has in him "such perfit learning, that without any experience, and again so great experience, that without any learning . . . [he] may well be any king's counsel."[37] As the penetrating analysis in Book I of England's economic and social disorders and, especially, of their close interrelation indicates, More himself was capable of applying his learning and his experience realistically to actual conditions.

It is More's realism, his ability to combine the abstract with the concrete, that permitted him to give the problem of counsel a more human form than Starkey's primarily scholarly mind was able to do. This is especially apparent when he is dealing with the limitations within which the intellectual-turned-counselor must operate. Although Starkey was not without experience at court, he did not have More's training or the experience in the actual affairs of government More obtained at an early age. Like Starkey, More was well aware of the selfishness and intransigence of human nature. "For it is not possible for all things to be well, unless all men were good. Which I think will not be yet this many years."[38] But he probably understood more clearly than Starkey how this constant factor of vice found expression in the world of affairs. Certainly he stated the problem with far greater clarity. Whereas Starkey repeats the truism that men are often blinded by "affects," and admits that the wise man who attempts to offer his advice "in time of tyranny, or in such a place where they that rule are bent only to their private weal" will surely be

35. *Utopia*, Everyman Ed., p. 34. Since it was not possible for me to make use of the new Yale edition of More's works, I decided to refer to this readily available edition.
36. *Ibid.*, pp. 34-35.
37. *Ibid.*, p. 19.
38. *Ibid.*, p. 42.

laughed at, More pictures the wise man actually trying to tell, say, the king of France to abandon his policy of conquest and attend to the welfare of his people as befits a Christian prince, or, again, rising to his feet in the council of a bankrupt monarch and announcing to him that his advisers, the men who in their mistaken loyalty have been devising subtle policies for squeezing money out of his subjects, are in fact seducing him from the path of kingly rectitude.   The picture is vivid.   In a flash of ironical, almost humorous realism the reader sees the dilemma of the humanist intellectual who would place his wis⁄ dom at the disposal of the state in the hope that he could thereby restore society to the ways of reason and Christian virtue.

Yet, if we are to interpret More's dialogue of counsel in terms of the decision he was earnestly debating in his own mind when he wrote the *Utopia*, the decision to leave his unattached position and enter the actual service of Henry VIII,[39] the message of the dialogue is again one of reason and realism—the realism of the practical idealist.   The dilemma cannot be completely resolved.   Human nature, being only in part governable by reason, will not permit a wholly reasonable solution.   Kings and princes are as human as the rest.   "Evil opinions and naughty persuasions can not be utterly and quite plucked out of their hearts."   Nor is the problem merely that of the old Adam in man.   Vice is social in its context and to some extent in its origin. "You cannot remedy as you would vices which use and custom hath confirmed."   The wise man must therefore make some compromise with the facts, both of human nature and history, if he is to be of any real use to his country.   "You must not leave and forsake the com⁄ mon wealth: you must not forsake the ship in a tempest because you can not rule and keep down the winds."   He must proceed tact⁄ fully, not trying to force "new and strange informations" upon people who are unprepared to appropriate them.   He must not run head⁄on into the prejudices and vested interests at court, but must "with a crafty wile and a subtle train study and endeavor . . . to handle the matter wittily and handsomely for the purpose, and that which you can not turn to good, so to order it that it be not very bad."   Yet this involved a compromise of moral principle.   It was not merely a matter of practical politics.   "Naughty counsels must be openly allowed and

39. For a penetrating discussion of More's personal problem, see J. H. Hexter, *More's Utopia: The Biography of an Idea* (London, 1952).

very pestilent decrees must be approved."[40] And all this business of "crafty wile" reeked of that very Machiavellian statecraft against which More seems to have aimed the greater part of this first book of *Utopia*.

Starkey also saw the need for compromise. The public-spirited intellectual must allow for the exigencies of time and place. If he tries to preach justice to a tyrant or zeal for the common weal to those who think only of their private interests, he will surely be ridiculed, perhaps even suffer exile or death. "It is therefore," says Pole, "no small difference in what time and place a wise man is born."[41] But this is a compromise of mere prudence rather than of conscience. It is merely a recognition of historical contingency, and one Lupset is not willing to accept as a sufficient reason for wise men to remain in retirement. If they look too long for the right time and place, if they look "for Plato's common weal; in such expectation they spend their life, as they think, with great politic wisdom, but indeed with great frantic folly."[42] All he will allow is the need for realism: "follow not the example of Plato, whose order of common weal no people upon earth to this day could ever attain," but rather "look you to the nature of our country, to the manner of our people, not without respect both of time and of place."[43] Only in this way can the advice offered be useful to the king—who, so it happens, is eager to put good counsel to effect![44]

Starkey's approach to the dilemma of the wise man in public life is thus by way of historical realism, and it is made with the good of the state primarily in mind. That of More involved a clearer awareness of the moral issue and of the cost of effective counsel in terms of personal integrity. But they both recognized, as those who viewed society from the morally absolute vantage point of the pulpit failed to do, the fact that the affairs of public concern could not wait for men to become virtuous. Indeed, Starkey makes it clear that a virtuous society can only be brought into being by "prudence and policy," by, that is, the application of the informed and experienced mind to the weal public. Like old Sir John Fortescue,[45] who, however, arrived at the same

40. For all of the above argument, see *Utopia*, pp. 41-43.
41. *Dialogue*, p. 41.
42. *Ibid.*, p. 38.
43. *Ibid.*, p. 40. See also below, chap. xiii.
44. *Ibid.*, p. 38.
45. See above, chap. v.

conclusion by way of an indigenous realism unassisted by the imported learning of the humanists, More and Starkey were willing to
take the fact of man's perversity as given, indeed as virtually constant,
and turned their minds to the practical problem of providing as sensible counsel as, in any concrete situation, could reasonably be expected to succeed.

ᔿ ᔿ ᔿ

The problem of counsel continued for most Tudor Englishmen
to be the core of the problem of government.   The two most remarkable pieces of political literature written during the reign of Henry
VIII, More's *Utopia* and Starkey's *Dialogue*,[46] both turn on the problem.   Indeed it seems to have preoccupied them almost to the exclusion
of any real discussion of political theory.   Both More and Starkey were
willing enough to accept the existing system of government.[47]   Both
were well aware of the dangers and at best the uncertainties inherent
in hereditary monarchy, especially when the monarch enjoyed a strong,
if by no means legally despotic, power.   But neither apparently felt
that there was anything so bad in the English system of government
that could not be remedied by informed and intelligent counsel,
conscientiously applied.   And there was no doubt in their minds
that they, as men of learning, experience, and presumably of wisdom
and virtue, bore a special responsibility to the commonwealth.   In
this they spoke for the generality of their fellow humanists.

The question remained for the intellectual who would discharge
this duty to the commonweal, in what capacity could he most effectively
do so? The early humanists were as a rule ready enough to live up to
their professed ideal by entering the direct service of the court.   More
found the decision difficult and waited to be asked.   Others, especially such less illustrious and self-supporting personages as Morison
and Starkey, who needed patronage as well as an opportunity to serve
the community, sought employment at court.   Even when their
decision was influenced by monetary considerations, however, there
is little reason for doubting the sincerity of these scholars' devotion to
the commonwealth of England.

46. J. W. Allen, *A History of Political Thought in the Sixteenth Century* (London, 1928),
p. 143.

47. *Dialogue*, p. 190; *Utopia*, p. 19.

This is especially true of Starkey who seems throughout his brief but turbulent career at court to have maintained a high degree of personal integrity.   In 1534 he commended himself to Cromwell in words that remained consistent with what we know of his subsequent career. He had, he wrote in what amounts to a comprehensive apologia for the ideal of the scholar-counselor, engaged in a wide variety of studies, from classical languages and philosophy to the Scriptures, and finally, "because my purpose then was to live in a politic life," the civil law; and in all these studies he had kept always before his eyes "this end and purpose at the last here in this commonalty where I am brought forth and born to employ them to some use."   Whatever he had learned, with God's help, he hoped to "apply it to the service of our prince, and thereby reckon myself to attain a great part of my felicity."[48]

This direct participation of the wise man in the service of the national monarchy was not, however, the only capacity in which the intellectual could serve, a fact to which the many pertinent pamphlets written by men who remained outside the formal structure of govern‑ ment attest.   The articulate citizen might contribute independently to that reservoir of information and constructive criticism upon which the prince could profitably draw as a supplement to the advice of his official councilors.   Although Starkey was being retained by the government when he wrote his *Dialogue*, he wrote it, as it were, on his own time; and the interlocutors speak as though they both were in‑ dependent citizens, simply seizing an especially opportune moment to discuss the affairs of the country.   After admitting that he could not justify remaining remote from such problems, Pole agrees to "devise" something "touching the order of our country and common‑ weal; to the which purpose the time exhorteth us, seeing that now our most noble prince assembled his parliament and most wise counsel for the reformation of this his common weal."[49]   Here again we find the idea of counsel being expressed in terms of extra‑parliamentary, unofficial discussion, the kind of thing that is foreshadowed, however dimly, by the author of *Mum and the Sothsegger*.[50]

The real problem Starkey was wrestling with in this preliminary section of the *Dialogue* remains, however, that of getting Pole, the

48. Herrtage, p. x.
49. *Dialogue*, p. 39.
50. See above, chap. iii.

personification of the intellectual, to admit his duty to serve the prince more directly. Indeed, it is service in some official capacity that prompted both of the classic discussions of the problem of counsel in early Tudor England. Starkey was actually concerned to get Pole into the service of Henry VIII,[51] a project which looks less likely in hindsight than it did in prospect. And More was debating in his own mind the choice that he himself must soon make whether to remain in a more or less independent position or to accede to the pressure being put on him by the king to enter his official circle.

In either case the issue is the same, and in either the element of choice becomes somewhat academic. But essentially the debate is the old one between the *vita activa* and the *vita contemplativa*, and in both dialogues it is resolved in favor of the active life—but with a curious reverse twist. Pole, the protagonist of the contemplative ideal in Starkey's *Dialogue*, gives in and admits freely that he should enter the king's service, the only question being whether he should wait to be called. The historical Pole, while not shunning active politics, refused to serve Henry VIII. Teh spokesman for the unattached intellectual in More's dialogue of counsel refuses to make the conces' sions that Starkey's Pole made and the conversation ends inconclusive' ly, yet More himself decided to abandon his independence and accept public office. It was, of course, a conclusion that emerges from be' tween the lines of that earnest discussion of England's actual problems in Book I, a discussion that belies the cynicism of Hythloday's remarks. In both dialogues the reader is left with no real doubt but that the life of contemplation does not in itself fulfil the obligation of the citizen to serve the commonwealth in whatever capacity he can. That ob' ligation must be fulfilled in a life of active citizenship. Starkey states the problem clearly and succinctly:

> . . . this is the mark that every man, prudent and politic
> ought to shoot at: first to make himself perfit, with all virtues
> garnishing his mind, and then to commune the same perfection
> to other. For little availeth virtue that is not published abroad
> to the profit of other; little availeth treasure closed in coffers which
> never is communed to the succor of other.[52]

51. Herrtage, p. xxii.
52. *Dialogue*, p. 24; cf. pp. 35'36.

The reader will remember that virtue, in humanistic thought, was the end product of knowledge.

Yet the antithesis between the active life and the contemplative is not absolute.   In fact the line dividing the two in these classic state, ments of the problem of counsel becomes, on closer observation, in, creasingly blurred.   Traditionally it had divided the life of the world from the life of religious meditation or of scholastic speculation.   It seems to have been in just such terms that Stephen Hawes, writing only a few years before More, had the central character of his allegory of the life of the knightly class make the initial decision of his career.[53]   In More's work and in Starkey's this is no longer true.   The alternatives are much closer together—so close indeed that the difference between them becomes less a matter of mutual exclusion than of emphasis.   For both men felt that even the most philosophical studies formed an essential part of the education and training of the wise man, considered in his capacity as citizen.

It is true that Lupset finds it necessary to shame Pole out of "the sweetness of his studies" where he was "drowned in the pleasure of letters and private studies" and to call to his attention his country's cries for help.[54]   But Pole manages to justify a certain amount of speculative endeavor on the reasonable ground that it is necessary for a man to know himself before he can govern others.[55]   It is true also that Pole pleads the precedent of "old and ancient philosophers" who believed that "knowledge of God, of nature, and of all the works thereof should be the end of man's life, and the chief point therein of all men to be looked unto."[56]   But Lupset has him in a corner forth, with by means of another of those practical, rational compromises the English humanist was so adept at making.   "Philosophy," he says, "as all men know, is far to be preferred above all worldly riches." Yet it is better "as Aristotle saith, for a man being in poverty rather to procure some riches than high philosophy."   And anyway, "meddling with the causes of the common weal" is the necessary means to the attainment of this more perfect life of the mind.[57]   In other words,

---

53. Ferguson, *Indian Summer*, p. 62.   For a more extended analysis of Hawes's work, see *ibid.*, chaps. ii and vi.

54. *Dialogue*, p. 22.

55. *Ibid.*, p. 23.

56. *Ibid.*, p. 23.

57. *Ibid.*, pp. 25,26.

the lives of the mind and of affairs are interdependent. And it would seem that it is the pleasure that Pole is deriving from his "private studies," as well as his reluctance to turn his philosophy to more immediate practical ends, that prompts Lupset's criticisms.

The antithesis is even less clear in *Utopia*. The imaginary state of the Utopians embodies the ideal of a government of philosophers and of a citizenship based on a natural wisdom, the product of studies that are both speculative and practical. And surely a man so experienced as Hythloday, and one withal so superlatively articulate, would not have finished his days in complete seclusion and utter silence, however distasteful he might have found a more active life at court. He preferred, he said, in answer to those who would have him enter some prince's service, "to live at liberty after my own mind and pleasure;" but we may be permitted to remark that he spent a long day on a bench of green turves telling of his experiences and giving to the not undistinguished company present the benefit of his highly critical views on specifically English problems. Such freedom to speak his mind, such intellectual independence, More himself no doubt found only too attractive. In the context of Renaissance life the obligations of citizenship could be discharged through public discussion as well as by service at court, if not perhaps with the promise of so immediate an effect. To an increasing extent the career of the intellectual who would apply his learning and experience to what Starkey called "the maintenance and setting forward of the true common weal," was becoming that of the pamphleteer.

ᖇ ᖇ ᖇ

The point was made at the beginning of the chapter, and I am sure it has become more and more apparent ever since, that the humanists approached their ideal of citizenship by way of education. If knowledge really did lead to virtue and virtue to a patriotic and active citizenship, then it mattered a great deal what knowledge was imparted and to whom. Now this is not the place to retell the story of Tudor education. It has already been told fully and at times brilliantly.[58] Since, however, it constituted such an important part of the humanist program and of the humanist outlook on public life, the new education can hardly be ignored. But I shall confine the discussion to those

58. See especially Caspari.

aspects of early Tudor education most pertinent to the problems of counsel and articulate citizenship.

The new education grew out of both philosophical and practical considerations, if indeed the two can be separated except for purposes of analysis, and thrived in a new social setting to which it was well fitted. On the philosophical side it grew out of the profound, though often naïvely optimistic belief of the humanists in the educability of man. It was an idea propagated widely in England during the earlier years of the century by Erasmus, and it came to be shared by most of the later generations of humanists. Something of its character we have already seen in Starkey's thought. It involved a strong belief in the importance of man's environment as the source of those influences which shape his mind, and in the concomitant belief that there is nothing innate in man, no tendency toward evil, for instance, so ineluctable that it cannot be overcome by education. As Erasmus put it, with characteristic exaggeration, "*homines non nascuntur sed finguntur.*"[59] It involved also a closely related belief in the rational nature of man and in his ability to shape his own environment through education and constructive criticism, though the latter carried with it implications of which the Tudor humanist was not always fully aware. Indeed only two things separated this Erasmian faith in education from the eighteenth-century idea of perfectability—also nourished as a matter of faith—namely the unwillingness of the humanists to bypass their Christian heritage in favor of a purely secular ideal of rational reform, and their failure to appreciate the dynamic implications inherent in their vaguely environmentalist position. Yet, vague as it was, even in the writings of a man of Starkey's capabilities, the idea carried with it the hint of change, the heady suggestion of an indefinitely continuous approximation to a state of perfection in this world.

The practical importance of a new education lay in the need for a governing class capable of adding the more complex duties of civil government and intelligent counsel (which had in fact for some time been taxing the limited intellectual resources of the English gentry) to the primarily protective, basically military function originally assigned to the knight. It was a commonplace of humanistic criticism to berate the nobility and gentry for their indifference to education.

59. Quoted in *ibid.*, p. 35.

These strictures were no doubt exaggerated by men whose own im-portance derived from their putative ability to remedy the situation.[60] But there were doubtless a good many among the governing class as a whole who were still being raised in the tradition of chivalric ap-prenticeship to which the old barbarian in Richard Pace's well-known story referred: "it becomes the sons of gentlemen to blow the horn nicely, to hunt skillfully, and elegantly carry and train a hawk. But the study of letters should be left to the sons of rustics."[61] Pace, how-ever, was able to have the last word, and on grounds which were coming to be more clearly understood as utilitarian. He answered, in effect, that, should a foreign ambassador come to the king, the learned sons of rustics would be called upon to answer him, the gentle-man's sons being able only to blow his horn.

A humanistic education had in fact been recognized as a pre-requisite for diplomatic service since the mid-fifteenth century. To a demand for this largely rhetorical skill was now being added the de-mand on the part of the government for men capable of using their knowledge of ancient history and philosophy as a supplement to the experience they were able to obtain in their own careers, and thus to contribute effectively to that reservoir of intelligence and informed common sense without which no government could properly function—especially one that depended to such an extent as did the English on its gentry and burgesses for local administration. If members of the governing class were not able to supply this demand, there were plenty of yeomen's sons and tradesmen's sons, men like Hugh Latimer and Thomas Cromwell, who could and would. And so it was partly in self-preservation that the English aristocracy took to a bookish edu-cation. It was becoming increasingly apparent that the society of hierarchy and aristocratic leadership depended on the ability of the aristocracy to lead, and that leadership required a new and broader education. English society was, we know, in a state of flux. As Sir Thomas Smith pointed out, gentlemen in England were made good cheap.[62] But even the new men adhered with anxious insistence

60. J. H. Hexter, "The Education of the Aristocracy in the Renaissance," *JMH*, XXII (March, 1950), 1-20. A good example of the standard criticism may be found in *Dialogue*, p. 123.

61. Ferguson, *Indian Summer*, p. 216. See also Caspari, pp. 136-137. Cf. [Sir Richard Morison], *A Remedy for Sedition*, ed. E. M. Cox (London, 1933), p. 55.

62. *De Republica Anglorum*, Book I, chap. xx.

to the due of birth and believed heartily in the importance of order and degree. By the early years of Elizabeth's reign there were signs that the government itself was trying to promote a better education for the governing class, if only to prevent the undue influx of new men to places of privilege and responsibility. And during the latter part of the century members of that broad class seem to have entered the universities to an extent that amounted to an invasion of those once exclusively clerkly halls.[63]

The new education thus involved a new social ideal. The knight was giving way to the gentleman. And the gentleman was being required to accept not only those responsibilities that traditionally devolved upon the knight, but also many of those that had hitherto been largely, though decreasingly, the preserve of the clergy. He must now exert an intellectual as well as a physical force in society. He must not only see that justice is done, but take part in the shaping of the laws and in their administration. He must not only be able to defend, if need be, the rest of society, he must also be able to share, if asked, in the formulation and elucidation of policy. And as a preparation for his new and expanded role in society the "gentleman-governor" must have a broad and bookish education in addition to one that retained such of the military and courtly values of chivalry as were still pertinent to his life.

The humanists were quite aware of this change in social ideals. They tended, however, to be divided in their loyalties. On the one hand they liked to think that status, dignity, and true nobility should come from virtue and accomplishments rather than from birth or inherited wealth.[64] On the other they held to the conservative ideal of a society of strict hierarchy. As scholars they could hardly help but see, like More's Utopians, that reason and the protean quality of human nature knew no class. As Renaissance Englishmen, they found it difficult, often impossible, not to recognize the customary social divisions and to fear an equalitarianism that they identified with

63. Hexter, "Education of the Aristocracy." Contemporary attitudes toward the education of the governing class are exemplified in the following: Roger Ascham, *English Works*, ed. W. A. Wright (Cambridge, 1904), I, 69; Sir Humphrey Gilbert, *Queene Eliazbethes Achademy*, ed. F. J. Furnivall, E.E.T.S., E.S., No. 8 (1869); William Cecil, *Considerations Delivered to the Parliament, 1559*, in Tawney and Power, I, 325-330.

64. The somewhat hesitant treatment of the Fulgens and Lucres theme in England is an early, but revealing example. See above, chap. i, and Baron, *Crisis*, pp. 625-628.

the wildest religious radicalism and saw periodically erupting in actual unrest, even rebellion.[65] As we shall see in later chapters, much of their thought on public affairs was determined by the constant danger of sedition. With the Pilgrimage of Grace in mind, Richard Morison argued that a properly educated aristocracy was in itself a powerful safeguard against sedition. "For as noble men be, so their servants are."[66] Moreover, as residual legatees of medieval culture, the human, ists still envisaged the "commonwealth," like the universe of which it constituted the microcosmic reflection, as hierarchically ordered. As a matter of fact, of course, the class structure was not so clearly marked in England, nor so nearly static as all this. But the larger fact remains that, in England as in other countries north of the Alps—and in Italy by the sixteenth century—the humanist tradition was profoundly con, ditioned by its association with a courtly, basically aristocratic society.

No doubt many observers recognized that the governing class was in fact a loosely knit affair, and, while conceiving the problem of education for citizenship mainly in terms of that class, were still more concerned to bring intelligence to bear on the affairs of the common, wealth. Cromwell enjoined the clergy of England in 1536 to see to it that all children should be set either to learning or a trade, the former so that "when need shall be" they may "profit the commonwealth with their counsel and wisdom."[67] Perhaps Cromwell had a somewhat more realistic attitude than his more aristocratic colleagues toward a social system in which he himself had risen from relatively low estate to the highest (and, for such as he, most treacherous) pinnacle of public responsibility. But the likelihood is that he was simply looking at the practical problem of assuring the state the necessary stockpile of intellect. Latimer lamented the tendency of the sons of rich and noble families to flock to the universities, thereby making it harder for yeomen to keep their sons at college, as his own father had done. Latimer's concern was, of course, with providing preachers, not gover, nors.[68] By contrast, the author of the *Discourse of the Common Weal* was very much interested in securing good governance through good counsel, and seems not to have cared very much where the counsel

65. See below, chaps. viii and ix.
66. *Remedy for Sedition*, p. 36.
67. Quoted in Zeeveld, pp. 194-195.
68. A. G. Chester, *Hugh Latimer: Apostle to the English* (Philadelphia, 1954), pp. 177-179.

came from.[69]   His Doctor is more disturbed over the possibility that half-educated men, who do not even know their own shortcomings, may reach positions of public responsibility than that those positions should be filled by men of the wrong social order.[70]   Roger Ascham wrote the *Schoolmaster*, so he said, in order that "the youth in England, specially gentlemen, and namely nobility," should receive the kind of education that would allow them to serve their prince and their country with wisdom, learning, and virtue.[71]   But he also tells us that he decided to use English, not because it was a very good language in itself, but because it would allow him to reach "the gentlemen and yeomen of England."

For the most part, however, the Tudor humanists looked with suspicion, if not horror, on the prospect of an indiscriminate education of all classes for a vocation of leadership that they believed still to be peculiarly fitting for the aristocracy and gentry and those already in a position of wealth and influence.   It was quite specifically to the nobility and gentry, whose sons "hereafter may be deemed worthy to be governors,"[72] that Elyot appealed in the interests of a better education. And his ideal of an elite of both learning and birth was typical and doubtless influential.   Starkey was so concerned for the education of the governing class that he proposed an academy to be organized for the specific needs of the aristocracy.   This institution would combine humanistic learning and chivalric exercises.   And it would become "the fountain of all civility and politic rule."[73]   A similar project was proposed in considerably greater detail several years later by Sir Humphrey Gilbert.[74]

Humanists of Elyot and Starkey's sort were not, of course, alone in their awareness of the close relationship between education and citizenship.   In their way, the reformers felt just as strongly. (We must include in this category many whose own background was humanistic, yet whose concerns had become primarily theological and evangelistic.)[75]   Yet theirs was a different way.   To such men as

69. *Discourse*, p. 11.
70. *Ibid.*, p. 30.
71. *English Works*, I, 63.
72. *Governor*, I, proheme, cxcii.
73. *Dialogue*, p. 169.
74. See above, n. 63.
75. An enlightening treatment of the relation between scholarship and religious reform

Latimer, Cranmer, Hooper, Lever, and Becon the good citizen is the godly citizen, for the state to which he owes allegiance is basically theocratic, its institutions the means through which the will of God finds temporal expression. Like the medieval commentators, they believed that the welfare of the secular community depended on the righteousness of the individuals that composed it—or, more accurately, they made little distinction between the secular life and the spiritual, for both depended in the long run on the same theologically sanctioned morality, and the same teleological interpretation of human endeavor as a pilgrimage toward salvation. Like them, too, they believed that the preacher performs a function essential alike to the secular and to the spiritual welfare of the community. His broadly based counsel it is that must underlie the more specific counsel upon which good governance rests. Where they differed was in the importance the reformers attached to reading the Bible and in their emphasis on a ministry capable not merely of moral criticism and exhortation, but of interpreting the Word of God to those who had presumably already read it.

On both accounts, they found it necessary to stress education. They hoped that not the least of the good results to be expected from the dissolution of the chantries and monastic houses would be the endowment of education. In this they were bitterly disappointed, and by the mid-century they were sharp in their criticism of what they believed to be the shameful miscarriage of an otherwise godly reformation.[76] All agreed that a knowledge of the Scriptures would lead to the general welfare. Nothing, Hooper declared, is more profitable to the commonwealth than the wide dissemination of such knowledge, for "then shall justice, peace, and concord reign, the door of idolatry be shut up, by the which hath entered all evil."[77] The crux of the problem, however, was less the basic minimum education for the Christian citizen himself than the higher education of the preacher who interpreted the Word and served as the voice of conscience for both public and private affairs. It was, indeed, more important to train good preachers than to educate the gentry in secular learning.[78]

may be found in H. C. Porter, *Reformation and Reaction in Tudor Cambridge* (Cambridge, 1958).

76. See below, chap. ix.

77. *Early Writings*, ed. S. Carr, Parker Society (Cambridge, 1852), p. 435.

78. E.g., *A Supplication to our most Soveraigne Lorde Kynge Henry the Eyght* (1544), ed.

The reformers generally regarded citizenship in the light of Christian virtue, expressed in the service of a theocratic society rather than of a classically inspired, more distinctly secular virtue, expressed in the service of the national state.   To them the prophetic figure of Jonah warning the people of Nineveh to repent of their sins or suffer the plagues of divine punishment had largely replaced the rational, thoroughly secular image of Cicero addressing the citizens of Rome in the interests of the *respublica.*

ꙍ   ꙍ   ꙍ

Although, after its slow beginnings in the fifteenth century, the new learning found brilliant expression in the small circle of Erasmian humanists, it is Sir Thomas Elyot who deserves principal credit for interpreting its meaning to the governing class as a whole.   More, it is true, had demonstrated in *Utopia* how classical learning could be applied with clarifying effect to contemporary conditions.   Concerned as he was to perpetuate the essential values of the Christian tradition, he had also showed how far a people like his Utopians could conceivably go without the Christian revelation and with no other cultural aid but the classics.   But it was Elyot nevertheless who undertook systematically to instruct the gentleman-governor.   Far from exciting, suffering in all but the utilitarian tests by comparison with its more sophisticated counterpart, the *Cortegiano* of Castiglione, Elyot's *Governor* remains a landmark in the history of "applied" humanism in England.

Elyot was well qualified for the task he attempted.   He had been a friend of More and had inherited the mantle of Erasmian humanism. Yet he was closer to those later "commonwealth men" who, by turning their classically inspired minds to the investigation of specific problems of English life, made the common characteristic of a large group of commentators what had in More been exceptional and confined largely to his early period.   Born into the landed class, he knew at first hand the duties and headaches likely to fall to the lot of the young gentleman.   He had himself served as justice of the peace and sheriff as well as in the central administration.   He knew what it was for a knight to be called upon to serve as "governor." Although, like More, he had earned the order of knighthood in the civil service of the state, he was born to a class in whose mind the memory of the chivalric past was still green and for whom the chivalric discipline still retained a certain value. And he was conversant with the Italian literature of courtly conduct and learning. He strove accordingly, in *The Book named Governor* (1531), to outline for the specific purposes of the English gentry an ideal of education that would combine whatever of value there remained in the chivalric tradition with whatever could be im- ported without damage from contemporaneous Italy, and to base it all solidly on the values of a Christian humanism.[79]

His purpose was thus strongly utilitarian, and in this respect he reflected a characteristic deeply ingrained in the thought of the early Tudor humanists, considered as a group. In this respect also it is important to notice that the essential link between humanistic learning and practical citizenship lay in the emphasis he and his fellow human- ists placed on experience. It was fortunate that the generation of Elyot and Starkey came at a time when the new learning had lost much of its academic and imitative character. They were therefore able to begin at a relatively early stage in their own development the application of classical precept and example to those problems of con- temporary life which tended to preoccupy them. In dealing with those problems they were forced to rely to a greater extent than their predecessors on experience, on what they themselves could observe and by analytical criticism understand. Naturally enough, therefore, they recognized in a classical education a means of extending this more immediate experience. The ideal citizen-counselor—More's Hythlo- day, if he only would, or the Pole of Starkey's *Dialogue*—is a man who combines both personal experience in the ways of the world and the extended experience that comes from a study of the thought and action of earlier ages.

ᴄ⌒ ᴄ⌒ ᴄ⌒

For this, if for no other reason,[80] the pamphlet literature of the early English Renaissance reveals a deepening appreciation of the uses of history. At this point, indeed, the scholarship of the humanists made its most fruitful alliance with their sense of active citizenship. Though

79. See Caspari, chap. iv; Ferguson, *Indian Summer*, pp. 218-221.
80. See below, chap. xiii.

not historians and not as a rule much interested in historiography as such (no scholar appeared for the next half-century to carry on the critical historiography of Polydore Vergil or that exemplified in More's *History of Richard III*), the early Tudor humanists were very aware of the usefulness of history, considered as experience. They never tired of quoting the Ciceronian definition of history. Elyot's version is typical: "history [is] the witness of times, mistress of life, the life of remembrance, of truth the light, and messager of antiquity."[81] And in his *Report of Germany*, an eyewitness account of German political history from 1550 to 1553, Roger Ascham demonstrated the ability of the humanist scholar to subject contemporary experience to searching analysis. Very probably meant for the ears of the king's policy advisers, the *Report* stands as something of a milestone in the history not only of Tudor historiography but of the scholar-counselor's pragmatic approach to history.[82]

The Tudor humanists did not, of course, introduce the idea into England, nor was humanism apparently a prerequisite to its growth. The confusing and depressing events which followed the close of the Hundred Years' War were in themselves enough to send the patriotic and realistic observer in search of something that might point the way out of the wilderness to which English public life appeared to be reverting. Fortescue,[83] to whom the learning of humanism seems to have been a closed book, examined the recent history of the national states with a realism that recalls the memoires of his equally non-humanist contemporary, Philippe de Commines, and with a similar confidence that such reflections would illuminate the present. Humanism did, however, create an atmosphere very conducive to the development of the historical sense, and the humanists seem to have entertained a more than ordinarily high regard for the power of historical study artificially to extend the experience of the individual and to serve as an inexhaustible mine of example upon which the more practical teachings of moral philosophy might be firmly founded.

"Experience whereof cometh wisdom," Elyot wrote, "is in two manner of wise." The one is the deeds of men which according to their success or failure prompt us to emulation or avoidance. "The

81. *Governor*, I, 82.
82. See Ryan, chap. viii, for a discussion of the place of the *Report* in both respects.
83. See above, chap. v.

knowledge of this Experience is called Example, and is expressed in history."[84] It encompasses the entire recorded past. It may be found in the ancient historians, in the Old and New Testaments, both of which are primarily historical, and, on occasion, the histories of recent events.[85] The other kind of experience is that "which is in our proper persons,"[86] and is gained by a "governor" in the actual discharge of his duties and in travel and general observation.[87] This experience is the means "whereby knowledge is ratified and (as I might say) consolidate."[88]

There were apparently those who did not appreciate this appeal to historical experience. Elyot found it necessary to defend history at some length against the charge that it was all "leasings and fantasies." Such critics "in contemning histories . . . frustrate Experience." For "there is no doctrine, be it divine or human, that is not either all expressed in history or at the least mixed with history."[89] The critics to whom Elyot referred were doubtless those who found it unsettling and perhaps dangerous to go beyond the data of Holy Writ, and it was probably for their benefit that he took pains to point out how essentially historical most of the Bible really was.

ⵦ ⵦ ⵦ

The entire program of the humanists seems, indeed, to have needed some defense. Extreme Protestants tended to proceed from their initial emphasis on faith and on the authority of the Scriptures to an anti-intellectual position in which reason counted for little and the ability to read the English Bible was all the education the average man needed. On the other extreme, barbarians of a more secular turn of mind, men like Pace's old nobleman and his horn-blowing son, or like the Capper in the *Discourse of the Common Weal*, could not yet understand the utility, large but indirect, of classical learning. How useful such knowledge seemed to the citizen, either in his private or his public capacities, depended pretty much on the amount of it he had. The young gentleman was beginning to see how learning could

84. *Governor*, II, 383-390.
85. *Ibid.*, II, 385-401; cf. I, 21-22.
86. *Ibid.*, II, 402.
87. *Ibid.*, II, 402-417.
88. *Ibid.*, II, 403.
89. *Ibid.*, II, 385.

lead to political advancement, and the chivalric prejudice against it was rapidly dying. But, then as now, the educator faced a dilemma. Unless a man were educated to some extent in the "useless" arts he would not be likely to appreciate how useful they could be, and unless he appreciated their usefulness he was not likely to study them.

A remarkably clear, concise, and utilitarian defense of the human, istic education as a preparation for citizenship is contained in the *Discourse*. It all comes out in answer to the Capper's attack on the utility of higher learning. That crusty artificer the author uses as the type of the aggressively ignorant, the "practical" man whose mind is closed like a fist about a notion of practicality narrowed to fit his grasp. He stands for an anti-intellectualism no doubt widespread among those of the common folk who had come to consider the English Bible as a sufficient education and who distrusted any public discussion of basic issues. He would, he said, have men trained mainly in languages so that they could communicate with neighboring countries (about the trade in English caps?) and read the Bible in English.[90] Beyond that, learning merely leads to controversy and controversy to confusion and sedition.

> . . . for the devil a whit the good do ye with your studies,
> but set men together by the ears. Some with this opinion and
> some with that, some holding this way and some that way, and
> some an other, and so stiffly as though the truth must be as they
> say that have the upper hand in contention. And this con-
> tention is not the least cause of these uproars of the people; some
> holding of one learning and some holding of the other. In my
> mind it made no matter if there were no learned men at all.[91]

This, of course, serves both as challenge to the Doctor and straw man for him to demolish, and so he launches into the only lengthy digression in that otherwise closely argued discussion of England's economic problems. Yet in a sense it is not a digression at all, be, cause Smith (if it was he who wrote the book) really believed in the efficacy of learning, and especially of learning which is set to the task of erecting an intellectual scaffolding for the builder of national policy. He had, in other words, to establish the credentials of the learned man

90. *Discourse*, p. 22.
91. *Ibid.*, p. 21.

as a counselor of princes before he could allow him to complete his analysis of the economic system.

In the best humanist manner the Doctor appeals to ancient history and also to that of England itself in support of the position, equally typical, that "an empire or a kingdom is not so much won or kept by the manhood or force of men as it is by wisdom and policy, which is gotten chiefly by learning." What that learning should be becomes quickly apparent. It is that which allows the individual man to extend his experience beyond what he himself could amass through his own activity and observation: "let that then be set for a sure ground, that experience doth further wisdom, and take it as it were the father of wisdom, and memory to be the mother."[92]

This experience, extended by memory, is a many-faceted thing. Nothing human is alien to it, and it goes well beyond mere *res gestae*. But there are some things more than others that make the truly learned man an effective citizen.

> Tell me what counsel can be perfect, what common weal can be ordered and upright, where none of the rulers or counsellors have studied any philosophy, and specially that part that teacheth of manners? . . . What part of the common weal is neglected by moral philosophy? Doth it not teach first how every man should govern him self honestly and profitably? Secondly, how he should guide his family wisely; and thirdly, it showeth how a City or Realm or any other common weal should be well ordered and governed, both in time of peace and also in war. What common weal can be without either a governor, or counsellor, that should be expert in this kind of learning? This concerneth the point that we now talk of; if men expert in this science were counselled and followed, the common weal should be ordered as few should have cause to complain. Therefore Plato, that divine philosopher, said that happy is that common weal where either the king is a philosopher, or where a philosopher is the king.[93]

Seldom in early Tudor literature was the humanist faith in the uses of learning more concisely or yet more eloquently stated. Much of

92. *Ibid.*, p. 24.
93. *Ibid.*, p. 28.

it reads like a precise of the pertinent chapters in Elyot's *Governor*.[94] Perhaps, indeed, by this time (ca. 1549) Elyot's own arguments, though themselves scarcely original, had become the common property of English intellectuals. But it is a statement unusual not only in its vigor but also in the utilitarian nature of its immediate context.

And it seems to have been provoked by what Smith felt to be dangerous tendencies at work in the England of his day undermining sound learning. There is that pernicious notion, for example, the one voiced by the Capper, that a knowledge of languages is sufficient as a basic education. This, he says in effect, is the fallacy of the half-educated, the error of those men "that esteem the bark more than the tree, and the shell more than the kernel."[95] Then there is the economic and social factor. Men "see no preferment ordained for learned men, nor yet any honor or estimation given them, like as hath been in times past." Smith may here be harking back to the unprecedented and, in its way, temporary attention paid by Cromwell to the humanist scholars. And he is no doubt indulging in the self-pity to which those trained in the humanities have ever since been prone, for he was writing at a time when he and his fellows were expressing themselves with unusual freedom. Be that as it may, his testimony indicates that the learned man of the mid-century had reason to feel that his qualifications in public life were being neglected. More than that, should he take part in public discussion, he was likely to incur grave danger. "Marry," exclaims the good Doctor, in a tone that rings of personal experience, "have you not seen how learned men have been put to trouble of late, within these xii or xvi years, and all for declaring their opinions in things that have risen in controversy?" And these, too, the "singularest fellows of both parties." No wonder, then, that a man "will rather put his child to that science, that may bring him to better fruit than this, or what scholar shall have any courage to study to come to this end?"[96]

∽ ∽ ∽

There is a passage in the letter Thomas Starkey wrote to Henry VIII as an epistle dedicatory to his *Dialogue* which epitomizes with uncanny

94. E.g., *Governor*, I, 92-96, 116, 131, 161-162.
95. *Discourse*, p. 30; cf. pp. 22 and 31.
96. *Ibid.*, p. 31.

accuracy the attitude of the humanist toward the responsibilities of citizenship. Explaining how he came to write such an analysis of the English common weal, he expressed himself in these words:

> After that I had spent part of my youth in the study of phi-
> losophy and thereby somewhat perceived the dignity of man's
> nature, inflamed I was with a great desire to take some ex-
> perience of the manners of other people in strange nation to the
> intent I might thereby of such things which I had in books read,
> gather and confirm a more stable and sure judgment: whereupon
> I went straight into the country of Italy, as to the place most
> famed both with great learning and good and just policy, by the
> reason whereof glad I was there certain years to be conversant as
> diligently as I could observing their learning there in high
> philosophy as [well as] their practice in common policy, by the
> which observation I was somewhat better instruct at my return
> into mine own country indifferently to consider and weigh the
> customs and manners of mine own countrymen with the policy
> used here in our nation, whereupon I looked as a stranger as me
> thought in no part corrupt by any affection, but indifferent
> judgment everything examining: and so well noting the manners
> here used at home and comparing them with other used in
> strange nation I have found great correction with much abuse in
> law and policy whereof by long observation I have gathered a
> certain commentary and compiled as it were a little book of the
> same.[97]

There is here the nice balance between learning and practical experience the later humanists had come to value above mere scholarly precision, the rational balance between the active and contemplative ideals toward which they strove. There is here also the almost compulsive urge to analyze their society, to find what made it the way it was, more especially to see it not so much in relation to an absolute ideal as in comparison with another, presumably more sophisticated society. Above all there is the sense of obligation to turn both learning and experience to the good of their mother country.

About the only thing this passage does not reflect is the dilemma of the unattached, or semidetached, intellectual. Although he knew well enough that his words might fall on deaf ears—as his own *Dialogue*

97. Herrtage, p. lxxiv.

seems to have done at court—or, worse still, might provoke dangerous hostility among those in authority, Starkey was confident in his ability to supply the quality of thinking, the element of mind, otherwise lacking in the newer monarchy, and he was only too conscious of the duty encumbent upon him to undertake the task of counsel. The humanists were finding out but slowly what some of them had always feared, namely that it is not possible for all things to be well, or reasonably ordered, unless all men are good and also reasonable—which, as Sir Thomas More said, will not be yet this good many years. The confused forties in fact failed to justify even the cautious optimism expressed by Elyot and Starkey in the thirties.

In a sense, however, the important thing is not that the humanist pamphleteers of the second quarter of the Tudor century failed to create a rational and virtuous society, but rather that, in the process of trying, they achieved fresh insights into the nature of the society in which they were actually living. And in the *Discourse of the Common Weal*, if nowhere else, their methods and assumptions made possible a quality of social analysis which remained to the end of the century virtually without rival and which went a long way toward justifying the faith these early Tudor humanists placed in the informed mind.

CHAPTER VIII. THE SEARCH FOR CAUSE: UTOPIA AND REVOLUTION

THOSE WRITERS OF EARLY TUDOR ENGLAND WHO subjected their society to critical examination differed from their medieval counterparts less in the broad frame of reference within which they conducted their investigation than in the character of the investigation itself. They accepted, for the most part, the world outlook of their ancestors, but asked fresh questions of their own society, questions whose implications led insistently away from medieval and toward modern thought.

With a few notable exceptions (noted in the first part of this study) the medieval critic of society failed to explore the vast area of tangible, to some extent manageable relationships that lie this side of Divine Providence, well within the reach of man's inquiring mind. Assuming that the social order was an organism, divinely ordained in form and determined in its life history, and that the function of government within that organism is essentially protective, he either ignored the dynamic tendencies already at work altering the very foundations upon which his society rested, or condemned them as mere manifestations of human perversity against which it was his duty to warn his fellows. His diagnosis of the public ills was therefore conducted on a moral or theological basis. Their causes he traced either to the fatal flaws in man's moral nature or to the inscrutable workings of Providence. In either case he saw little reason to explore the more tangible, secondary causes. Virtue, considered primarily as the avoidance of vice, thus became for him the means not only of personal salvation but of health in the body politic.

It is here the writers of the Tudor era differed most fundamentally from their predecessors. Anyone who doubts that this was a new era in cultural as well as political history, anyone, that is, who insists too strongly on the continuity of medieval thought, should pay close attention to the emphasis placed on causal analysis by a succession of pamphleteers in the reigns of Henry VIII and Edward VI. Im-

pelled by the speed of change itself, already accustomed by generations
of realistic social criticism to accurate observation of fact, in varying
degrees under the influence of a new education, these men achieved
a new insight into the workings of their society. Within the broad
limits of an inherited intellectual system which gave little room for
any concept of change other than that of sickness within the body
politic or its restoration to health, they undertook, paradoxically, to
examine those evidences of change they could hardly escape observing in actual life, and to search out their causes.

Their approach to the issues of public concern was conditioned
by certain related assumptions: that society constituted an area of
experience capable of being investigated rationally and worth investigating in itself, without necessary reference to the theological or moral
ultimates; that virtue, considered primarily as the product of knowledge
and expressed in the service of the commonweal, was a positive rather
than a negative factor in social causation; that the ills of society could
be diagnosed and their causes determined within the context of observable fact; and that, once the causes had been located, it was possible
by intelligent policy to remove them and so restore the community to
health, perhaps even to reshape it to meet the challenge of change
itself.

Although this tendency of theirs can be explained to some extent
in the context of English experience and conditions, it was also part of
a larger pattern characteristic of Renaissance culture. The articulate
citizen of Tudor England had, for example, been preceded along the
road they were traveling by the civic-minded humanists of Renaissance
Italy, and by more than a century.[1] But it is important to recognize
that their purpose in making the journey was somewhat different and
that they in fact arrived at a somewhat different destination. The
Florentine humanists of the late fourteenth and early fifteenth centuries
point, it is true, toward a new realism in the analysis of society, but it
is toward Machiavelli that they face rather than the commonwealth of
Tudor thought. Their efforts were directed toward the analysis of
political rather than of social and economic experience. They looked
first of all—and perforce, considering the nature of Italian politics—
for those personal factors which constitute the moving parts of the
political situation and in which the deeper social forces find overt

1. See Baron, *Crisis*, especially pp. 112-142.

expression rather than, as was the habit of the more advanced among the Tudor commentators, for the impersonal principles at work within the social mechanism itself. The Italian writers tended to think in terms of a statecraft dedicated to the maintenance of princely power, the English in terms of policies meant to promote the welfare of the national community.

The literature of comment and criticism in early Tudor England reveals a marked preoccupation with cause. From the least of those letters written by private persons to the king and his council in that newly kindled spirit of participation in counsel which marks early Tudor public life up to the most sophisticated treatises written by men of position and influence, that literature follows with remarkable consistency the simple formula *sublata causa, tollitur effectus.* As one writer put it, "when a man doth perceive his grief, and the occasion also of the same, he is in good way of amendment." Obvious as this appears to the modern mind, when applied to the secular affairs of the national community it revealed a process of considerable subtlety and of fundamental importance in the history of modern thought.

True, they often spoke in the language of an earlier day, one, indeed, not at all fitted to the exploration of social phenomena, and to that extent they seem at times not to be as clear as they might have been regarding the processes they were examining. It may even be that inherited formulas actually inhibited them in their analysis. They found it hard, for example, to escape the habit of viewing society as an organism. The analogy of the body politic had colored, perhaps even shaped much of medieval social and political thought. English critics of the early Renaissance continued, almost without exception, to picture themselves laboring to find the cause of disease in the political body just as physicians diagnose ailments in the body natural. "Sedition," Crowley wrote in 1550, "being a dangerous disease in the body of the commonwealth, must be cured as the expert physicians do use to cure the dangerous diseases in the natural body. And as the most substantial way in curing diseases is by putting away the causes whereof they grow, so it is in the pulling up of sedition."[2] Taking, as was his custom, a more comprehensive and a more philosophical view of society, Starkey makes even more use of the same analogy. It will, Pole says in the *Dialogue*, be the principle of the discussion of the

2. *Way to Wealth*, p. 131.

commonwealth he and Lupset are about to conduct to "take nature for our example" and to treat of the state as a politic body, "this general rule of expert physicians in curing of bodily diseases as much as we can ever observing—that is to say, first to ensearch out the cause of the diseases, without which the applying of remedies little availeth."[3] Not until the remarkable *Discourse of the Common Weal* do we find a writer willing to abandon the organic analogy and, as we shall see later, to adopt for purely illustrative purposes the mechanical analogy of the clock.

Now this all could be considered a harmless, if clumsy, rhetorical device were it not for certain implications that cling persistently to the organic analogy.   One arose from the very habit of thinking in terms of analogies.   It is hard for a modern person, accustomed to thinking of cause and effect, of "linear" relationships, to appreciate how little meaning such relationships had to the medieval mind and how satisfying it found those "lateral" relationships based on similarity and reflection.   Renaissance Englishmen continued to envisage all created things as in one way or another reflecting the divine purpose and in the process presenting a complex series of divinely ordained comparisons. And the use of symbols, so inveterate a part of medieval thought, still tended to call attention to parallelisms rather than causal connections. Relationships of this sort were, within the framework of a Providential history, essentially static.   Static also was the idea of society as an organism in which each member has its appointed place and function. And it is also profoundly conservative, for place must be maintained and function dutifully performed if the whole body is to be kept in health.

Likewise inhibiting was the habit, almost as characteristic of the sixteenth-century preacher as of his medieval predecessor, of tracing all social and political evils at once to their moral or Providential origin, thus bypassing those more tangible secondary causes quite observable within the social system, even when the latter was considered in organic terms.   It might even be that the Reformation, by in-ducing the Protestant preachers and writers to adopt a more than ordinarily theocentric view of society and a more than ordinarily pessimistic view of man, actually increased this tendency.   The Bible

3. *Dialogue*, pp. 136-137. Cf. *An Exhortation to Styrre all Englyshmen to the Defence of theyr Countrye* (London, 1539), sig. Aii.

of the reformers seems, in fact, to have served as an effective counter-poise to the more secular influence of the classics during the middle decades of the century, even among those reformers whose early training had included a thorough grounding in *literae humaniores*. In the Old Testament especially those ardent evangelists, sensitive to social maladjustments as to matters of faith, found a wealth of examples telling of peoples who had sinned and had accordingly suffered the temporal disasters God visits upon those who turn their face from Him. And there, too, were the promises made to those who repent, promises, incidentally, which by no means excluded worldly prosperity.[4] Noth-ing was less likely to inspire realistic analysis, even among these men who were often realistic observers of social fact, than the belief that God, working directly through men, is the mover of all things and hence the only causal force worth the serious attention of the citizen-counselor.

So it was that much of the literature of social criticism in this period remains in the purest tradition of the medieval moralist, and, as in the fourteenth century, written criticism echoed the accents of the pulpit. Robert Crowley's pamphlets recall with curious exactness the attitudes of John Gower. Nor is it surprising that *Piers Plowman*, with its powerful compound of social criticism and religious mys-ticism, should have found a new and enlarged audience in an Eng-land preoccupied with social and religious crises roughly parallel to those of Langland's own day.[5]

No one, of course, denied that man's search for cause must sooner or later come up against the ultimate factors of Providence and the moral nature of man. And, among the humanists, Starkey, at least, was willing to add to the factors limiting the analytical quest the more exotic and not very orthodox concept of fortune, borrowed from the most unimpeachable ancient authority.[6] He does not, however,

4. See, for example, Lever, *A Sermon preached the thyrd Sondaye in Lente* . . . *1550* (London, 1550), *STC* 15548, sig. Aii-iii and *A Fruitful Sermon made in Paules Churche* . . . *1550* (London, 1550), *STC* 15543, sig. Av; Thomas Cranmer, *Miscellaneous Writings*, ed. J. E. Cox, Parker Society (Cambridge, 1846), pp. 190-191; Hooper, *Early Writings*, p. 449.

5. Helen C. White, *Social Criticism in the Popular Religious Literature of the Sixteenth Century* (New York, 1944), chap. i, deals in some detail with the vogue of *Piers Plowman* in the early sixteenth century.

6. *Dialogue*, pp. 66-68.

insist upon it; his toying with the notion simply indicates that he recognized an element of indeterminism in the affairs of men which will always limit their freedom of action, yet which can always be hedged against to some extent by prudent policy.

These limitations must not, however, obscure the fact—indeed they help establish it—that the early Tudor writers on matters social and economic were preoccupied with cause. Nor should they obscure the fact, of still greater importance, that many of them sought the answer to questions of social causation in an exploration of the moving forces they saw, or thought they saw, operating within society itself, forces which they were beginning to recognize as in large part impersonal.

In a sense, the habit of analysis was itself simply an advanced manifestation of that older and more general trend toward reality apparent in all aspects of late medieval English culture. It had left its mark on the art of the period, with its increasingly naturalistic treatment of flowers, birds, animals, and patrons. It had infiltrated academic thought by way of a neo-Aristotelian theory of knowledge based on sense perception, culminating in the concretizing tendencies of the Ockhamist tradition.[7] It was expressed, as we have seen, in the political literature of fifteenth-century England. In the early sixteenth century it finds expression also in a curiously naïve, but firm, faith in statistical fact. Figures, especially, seem to have fascinated the Tudor commentator. From the modern point of view there is nothing remarkable in a person's supporting arguments concerning economic matters with data that lends itself to statistical analysis. Medieval English writings, with the partial exception of the *Libel of English Policy*, will, however, yield few such examples.[8] By contrast, the pamphlet literature of the sixteenth century teems with figures.[9] For the first time English commentators seem generally to have been

7. For interesting light on this subject, see H. A. Oberman, "Some Notes on the Theology of Nominalism: With attention to its Relation to the Renaissance," *HTR*, LIII (Jan., 1960), 47-79.

8. See, for example, *Libel*, p. 22.

9. Examples are too numerous to be worth citing; but it is interesting to notice how the author of *Piers Plowman's Exhortation*, under the guise of tradition, substantiates his very practical proposals for economic reform with suspiciously round, but still impressively concrete figures on external trade, and how William Forrest adapts the traditional "mirror of princes" to English conditions with a similar appeal to figures, *Pleasaunt Poesye*, pp. xcvi-xcvii.

conscious of the value of statistics as the kind of evidence ostensibly most specific, most concrete, and hence most nearly irrefutable. Un-happily, they were generally egregiously inaccurate, at times gullible, even irresponsible.[10] But it is the value they placed on such evidence rather their use of it that is important at this point in the history of their thought.

Even the Tudor humanists owed a good deal of their charac-teristically utilitarian bent to an indigenous realism. They seem at times to have subjected even their cherished classical sources of in-spiration to the test of practicality. Starkey, for example, is at pains to make it clear to his reader that he is not shaping the discussion of the true commonwealth in his *Dialogue* after the model of Plato "whose order of comon weal no people upon earth to this day could ever yet attain," but with strict reference to England and to the realities of "time and place."[11]

To this general trend toward the concrete, the tangible, the practical, and the observable,[12] the Tudor humanists nevertheless added a fresh emphasis on life in this world of time and place, an emphasis derived in large part from their reinterpretation of the ancients. In the image of classical antiquity they had caught a glimpse of what they took to be a reasonable society in which man was free to realize his earthly potential, a society in which the inquiring and creative intellect could be brought to bear on its immediate environment, free from any neces-sary or exclusive commitment to an otherworldly ideal. The Tudor humanists had come to recognize the possibility of analyzing the work-ings of their society in terms not necessarily or constantly related to the great questions of salvation or morality.

We must be careful, of course, not to exaggerate this tendency or to strip it from the context of Christian values in which it found ex-pression. The English humanists were as concerned as their pred-ecessors with moral conduct. If they differed in this respect—and they did—it was only to emphasize a distinctly worldly, civic virtue, virtue that comes not so much from the avoidance of sin as from knowl-

10. See Lipson's criticism in *The Economic History of England* (London, 1956), I, 180. See also below, concerning Simon Fish's use of statistics in his *Supplicacyon for the Beggars*.

11. *Dialogue*, pp. 39-40.

12. On this subject, see M. H. Carré, *Phases of Thought in England* (Oxford, 1949), chaps iv-v, especially pp. 134-156.

edge of things human, interpreted by right reason and expressed in the active service of the commonwealth. If they considered even this aspect of human nature a factor limiting their search for tangible causes, they seem nevertheless to have been more optimistic than their more theologically oriented contemporaries. Civic virtue was after all capable of being cultivated by education and persuasion, in which the humanists placed immense faith, whereas the preachers them-selves seem to have expected little immediate result, certainly not in worldly matters, from their exhortations to repentance. To an increas-ing extent, however, the humanists of the thirties and forties preferred to concentrate on forces more amenable to control through policy and on man's potentiality for positive, constructive action. Some, to be sure, had not gone as far in this direction as others. Some became involved in the religious and ecclesiastical controversies and tended therefore to revert to an attitude toward the world of affairs more characteristic of the medieval preacher than of the Renaissance scholar. All were eclectic in their willingness to call upon either the classical or Christian elements in their background for whatever inspiration might serve as a guide to action at any given moment. The great contribution of the Tudor humanists was to give form and substance to the search for reality and, in particular, to broaden and define the area of experience that could properly be investigated, and investigated primarily, if not exclusively, with the tools of reason and experience.

ഗ ഗ ഗ

It would be reasonable to suppose that the story of the Tudor intellectual's response to the accelerating tempo of public life would begin with that small but famous group of humanists who gathered in London in the early years of the century. In a sense it does. The "Erasmian" generation of humanists,[13] of which Thomas More was the most brilliant native product, had a message to deliver to the world of their day. It was at first an optimistic message. Despite the change and decay that (like their predecessors) in all around they saw, they had caught the vision of a new world, remade on rational and Christian lines. Their scholarship, both in its study of pagan anti-

13. Of the several books relating to this group, the most recent, and from the point of view of this study the most relevant is Robert P. Adams, *The Better Part of Valor* (Seattle, 1962).

quity and in its re-evaluation of the Christian transition, had shed a
newly revealing light on the world of the present. And, in the England of the young Henry VIII, an England in which scholarship
seemed at last to be valued as an aid to citizenship and which Erasmus
could still believe to be in truth a fortunate isle, they had the not
unreasonable hope of realizing the civic ideals of ancient Rome, tempered by the *philosophia Christi.*

Yet, to this study of the English public mind, the Erasmian
critique is relevant only in an indirect way. For the most part the
Erasmian group placed contemporary problems in a philosophical
rather than a practical context, and, their purposes being nonetheless
practical, to appeal to the mind of the intelligentsia in the interests of
peace and justice rather than more directly to governors in the interests
of specific policies. With energy, and for a while with confidence,
they struck out at the vicious folly they saw at work undermining the
edifice of an ordered Christendom, at the calculating brutality of a
diplomacy that depended on war, at a statecraft devoted to ends of
power and dynastic aggrandizement, and at a social ideal that placed
individual profit before the common good. Yet these were ills to
which all Christendom was heir; and, except for *Utopia* the critique
itself smacked more of the teacher, the *philosophe,* than of the citizen-
counselor. Once disillusionment set in, when in particular Henry
VIII began to lose his knightly shirt at the poker table of Renaissance
power politics, Erasmus withdrew to the Continent to continue his
fight on what was for him the indivisible stage of a Christian Europe.
Vives, who came late to the group of London reformers, also found
England eventually uncongenial to the international scholar, and,
although he contributed to the solution of England's problem of poor
relief, it was indirectly through a plan he worked out for the city of
Ypres.[14] More, alone, brought the Erasmian vision to sharp focus on
the facts of English life—and he was soon forced by the pressures of
public office to abandon his earlier role as publicist.

The generation of More and Erasmus did not, however, labor in
vain. What they were able to do—and do more effectively than those
will admit who talk about the "arrest" or the "defeat" of English
humanism[15]—was to transmit to later generations something of their

14. See below, and chap. xi.
15. See J. S. Phillimore, "The Arrest of Humanism in England," *Dublin Review,*

humane vision and their faith in the power of reason, inspired by civic virtue, to cope with the dislocations of their society. Their successors in the capacity of citizen-counselors, those men especially who observed English society in the revolutionary decades of the thirties and forties, were able to bring an Erasmian quality of vision once more to focus upon the realities of the national life and to follow up, perhaps consciously, the critical insights More achieved in the analytical portions of *Utopia*. Freed from a too exclusive preoccupation with the fate of Christendom by a schism in the universal church and by a quarter-century of foreign policy generally disastrous to English interests, these shrewd observers were able to turn their humanistically trained minds with unprecedented consistency to the problems peculiar to the commonwealth of England.

∽ ∽ ∽

More himself was in many ways ideally fitted to bridge the gap that separated the medieval critic of society from the articulate citizen of the Renaissance. Whatever his personal influence on those who came after him—and it may well have been more pervasive than has usually been thought—the fact of immediate importance is that he stood at the exact point where the two worlds met. Moreover, he seems to have been quite aware of his position. Indeed, it is his ability to look both backward and forward and see in some perspective the shifting relationships in the society of men that, despite the ambivalence of his position, places him irrevocably among the company of Renaissance thinkers. He was quite capable of viewing society, like the medieval commentator, in the context of eternal values, yet at the same time in relation to other societies (both real and imagined) of other times and other places and to the ever unfolding fact of change. He could entertain the vision of a world remade on humane and rational lines, yet accept with disconcerting frankness the constant factor of human frailty. He was able to recognize the values he believed essential to the vitality of the Christian world as he knew and valued it and to separate them from the institutions and customs which,

CLIII (1913), 1-26; R. W. Chambers, *Thomas More* (New York, 1935), pp. 378-382; Adams, pp. 86-87 260-261. Cf. Douglas Bush, *The Renaissance and English Humanism* (Toronto, 1939), pp. 73 ff.

since they were the creatures of time and place, must be considered changeable, susceptible to the inventive genius of man.

More's mind, like that of most humanists, was a synthesizing mind. He hoped to reconcile the Christian and classical traditions, the old values with the demands of a new order. But synthesis had to be preceded by analysis, and understanding was a necessary condition for reconciliation. Hence the realism that underlies so much of More's idealism. Hence his concern, unique among Englishmen of his generation, for causal analysis, for "relating disparate social and political symptoms to a central cause."[16]

More was especially and acutely disturbed by two tendencies in his society. One was the new statecraft which was taking shape to meet the needs of a newly competitive international order, a statecraft that combined an amoral, thoroughly Machiavellian realism with the less reputable values of a perverted chivalry. The other was the acquisitive spirit of private economic enterprise. Both were dynamic forces, the one tending toward ends of dynastic power and prestige, the other toward those of wealth.

It is possible that More was in 1516 looking with a slightly less jaundiced eye at the statecraft of his own king than he would have a few years earlier. Henry VIII had just emerged from a series of military and diplomatic adventures in which he had lost the fortune his father had amassed for him and had gained little more than a salutary lesson in *Realpolitik* at the hands of the most accomplished masters of the art in Renaissance Europe. Whether he had learned those lessons well enough—or too well—remained to be seen. More was apparently hoping for the best. But he had learned his own lessons from the events of the preceding years. He had watched with the most profound misgivings while his king had become embroiled in Continental policies. He had become painfully aware of the amoral realism of contemporary diplomacy and the pseudo-chivalric lust for military renown which, more than realistic calculation, had prompted the younger Henry.

16. Paul Coles, "The Interpretation of More's 'Utopia,'" *Hibbert Journal*, LVI (July, 1958), 365-370. In this regard it is interesting to notice Erasmus' statement that More published the *Utopia* "for the purpose of showing what are the things that occasion mischief in commonwealths, having the English constitution especially in view, which he so thoroughly knows and understands." Quoted in A. L. Morton, *The English Utopia* (London, 1952), p. 45.

And so, during the period *Utopia* was taking shape in his mind, he had apparently been subjecting the issues of the day to a really agoniz' ing re-appraisal in the light not only of his Christian humanist values but also of his own impending decision to enter the service of the king.[17] Falling as it did from divergent directions, this light was starkly revealing. It showed up with pitiless clarity the folly of man and his moral weakness, the pride of a misdirected knight-errantry, as well as the ruthless ambition of the new politics of power and of expediency, untempered by the humane values common to both the Christian and the classical traditions. It also revealed the emerging system of com' peting states, each recognizing no human authority superior to its own. It was a world the statecraft of which More understood as well as did Machiavelli, but which unlike the more pragmatic Florentine, he could not accept on its own terms. It was in this light, generated in almost equal proportions by idealism and realism, that More placed his analysis of foreign policy in Book I of *Utopia* and developed the satire of Book II.

More developed his analysis of contemporary statecraft with prudent indirection and on the basis of supposed instances: what the French king and his council might perhaps do, or some quite hypothetical European prince, or even the ruler of one of those entirely fictional peoples who inhabited that land of nowhere with which the traveler, Hythloday, was alone familiar. Yet it is basically as realistic as Machiavelli's in its grasp of the principles upon which this statecraft is actually founded. It has been rightly said that in this respect the *Utopia* reads like a commentary on the *Prince*. More's purpose, how' ever, was diametrically opposite to that of Machiavelli. He was con' cerned not with the results of the policies he treats, but with the ethical principles underlying them. He recognized as clearly as Mach' iavelli the real, though seldom admitted, premise of Renaissance statecraft, namely, that power is an end in itself, but again he refused to accept current practice as inevitable, much less right. He was consequently unable to content himself with a more or less objective analysis of those purely political or material factors which contribute to the success or failure of a policy. And, by the same token, he was unable to achieve that appearance of empiricism, of scientific analysis on the basis of facts objectively observed and evaluated without

17. See Hexter, *More's Utopia*, and above, chap. vii.

reference to prior moral commitments, which gives to the work of Machiavelli a recognizable, if somewhat deceptive, air of modernity.

Moreover, the basic motives as well as the ends, in political life as well as in other social relationships remain, for More, ethical. It is pride, as the Christian moralist would call it, or ambition as the same thing became in countless Elizabethan commentaries, that impels princes to unprovoked aggression and to unjust wars, just as it is pride that drives the citizen to enter the contest for private wealth.[18] Man, however, also retains moral choice. The good counselor, the only likely substitute for the philosopher-king, can do something by his virtuous advice at least to mitigate the effects of these strivings and at least partially divert them into more humane and rational channels.

Similarly, by the exercise of that quality of right reason which is common to all men, the Utopians had managed to some extent to counteract the tendency of states to be drawn into the kind of barbarous anarchy that could only end in war. They could not always avoid war, for some wars were just.[19] But they could, by understanding its causes, do much to alleviate its effects. Like Erasmus,[20] More found in human nature the basic causes of war: the blood lust of those who slaughter animals for sport,[21] the honors given in the chivalric tradition to those who are most proficient at the slaughter of men,[22] and the ambition of princes who hold the values of civilized life of lower importance than their own aggrandizement.[23] Yet he seems not to have shared the pessimism of Erasmus who traced the origin of war to a progressive degeneration in human society from a primitive golden age to its present depravity. The Utopians, at least—and we may reasonably suppose that in this instance they personify More's still lively hopes for the race—have managed to neutralize among their own people most of the evil passions that lead

18. Hexter, *More's Utopia*, p. 72; cf. Russell Ames, *Citizen Thomas More and his Utopia* (Princeton, 1948), p. 176.

19. See Adams, chap. ix, for a detailed analysis of More's attitude toward war. *Utopia*, pp. 91-92.

20. *Erasmus Against War*, ed. J. W. Mackail (Boston, 1907), pp. 18-24. See also Adams, pp. 98 ff.

21. *Utopia*, pp. 76-77. Here More implies what Erasmus makes explicit concerning the tendency for this weakness in man's nature to lead to war.

22. *Ibid.*, p. 91.

23. *Ibid.*, also p. 35. See also *The Dialogue Concerning Tyndale by Sir Thomas More*, ed. W. E. Campbell (London, 1927), pp. 307-308.

to war.   And, where they could not avoid war, they followed a policy of calculated realism, deliberately antithetical to any sort of chivalric idealism, that avoided many of its more vicious effects.[24]   More than that, these other islanders had analyzed, with a shrewdness some modern German writers[25] have found only too characteristic of a later British imperialism, the strategic advantages of an insular position, advantages which make it possible to exercise economic rather than crudely military power.

ༀ ༀ ༀ

Keen as it was, More's political analysis remains one step removed from specific cases.   The same can not be said of his treatment of social problems.   Here he proceeded on the basis of specifically English facts, and in his analysis of them he anticipated by a generation that of the "commonwealth men" who may be said to have established the habit of social analysis among English pamphleteers.

The trouble, as More saw it, centered on the dismal fact of poverty. It was by no means a new problem, although of recent years seriously aggravated.   Nor was it simple, for it involved the related evils of idleness (meaning both sloth and involuntary unemployment), vagabondage, with all its dangers to the peace and security of the community, beggary in its many distressing forms, and crime, to More the product less of private vice than of a vicious social system. And that social system was rooted deep in the economic soil.

The period into which England was moving was, in fact, one of rapid change in the economic habits and ways of life.   It was one of unparalleled opportunity and correspondingly frightening insecurity. Caught since the beginning of the century in the increasingly tight grip of a price revolution, Englishmen had to revise many of their customary ways of making a living.   Capitalistic enterprise was, to be sure, no novelty in More's day.   For the better part of two centuries it had been eating away at the underpinning of a society based on custom and status and had by the end of the preceding century already gone a long way toward creating a society of economic individualism, of relatively free contract, and of corresponding instability.

24. *Utopia*, pp. 89-99.
25. E.g., Gerhard Ritter, *The Corrupting Influence of Power*, trans. F. W. Pick (London, 1952), pp. 74-89.

Now, however, the change was being speeded up by the rise in prices. In the resulting confusion of what was to become a social revolution many, less fortunately placed than others, fell into destitution. Of these, the most widely advertised were the people who were evicted from their tenancy of land by enclosing landlords, or who became victims of the general effort of the landed gentry to revise customarily fixed rents by "rack-renting" methods. That this should be so was natural enough in a country where 90 per cent of the population still earned their living from the land. And it is not necessary to take the excited comments of contemporary social critics entirely at their face value to appreciate the shock to their essentially conservative minds produced by these agrarian changes. The results of enclosure could be dramatically and disastrously apparent in any given locality; it did not take more than one or two depopulated villages to magnify the evil to startling proportions in the eyes of anyone who happened to be on the spot.

The spectacle of poverty, and in particular the ubiquitous and loathsome race of beggars, was ideally calculated to arouse the reform-ing instinct so characteristic of the Erasmian group of humanists among whom More reached intellectual maturity. And the threat to respect-able men posed by the army of vagabonds and rogues elicited also their equally characteristic sense of civic responsibility. Social phenomena of this sort also piqued the highly susceptible curiosity of these humanist critics. They called out for explanation, for it was becoming clear that they were merely superficial sores on the body politic, distressing enough in themselves, but symptoms of a more deep-seated disorder. In the process of diagnosis the reformer no doubt exag-gerated the incidence and virulence of the disease. If men become in-creasingly sensitive to an evil, they are likely to assume that it is the evil itself that is increasing. There remained, however, only too much in the society that More surveyed to warrant the deepest concern.

The problem of poverty lies at the heart of More's indictment of the society of capitalistic enterprise. With a lawyer's insight he recog-nized that the prevalence of crime provided a pretty good indication of a country's general health. And so it is by way of a discussion of crime and punishment that, in the first book of *Utopia*, he leads his readers into an examination of the underlying problem of poverty. For, Hythloday argues, there is no punishment so horrible "that it can keep them from stealing, which have no other craft whereby to get their living." Attention should therefore be given not to raising the legal sanctions against theft but to creating an environment in which men are not driven, in desperation, "first to steal, and then to die."[26] Having thus fairly raised the issue of poverty in a broad and essentially secular context, More proceeds to explore that context in an effort to clarify the causes of poverty.

He finds the immediate cause in the failure of his society to provide a job for all men who are willing to work. But he then proceeds to go still deeper into the social texture and to analyze the economic factors that underlie involuntary idleness. Most serious are those affecting agrarian life, enclosures in particular. Sheep, he wrote, "consume, destroy, and devour fields, houses, and cities." In the finest wool-growing areas, noblemen and gentlemen "yea and certain Abbots," not content with their customary income from rents, "enclose all into pasture," with the result that the husbandman must be evicted "by one means therefore or by other, either by hook or by crook," for "one shepherd or herdsman is enough to eat up that ground with cattle, to the occupying whereof about husbandry many hands were requisite." The fate of these displaced persons, with only the pitifully small sale price in their pockets, thrust forth in a society still not accustomed to absorbing masterless men, is likely to be dismal indeed. For them, More says, the alternative is either stealing or begging.[27]

More also recognized that enclosures acted indirectly to increase poverty by contributing to the cost of food. Indeed, the converting of arable land into sheep-runs was quite generally believed to be a major cause of that "dearth" (meaning "dearness"—"inflation" to us) which was the most obvious and distressing economic trend of the age and which clearly contributed to the plight of the poor. Enclosures, More states, are "also the cause why victuals be now in many places dearer." But, he sees, this question of price is not a simple one.

> Yea beside this the price of wool is so risen, that poor folks, which were wont to work it, and make cloth thereof, be now able to buy none at all. And by that means very many be forced to forsake work, and to give themselves to idleness.
> . . . And though the number of sheep increase never so fast,

26. *Utopia*, p. 21.
27. *Ibid.*, pp. 23-24.

yet the price falleth not one mite, because there be so few sellers. For they be almost all come into a few rich men's hands, whom no need forceth to sell before they lust, and they lust not before they may sell as dear as they lust.

The same speculative enterprise is apparent in other kinds of cattle. Rich drovers buy up and fatten cattle rather than conduct less im/ mediately profitable breeding operations. This, again, raises the cost of food, forces men to cut down their staff of servants, which, in turn, swells the ranks of the unemployed.[28]

In his final appraisal More seems to abandon this startlingly realistic analysis by finding the prime mover in the whole complex of economic relationships in "the unreasonable covetousness of a few." Yet, reminiscent as it is of the medieval critic and also of future Protestant spokesmen like Latimer and Crowley, this resort to moral fundamen/ tals is not so unrealistic as it appears, for it is coupled with the starkly realistic observation, voiced by Hythloday, that such vicious pro/ pensities would always be fostered in a society based upon the institution of private property. Here More reveals the conflict which shaped both his thought and his career and which symbolizes in a sense that society of transition in which he lived. Recognizing with the utmost clarity the bleak fact that this society was becoming in/ creasingly competitive, and that competition and the profit motive back of it were inevitable so long as private property existed, yet quite aware, as any common lawyer must have been, that private property, though not the only conceivable economic system, was for the foreseeable future ineradicable, More nevertheless refused to justify these facts and chose instead to adhere in principle to the values traditionally expressed in the ideal of a Christian commonwealth. From this point of view, then, his resort to moral explanations, as well as his indictment of private property, becomes simply the logical conclusion to an argument already concluded for practical purposes by a ringing, if not very optimistic, demand for remedial, regulatory legislation. "Make a law," his spokesman cries, "cast out these pernicious abominations." Though promising at best only partial success, doomed by the nature of man and the virtually unreformable character of property law to at least partial failure, here was the only intelligent course, the course of

28. *Ibid.*, pp. 24/25; cf. pp. 21/22.

active policy, the course which, despite his misgivings, More himself chose.

Man, in short, need not be utterly the slave of his passions. He can always do something to curb or neutralize them. His moral nature is constant, and his values eternal, but his propensity to err is to a considerable extent determined by an environment over which he himself has some control. More was far from optimistic about man's ability to do much about his environment. He seems to have recog-nized in the system of private property a supra-personal force that would be hard indeed to deflect from its path. Nor was he as ready as some of his successors, the author of the *Discourse of the Common Weal* for example, to accept self-interest as a normal and constant factor in human affairs, to be analyzed, allowed for, even to some extent harnessed in the common interest. But he retained a stubborn faith in the regenerative, even the creative ability of the mind. If English-men were not in fact likely to remake their environment in a sufficient-ly radical way to curb their vicious tendencies, they could at least make things a little better by trying. And where they failed, More's own Utopian brain-children succeeded. By removing the means of material competition and conspicuous consumption, they had effective-ly neutralized the effects of pride, and of the closely associated vices, greed and envy.[29] Though there is little reason for hope in it, the fact remains that, within the not too restricted limits of his little world, within the province left to him in God's plan, man was the master of his environment, the primary causal force.

The fact that others followed close upon More's heels in search of the causes of poverty must not obscure the freshness of his analysis. Although the thesis that unemployment, poverty, and crime stemmed from enclosures was never more than a half-truth, it represented a serious attempt to understand the dynamic element in English society, and it was, moreover, not in 1516 the commonplace it became soon afterward.[30] Subsequent commentators indeed added little to More's analysis. When, however, a younger generation of English humanists turned its attention to poverty, it was forced to examine it in the broader context of social and political revolution and to advise a government

29. Hexter, *More's Utopia*, pp. 60-66, 72.
30. J. A. Schumpeter, *History of Economic Analysis* (New York, 1954), pp. 207-208.

now required to assume the responsibility for poor relief hitherto
carried by the church.

ᔕ   ᔕ   ᔕ

Meanwhile, the Henrician revolution preoccupied commentators
to the virtual exclusion of less dramatic problems.   That revolution,
however, involved much more than the politico-ecclesiastical considerations immediately related to Henry's dynastic policies.   It meant
disturbing roots that had reached into every part of English life.   The
result was social and economic change of equally revolutionary
proportions.   Anyone, therefore, who was able to observe this fast
moving situation with any degree of critical detachment must have
found much in it to stir his curiosity and prompt him to some sort of
investigation.   It was, in short, not so much the event itself that
stimulated the analytical mind as the repercussions that emanated
from it in ever widening circles throughout English society.

These non-religious, largely social and economic implications of
ecclesiastical reform did not become fully apparent until the actual
break with Rome and, in particular, until the dissolution of the
monasteries and the Pilgrimage of Grace had demanded the attention
of all public-spirited observers.   The Reformation had, however,
been preceded by an intensified anticlerical agitation focused on the
corporate wealth of the clergy.   Like their Lollard forerunners, the
anticlericals of the 1520's saw in clerical property the root of those
worldly entanglements that prevented the church from performing its
spiritual duties as faithfully as it should.   Like the Lollards, too, the
sixteenth-century critics of the clerical endowments found themselves
exploring these economic and social relationships.   But there is little in
the resulting literature prior to the articulate thirties that need detain
anyone interested primarily in the rise of social analysis.

An interesting, if minor, exception is the strange pamphlet con-
frontation between Thomas More and Simon Fish.   The latter, one
of the group of young men who saw in Cardinal Wolsey, despite his
own efforts at reform, the embodiment of clerical wealth and worldly
entanglement, undertook in his *Supplication for the Beggars* [*ca.* 1529][31]

31. Simon Fish, *A Supplicacyon for the Beggars*, ed. F. J. Furnivall, E.E.T.S., E.S.,
No. 13 (1871).   On the subject of criticism of clerical wealth in general, see Helen C.
White, chap. iii.

to attack the whole system of clerical endowments. Though influenced by Tyndale and the Continental Protestants, and accordingly
against endowments on the theological grounds as both the morbid
sequelae of the doctrine of salvation by works and one of its main supports, Fish felt constrained, like the Lollard pamphleteers,[32] to point
out also their economic implications. Like the Lollards, too, he was
probably not above recognizing the attraction a policy of disendowment might have for a land-hungry governing class. At any rate he
chose to concentrate on the social and economic problems presented
by the large number of chantries dedicated by their founders to perpetual prayers for the dead. He wrote his pamphlet as though it were
a plea by the poor against those clerical mendicants they considered
unfair competition for the alms of the laity and, more generally,
against a class pictured as essentially parasitic.

It was crude and unscrupulous propaganda, even judged by sixteenth-century standards. But it is interesting for present purposes
because of its author's evident regard for what he took to be statistical
analysis. His figures are scandalously fishy. But his use of them tells
us a good deal about the public for which he wrote, the anticlerical
Londoner in particular. Even so the pamphlet, though widely
circulated and subsequently remembered, would hardly be worth our
attention had not More found it necessary to take his valuable time to
answer it, and moreover to devote the whole first part of his *Supplication
of the Poor Souls in Purgatory* to a systematic critique of his adversary's
facts and method. By doing so he tacitly admits that both carried
weight among the kind of people likely to read the book.

Characteristically, More has also a good deal of amusement at
Fish's expense. It was not hard to point out the mendacious exaggeration of his facts. But it was ridiculously easy for a man of More's
satirical ability to uncover the fallacy in his method. Fish's conclusion
that begging friars take annually 43,333 pounds, sixteen shillings, eight
pence from 52,000 English parishes is, More says, "grounded upon
two false grounds, one upon fifty-two thousand parish churches, the
other that every of the five orders hath every quarter of every household
a penny." Thus the whole thing is, More continues, burlesquing
Fish's ponderous reckoning, "as if he would make a reckoning with
you that every ass hath eight ears. And for to prove it with, bear you

32. See above, chap. iv.

first in hand that every ass hath four heads, and then make, *summa,* four heads. Then might he boldly tell you further that every ass head hath two ears, for that is commonly true except any be cut off. *Summa* then, two ears, and so *summa totalis,* eight ears." This, More claims, is silly enough, but it is based on only one false figure, whereas Fish uses two. Then, he continues, to compound the trouble Fish adds his total 43,333 pounds, six shillings, eight pence that the friars exact to what he claims the rest of the clergy take, "which he summeth not," and then proceeds to say that they "together amount unto more between them than half of the whole substance of the realm. And this he af-firmeth as boldy as though he could reckon the whole revenues and substance of all England, as readily as make the reckoning of this beggar's purse." And so on, until he has subjected Fish's analysis to a thoroughly damaging criticism.[33]

More's exchange with Fish, slight as it appears now in relation to the magnitude of the events even then in the process of gestation, shows how difficult it was for the religious issue to be separated from its social and economic context. Matters of pure theology could be, and were, debated *in vacuo,* but insofar as the religious life required external institutions for its expression in organized society, it could hardly be separated from the closely woven web of relationships which made up that society. Anticlericalism stemmed initially from spiritual dis-content. But it found essential nourishment in the secular soil of English life, especially in those economic relationships which, in turn, had arisen from the character of the church as an endowed corporation, necessarily dependent for its maintenance on the efficiency of its fiscal system. Accordingly we find Simon Fish attacking the doctrine of purgatory by means of a critique based almost entirely on social, economic, and political considerations, and More defending the same doctrine, in part at least, by carefully discrediting his adversary's social, economic, and political data.

The king's divorce proceedings tended for a while to divert atten-tion from the social and economic background of the Reformation to the more dramatic events that for a while dominated the political

33. *Supplication of the Poor Souls in Purgatory,* ed. Sister Mary Thecla (Westminster, Md., 1950). See also his criticism of Fish's facts regarding Parliament (p. 301), the problem of poor relief (pp. 301-302), the problem, considered in its social aspects, of clerical marriage (pp. 306-307), and history (pp. 296, 311-312).

scene. Those events, the legislative activity of the Reformation Parliament, the divorce itself, the assumption by the king of the supreme
headship of the church in England, and finally the dissolution of the
monasteries, constituted in themselves a revolution which could not
be ignored. The resulting spate of pamphlets, independently authored
as well as officially inspired, constitute a landmark in the history of
public discussion in England. But the Henrician propaganda, insofar as it was confined to the ecclesiastical and political issues themselves, does little to illuminate the inquiring mind of these Englishmen
of the early Renaissance, nor does it throw much light on their changing attitudes toward government as a functioning thing. In their
handling of the basic problem of church and state, the Henrician
publicists generally showed little originality. They drew mainly on
the stock of ideas common to late medieval Christendom and spent
most of their ingenuity in a desperate and pragmatic search for the
most impressive precedents and the most useful authorities.

But in the process they were also forced to examine their policies in
the light of history. They were forced, that is, to demonstrate how a
really unprecedented policy such as the Royal Supremacy could be
rationalized within the framework of traditional thought and in the
eyes of a public still largely committed to the old order. This line of
investigation led to what might be described as a kind of historical
casuistry which, at its best, made it possible for a few acute minds to
arrive at a more mature understanding of society as a changing thing.
At Cromwell's behest, Thomas Starkey took up the task of justifying,
on grounds other than precedent or mere expediency, the Erastian
church polity on which Henry had embarked. By adapting for English use the distinction already made by Continental reformers between those things that are essential to salvation, and hence timeless,
and those that, however important to the life of religion, are not
strictly essential but are subject to the contingencies of time and place,
he managed to lay the theoretical foundation for the Anglican *via
media* with remarkable firmness in the apparently shifting sands of historical relativism.[34]

Henry's publicists had scarcely finished the initial task of rationaliz-
ing the Royal Supremacy before they were called upon to argue the
king's case in an issue which, by revealing the complex relationships

34. On this subject, see Zeeveld, *passim*.

between the politico-ecclesiastical revolution and the social and economic interests of the country, did considerably more to foster analytical thought. The trouble arose particularly in the north and culminated during the late months of 1536 in the rising known as the Pilgrimage of Grace, an event that came close to upsetting not only Cromwell's policies but Henry's throne. Its causes were complex. For years the northern counties had been seething with unrest. The Tudor monarchy, with all its centralizing policies, had never quite succeeded in counteracting the centrifugal force still exerted by old feudal loyalties and the jealous resentment of the northern lords against the more prosperous, politically favored south and especially against the increasing interference, financial and administrative, of the central government. The conservative northern lords and gentry also saw in men like Cromwell and Cranmer, men chosen, with typical Tudor realism, rather for their innate ability than for their birth or social connections, a deliberate threat to those chivalric values that alone gave meaning to secular society as they understood it. Their tenants on the other hand accused them, with equal justice, of destroying the custom of the manor by enclosing the open fields and by arbitrarily raising rents. Poverty was, in fact, widespread in the north. In reality, both gentry and tenants were struggling in the ever tightening grip of economic forces that transcended the personal relationships and regional jealousies with which they were familiar and beyond which they could not see. Not much was needed to crystallize this fluid discontent into open rebellion, and for a brief moment to unite in frustration and despair elements that had little else in common.

As it happened, Henry and Cromwell provided much more than was needed by dissolving nearly four hundred of the lesser monasteries, a disproportionate number of which were located in Yorkshire and Lincolnshire. The men of the north found this ruthless, though not unprecedented, act the one thing they could agree upon. The monasteries meant a great deal to them in a practical way—probably more than elsewhere—by virtue of the services they rendered, or were supposed to render, as sources of poor relief and hospitality. They were also symbols of a way of life these men of the agrarian north felt was disintegrating in the fast moving world of Tudor politics. They stood, of course, especially for the old religion, now clearly challenged by a politically supported heresy born in the more commercial south.

It is useless to inquire into the merits of the case against the monasteries. Even if they had been as black as Cromwell's visitors painted them, which they certainly were not, their fall would doubtless still have rallied the otherwise disparate malcontents of the nothern counties.

The crisis was soon over. The rebels lacked a clear program and steady leadership, and the king acted with speed, skill, and a char' acteristically ruthless disregard for scruple. But the danger to his throne had been real while it lasted. Dependent as he was on popular support, he had to use persuasion as well as strategy, and so he turned again to the men who had served him so well in his battle with the papal hierarchy. This time Richard Morison was given the chief responsibility for stating the king's position.

It would have been easy enough for him simply to have rehearsed the old case for obedience to constituted authority. By 1536, after the heavy artillery of the Henrician bishops had already been expended freely in its defense, the idea of obedience in church and state was familiar enough. Or, if additional argument were needed, English' men, in whose own historical memory the Wars of the Roses were still fresh, could readily be aroused by examples taken from the more distant past illustrating what happens to a house divided. Rebellion could easily be made to seem unpatriotic, unchristian, unwise, and unnatural. Morison did just that. In two pamphlets, now recog' nized as his,[35] he labored these old themes with a vigor and vividness of style that no doubt recommended him to patrons who were by this time connoisseurs of the art of propagandist writing. In them, too, he turned his well nigh unrivalled knowledge of ancient and contem' porary history[36] to the practical uses of persuasion. But he did much more than that, and therein lies his value for our purposes. In the second of these tracts, *A Remedy for Sedition*—and incidentally the one he appears to have polished with special care, presumably for more reflective reading by an intelligent public—he brought his scholarship, his critical intelligence, and his first'hand acquaintance with other

35. C. R. Baskerville, "Sir Richard Morison as the Author of two Anonymous Tracts on Sedition," *Library*, 4th series (1936), No. 1, pp. 83'87. Baskerville's findings are accepted and confirmed by Zeeveld (see p. 174). The first of these tracts was entitled *A lamentation in whiche is shewed what Ruyne and destruction cometh of seditious rebellyon* (London, 1536), STC 15185, the second, *A Remedy for Sedition* (London, 1536), ed. E. M. Cox (London, 1933).

36. Zeeveld, p. 183.

lands to bear on the problem of uncovering the causes of the late rebellion.

These he found in the social background of the risings. The problem, he recognized, was not limited to the simple conflict between loyalty and disloyalty. It was not exclusively, not even in a sense primarily, a political problem. Although the voice of popular discontent had been largely drowned out in the formal pronouncements of the rebels by that of the more articulate clerical and aristocratic elements, no one in the England of 1536 who was willing to listen could have failed to catch the steady undertone of economic distress. "Some," Morison wrote, "say poverty is the cause," and, as far as it went, Morison was willing to agree with that estimate. But it did not go far enough. To say that poverty was the cause meant little more to him than to say that disobedience was the cause. "For," he continued, "I know divers realms, where poverty reigneth much more than in England, yet rebels there be none. The root is lower, dig deeper, ye may perchance find it."[37]

The real cause he found in the failure of England to make use of her natural endowments which were, he believed (and he spoke as one who had traveled), not only rich enough to support her people but greater than those of her most prosperous neighbors—perhaps, indeed, too great for the proper moral discipline of her own people.[38] This failure he laid at the door of English education. "Education, evil education, is a great cause of these and all other mischieves, that grow in a common wealth." It was natural that Morison, the humanist, onetime protégé of Pole, the friend of Starkey, whose mind had matured under the warm sun of Italian culture, should have seen in bad education a universal cause and in good education a panacea. Like Starkey and others of his humanist contemporaries, he found in the mind the source of mankind's potentiality. "There is a part in man, which is named the mind, that is of this nature, if it be galiard and lusty, either to do much good, or contrary, to do much hurt. If this lack good institution, . . . men may lack sedition, but they can not lack a thing within them to stir them to sedition."

37. *Remedy*, p. 35. Except where otherwise indicated, the following argument may be found on pages 3536.

38. *Ibid.*, pp. 35, 4748.

But Morison was not, like Elyot or Starkey, concerned with the more advanced training of the upper classes. That, to be sure, is important. "I long have supposed, that as the bringing up of the nobles is a safeguard of a common wealth, so their evil education is the ruin thereof. For as noble men be, so their servants are." Here, however, he hoped rather to provide the kind of practical training that would give every man who was capable the ability to earn a living. "For where so many lack honest occupations, where by all men, that can not otherwise live by their lands, ought to maintain themselves, how can we lack any kind of mischief?"[39] No man is born a crafts-man; he must be trained. Without honest crafts there is idleness, and idleness, if not "the whole cause of sedition," yet breeds rebels just as it breeds thieves and beggars. In short, the problem facing the English government was to make use of the potential latent in its subjects for productive work. In this respect, Morison suggests, England could learn from her industrious and frugal neighbors.[40]

This, however, was not a consideration uppermost in the minds of the more aristocratic of the rebel force. Rather, they were upset over the presence in the king's council of men of mean estate. In Henry's tendency to raise to positions of power and status men like Cromwell whose credentials were exclusively those of personal ability, and to pass over the "natural governors" of society, the northern nobles rightly saw a challenge to the chivalric values which still served them as the measure of secular life. The Tudors had learned to use talent where they found it, and to rely on an education no longer limited, like that of the schools, largely to clerks, or like that of the knightly tradition, to the sons of the aristocracy. Henry was here in the curious position of the revolutionary against whose policies rebels appealed in the name of sacred tradition. As so often in his policies during the mid-thirties, Henry was being pushed by the dictates of expediency into positions too radical in their implications to be entirely congenial to his basically conservative temper. In the rapids of revolution no current runs straight. For the moment the king's spokesmen were forced to follow at the same time two contradictory lines of argument. They had to justify the promotion of men like Cromwell on the ground of careers

---

39. Cf. Armstrong, *A treatise concerninge the Staple* in Tawney and Power, *Tudor Economic Documents*, III, 112.

40. *Remedy*, pp. 47-52.

open to talent; yet they had also, like any other government of the period when faced with rebellion, to preach the generally accepted doctrine of obedience within a society of order and degree.

Morison saw more clearly than most the real implications of what was going on in English society. Himself a man of poor origins, trained in the society of Renaissance Italy where an ideal of *virtù* had long been accepted in theory and was to a significant degree vindicated in practice, he saw in English society and in Tudor policy similar tendencies. Thus he recognized, perhaps more fully than the king, that the governing class was in fact no longer a strictly hereditary caste, primarily military in its training and protective in its social function, but rather a class actually open to men of ability, a class whose function was now primarily civil, and one which demanded above all a trained and resourceful mind.[41] Morison was able for a moment to see clearly outlined in the flames of rebellion the meaning of social facts that had considerably outrun social theory. And so he undertook to state in specific terms—and for the first time in anything like an officially sanc- tioned paper—the familiar Renaissance idea that nobility depends on character and ability expressed in the active service of the common- wealth rather than on birth or inherited wealth.[42] And the implication is clear that the virtues to which he is referring are those of the educated gentleman rather than those traditionally ascribed to the knight. King Henry, he wrote,

> hath evermore well declared that true nobility is never, but where virtue is; and hath evermore from the first of his reign, hitherto, both by his own great study, to attain learning, wisdom, and other princely qualities, and also in giving offices, dignities, and honor, well testified, that he will all his subjects to contend, who may obtain most qualities, most wit, most virtue; and this only to be the way to promotion, and here nobility to consist."[43]

If in running, wrestling, archery, or horsemanship a man should fail to distinguish himself, it would mean nothing that his father was adept at these sports. How much more should the government of a commonwealth be placed in the hands of those who have demon-

41. See above, chap. vii.

42. For discussion of this subject and for bibliographical references, see Ferguson, *Indian Summer of English Chivalry.*

43. *Remedy*, pp. 16-17; see also p. 55.

strated, not their fathers' ability, but their own? Following Plato, Morison asserts that civic honor should go first to qualities of the mind, secondly to physical prowess, and only thirdly to such externals as family and possessions.[44]

In thus stressing the quality of a man's mind as the most important basis for his advancement, Morison was not alone. The humanists of his generation, although aristocratic in their social ideal and perfectly willing to accept in theory the principle of degree as the skeletal struc-ture on which a stable society must be built, leaned toward the notion of an aristocracy of merit. They had, as we have seen, a deep and touching faith in the educability of the mind and in its power, once properly trained. Writing only a little while before Morison wrote the *Remedy*, Elyot repeatedly expressed the idea that men of under-standing should have pre-eminence in a commonwealth[45]—and this within the context of a social ideal, classic in its adherence to the principle of degree.[46]

This was a position the implications of which Henry, had he been aware of them, would have repudiated. And Morison himself, with the king almost literally looking over his shoulder as he wrote, was at pains also to state the more orthodox theory: "Lords must be lords, commons must be commons, every man accepting his degree, every man content to have that that he lawfully may come by."[47] If there is any possibility of reconciling these two theories, and for Morison I think there was, it lies in that last phrase. He appears here to be advocating a society of class and degree, yet allowing for the irrepres-sible dynamism of individual enterprise, to be guarding against sedition, not personal ambition. Such a position should not be too surprising in one whose thought followed the bias of humanism. Elyot said something very similar when he wrote "They which excel other in this influence of understanding, and do employ it to the detaining of other within the bounds of reason, and show how to provide for their necessary living; such ought to be set in a more high place than the residue."[48] To Morison and Elyot, and, as we have seen, also to Starkey, man and his society appeared possessed of an inexhaustible

44. *Ibid.*, p. 18.
45. *Governor*, I, 6; II, 376, 378 ff.
46. E. M. W. Tillyard, *The Elizabethan World Picture* (New York, 1944), pp. 11-12.
47. *Remedy*, p. 22.
48. *Governor*, I, 6; see also I, 28.

potential which always tended to belie the static terms in which formal and accepted theory was generally expressed—even by themselves. And not the least of the results of the Pilgrimage of Grace was the brief but powerful stimulus it gave to a more profound exploration of that potential.

∽ ∽ ∽

The risings of 1536 again called attention to the problem of poverty. By showing how it was related to sedition, Morison gave it a new and politically alarming dimension. Meanwhile other critics of English society were examining it, together with the related evils of idleness, vagabondage, and beggary, with renewed interest.[49] The paradox of indigence and "dearth" in a land more than ordinarily endowed for the maintenance of man had for some time plagued such socially conscious critics. By the 1530's the government itself was beginning to accept the responsibility for at least the relief of the poor and to recognize the need for specific legislation.

In this investigation of poverty, the humanists again took the lead, following in the path already well marked in the realm of theory by More in *Utopia* and, in a more immediately practical context, by Vives, who wrote his influential treatise *De Subventione Pauperum* in 1526 while sojourning in England. During the thirties, the example of More was followed most notably by Starkey and Morison, the former in his *Dialogue*, the latter in the *Remedy*. Both had a good deal to say about the roots of poverty in the course of a broader analysis of the national scene. William Marshall was apparently influenced directly by Vives, but achieved a mature insight of his own in a draft, now attributed to him,[50] of a bill for the relief of the poor. Public concern was not, however, the monopoly of the humanist critics. Clement Armstrong, who can hardly be so classified, was also drawn to the problem of poverty in the course of the pamphlets in which he took it upon himself to analyze the entire economic structure of England.[51] All of these men, in their way, agreed with Vives that the

49. F. R. Salter (ed.), *Some Early Tracts on Poor Relief* (London, 1926) contains pertinent materials. See also E. M. Leonard, *The Early History of English Poor Relief* (Cambridge, 1900); W. K. Jordan, *Philanthropy in England, 1480-1660* (New York, 1959); Helen C. White, chap. vi.

50. G. R. Elton, "An Early Tudor Poor Law," *EcHR*, 2nd Ser., VI (1953), 55-67.

51. *How the Comen People may be set to worke an Order of a Comen Welth*, in Pauli, *Drei*

health of a society depended in large part on its ability to care for the poor and to eradicate idleness, voluntary or otherwise.

Whether the increasing attention being paid to poverty and its related evils resulted chiefly from an actual increase in the incidence of those evils or from the fact that they were being examined for the first time by critics more than ever before equipped by virtue of their education, travel, and experience in public affairs to anatomize such problems is a question difficult to answer, and one not entirely ger⁄main to this study. Unquestionably, however, these critics of the thirties had plenty to criticize. The social and economic forces which More had examined with both prescience and misgivings had not abated. The price revolution was proceeding at a constantly ac⁄celerating pace. The profit⁄minded gentry had lost nothing of their desire to turn their lands to good account, regardless of social con⁄sequence. And the redistributed monastic lands provided the means of still more rapidly accelerated change.

It was not, however, the fact of poverty that concerned the critics of the 1530's so much as its social origins. Like Thomas More (to whose analysis they added little), they saw it as a social phenomenon, the product of observable, moving forces. This is where both they and More differed from their predecessors. Sensitive as these earlier critics were to the plight of the poor, and ready at times to preach a social gospel in which the poor man was given almost Christ⁄like attributes, subtle as were the canon lawyers in defining the obligations of the community for the relief of the poor,[52] the medieval mind failed to see the necessity of investigating the causes of poverty. The poor were a constant element in the society of chronically sinful man. No reasons needed to be sought to account for their condition other than the failure of the rich to perform their eleemosynary duty toward the deserving poor and the failure of the "sturdy" poor to seek their own welfare through the avoidance of vice and the cultivation of industrious habits. Moreover, except where poverty gave rise to crime or va⁄grancy, it remained a subject to be examined primarily within a moral and ecclesiastical frame of reference. In contrast, the early Tudor humanists could hardly think of the problem without looking also

---

volkswirthschaftliche Denkschriften and *Howe to Reforme the Realme in settying them to worke to restore Tillage*, in Tawney and Power, *Tudor Economic Documents*, III.

52. Brian Tierney, *Medieval Poor Law* (Berkeley, 1959) is indispensable on this subject.

for its causes, and, be it remembered, for those causes which could be reached by remedial policy; for what set them, here as elsewhere, to looking for the causes of social evils was their faith in the possibility of remedy through constructive policy. Although the social context of poverty had been changing for generations, it was only in the early sixteenth century that English commentators recognized at all generally that discussion of the problem must take the several moving forces responsible for social change into account. And, since jurisdiction of the church was being eliminated by the maturing monopoly of all jurisdiction by the sovereign state, any discussion of remedial policy must be carried on in basically secular terms.

This concern for practical measures helps, incidentally, to explain why these writers tended to trace poverty to idleness, and there to rest their case rather than to pursue their analysis any further. Idleness, a favorite *bête noire* of the medieval commentators, continued to preoccupy those of the sixteenth century. But, like so many words used in that latter period of transition, its meanings lead in two quite divergent directions. It could indicate, as it did to the medieval moralist, a weak/ness in the moral fiber of the individual. Or it could mean the kind of involuntary unemployment which More found to be the product of changes in the organization of economic life. In the former sense it could be coupled nicely with the avarice or covetousness of the propertied classes to become the double/edged cause of all poverty. This moral explanation continued to be voiced by sixteenth/century analysts. It was naturally enough most common among the reforming preachers who in many ways perpetuated the habits of mind typical of their medieval brethren. Yet even to them poverty was only in part a moral problem; nor had they by the mid/century mark succumbed to the virulent and theologically fortified moralism of the later Puritans which made the poor, through the shiftlessness peculiar to those from whom God had turned His face, the predestined authors of their own misery. Poverty to them remained a social problem, a challenge alike to the public conscience and to the ingenuity of the public authorities. It was, after all, Latimer's support of the reforming element in the government of Edward VI, the "commonwealth" group who hoped by legislative action to remove the social causes of poverty, that in/curred the suspicion of the landlords, one of whom singled him out as a "seditious fellow."[53] It is in this social connection that idleness achieved its most advanced and significant place in early Tudor discussions of poverty. It bulks large not so much because the commentators failed to see the possibility of, as Morison suggested, digging deeper for the roots, but because they saw in providing all willing workers with the means of working out their livelihood the practical starting point toward achieving a remedy for poverty.[54] The ingenuity expended in devising schemes of this sort, and also for seeing that those who were work-shy were required to labor for the common good, was surprisingly great—surprising, that is, if it is not seen in relation to the intelligent concern revealed in this literature to get at the causes of poverty. But we shall have to examine this constructive side of the commentator's mind more thoroughly in a later chapter.

Starkey, who, however, was more concerned with the "ill-occupied" (his term for those who pandered to the more frivolous tastes) than the unemployed, was able to use the term in both senses. To him idleness was both a moral failing, to some extent up to the individual to remedy, and a social problem over which the individual had little control and for which the cause must be sought still deeper in the body politic. If, the Thomas Lupset of his *Dialogue* asserts, poverty is indeed widespread in England, if, as is agreed, there are more beggars in England "for the number of people" than in any other Christian country, the fault lies in "much idleness and ill policy."[55] But, like both More and Morison, it is the ill policy with which he is primarily concerned, the failure, that is, of those in authority to devise plans to prevent the spread of this social canker.

Simple as the humanist analysis of the causes of poverty seems to modern eyes, it ran nevertheless far ahead of that which the men actually saddled with the formulation of policy could manage.[56] It was not hard for the intellectual, whether his point of observation lay within the circle of the royal court or safely beyond it, to see idleness as a social problem as well as a personal one, the result of economic

53. Hugh Latimer, *Seven Sermons before Edward VI*, ed. E. Arber (London, 1895), pp. 4-6.

54. See, for example, Armstrong's pamphlets referred to above, n. 51; also *LP*, V, No. 1501.

55. *Dialogue*, p. 89; see also pp. 90-93, 142-145.

56. R. H. Tawney, *Religion and the Rise of Capitalism* (Penguin edition, 1947), pp. 217-218; see also pp. 100-101.

distress as well as of shiftlessness.   The administrator could hardly avoid considering idleness primarily in terms of vagrancy and vagrancy in terms of public safety.   In a day of ridiculously inadequate police protection, the vagrant was a potentially dangerous character; the men responsible for measures to control vagrancy thought only of treating him as one personally responsible for his own condition. And so the brutally coercive legislation which for the first time at/tempted to cope with poverty on a national and secular scale reflected little of the analytical subtlety of the humanist reformers regarding the social origins of poverty.   The act of 1536, though reflecting some of the ideas incorporated in William Marshall's draft, reflects none of the humanist's concern for cause.[57]

∽ ∽ ∽

The men of early Tudor England recognized in the absolute indigence of the beggar merely the extreme manifestation of a general lack of plenty, a "dearth" which affected all of their countrymen in one degree or another and made itself most particularly apparent in the disturbingly rapid rise in prices.   Thus the problem of poverty merged in their minds easily with that of "wealth"—the term used not in a modern, capitalist sense, but in the sense of welfare, the "weal" of a society still thought of ideally as one of hierarchy, the plenty out of which all men might derive the means necessary for the kind of life appropriate to their station.   It is this preoccupation with "wealth" that gives to the term "commonwealth" a social and, even more narrowly, an economic meaning rather than, or in addition to, a political meaning.   And it is for this reason that so much of the so/called political literature in early Tudor England turns upon economic rather than strictly political issues.

So it is that idleness, instead of being treated strictly in connection with the plight of the poor, becomes a matter of concern to the entire national welfare, for it involves the ability of England to develop the resources with which God had endowed her.   That God had been generous to His Englishmen, no one seemed to doubt for a moment. Morison, as we have seen, was convinced that life in England was, in comparison with that in other countries, a little too easy,[58] a fact

57. See below, chap. xi.
58. *Remedy*, pp. 47/48.

which helped in turn to explain the idleness of Englishmen and their consequent failure to realize their economic potential.   Starkey is even more specific.   "This realm," Lupset says in the *Dialogue*, "hath been called ever rich, and of all Christendom one of the wealthiest.   For as touching wool and lead, tin, iron, silver and gold, yea and all things necessary for the life of man, . . . I think our country may be compared with any other."[59]   Armstrong, who no doubt knew a bit more about the economic life of the country than the scholarly Starkey, is equally specific and considerably more accurate.   God's endowment of England lay mainly in the ability of the English soil to produce a quality of wool superior to any other wool in the world.   But England does not have certain other commodities, the "fruits of olives, figgs, almonds, dates and oranges," for instance, that come out of Spain.[60] Above all, she does not mine her own gold and silver, and therefore is dependent upon other countries for coinable metals.[61]   Yet these deficiencies, Armstrong argues, need not embarrass England, provided she make the most of her own special endowments by eliminating idle- ness, eschewing unnecessary imports, and seeing to it that her wool and cloth command the kind of market they deserve.

Yet these optimistic statements are made in the course of discussions which have been prompted in the first place by an acute awareness of scarcity and a feeling that the foreign countries were competing on terms steadily disadvantageous to England.   The problem of poverty is indeed a national one and it is getting worse, not better.   Pole answers Lupset's confident assertion by pointing out that, while it was undoubtedly true that England was once the "most wealthy and rich isle of Christendom," that was "many years ago."   Now, "if you hearken to the plaint of all states [estates] and degrees you shall doubt of this matter nothing at all.   The ploughman, the artificer, the merchant, the gentleman—yea, lords and princes, bishops and prelates—all with one voice cry they lack money, and that they be nothing so wealthy and rich as they have been in time past."   Who, he continues, could deny "when he looketh to the great dearth of corn, cattle, victual and of all other things necessary, a common dearth argueth great lack? If there were abundance and plenty, it could not be long so dear,

59. *Dialogue*, p. 88.
60. *A treatise concerninge the Staple*, III, 98-100; cf. *How the Comen People*.
61. *Howe to Reforme*, III, 115.

for abundance ever maketh everything good cheap." Pole is forced to agree, however, that, despite this general dearth and poverty, England is still better off than other countries, her commons "wealthier" than those of France, Italy, and Spain.[62] But this, he insists, is not the issue. If Englishmen lack what they are accustomed to enjoy, it is a matter for public concern regardless of how much better off they are than others. And so it is agreed that England must solve the dearth that makes her people complain with justice of poverty, however relative it may be.

Starkey is less at home amidst the complexities of economic life than in the realm of political and legal theory. At one point in the *Dialogue*, he seems ready to blame everything on despotism and on the threat of tyranny that he, like Fortescue, believed implicit in it.[63] He is considerably less familiar with the business world than old Armstrong who had been raised in the rough-and-tumble world of London business. He fails in particular to see the close relationships of economic problems and tends to treat them each in semi-isolation. But the reader should be able to read between his lines a groping effort to explain why England (so he and his contemporaries believed) is not so wealthy as in former times. He seems to find the key to this large question in her failure to employ her manpower effectively and to foster a high level of discipline in her people. If ploughmen were as industrious as in other countries, the land would yield a greater plenty of food, and waste lands could be utilized for the support of a larger population, which, he contends, is essential to the prosperity of a great state. Like most of his contemporaries, he was preoccupied with what he considered to be the fact of continuous depopulation. Similarly, artificers and craftsmen are negligent "in the use of their crafts." Then there are those who are idle, either voluntarily or through force of adverse circumstances, and those who might just as well be because they are "ill-occupied"—serving men in the retinues of nobles, monks, friars, and the hangers-on of the religious houses, artificers engaged in pandering to the taste for "new-fangled things" and to the "vain pleasure" of the body, providers of light

62. *Dialogue*, pp. 88-90.
63. *Ibid.*, p. 100.

entertainment, and merchants who trade necessaries for "vain trifles and conceits" from overseas.[64]

On one point only does he demonstrate more than a layman's understanding of the economic situation. He appreciated better than most of his reforming friends the complexity of the problem of enclosures. Ready enough to admit that irresponsible enclosures depopulated villages and created scarcity of grain, he argues in favor of moderate enclosure in the interests not only of sheep, "by whose profits the wealth and pleasure here of this realm is much maintained," but of all livestock.[65] Perhaps he was here speaking not only in behalf of a balanced economy—which I think was his primary concern—but also for the interests of the landed classes. There is an element of aristocratic conservatism in Starkey's social thought that sits uneasily beside the radicalism of his political preference for a monarchy ruling by consent of the governed. In this connection it might also be noted that one of the social and economic maladjustments through which both the "common wealth" and the social system is most endangered is the tendency of men to eat, dress, and build beyond their means and their social status.[66]

The important thing about this otherwise not very penetrating analysis of Starkey's is that it was carried on within the range of the observable and in terms of the concrete and ponderable. Moral considerations obviously underlie human actions. Sloth, gluttony, pride, and avarice are to Starkey very real and powerful forces. But he treats them as forces to be controlled by policy rather than by preaching, for they are of public as well as of private significance. Indeed Starkey's moralism culminates, not in a Jeremiad directed to individuals in the hope that they might mend their ways, but in the policy of a paternalistic government which accepts as its basic function the regulation of private interests and the disciplining— meaning restraining—of private folly in the common interest. Despite his philosophical opposition to despotic monarchy and his practical fear of all tyranny, he apparently saw no alternative but to give the

---

64. *Ibid.*, pp. 75⸓87.

65. *Ibid.*, pp. 95⸓97. A similarity between this passage and one in the *Discourse of the Common Weal* has been noticed; A. Tersen, *John Hales, Économiste Anglais du milieu du XVIᵉ Siècle* (Avallon, 1907), pp. 86⸓87.

66. *Dialogue*, pp. 93⸓95.

paternalistic state the responsibility for manipulating the causal forces in economic life.

And so he falls back on the crude mercantilist principles that had been taking shape since the mid-fourteenth century. He finds a serious threat lurking in the tendency of English merchants to export such necessary commodities as "cattle and corn, wool, tin and lead and other metal whereof we have no such abundance that our country, with commodity, may lack so much," and to import such things "as we may not only lack right well, but such as be the destruction of our people and of all diligent exercise of arts and crafts in our country— as, many sorts of delicate wines, fine cloths, says and silks, beads, combs, girdles and knives and a thousand such trifling things which other we might well lack, or else, at the least, our own people might be occupied with working thereof, which now, by the reason thereof, are much corrupt with idleness and sloth."[67]

The same mercantilist arguments based on the same assumption that the national state is a sort of giant business enterprise, its collective interest superior to the private interest of the citizen, finds expression in Armstrong's pamphlets. In them, too, moral considerations, though never far from the writer's mind, become factors to be reckoned with by the secular government. Armstrong, indeed, tends to lump them all together in the general formula stated more forcefully than elegantly in the following sentence: "No man in England never seeketh for no common weal, but all and every for his singular weal."[68] Himself a business man, and apparently a shrewd and successful one, he nevertheless looked upon private enterprise and the profit motive with traditional suspicion: or perhaps it would be more accurate to say that he transferred the dynamism obviously inherent in capitalistic enterprise from the individual to the state. By so doing he also transferred the moral criticism traditionally levelled against such enterprise from a religious to a secular context with government as the moderating, the disciplining agency.

And, although a most pious man, given in his later years to concocting sermons as well as conducting economic investigation, he considers the province of governmental policy to be an extensive one, bounded only by the broad outline of God's plan. God has estab-

67. *Ibid.*, pp. 92-93.
68. *A treatise concerninge the Staple*, III, 114.

lished the basic laws according to which economic activity must proceed. He has endowed nations differently, but he leaves it to them to work out a method of trade whereby their various and peculiar endowments can be exchanged to their mutual advantage.[69] He has decreed that all common people must work for their living,[70] and it is God's plan that the "whole wealth of the body of the realm riseth out of the labor and works of the common people."[71] But it is up to the national government to see that they are properly employed for the common good.[72] God is even back of the bullionist principle that is the main support of Armstrong's economic world: "for God hath ordained that gold and silver should be brought out of other countries into England for woolen cloths and for other commodities, which God giveth yearly to the realm."[73] Nor is God against a reasonable increase. The king and his lords must endeavor to bring the realm not merely to its former prosperity, but "to a more wealth than ever it was in, as much as God hath not otherwise ordained it."[74] God, in short, has established the laws of economic life and also the rather broad limitations within which man can labor constructively.

It is important to notice in addition that, within these divinely ordained limitations, there lies the whole range of more specific relation‑ships which must be understood as a prerequisite to the formulation of policy, and analyzed in order to be understood. To this more particular task Armstrong brings a wealth of data, drawn from his own observation and experience. Here the difference between the old business man and the humanist scholar becomes glaringly apparent. Armstrong undoubtedly knew much more about his subject than Starkey. In addition, if his vision of England's economic profile is at times distorted, he must be given credit for marshaling his data in such a way as to develop a coherent theory. Whereas the reader must search for the key to Starkey's explanation of England's supposedly declining "wealth," must indeed put two and two together to deter‑mine that it is this general "poverty" that is the chief ground of Starkey's anxiety, he is left in no doubt about the lines of cause and effect to

69. *Ibid.*, pp. 98‑100; *Howe to Reforme*, III, 128‑129.
70. *Howe to Reforme*, III, 127.
71. *Ibid.*, pp. 115‑116, 127.
72. *Ibid.*, p. 115.
73. *Ibid.*, p. 117.
74. *Ibid.*, p. 115.

which Armstrong calls his attention—and that despite the fact that they often lead through a veritable jungle of facts and figures and grammatical anomalies.

To follow Armstrong's more detailed analyses would be tiresome, and unnecessary for immediate purposes. Suffice it to say that he finds the key to most of England's economic ills in the existence of an inordinate number of merchants who, because of the fact that there is no staple in England, operate free from any close governmental control, trafficking in buying and selling, and, as middlemen, con‚ tributing nothing to the productive capacity of the country, while profiting privately at the expense of the commonwealth. These are the men who, by exploiting the overseas market for English wool, have so raised its price that English farmers have rushed headlong to enclose arable land for pasture, thereby depopulating villages and raising the price of food, and, by bringing into use the wrong kind of pasture, adulterating the quality of the wool itself.[75] They also trade good English commodities for foreign‚made goods, for many of which, especially luxury items, Armstrong shares Starkey's stern disapproval. By so doing they make it hard for English industries to thrive and for English craftsmen to find work. Worst of all, to this convinced bullionist, they deal to a large extent in goods, exchanging English for foreign products rather than for hard cash. That is of fundamental importance, for "the whole wealth of the realm is for our rich com‚ modities to get out of all other realms therefore ready money; and after the money is brought in to the whole realm, so shall all people in the realm be made rich."[76]

It is in this area of concrete fact and observable relationship that, according to Armstrong, policy‚makers fail, and they fail because they do not pursue the technique of causal analysis. "The lords in Eng‚ land hath enough to do to harken always to mischiefs done in the realm daily for lack of a right order of life in the whole commonalty, but they never search to the original cause, to know what is the very

75. Cf. *Dialogue*, p. 96, where a similar recognition is made of the natural conditions governing the growing of fine wool.

76. *A treatise concerninge the Staple*, III, 105. Though bullionist in his main emphasis, Armstrong was groping his way toward a concept of the balance of trade. See *ibid.*, 105‚106 and *Howe to Reforme*, III, 128‚129. The above arguments represent only very sketchily and in oversimplified form what Armstrong develops principally in this work on the Staple, but also in *Howe to Reforme*.

root of the whole need, necessity and scarcity of the whole realm."[77]
Devoted by habit to the protection of the community from disorder,
they fail to see the economic system as a whole. They cannot see the
wood for the trees. And there, Armstrong seems to imply, is where
the likes of himself can make their special contribution. He may
have underrated the men actually engaged in government: such self-
appointed consultants usually do. But it remains extremely important
to notice the emergence of so clearly conscious an appreciation of the
necessity of analysis in search of what makes the economic system
move. Indeed it is a matter of considerable significance in itself that
a man like Armstrong should have become so clearly aware of the
existence of such a mechanism of impersonal, manipulatable cause
and effect. Once again we are permitted to remark how readily the
observation of economic relationships, especially first hand observation,
could lead the observer into the maze of causal analysis, and with
what relative sharpness it brought into focus the inherent dynamism
of Renaissance life.

ʕ ʕ ʕ

Starkey wrote the *Dialogue* before the dissolution of the monasteries
had set in motion a process which profoundly affected the "wealth"
of England. The historian knows that Henry's decision to suppress
the religious houses and confiscate their lands, a decision taken for
fiscal, political, and religious reasons (and pretty much in that order of
priority), did more than any other of his enactments to change the
secular habits of Englishmen and in the long run to alter the structure of
English society. It should therefore be interesting to inquire whether
Starkey, or any other of the men who have left us the fruits of their
observation of English society in that revolutionary decade, were able
to catch the significance of his decision—its social and economic
significance in particular, for its religious meaning was plain for all to
see. We have already noticed that Morison had been required to
cope intellectually with the first of the overt repercussions. But he had
perforce to deal primarily with the problem of sedition and with social
conditions only as they helped explain why the commons took part
in the risings. If he recognized the important part the dissolution of
the monasteries had played in the northern discontent he did not find

77. *A treatise concerninge the Staple*, III, 94.

place for it in his otherwise perspicacious *Remedy*. The risings had followed hard upon the initial movement toward suppression, leaving little time for even so keen an observer as Morison to appreciate its implications. Only a year later, however, we find Starkey including in an unsolicited letter of general counsel, addressed to the king, a lengthy comment on the whole policy.

It throws a good deal of light on Starkey's grasp of social and political reality, for it indicated that he already had a pretty good idea where that policy was leading. He of course applauded its ostensible purpose in cutting away the last vestiges of Romanism. He seems quite sincerely to have felt that the monasteries had, in the light of the new theology, no longer any religious reason for being, and that, as far as their social function was concerned, they had become parasitic or worse. But he was apparently well aware of Henry's main purpose, namely to recoup a depleted treasury.[78] He saw also (he claims, no doubt for self-protection, that it was "openly judged and commonly thought") that the confiscated monastic properties were likely to pass out of the king's hands and into those of such people as would pay for them: "great lords and gentlemen of much possessions and to them which have thereof no great need at all." This, he argued stoutly, would greatly reduce the "public utility" (the phrase has an oddly modern ring!) of the act, whereas if the lands were "leased to copy-hold, and of a mean rent, to younger brethern living in service un-profitably, and to them which be of lower estate and degree," the effect would be to "set forward Christian civility and much increase the number of your people."[79] This, the relation of the welfare of a country to the size of its population, was a favorite topic of Starkey's. In the *Dialogue* the speakers agree that no country can be healthy wherein there are either too many or too few people,[80] and that in England the problem is rather too few than too many.[81] And, among other measures to increase the rate of legitimate births, they discuss the possibility of modifying the law prohibiting the secular clergy, at least, from marrying.[82] Now Starkey sees a further pos-

78. Herrtage, pp. liii-lv.
79. *Ibid.*, p. lviii.
80. *Dialogue*, p. 56.
81. *Ibid.*, pp. 75-76.
82. *Ibid.*, p. 140.

sibility in the wholesale marriage of the regular clergy.[83]   But the greatest benefit, he argues, would come from the use of the monastic lands for what he rather vaguely calls the "setting forth and increase of all virtue and honesty." That appears, on explanation, to involve the encouragement of two classes of people, namely "men of letters and learning, and men exercised in feats of arms and chivalry, of the which as the one sort is necessary for war, so the other must needs be had in time of peace."[84] It all adds up to the humanist plea for better education, with the emphasis implicitly, though unmistakeably, placed on secular education.

Starkey's determination to discuss this primarily ecclesiastical problem in terms of its impact on the secular life of the national community no doubt sets him apart from most of his contemporaries. At least no similarly systematic and penetrating analysis appears to be extant. But the many implications of the suppression could hardly have been lost on the intelligent observer. The possibilities inherent in such a policy had provoked speculation from the time when disendowment was first thought of as a purgative for whatever ailed the church.[85] Simon Fish, for all his exaggeration, saw at least how advantageous it could be for his purposes to stress the social aspect of his proposal to disendow the clergy. Now, after it had begun, Bishop Latimer viewed the dissolution with both hope and misgivings. Like Starkey, he hoped that the lands might be used for social purposes, and in a sermon before the king he urged Henry to "revert the abbeys and priories to places of study and good letters and to the continual relief of the poor."[86] That he felt it necessary to preach such a sermon indicates, however, that he also shared Starkey's deep suspicion that such was not likely to be the final disposition of these properties.

As time went on, and as the abbey lands went in fact to individuals whose acquisitive instincts were more in tune with the times than was the idealism of the reformers, hope languished and suspicion ripened into disillusionment. During the last half-dozen years of Henry's life at least three pamphlets were written which confirm Latimer's fear that, so far from contributing to the general welfare, the suppression

83. Herrtage, p. lviii.
84. *Ibid.*, p. liv.
85. See above, chap. iv.
86. Quoted in Chester, *Hugh Latimer*, p. 126.

had set in motion tendencies that worked in the opposite direction.[87] With these we shall have more to do in the next chapter.

↶ ↶ ↶

The years of Henry VIII's reign that followed the execution of Cromwell proved comparatively barren of analytical discussion. Confessional controversy continued, though within strictly cir/ cumscribed areas. But the eagerness of the men of the thirties to anatomize the political body in an effort to understand its natural processes is not nearly so apparent in the writings of the early and middle forties. The group of scholars who had gathered at the court seems to have broken up. Starkey died shortly after Cromwell's fall. We hear little thereafter of William Marshall. Although Morison continued for a while to write in support of the king's policies, his productive literary career was virtually over by that time.[88] And the younger scholars like Thomas Smith and John Cheke who were able eventually to carry the humanist influence into the reigns of the mid/ century, though still enjoying royal patronage in the form of academic preferment, were not as yet encouraged to express themselves on matters of public concern. Then, too, some of the best minds of the period were turned from the critical study of society to the more im/ mediately pressing business of government. Stephen Gardiner, for example, turned a mind unusually well grounded in humane letters and in Roman law almost exclusively to the task of maintaining some equilibrium in a government committed both to an orthodox theology and an Erastian polity. Any concern that he and the rest of the con/ servative prelates might have had for social or political reform was consequently tempered to the point of extinction by dictates of ex/ pediency and by an ever/present fear of popular uprising.[89]

The urge to inquire and to counsel did not, however, languish utterly. Indeed, when we see John Hales, the public/spirited and largely self/educated gentleman who was to serve so faithfully the quixotic cause of the Protector Somerset, already in the early 1540's seeking to bring his unsolicited defense of the English Common Law

87. In addition to Brinkelow's *Complaint*, pp. 9/10, see *A Supplytacion to our most Soveraigne Lorde Kynge Henry the Eyght*, pp. 38/44, and *A Supplication of the Poore Commons*, pp. 79/81, in *Four Supplications*.
88. Zeeveld, pp. 233/234.
89. L. B. Smith, *Tudor Prelates and Politics, 1536/1558* (Princeton, 1953), pp. 52/57.

to the attention of the king,[90] and when, in 1542 we find Thomas Becon deviating sufficiently from his early career as an apologist for the reformed religion to compose a likewise unsolicited pamphlet on the conduct of an apparently impending war with France,[91] we become aware that a new generation of citizen-counselors is ready to take the place of the scholarly Starkey and the garrulous Armstrong, the ambitious Morison and the practical Marshall. Likewise earnest of things to come, and by no means unimportant in itself, is the fact that the last few years of Henry's reign witnessed the appearance of the first of those tracts in which the more extreme Protestant group vented their disappointment at what they had already come to believe was the miscarriage of a great and godly revolution. Of the often penetrating comment of Henry Brinkelow, especially, we shall have more to say anon. A cloud of like witnesses was to follow in the reign of Edward VI. But before the death of Henry he stands, if not alone, at least among those who were the exception, and it is perhaps significant that his writings were first printed, not in England, but on the Continent.[92]

90. *LP*, XVII (1542), Appendix 1.
91. Becon, *The Policy of War*.
92. See Cowper's introduction to the *Complaint* and the *Lamentation*. See also tracts referred to in n. 87, above.

CHAPTER IX. THE SEARCH FOR CAUSE: THE AFTERMATH OF REFORM

ALTHOUGH IT WAS TO BE SOME TIME BEFORE THE articulate citizen could enjoy anything like the encouragement given him by the Vicar General—not really until Somerset's protectorate—the last few years of Henry's reign and the first half of Edward VI's witnessed the advent of a new generation of commentators, willing and able to subject the problems raised by the Henrician revolution to an analysis, profuse in quantity if uneven in quality.

It is difficult to generalize in describing the mood of this new generation; for, unlike their predecessors, they did not all speak in basically similar terms. The men of the thirties who undertook to anatomize the body politic spoke a common language derived from the closely related traditions of Erasmian humanism and native realism, a language well suited to the discussion of secular issues. That language continued to be used, and, indeed, in the most penetrating analyses of social and economic problems made during the midcentury period. In the decade of the forties, however, those same problems were also discussed in the atmosphere of embattled theology and in terms of repentance and the wrath to come. The attempts at social analysis made at this time thus reflect two curiously, at times deceptively, divergent tendencies: the one characterized by a predominantly humanistic secularism, tempered by a devout concern for the spiritual welfare of the community, the other by the zeal of the Protestant reformers, tempered by a strong social consciousness and by the lingering effects of a humanistic education. What gives a certain unity to their thought is a common and profound belief in the ideal of the commonwealth, that touchstone of all early Tudor social and political thought. In the name of the "very and true commonweal," an ideal largely medieval in origin and conservative in its implications, the most zealous Protestant and the most secular humanist could attack the same problems, confident that they were both striving toward the same good end.

One other thing they had in common. Both regarded the trend

of affairs in the England of their day with more than the usual misgivings of the social critic.   The reform of religion had not fulfilled
the hopes of the Protestant party.   What seemed in its inception so
godly a reformation had by the forties somehow misfired.   It had
failed to hit the old religion with the deadly accuracy its more extreme
proponents had hoped for, and it had inadvertently damaged the
social order to an extent that seemed to the conservative social consciousness of the reformers nothing short of disastrous.   Yet the religious
reformers were quite prepared to accept as natural and desirable that
changes in doctrine or ecclesiastical polity were bound to bring in
their wake changes in the rest of society.   Indeed they would have
considered odd and misguided any attempt to separate the two aspects
of man's activity, so deeply were religious practices and institutions
still embedded in the social soil, and so completely was the life of man
subordinated in their eyes to the will of God.   The reforming preachers
of the early Tudor period believed that the new dispensation in religion should therefore find its reflection in a more just and humane
society, which is to say a more godly society.   When, as it turned out,
their hopes seemed indefinitely deferred, they asked, in their sickness
of heart, why? Those critics who were more capable of separating
religious and secular concerns, if only for the purpose of analysis,
turned their attention to the same social conditions.   Like the religious
reformers they were profoundly disturbed at the apparent decay of the
functional, organic society idealized in the concept of the commonwealth.   But, whereas with the former the commonwealth assumed
a quasi-theocratic character, with the latter it was a primarily secular
ideal, or more accurately, one which could be studied profitably,
perhaps primarily, in secular terms.

What alarmed all observers, regardless of their point of view, were
the many manifestations of the pervasive and expanding spirit of private
enterprise.   To their essentially conservative minds that spirit seemed
to be subverting all that had been valued in the company of right
thinking men.   And they were quite accurate in observing that the
old social and economic order was changing more rapidly than ever
before, even within the memory of men already more accustomed than
were their ancestors to the phenomena of change.   Prices continued
to mount.   By harnessing the inflationary tendencies and making
them work for their own profit, the propertied classes continued to

protect their interests whatever the results might be to the customary economic relationships or to the commonweal as it was traditionally conceived. Merchants continued to manipulate the staple trade in wool in the interests of the quickest profit, thereby increasing the in-centive to enclose commons and arable land for pasture, which, in turn, defied the immemorial custom of the manor, depopulated some villages, and generally deranged the life of the communities affected.

Serious enough to begin with, the situation was now complicated by the fact that all of these tendencies toward economic and social change had been dangerously aggravated by the events of the preceding decade. The dissolution of the monasteries involved a widespread redistribution of land among the kind of men who were to contribute in a major way to the building of a new England, but who in their own generation typified the very tendencies against which preachers and pamphleteers expended the heaviest ammunition in their critical arsenal. Yet these "greedy cormorants," as Crowley called them, were themselves being driven, as well as tempted, by the general rise in prices; it is there that the government's fiscal policy contributed a final and, as at least one perspicacious observer recognized,[1] a decisive impetus. In a desperate effort to avert bankruptcy, Henry had resorted to the shot-in-the-arm policy of debasing the coinage. The results were disastrous. Without giving more than temporary financial relief, the policy of devaluation spread like a virus through the bloodstream of the body politic, aggravating as it went every disorder from which it already suffered and creating some wholly new ones.

The England that emerged from the era of Henry VIII must have presented to the public-spirited observer (if we may be permitted to create a composite figure out of very disparate materials) a spectacle at once confusing and exciting, to his still medieval feeling for stability, ominous, to his Christian humanist feeling for rational reform, burst-ing with potentiality. The old order was changing with measurable rapidity, a fact now almost as clear to him as it has since become to the historian, even if he did not so fully understand the reasons. Perhaps this increasingly acute awareness of change might by itself have given rise to the critical and analytical comment that spilled from his pen, but it is unlikely. The times were probably as bad before 1547 as they were after that date, yet the concern of the observer did not then

1. [Sir Thomas Smith], *A Discourse of the Common Weal*. See below, chap. xi.

so frequently achieve written expression, nor so comprehensively. Insofar as they affected the analytical discussion of social problems, the early years of Edward VI's reign differed from the latter part of Henry VIII's less in the gravity of the issues than in the encouragement once more given to the articulate citizen by the government.[2]

Whether that encouragement was tacit or explicit, the important fact is that, during the short ascendancy of the Protector Somerset, the articulate citizen once again found his voice and in a rush of words expressed himself on most of the issues affecting the common weal of England. Somerset's program of reform included a relaxation of the strict treason laws of the preceding reign. In its broad outline it was conceived—or misconceived—much in the spirit of Starkey's *Dialogue* (the similarity is no doubt accidental, but it is interesting to speculate on the possibility that Somerset may have been one of those privileged to read the unpublished manuscript of that manifesto of English civic humanism) and the documents enacting it reflect at times not merely the mood and bias of the "commonwealth men" but their language as well.[3] Tragic as was its failure in most respects, the prematurely liberal rule of Somerset made it possible for a new generation of scholar-counselors to express themselves for a short while with unprecedented freedom.

ကာ   ကာ   ကာ

It is not, however, to these rare minds that we shall turn our attention immediately. They will have to wait until the next chapter; for the most obvious, and in many respects the most significant change in the general character of discussion during the late years of Henry VIII's reign and those of his son was the growing concern for the worldly welfare of English society on the part of the religious reformers and their increasing appreciation of the relationship between religious reform and social change. Whereas the earlier diagnosis of the nation's ills had been attempted largely by humanist pamphleteers, either independently or as a sort of volunteer service in addition to their official duty as consultants and propagandists, such social analysis in the reign of Edward VI was undertaken as much by partisans

2. See above, chap vi.
3. E.g., Somerset's proclamation concerning enclosures, 1 June 1548, Pollard, *Somerset*, pp. 218-221, and preamble to the act repealing the heresy and treason laws, 1 Edward VI, c. 12.

of the new theology as by the more secularly inclined writers who carried on the tradition of Starkey, Morison, and Marshall. Indeed, if we count the published sermons of Latimer, Lever, Hooper, and Cranmer as well as the pamphlets of Brinkelow, Crowley, and Becon, the sheer volume of comment from this quarter considerably outweighs the generally more penetrating work of the secularly oriented pam-phleteers. Whatever the comparisons, the initial fact of importance is that during this period it is possible to distinguish two quite dif-ferent approaches to the problems facing the secular authorities. Both are made in the name of the commonwealth, and are animated by the same conservative, essentially medieval social ideal. Yet, despite the fact that their exponents stand on pretty much the same ground, and for the purposes of exerting political pressure presented a unified front, the one group looks backward and the other forward. The one faces back not merely to the corporate, functional, and hierarchical social ideal of the Middle Ages but also to its theological sanctions. The other is preoccupied with the practical problem of secular govern-ment in the present; to the extent that it believes in the power of rational analysis to lay the basis for constructive policy, it faces the future—more squarely, no doubt, than its members always realized.

What, then, accounts for the increased activity of the Protestant reformers in their adopted role of analysts? Looked at from one point of view the fact that they undertook to excoriate the social evils of the day in addition to preaching the newly interpreted gospel needs little explanation. They inherited the social ideal of medieval Christen-dom pretty much in its totality. It was an ideal that maintained as its final objective the welfare of the community, defined, not as the attainment of ever increasing wealth, but the maintenance of each man in the status to which he was born, free from want and injustice, and capable of leading a life of virtue and contentment rather than of ambitious striving. This ideal embraced all classes, but it naturally tended to be construed in favor of those who could not protect them-selves and who were therefore most likely to suffer from the injustices of the propertied classes. It was especially antithetical to the acquisitive spirit that animated the emerging society of capitalism. Whatever compromise the Protestant reformers eventually felt constrained to make with that spirit, these first generations of Protestant publicists were forthright in their criticism of it. To them, as to the medieval preacher, social maladjustment reflected the sinful nature of man and thus came naturally within the province of the church.

But to their traditional social theory had been added new ingredients. The strongly theocentric tendencies of Protestant thought served to intensify the traditional approach to social problems and give it new dimensions. The contrast drawn by the more rigorous Protestant theologians between the helplessness and native depravity of man and the omnipotence of God led as logically to a theocratic ideal of society as it did to a predestinarian doctrine of personal salvation. To be sure, few Protestants, especially in England, were as logical as all that, and there remained convenient stopping points before the end of either road. But the road to theocracy was there for those to travel who would.

Thus in an England torn by political rivalries and religious discord, and rocked by the seismic disturbances of a social and economic revolution, the more zealous Protestants, the preaching prelates of Latimer's kind and publicists like Robert Crowley, conceived it their duty to act as emissaries of a God in whose mind and will resided the real government of mankind. They did not, of course, go so far as to advocate for England, or even to contemplate, a government such as that of Calvin's Geneva. They were committed to the Erastian principle established by Henry VIII, and, in the fervent hope that theirs would be a truly godly prince, they continued to preach the political doctrine of obedience.[4] Not until the Catholic counterattack bade fair to destroy the Protestant cause entirely was a doctrine of resistance seriously explored. The Edwardian Protestant leaders nevertheless believed so wholeheartedly, and in a sense so literally, in the sovereignty of God that they tended in their analysis of secular affairs to ignore the factors of natural and impersonal causation and to look to preaching rather than policy as the source of all remedy. They nourished the partisan feeling that a country which had eradicated the alien and iniquitous jurisdiction of the Bishop of Rome should show in its temporal life the fruits of such cataclysmic virtue. They accordingly felt the more dismay at the injustice and disorder they believed to be still rampant in English society. More than that, they seem really to have been convinced that such evils were plagues visited upon a sinful people by a stern deity, and that the only way to

4. On the doctrine of obedience see Baumer, *Early Tudor Theory of Kingship*.

escape national catastrophe was by nationwide repentance. In any event they felt it their duty to speak out, and in doing so they became, inevitably, leaders in the movement for social and economic reform as well as "apostles to the English."[5]

Most of them had a genuine interest in social reform for its own sake, an interest which can neither be explained entirely by their religious preoccupation nor by their sense of duty as public monitors. There is in it something of that tendency toward realistic observation and practicality we find to an increasing extent in the literature of the late medieval and early Tudor periods. There is perhaps even more in it of the civic consciousness that stems from the humanist tradition. Most of the reformers were, after all, university men and in the universities, especially at Cambridge,[6] the Erasmian influence remained strong. Unfortunately, we know a good deal more about where and when these men went to school than what they studied. But they no doubt absorbed many of the same influences that shaped the more secular minds of Starkey and Morison, and later of Smith and Cheke. No doubt they also learned to respond to the example of civic virtue to be found in classical culture as it was reinterpreted by the humanists and to respect the powers inherent in the human mind for projecting intelligent reform on the basis of rational criticism. These impulses were merely overlaid by the apocalyptic theology of an embattled Protestantism, the small voice of a rational humanism scarcely audible in the noisy confessional debate.

Certainly the sermons of the reformers and the pamphlets written in the same spirit represent a noteworthy advance in social analysis over analogous utterances of the preceding centuries. The medieval preacher and the poet-commentator who followed in his footsteps remained content to castigate piecemeal the failings of each order and had nothing significant to say about the causal relationship immediately underlying the workings of their society. Nor, except for a while in the late fourteenth century when the Lollards were advocating the Wycliffite program of disendowment, did they think in terms of a policy which would comprehend a whole complex of such criticisms. Now the speed of change had greatly accelerated, and to a consideration of the resulting problems the Edwardian Protestant reformers brought

5. Chester's treatment of Latimer's career gives the best insight into this process.
6. Porter, *Reformation and Reaction in Tudor Cambridge.*

minds conditioned in part by the utilitarian bias of English humanism
and accustomed to some analytical subtlety in the discussion of social
problems. Like their medieval prototypes, they considered none of
these problems alien to them. Yet their critical vision was bounded
by the sea to an even greater extent than was that of the medieval
Gower whose sense of national identity, strong as it was, did not
prevent him from reverting almost automatically to the formulas of a
universal Christendom.[7] They had committed their faith and mort-
gaged their future to the policy of a national church; so to their sincere
patriotism was added the practical necessity of looking to the national
government as the source of all reform measures. Of the need for
such measures they were painfully aware. Whatever its virtues, however great its natural endowments, their little Eden was still a good
deal less than half a paradise.

It was not, however, the mere multiplicity of England's problems
that turned these men from simple, piecemeal criticism of individual
evils to the analysis of causal relationships. Had such been the case
the Protestant reformers might have devoted more time to criticisms
than had the medieval social critics and might have been a trifle more
realistic in their comments, but they would hardly have advanced
beyond them in the direction of social analysis. Even as it is, men of
Brinkelow's cast of mind, or Crowley's, bear at first glance a more
than fortuitous resemblance to the critics of earlier generations. The
difference lay in the fact that the religious revolution from which the
reformers had hoped for so much had, to their way of thinking,
miscarried. True, it had accomplished much. The very act of
cutting away the jurisdiction of the pope they saw as an event of the
greatest historical magnitude. But its promise seemed to be only
partially fulfilled, and, worse still, it had accomplished some things
that the reformers believed to be positively bad. Somehow, somewhere, something had gone wrong. Rather than resembling the
hoped for society made virtuous and just through the spiritual regeneration of its members, England looked discouragingly like its old self,
only worse. Too many of the old devils still flourished and new ones
seemed to be rising to take the place of the few that had been exorcised.
Disappointment can serve as a powerful incentive to investigation, if

7. See above, chap. ii.

only in order to find a convenient scapegoat, and even the search for a scapegoat involves the asking of searching questions.

So it was that, beneath the familiar words of even the most help-less "lamentation" there stirred, ever so slightly, a new spirit of inquiry. The medieval mind was not much given to asking, why?—not, at least, of things tangible. Having once established the divine purpose under which all lesser purposes must be subsumed, the question had really been answered, and in this most comprehensive answer all lesser forms of the question were automatically answered. From this habit of thought the Englishmen of the Renaissance moved slowly and, in the case of the religious reformers, with apparent reluctance. But the challenge of the times was imperative. The old order had changed—officially—and it was no longer satisfactory merely to trace the evils that somehow still plagued the new order to the seven sins or to any particular combination of them. That the moralistic formulas still appear and, especially in the sermon literature, bear more than their share of weight is attributable in part to habit, in part to the conservatism of the clerical mind, and in part to the rigorously theocentric character of Protestant thought. In any case they must not be taken always at their face value.

We are not here concerned primarily with the religious controversies as such. It is, however, very relevant to see how, in their disillusion-ment at the apparent misfiring of a Reformation so godly in conception, the Protestant preachers and pamphleteers were forced to explain that deplorable situation, and in particular to trace, often with considerable care, the effect of the new dispensation on the social and economic life of the country. For much of the social criticism that figures so largely in the writing of these essentially religious reformers stems from this sense of necessity rather than from the social consciousness of the authors, if, indeed, it is possible to separate their awareness of social needs at all clearly from their fundamental concern with the refor-mation in religion.

Let us take as an example, the best example, the problem of the monastic properties. Much of the agitation for reform had been directed against the wealth of the clergy, for centuries considered a major source of those worldly entanglements from which the church must extricate herself, or be forcibly extricated, before she could prop-erly perform her spiritual duties. Of that wealth the monastic houses constituted the most notorious instance. They remained in the eyes of the reformers the classic case of clerical parasitism; for, in its more rigorous interpretation, Protestant doctrine left no place for monastic asceticism, and the practical usefulness of the monasteries as sources of poor relief, education, and hospitality was at least open to question, especially by men who could readily conceive of alternative means that might reasonably be supposed to perform these functions better. In addition, the monasteries owed allegiance to a foreign potentate whom the more extreme Protestants identified with Antichrist. The more radical Protestant group therefore hailed the dissolution as in itself a most meritorious act and one which, properly administered, should contribute greatly to the temporal as well as to the spiritual welfare of the national community. The resulting changes that took place in property-holding in fact reshaped to a perceptible degree the profile of English society, gave a decisive slant to the Reformation itself, and affected for generations the character of English government.

These results were, however, neither anticipated nor, certainly, desired by the religious reformers. As we saw in the preceding chapter, some had misgivings from the very beginning. Hugh Latimer, to say nothing of the more secular Starkey, saw quickly enough that the wealth of the monasteries was being confiscated, not solely for the purposes of reform or even in the public interest, but to replenish the king's treasury, and they were shrewd enough to see (it must have been pretty obvious) that the lands would be sold or other- wise alienated into the hands of the rich and enterprising rather than used for the purposes of social betterment. But the social and economic effects of the suppression did not become apparent at once. By the end of Henry VIII's reign they had, and it is consequently then and during the succeeding reign that the entire process could be assessed for the first time.[8]

The following excerpt from a sermon of Thomas Lever (1550) summarizes admirably what he and his Protestant colleagues believed to have been the king's purpose in dissolving the monasteries and what the reformers hoped might be done with the proceeds.

> For in suppressing of Abbeys, Cloisters, Colleges, and Chan-
> tries, the intent of the king that dead is, was and of this our king
> now, is very godly, and the purpose, or else the pretence of other,

8. See Helen C. White, chap. iii, for fullest treatment.

wonderous goodly: that thereby such abundance of goods as was superstitiously spent upon vain ceremonies, or voluptuously upon idle bellies, might come to the king's hands to bear his great charges, necessarily bestowed in the common wealth, or partly unto other men's hands, for the better relief of the poor, maintenance of learning, and the setting forth of God's word.[9]

It had been a worthy process, both godly and, ostensibly at least, statesmanlike. But Lever's words also provide us with a stick wherewith to measure the disappointment he and his fellows were suffering by that date.

As part of their responsibility the monasteries had undertaken to relieve the poor. Indeed, the Protestant reformers, unwilling to grant them any real spiritual function, tended to assume that it was their sole reason for being.[10] That function had now to be exercised elsewhere, and the most reasonable policy was to use part of the confiscated properties for that purpose. But the consensus seems to have been at the mid-century that, however badly the monasteries had done their work, the poor were better off with them than with those into whose hands the abbey lands had fallen. One anonymous pamphleteer laments that the poor have "failed of their expectation, and are in more penury than ever they were." The monks bled their charitable patrons, "yet had the poor impotent creatures some relief of their scraps, whereas now they have nothing. Then had they hospitals, and almshouses to be lodged in, but now they lie and starve in the streets. Then was their number great but now much greater."[11] Brinkelow, giving the devil his due, admitted that the monks had done their fumbling best to help the poor and to provide hospitality for wayfarers. "But now that all the abbeys with their lands, goods and impropered parsonages, be in temporal men's hands, I do not hear tell that one halfpenny worth of alms, or any other profit, cometh unto the people of those parishes." This, he concludes, "is a fair amendment"![12]

9. *A Fruitful Sermon*, sig. B v-vi. Cf. Henry Brinkelow, *The Complaynt of Roderyck Mors*, ed. J. M. Cowper, E.E.T.S., E.S., No. 22 (1874), pp. 9, 22-23.

10. Helen C. White, p. 88.

11. *Supplication of the Poore Commons*, p. 79. On the authorship of this tract, see *Four Supplications*, ed. Cowper and Furnivall, p. xiv. Thomas Becon expresses the same sentiment. *The Jewel of Joy*, in *The Catechism of Thomas Becon*, ed. J. Ayre, Parker Society (1844), p. 435.

12. *Complaynt*, pp. 33-34. See also Crowley, *One and thyrtie Epigrammes* in *Select*

Some felt even more strongly about the loss, both actual and poten-tial, to the cause of learning.[13] Tudor education depended to a large extent on endowments made within the monastic system as it was broadly interpreted for the purposes of confiscation. The suppression of the chantries in 1547 added a final touch to a process the Protestant observers described, with some rhetorical exaggeration, as a disaster to English education. Lever was especially vehement in his denun-ciation of the failure to implement official policies concerning the use of monastic properties in the interests both of the universities and of the grammar schools.[14] No doubt most of the reformers retained a humanistic regard for lay education. But their concern for the maintenance of education in general stemmed rather from their even more profound concern for the spiritual welfare of the community. The latter depended on good ministers, men, that is, able and willing to preach the word of God; and good ministers could not be made from ignorant men.[15] The entire cause of religious reform was, there-fore, in jeopardy because the monastic wealth had not been in sub-stantial part diverted to the endowment of schools and universities and to the subsidization of poor scholars. Still worse, the new lay propri-etors were placing men of their own choosing, ignorant and under-paid, even in some cases men hostile to the new theology, in benefices over which they now had control.[16]

It is this consciousness of opportunity almost, but not quite, lost that helps explain the difference in attitude between the religious reformers of the Tudor period and the medieval social critics. What with the latter might have remained simple complaint about things as they are, has now become a more or less analytical criticism of a process, in-formed by experience in the actual circumstances of revolution, and animated by a new sense of potentiality. The difference becomes even more apparent when these Tudor pamphleteers and preachers attempt

---

Works, pp. 7-12; Lever, *A Sermon preached the thyrd Sondaye in Lente* . . . *1550* (London, 1550).

13. Opinion, both contemporaneous and historiographical, concerning the effect of the dissolution on education is reviewed critically in Douglas Bush, "Tudor Humanism and Henry VIII," *UTQ*, VII (1938), 162-177; see especially p. 165.

14. *Sermon, 14 December, 1550*, in *Three Fruitful Sermons*, sigs. Lv-Mi; *Sermon . . . thyrd Sondaye in Lente* . . . *1550*, sig. Ei.

15. Helen C. White, pp. 102-103.

16. Lever, *A Fruitful Sermon*, sig. Bvii; Brinkelow, *Complaynt*, p. 34.

to find a social explanation for the disappointing tendencies in the new dispensation and when they trace the social and economic maladjust'ments that accompanied the redistribution of the abbey lands. For if the dissolution had taught them anything it taught them that even the most idealistic reform must take place in a social context and that, if spiritual regeneration depends on rearranging customary property tenures, its exponents cannot ignore the effects that are bound to follow in the economic life of the community.

In assessing blame for the failure of the policy of disendowment, the reformers naturally tended to look first for a convenient scapegoat. The king himself was, of course, ultimately responsible. But Lever, for one, prefers to blame "covetous officers" who have turned the goods of the monasteries to their own worldly ends. The most common formula was, however, to blame the "possessioners," the gentry and wealthy merchants who knew a good thing when they saw it and who were in no way inhibited from pursuing their private interests. Since those interests were hardly likely to coincide with the objectives of social service the reformers had in mind, the new proprietors were in a quite real sense the agents through whose efforts the policy of disendow'ment became so badly warped. The dissolution had, in fact, con'tributed substantially to the rise of the landed gentry to political and economic importance. Land still represented the safest, and socially the most advantageous, investment for any person with capital. Not only did it still constitute the measure of status and influence, but, to a degree never before possible, it provided opportunities for profit. By hard, sometimes ruthless management, especially by raising rents and enclosing land for sheep walks, the enterprising purchaser could turn the steady rise in prices that bedeviled the rest of the community to his own benefit. This, of course, involved considerable social dislocation and the gradual destruction of the customary safeguards which, though for long in decay, had served after a fashion to protect the interests of the tenant. All of which the religious reformers recognized, deplored, and no doubt exaggerated. What concerned them even more, how'ever, was that, in buying up so much of the confiscated land and managing it so exclusively for their private profit, they to that extent made it impossible for the monastic wealth to be used for poor relief, education, or the spread of the new religion.

But the reformers failed to press their investigation of the causes beyond blaming the "possessioners." The new lay proprietors they held personally responsible; for it was the covetousness of these "greedy cormorants"—or, as Becon even more picturesquely described them, "caterpillars of the commonweal[17]"—that moved them to take private advantage of what should have been an opportunity for public bene‐ fit. They would not, probably in most cases could not, recognize the impersonal forces inherent in an inflationary economy both impelling and inducing the landlords to make the most of whatever opportunity for profit they could see. Perhaps they recognized more clearly the spirit of capitalism, but, if they did, they disposed of it as a supra‐ personal factor by identifying it in thoroughly traditional manner with the sin of avarice. Referring specifically to the misuse of the abbey lands, Lever asked "Be we in better case than we have been before time, because papistry amongst us is kept under, or else worse than ever we were, because covetousness reigneth at liberty? That which pa‐ pistry abused, hath not covetousness destroyed?"[18]

The fact remains, however, that they were keenly aware of the dispersal of monastic wealth as a process, one that was altering the metabolism of the body politic and hence bound to affect the health of the entire organism. Henry Brinkelow offers an unusually sys‐ tematic analysis of this process. Naturally enough, pamphlet writers such as he were able to develop such arguments with greater care than the preachers whose treatment of matters of this sort had always to be subordinated to the peculiar demands of the pulpit. Brinkelow, moreover, was in a better position than most of the preachers to trace the economic implications of his subject, for he had left the clerical estate and had become by this time a mercer in the city of London. In the course of a rigorous diagnosis of all that ailed the national body, he explains how the dissolution aggravated existing economic evils.[19] Although he assumes that they all are ultimately moral in origin, he has faced the practical necessity of making up his mind about the sequence of purely economic and social causes and effects. Among these secondary causes, the prime mover, he has concluded, is the raising of rents. And here the new proprietors, to whom the king

17. Becon, *Jewel of Joy*, p. 432.
18. *Sermon, 14 December, 1550*, in *Three Fruitful Sermons* pagination uncertain; cf. *A Fruitful Sermon*, sig. Cvii.
19. *Complaynt*, pp. 9‐12. Cf. *Supplication of Poor Commons*, pp. 79‐80, in which a very similar argument is developed.

has "given and sold the lands of those imps of Antichrist, abbeys and nunneries," have been the chief offenders. Just why that should be he fails to inform us, but he is clear enough regarding the consequences. They are all familiar. The rack-renting landlords drive the defenseless tenantry into poverty and crime.[20] By using every opportunity to raise rents they force all prices upward so that no one, not even the rent-raiser is better off. The trouble can not, therefore, be confined to the landed interest. No doubt from personal experience, Brinkelow shows how the cloth trade will suffer, and in the long run the prestige of England in overseas markets, unless something is done to lower prices. All these problems have, he implies, been intensified to a critical degree by the endowment of a new class of capitalist landlords. And he is forced to the painful admission that, "but for the faith's sake . . . (for the which they were justly suppressed), it had been more profitable, no doubt, for the common wealth" if the abbey lands had remained in the hands of the religious.

If Brinkelow was able to speak with equal fluency the language of the mercantile world and of a militant Protestantism, his primary commitment was still to the latter.[21] In another tract of the period this situation is reversed. The anonymous author of *Piers Plowman's Exhortation* addresses himself to the legislative organ of civil government in the interests of specific measures calculated in large part to cope with the economic consequences of the dissolution. Only a few, largely peripheral, facts remind us that he was probably a man whose mind had been formed somewhere within the wide circle of influence exerted by the new religion. He had nothing to say in favor of the suppressed monastic houses. He admits, though perfunctorily, that the "worldly policy" he has spent virtually all of his book discussing will be of no avail unless "we mend our sinful living. For if God be determined to plague us for our offences, what can worldly policy prevail to the contrary." And he clothes his rather sophisticated counsel in the pseudo-simplicity of the reconditioned Piers Plowman tradition, then much in vogue among the latter-day exponents of the social gospel.

20. In another passage he points out that the suppression of the abbeys has left the poor and dispossessed without even the half-hearted relief they had been able to count on under the old order. *Complaynt*, pp. 32-34.

21. Although basically religious in nature, Brinkelow's *Complaynt*, it is interesting to note, has more pages devoted to the problems of the commonwealth than to strictly religious polemic.

But these are formulas which should not obscure the primarily secular, utilitarian emphasis made by this man, and the sense of active citizen⁄ship that permeates his work.

Despite his thin and conventional disguise of rusticity (it may well have contributed to the undeserving neglect this pamphlet seems to have suffered) and despite more than the ordinary disclaimer of any special ability which might give him a right to offer his counsel to Parliament, this author manages to see more clearly than most of his contemporaries the nature of the economic process set in motion by the suppression of the monasteries. Like Brinkelow, he tries to find the key factor in that process; but he looks for it, and finds it, more deeply imbedded in the situation. Reverting to the economic pre⁄occupation of those who in the 1530's undertook for the first time to make a systematic public attack on the problem of poverty, he sees it as a question of labor. It is a complex one. The erstwhile members of the monastic communities now must have land to work on or be idle, for, he points out, they cannot all be made soldiers. Moreover, the former celibates, being now free to marry, there will be more children born, which again will mean more men to be employed, presumably as farmers. Yet with the current high rents and prices only those farmers already reasonably well off, and childless to boot, can make ends meet. The whole laboring class is in poverty. Thus at a time when there are more laborers there is less work to be had and fewer farms. To make matters still more difficult, the men who bought or leased the abbey lands are mostly men who had lands of their own to begin with and who, through desire for profit and lack of facilities to manage the large number of laborers needed to keep the new lands in tillage, turn to pasture. And so the dispersal of monastic properties has contributed to the critical lack of agrarian jobs; for, he estimates, a dozen shepherds and four neatherds can look after pasture land which it would require five hundred ploughmen to till. The problem, then, is to provide enough work to turn the idle from a lia⁄bility to a national asset. That is the duty of Parliament, the author contends, but he is willing to make some suggestions, and does so in certain "rude bills."

So runs the analytical portion of the argument in this remarkable tract. Whether it is valid in any absolute sense is not at the moment important. It is, however, important to recognize this man's ability to follow the mechanism of cause and effect within a complicated process. It is worth noticing that, unlike Brinkelow, he makes a real effort to understand what purely economic factors, quite outside the area of moral choice, impelled the new landlords to work their new farms in such a way as to complicate the already serious agrarian problem. Nor is it insignificant that he ends his *libellus*, so predominantly secular in general tone, on a thoroughly nationalistic note. If Parliament will only follow both godly and worldly policy "this little realm is like to flourish and excell in wealth and prosperity all the realms in the world."

Having made the acquaintance of this latterday Piers Plowman, a character who bears no resemblance whatever to the central figure of Langland's poem, we have seen just about the full range of analytical thought provoked by the specific issue of the monastic lands. With him we have again arrived at an attitude of basically secular realism, and of undoctrinaire, almost instinctive empiricism which remains, even through these years of religious tension and evangelical enthusiasm, the most nearly constant element in the discussion of social and economic affairs. That such an attitude does not appear oftener in the discussion of the problems arising out of the dispersal of the monastic properties may at first glance seem odd. The answer is simply that most of the more secularminded writers preferred to treat England's social and economic problems as a whole rather than to deal with the abbey lands in particular. Enclosures, rackrenting, the general "dearth," these were all problems of the first magnitude; to men concerned primarily with the economic good of the country it was a matter of incidental importance that they were accentuated by the suppression. The dean of them all, the author of the penetrating *Discourse of the Common Weal*, deliberately plays down the importance of the sale of abbey lands as a cause of "dearth";[22] and in his discussion of the decline of learning he fails even to mention the reformers' favorite theory that it resulted from misuse of the confiscated ecclesiastical wealth.[23] The religious reformers, on the other hand, found that fact of great significance. And embarrassing as well, for not only did the deplorable results arouse their inherited sense of Christian justice, the fact itself

22. *Discourse*, p. 85.
23. *Ibid.*, pp. 2832.

demonstrated with cruel clarity that their great reform had, here at least, gone badly awry.

Other economic issues arising out of the Henrician Reformation likewise drew them from purely spiritual reform to the investigation of social processes.[24] The matter of the monastic lands offers, however, by far the best example and one that will have to suffice.

∽ ∽ ∽

If the history of the great disendowment made the more idealistic Protestants a little wiser as well as a good deal sadder, the events of 1549 filled them with utter dismay and gave them considerably more to think about. The disorders of that year made, of course, a deep impression on all thoughtful observers. The rebellions themselves demanded explanation, and their results called for analysis. For they marked a crisis in the movement for both religious and social reform; and the choice of a way out of the whole depressing situation depended on an understanding of the causal forces at work in it. But the risings seem to have been more than ordinarily disturbing to the religious reformers, and in large part for social and political reasons. The righteous, they had told themselves, are known by their fruits, and the more tangible fruits of religious reform they confidently expected to take the form of a just and humane social order. To that end they had accordingly devoted much of their reforming energies. They had taken up the social gospel, even as their predecessors had done in earlier times of discontent. Recognizing their kinship with the men who had stirred the social conscience of fourteenth-century Englishmen in the days of the great Peasants' Revolt, they reverted consciously to the tradition of Piers Plowman and with it a good deal more of the spirit of Christian equalitarianism than Langland would ever have accepted. Hugh Latimer, with his peculiar ability to sum up a point of view in a single striking sentence, put it like this: "the poorest plough-man is in Christ equal with the greatest prince that is."[25] They tended, however, to see the entire agrarian problem exemplified in its most extreme cases. We know that many of those who took part in the Norfolk rising, and even in the more religiously inspired revolts in

24. See, for example, Brinkelow, *Complaynt*, p. 39. Other examples are mentioned in Helen C. White, chap. iii.

25. Quoted in Helen C. White, p. 123.

Devonshire, were farmers of some substance, capable in cooler moments of pursuing their cause against grasping lords in the king's courts, men moved by indignation over the violation of customary rights rather than by hunger. Yet it is probably true that men of property had never before been in a better position to exploit those dependent on them, nor more generally inclined to do so. That, in fact, was the burden of the message the reforming preachers and writers had been bringing to those of their countrymen who were suffering as casualties in the transition from a society of status to one of contract, from a society that could still be fitted, though with difficulty, into the values of a corporate, functional commonwealth to one that must eventually be rationalized in terms of the sovereign state and the acquisitive individual.

The trouble was, however, that these men, in their enthusiastic hopes and deep despairs, failed not only to recognize these vast impersonal factors—for that they can certainly be excused—but also to appreciate the more immediate complexities of the situation. This is especially apparent in the area where religious radicalism impinged on the problem of maintaining peace and order. Men more experienced in the affairs of state and more accustomed to the language of political realism, men like the Henrician bishops, Gardiner and Bonner for example, might have told them what to expect and may, indeed, very well have done so.[26] From the very beginning of the Reformation the more politically responsible observers had expressed fears that religious radicalism was likely to bring social radicalism in its train and the danger of actual rebellion. It had happened before, in the England of 1381 and in more recent Continental experience, and it could quite conceivably happen again.[27] But the reformers refused to listen to such warnings—"belly wisdom," Latimer called it—[28] and persisted in treating social and economic maladjustments primarily as the expression of a simple conflict between good and evil, a conflict, moreover, being fought out in the breasts of individual men.[29] By no means unrealistic in their assessment of these maladjust-

26. L. B. Smith, *Tudor Prelates and Politics, 1536-1558* (Princeton, 1953), pp. 278-279.

27. *Ibid.*, pp. 95, 99, 103-104, 239. Chambers notes that More, as chancellor, was concerned with heresy primarily as a cause of "sedition, tumult and civil war." *More,* pp. 281-282. See also M. M. Knappen, *Tudor Puritanism* (Chicago, 1939), pp. 44-45.

28. Letter, Latimer to Henry VIII (1530), in Latimer, *Works,* II, 303.

29. See L. B. Smith, *Tudor Prelates and Politics,* especially chap. iv.

ments and of the suffering they caused, these earnest reformers allowed their righteous indignation to paint both villains and victims in sharp, primary colors. The result was a message more likely to incite to vio' lence than most of its exponents intended it to be.

The actual causes of discontent, though unprecedented in intensity, were not new in kind. Agrarian problems continued to account for most of the social unrest, especially in those areas where enclosures had created the most obvious break with manorial custom.[30] Whatever the underlying economic causes, most of which lay too deeply embed' ded in the social organism to be readily discerned, especially by the untutored, the enclosure of open fields and the attendant rack'renting and eviction of tenants was enough to stir to the point of explosion the feelings of a peasantry who had come to believe in the inviolability of customary right. Just so it had stirred the feelings of the reformers, both clerical and lay.

What the reformers failed to recognize was that the village com' munity nourished within itself the potentiality for violent action in behalf of its traditional way of life. Intensely conservative, it was capable of expressing itself in times of crisis in terms of a radicalism strangely out of keeping with the traditional view of society which accepted inequality as divinely ordained and the protection of property as the chief end of government. Moreover, to what Tawney has called the "spontaneous doctrineless communism of the open field village,"[31] was added the incitement of the social gospel, often, it would appear, stated in unusually extreme form, perhaps under Anabaptist influences, in any case charged with implications of antinomianism and primitive Christian communism. The result was that the well' meaning preachers and publicists found themselves faced by a rebel' lion they had neither asked for nor anticipated and one which, in fact, violated their still cherished ideal of a society of hierarchical degree, yet one also for which they could not wholly repudiate responsibility.

The writings of Robert Crowley illustrate the attitude of the Prot' estant reformers of the mid'century at its most typical, or rather at its

30. For background, see Frances Rose'Troup, *The Western Rebellion of 1549* (London, 1913), and A. R. Mason, "Rebellion in Norfolk, 1549," *CR* (March, 1959), pp. 164' 167.

31. R. H. Tawney, *The Agrarian Problem in the Sixteenth Century* (London, 1912), p. 338. On the anabaptists, see G. H. Williams, *The Radical Reformation* (Philadelphia, 1962), pp. 401'403, 778'790.

most obtuse. In 1548 he published a pamphlet entitled *An Infor^
mation and Petition against the Oppressors of the poor Commons of this
Realm.* In it he undertook to call the attention of Parliament to the
plight of the poor and to rally the members to their public duty. That
was the year before the rebellions. The year following, he published
another pamphlet, this time entitled *The Way to Wealth, wherein is
plainly taught a most present Remedy for Sedition.* As the title suggests,
this second pamphlet grapples with the problem of rebellion itself,
yet without abandoning the field to the evil agencies to whose con^
fusion the earlier one had been devoted, to wit, the "possessioners."

It is a very practical problem he lays before the Parliament as it sat
in 1548. Without preamble he lets the Lords and Commons know
what is on his mind.

> Among the manifold and most weighty matters (most worthy
> counsellors) to be debated and communed of in this present
> parliament, and by the advise, assent, and consent thereof speed^
> ily to be redressed, I think there is no one thing more needful to
> be spoken of than the great oppression of the poor commons by
> the possessioners, as well of clergy as of the laity.[32]

Accordingly, he sets forth the grievances of the agricultural tenant and
laborer much as, despite his assertion to the contrary, they had been
set forth in innumerable tracts and sermons during the previous two
decades—one might almost say during the previous two centuries.
Nor does his presentation involve subtle analysis. It is for the most
part simple complaint, more in the tradition of the medieval preacher
than of the Renaissance pamphleteer. Yet it shows with quotable
clarity how the Protestant idealists were able to press their social criti^
cism to the brink of rebellion without appreciating the danger in such
a course of action.

Despite his very direct appeal to Parliament as the agency through
which practical reforms must come, and despite the specificity of the
grievances he reports, the basic assumptions of the *Information and
Petition* are theocratic. All lordship of property is held as a trust
from God. Possessioners are "but stewards and not lords over their
possessions." They must administer their trust in the interests of the
"multitude" and are accountable to God for the results.[33] Otherwise

32. *An informacion and peticion* in *Select Works,* pp. 153^156.
33. *Ibid.,* p. 157.

they have no natural right to anything but what they "shall get with the sweat of their faces."[34] This was a doctrine of dominion based on the performance of divinely appointed duty, not one of communal ownership (he takes pains to repudiate any such notion),[35] and there, fore in the tradition of such adaptations of feudal law as those out of which Wyclif's doctrine of dominion had emerged. It was meant to challenge the acquisitive spirit of agrarian capitalism in what Crowley believed to be the most irrefutable of terms. But it failed to make clear why lords who had obviously failed in their stewardship retained any legitimate authority over their lands and tenants, and, although he certainly implies that Parliament is the agency through which any disciplinary action and actual reform measures must pass, the lan, guage he uses could easily be mistaken for a call to rebellion in the name of a higher authority.

Much of what Crowley says should not, of course, be taken quite literally. Like many of his fellow preachers and pamphleteers, he speaks habitually in the accents of the prophets. Quite unencum, bered by modesty, false or otherwise, he asserts that, even as Jonas was sent by God to the Ninevites and Daniel to the Babylonians, yes even as Christ was sent to the Jews, so he, Robert Crowley, was sent to tell the propertied classes of England to repent and restore to the poor their rightful measure of sustenance and protection.[36] Yet language of this sort could only come from a mind to which the more realistic analysis of social behavior had become unnecessary and irrelevant. By the same token a mind like Crowley's was not likely to appreciate fully the effect his words might have on those less sophisticated than him, self who were now, after a generation of Protestant preaching and social criticism, ready enough to take their message literally.

When, after the year of rebellion, Crowley came to write *The Way to Wealth*, he could not help but face the practical issue of sedition. But it is surprising how little effect it had on his habits of thought. True, he was shocked by the violence of the preceding year's events. Perhaps he had become a trifle humbler in his role of God, sent prophet to the English—at least he is now careful to point out that his biblical prototypes were also men of simple estate whose message was nonethe,

34. *Ibid.*, p. 163.
35. *Ibid.*, p. 156.
36. *Ibid.*, pp. 159,160.

less worth listening to.　But he finds the cause of sedition about where we should expect him to find it, namely in the failure of all concerned in the late uprisings to behave as it was the duty of men in their re/ spective stations to do.　Although he reserves his sharpest condem/ nations for the landlords,[37] he also takes the peasants sharply to task. Though unquestionably oppressed, they should have borne their burdens patiently instead of taking matters into their own hands and rebelling against their king and their natural superiors.　Indeed he tells them that it was their own sin that caused them to rebel.　"For sedition is poured upon thee to plague thy former sin withall."[38]　The logic of all this may perhaps have escaped the simple country folk—it may not even persuade the modern reader, but it was recognizable enough to men of Crowley's own circle.　For, beneath his notion of lordship conditional upon the performance of social duty, lay the bed/ rock of medieval functionalism, the divinely ordained rigidity of a hierarchical social order.　The supreme lordship of God did not for practical purposes invalidate lesser lordships even when these latter were unjustly administered, nor did it deprive the civil government of the right to exact obedience.　The idea did, however, cause Crowley to pass over causal relationships a less theologically oriented mind might well have observed.

At one point only does his experience seem to have given him in/ sight into the causes of rebellion.　He seems to have been convinced that the unruly conduct of the peasantry in the disturbed areas was in part the result of the poor or even downright vicious leadership given them by their local clergy.[39]　It is hard to tell whether he arrived at this conclusion as a result of detached observation or by deduction from an unquestioned premise, namely that a healthy community needs good preachers and, conversely, that a godly pastorate will bear fruit in a godly society.　Perhaps he was trying to counter argument made by the men of property to the effect that the risings had been caused by preaching similar to the kind of social gospel Crowley him/ self had published in the *Information and Petition*.　At any rate, he blames ignorant and perverse ministers for much of the trouble.　He may here have been referring to preachers of antinomian and com/

37. *Way to Wealth*, in *Select Works*, pp. 143/145.
38. *Ibid.*, p. 142.
39. *Ibid.*, pp. 133/134, 140/141.

munal tendencies.[40]   Or he may have seen how ignorant and under-
paid vicars serving in place of absentee, sometimes pluralistic patrons
could identify their own discontent with that of their parishioners.
Certainly he recognized how closely this latter problem was tied up
with the practice of lay appropriation of benefices.[41]   It is not impossible that Crowley was capable of learning from experience, and the
rebellions of 1549 may well have given him a deeper insight into the
workings of society.   Certainly they caused him to pause in his busy
career of printing, writing, and preaching to examine, if only in passing,
the relationship between his idealism and the realities of national life.

If the rebellions could bring a mind like Crowley's to a slightly
deeper appreciation of such relationships, they naturally proved still
more provocative to those among the reforming group who, perhaps
because they were in a better position to see the implications of both
popular and governmental action, adhered less stubbornly to the
formulas of the social gospel.   The great preaching prelates, Latimer,
Lever, Hooper, and Cranmer, and that most voluble of the Protestant pamphleteers, Thomas Becon, were close to the government of the
Protector Somerset.   Whereas Crowley wrote as a citizen volunteering
his counsel, they spoke to some extent for the government itself.   No
statesman of the period could afford to overlook the potential propaganda value of the London pulpits, especially when the sermons could
be, and were, so readily and so promptly made available to a broader
public through the press.   And Becon's value as a writer of propagandist pamphlets no doubt commended him in this respect, as well
as in more strictly doctrinal matters, to the Protector in whose household he served as chaplain.[42]

Without for a moment excusing the propertied classes for their part
in provoking the peasantry to seditious actions, the burden of their
message had now shifted to the threat such actions constituted to the
established order.   As Lever pointed out, there is no canker so dangerous to a commonwealth as rebellion.[43]   No matter how badly English

40. Crowley has the landed class accusing the peasants of just the kind of thing the
Anabaptists were supposed to advocate. *Ibid.*, p. 142.
41. *Ibid.*, pp. 145, 148-150.
42. D. S. Bailey, *Thomas Becon and the Reformation of the Church in England* (London,
1952), p. 54.
43. *Sermon . . . thyrd Sondaye in Lente . . . 1550*, sig. Diii. Cf. Cranmer, *Sermon*

agrarian society needed reform, the immediate problem was the threat from below. Accordingly they preached the orthodox droctrine of obedience: be subject unto the powers that be, for they are ordained of God. Becon is a case in point. Few had spoken out more eloquently than Becon against the enclosing landlords, yet in the face of actual rebellion he wrote with equal eloquence against the sin of disobedience.[44] Latimer, it is true, had the courage to continue his emphasis on the sufferings of the peasantry and the responsibility of the landlords to relieve them, but his efforts may well have contributed decisively to his eventual fall from favor at court.[45]

But what had caused this "unnatural disposition," as Becon called it, of the "inferior to rise against his sovereign"? How can obedience be obtained? Nothing very clear on these points emerges from the turgid flow of homilectic rhetoric. But it appears that obedience can be induced by those in authority giving justice to the common folk, or it can be exacted by enforcement of the laws enjoying a strict social discipline. Hitherto the emphasis had been on the former alternative and it continued to occupy a prominent place. But the latter received increasing attention. There is therefore in the sermons of 1550 a new tone of severity[46] that seems to argue a degree of disillusionment with the humane aims of Christian humanist thought and the compassionate teachings of the traditional social gospel, perhaps more specifically with the liberal policies of the Protector Somerset. The magistrates, Cranmer asserts, have been lax in punishing offenders, and have been deluded by a mistaken notion of clemency.[47] Poverty is no excuse for rebellion, nor is it a sufficient cause. Rebellion, indeed, is itself the cause of poverty.[48] The king and the governing class bear the sword, says Lever, in order to cut out cankered members of the political body in the interests of the entire organism.[49] The kind of discipline these

---

Concerning the Time of Rebellion, in *Miscellaneous Writings*, ed. J. E. Cox, Parker Society (1846), pp. 190-202.

44. Becon, *The Fortress of the Faithful* in *Catechism*, pp. 593-594.

45. See especially, *Works*, I, 248-249. Chester, pp. 170-179, 182-184; H. S. Darby, *Hugh Latimer* (London, 1953), chap. vii.

46. *Sermon . . . thyrd Sondaye in Lente . . . 1550*, sig. Diii-iiii; Hooper, *Early Writings*, ed. S. Carr, Parker Society (1852), pp. 473-484; Cranmer, *Sermon on Rebellion*, in *Miscellaneous Writings*, pp. 191.

47. *Sermon on Rebellion*, p. 191.

48. *Ibid.*, pp. 193-194.

49. *Sermon . . . thyrd Sondaye in Lente . . . 1550*, sig. Diii.

men called for made, to be sure, no distinction between action which might have direct repercussions in public life, such as neglect of duty, and those, such as adultery, gluttony, and blasphemy, which would today be restricted to the private sphere.[50]

Hooper speaks especially bluntly about the folly of "over much lenity and preposterous pity" in the enforcement of the law.[51] Hang every thief, he urges, in a passage that would have saddened the heart of Thomas More.[52] Clearly the problem of order in the common-wealth had by now overshadowed that of the relation of poverty to crime, and had diverted these men, social reformers by principle, from the subtler forms of social analysis.

But obedience, the preachers recognized, was not the only issue. Indeed it was only the more tangible aspect of a larger issue, namely, that of maintaining the social as well as the political order, of main-taining each man in his vocation as well as in obedience to the powers that be.[53] Profoundly conservative in their social doctrine, the Protes-tant leaders correctly sensed that there was another, and correspondingly radical, spirit abroad. This spirit could take the form either of ac-quisitive private enterprise or of the kind of primitive communism preached by extremists of Anabaptist leanings. As concerned as ever with the former, the preachers now tend to take special cognizance of the latter. Lever, in particular, stresses the evil effects of such preach-ing as twists the scriptural references to community of goods among the apostles into a justification for rebellion in the interests of a com-munal social order and the leveling of all class barriers based on prop-erty.[54] Indeed there is discernible in his attack on this leveling doctrine a tendency, significant as an indication of the direction in which thought at the time was going, to interpret the body politic in terms of economic inequality as well as of the functional diversity of its organs. Such men, Lever says, "that would have like quantity of every thing to be given to every man, intending thereby to make all alike, do utterly destroy the congregation, the mystical body of Christ, whereas

---

50. Cranmer, *Sermon on Rebellion*, p. 191; Hooper, *Early Writings*, pp. 454 and 476.
51. *Early Writings*, p. 473; see also pp. 481-482, 484.
52. *Ibid.*, pp. 481-482.
53. *Ibid.*, pp. 452, 454, 460-461, 466 ff.; Lever, *Sermon . . . thyrd Sondaye in Lente . . . 1550*, sig. Biiii; Cranmer, *Sermon on Rebellion*, p. 192.
54. *A Fruitful Sermon*, sig. Bi-ii. Cf. Cranmer, *Sermon on Rebellion*, p. 197.

there must needs be divers members in divers places having divers duties."[55]

Lever was thus more inclined than Crowley or Latimer or even Becon to credit the charge that radical and irresponsible preaching had caused the rebellions. Latimer, indeed, continued to maintain in his last sermon before Edward VI that such a charge was false. Perhaps he may conveniently have forgotten that there had been preaching of a dangerously inflammatory kind that reached in its leveling doctrine beyond the simple social gospel to which he still heartily adhered. Be that as it may, he attacked with characteristic humor and gusto the logic of those who would blame preaching in general for the risings. "Here was preaching against covetousness all the last year in Lent, and next summer followed rebellion; *ergo*, preaching against covetousness was the cause of rebellion." This, he adds, is "a goodly argument." It reminds him (Latimer always had an apt story in his bag of homiletic tricks) of the old story about the aged citizen of Sandwich who, when interviewed by commissioners sent to inquire into the cause of the Goodwin sands that had stopped up Sandwich haven, answered that it was Tenterton steeple that had caused Goodwin sands; for, he said, I am an old man and remember that before the building of Tenterton steeple no sands stopped the haven, and therefore I think that Tenterton steeple is the cause of the decay of Sandwich haven.[56]

All the reforming preachers had, of course, an ambivalent attitude toward this problem. They were, after all, committed to the ideal that good preaching was necessary for the achievement of a good society.[57] But even good preaching could lead to politically embarrassing conclusions, and the preaching of radical doctrine could be positively evil, not only to the souls of men but to the commonwealth.

Thus the rebellions of 1549 continued to divert the attention of religious reformers from purely spiritual considerations, which they would have preferred to think the only ones, to considerations of

55. *A Fruitful Sermon*, sig. Bii-iii.

56. *Works*, I, 250-251. More had told the same story, and for similar purposes of logical criticism, in his controversy with Tyndale. *Dialogue Concerning Tyndale*, ed. W. E. Campbell (London, 1927), pp. 306-307. Cf. Becon, *Fortress of the Faithful*, p. 596; Sir Thomas Smith, *Discourse*, p. 100. This and similar versions seem, in fact, to have been popular in this generation dedicated as it was to the exploration of causes.

57. Lever, *Sermon . . . thyrd Sondaye in Lente . . . 1550*, sig. Fiii.

a social and political nature.   In 1550 we see them poised in variously uneasy postures between a religious revolution which was, by their definition, good and a social revolution which was, by definition, bad—and would have been bad even if it had not erupted into overt rebellion.   In their distress they unquestionably achieved a more mature understanding of the complex relationships that were being established and re-established in their changing world.   On the other hand it must be admitted that they rejected the validity of change and sought only reform within the framework of a traditional and pre-sumably static social order.   And they agree that the basic cause of sedition is sin—covetousness in particular—or, more accurately, the vengeance of God wreaked upon the English people for their sins.[58] Their awareness of the existence of an area between sin and govern-ment that could yield a portion of the truth to those who would explore it was their only important discovery, and it was all that really sep-arated them from their medieval prototypes.

ఆ ఆ ఆ

The religious reformers were not, of course, alone in their concern for the events of 1549, nor were they as penetrating in their analysis as certain of their more secularly oriented contemporaries.   Somerset's program of reform owed its spirit and probably much of its form to men who, like John Hales, had matured under the influence of Eras-mian humanism.[59]   These men were as secular in their attitude toward the world of affairs as it was possible for intellectuals to be in that confessional age and in the prevailing atmosphere of an only partially outgrown medievalism.   Unlike the clerical reformers whose interest in social reform was always secondary to their preoccupation with the reform of religion, and to a large extent a corollary of it, these men were interested primarily in the welfare of society.   Both groups called for a more equitable society, freed from the oppressive and unsettling effects of a dynamic materialism.   Both invoked the commonwealth as their social ideal, with all its heritage of social values derived from the medieval past.   But, whereas Latimer preached that ideal from

58. E.g., Lever, *A Fruitful Sermon*, sig. Aiii-iv, *Sermon, 14 December, 1550* in *Three Fruitful Sermons*; Hooper, *Early Writings*, pp. 449-450; Latimer, *Works*, I, 247.

59. Into this category falls the author of the anonymous "sheep tract" entitled *Certain Causes Gathered Together wherein is Showed the Decay of England*, ed J. M. Cowper in *Four Supplications*, E.E.T.S., E.S., No. 13 (1871).

the pulpit and in the context of ecclesiastical revolution and in the language of moral exhortation, Hales undertook to give practical expression to it in the context of actual agrarian life. The rebellions and the subsequent fall of Somerset put an end to the reform movement alike in its propagandist and in its practical phases, and both preachers and humanist laymen were forced to explain the miscarriage of their hopes. But the latter, as might be expected, were more willing than the former to explore the purely secular relationships and to treat the whole affair as one lying primarily within the province of secular government.

Hales undertook to explain the rebellions not only because, as the immediate reason for the defeat of his plans for reform, they needed explanation, but also because he was forced to vindicate his own part in the events that led up to the risings. Like Latimer and the more socially conscious preachers, he had become identified with the reform agitation and shared with them the suspicious and vindictive scrutiny of the landed magnates. Now supported by the rising power of the unscrupulous Northumberland, the leaders of the landed interest turned on all those who had attempted to halt the process of agrarian change and accused them of fomenting sedition. They accused the preachers of encouraging equalitarian ambitions among the common people. But, except in the case of a few extremists, they no doubt found it hard to do more than criticize; for to condemn eminent and in many quarters beloved churchmen like Latimer for preaching a doctrine of Christian justice and traditional morality was to become indeed devil's advocates. Hales, on the other hand, they could and did accuse of specific acts within the realm of secular affairs, acts to which the partial immunity of the pulpit could not be made to extend.[60] Along with most of the "commonwealths," clerical or lay, Hales believed that enclosures were the cause of the prevailing "dearth." In this belief they received the support of Somerset who, in 1548, issued a ringing proclamation against enclosures, couched in just such language as the commonwealth men were accustomed to use in their sermons and tracts. Commissions were accordingly appointed to survey the situation in the counties and to hear complaints. Hales headed one of them—the only one, incidentally, that seems to have

60, See Lamond (ed.) of the *Discourse*, appendix to introduction, and Hales's *Defence*, in *ibid.*

pursued its duties with any vigor. His work continued through the summer of 1549. During that time he also wrote pamphlets and prepared drafts for parliamentary legislation on the subject of enclosures and their relation to the mounting inflation. Unfortunately for his hopes and for Somerset's policies, these investigations were accompanied by popular disturbances. Villagers in some parts of the country took the law into their own hands and tore down the hedges that were destroying the open fields and the immemorial custom of the manor. For these actions the commissioners were not unnaturally blamed, and when, in the summer of 1549, the disorders spread from the midlands to the western and eastern counties, the work of reform became completely discredited in the eyes of the landed gentry. In September of that year Hales felt constrained to defend his part in the affair. After the subsequent fall of Somerset he retired, prudently, to the Continent.

In his eloquent *Defence*, Hales looks for ultimate causes in the same quarter as did the preachers. "War, sedition, scarcity, famine, sickness, be plagues of God, which he sendeth for two causes chiefly. The one where the people do contemn His word and the other where they receive it and will not follow it."[61] Stated more specifically, the fault lies in the greediness of the landlords.[62] Where he differed from his preaching colleagues was in his willingness to accept covetousness as a fact, deplorable but for practical purposes inescapable, a ponderable fact which must be taken into account by civil government as well as by the church and dealt with, like any other menace to the common "wealth," by means of policy. Covetousness, he recalls, was the destruction of the Roman Empire and he warned that it would "have the like effect in this realm of England, if the king's majesty and his council do not the sooner put to their helping hand." For, he continues, "who will maintain husbandry which is the nurse of every country, as long as sheep bring so great gain? Who passeth on breeding of beasts, whereof no gain can be felt within three or four years, when of his sheep he shall be sure of his profit once every year?"[63] Here is the crux of the matter. Here lies the duty of the government, to apply regulation such as will restrain in the common interest the enterprise

61. *Defence*, p. lxvi.
62. *Ibid.*, pp. lviii-lix.
63. *Ibid.*, p. lxiv.

of individuals which, men being what they are, will otherwise simply follow the dictates of economic expediency.

Compared to considerations of this sort, the more immediate effect of spoken or written words Hales seems to consider of minor significance. True, he follows the popular argument to the extent of tracing the rebellion to the agitation of papists and Anabaptists as well as to the simple and desperate efforts of poor men to obtain what they considered their just due. But it is to the last of these three sources of dissatisfaction that he addresses himself in the body of the document.[64] Though no more willing than the preachers to condone a doctrine of communism or equalitarianism based on a crudely primitivistic, or perhaps merely mischievous, interpretation of the Scriptures (the poor, he argues, had a prescribed and necessary place in the political body),[65] Hales did not share their faith in preaching, whether for good purposes or subversive, and preferred apparently to believe that preaching of the latter variety would be effective only if the social organism continued to be deranged by the aggressive spirit of agrarian capitalism.

If Hales's disillusionment stemmed rather from the failure of the government and of the governing class as a whole to recognize their responsibility than from the ideological vagaries of the common people, Sir John Cheke agreed with the preachers that a dangerous doctrine of equalitarianism had in reality seduced the rebels. Cheke, however, was not concerned solely, or even primarily, with the causes of sedition. It was sedition itself—the Norfolk rising in particular—that interested him, and more especially its impact on English society. He, alone among those who commented on the rebellion, tried to analyze the rebel mind and to treat rebellion as in itself a causal factor.

That he should have made this kind of approach to his subject is not surprising. By training a humanist scholar, he carried on into the mid-century the tradition of "applied" humanism to which Starkey and Morison had devoted their energies in the preceding decade. He was one of those public-spirited intellectuals who felt it their opportunity and duty to understand the forces at work in their society, and to do so not merely for the intellectual satisfaction of understanding, but in the hope that through understanding might come reform. He also followed the example of those older scholars who plied their pen

64. *Ibid.*, pp. lvii-lix.
65. *Ibid.*, pp. lx-lxi.

in the service of the monarchy. His pamphlet, *The Hurt of Sedition*, was no doubt officially inspired for the purpose of discrediting the very idea of rebellion. But it was probably Cheke's own idea to combat sedition by demonstrating its evil effects on the body of the common-wealth rather than merely to seek out and blame those who started it. I hope his shades will forgive me if I venture to ask whether, after the fashion of academicians, he sought to avoid direct conflict with the authorities and, under the increasingly ominous shadow of North-umberland's rule, preferred to trace the *sequelae* of a rebellion no one was likely to defend rather than to probe more sensitive areas of public life in search of the causes. Whatever his motives, his tract stands out in a period of unusually brisk discussion as not only an effective piece of propaganda but an unusually thoughtful essay in social analysis.

As for the rebellion itself, what seems to have troubled Cheke most deeply was the fact that the Norfolk rebels had perverted the ideal of the commonwealth, around which the more responsible reformers had rallied, and that, by taking matters into their own hands, they had jeopardized a program of reform Cheke tells us was actually on the point of being worked out by the duly constituted authorities. This they had done in response to a doctrine of equality which Cheke felt would, if put into effect, have destroyed all order and degree, and eliminated all of the natural inequalities inherent in the orthodox notion of the commonwealth as a political body. The rebels of 1536 had also talked of equality, but, as Morison had recognized, what they wanted was the opportunity to better themselves, and so to rise in the social hierarchy. According to Cheke, the Norfolk rebels of 1549 wanted the leveling of all rank and degree.[66]

The rebels, he maintains, "pretend a commonwealth," but actual-ly ask for changes that would destroy a true commonwealth, and all out of a misdirected feeling of envy and ambition. "If riches offend you, because ye wish the like, then think that to be no Common-wealth, but envy to the commonwealth. Envy it is to appair an other man's estate without the amendment of your own. And to have no gentlemen, because ye be none yourselves, is to bring down an estate, and to mend none." Then he repeats the standard argument against equality of wealth: "Would ye have all alike rich? That is the over-throw of labor, and utter decay of work in this realm. For who will

66. See Zeeveld, pp. 222-225.

labor more; if when he hath gotten more, the idle shall by lust without right take what him lust from him, under pretence of equality with him. This is the bringing in of idleness, which destroyeth the common/ wealth; and not the amendment of labor, that maintaineth the common/ wealth." Then putting his finger on what he, like Morison before him, considered the legitimate expression of social ambition, he adds: "If there should be such equality, then ye take away all hope from yours to come to any better estate than you now leave them. And as many mean men's children do come honestly up, and are great succour to all their stock: so should none be hereafter holpen by you, but because ye seek equality, whereby none can be rich."[67]

We need not take Cheke's fears of the leveling propaganda entirely at their face value. We know that there was a substantial element among the Norfolk rebels. The articles which Ket and the other leaders drew up for the consideration of the government reflect a pro/ foundly conservative view of society. [68] They demanded not a "new deal" but the restoration of an old order in which their rights had been guaranteed by law and custom. Cheke may well, indeed, have been led to exaggerate the Anabaptist element in the popular agitation. Like his friends, the reforming preachers, he was keenly aware that such extremists had reflected discredit on all preaching of the new religion, with the result that the latter had, erroneously, been in some quarters blamed for the uprisings.[69] And, as in some capacity the spokesman for the government, he no doubt fell prey to that tendency, familiar enough in our own day, to brand all radicalism with the stigma of the extreme left.

Cheke was nevertheless able to see more clearly than most of his contemporaries that there was a dynamic element in his society, an element which could not be ignored nor wholly condemned. That element was individual initiative and its result the social mobility increasingly evident in actual life. And the only equality that could be reconciled with it was equality of opportunity within a society of unequal status and hierarchical degree. Even so, it is a factor Cheke prefers not to dwell upon. He is realistic enough to accept it as a fact,

67. Cheke, *The Hurt of Sedicion* in *Holinshed's Chronicles*, ed. H. Ellis (6 vols.; London, 1807/1808), III, 989/1011; see pp. 989/990.

68. Tawney, *Agrarian Problem*, pp. 338/340.

69. *Hurt of Sedicion*, p. 1002.

but he is not ready to justify it completely in theory. In the paragraph immediately following the one from which the above quotations were taken he condemns the rebels in the language of orthodox social theory for being "not content with your estate." The rebellion seems none-theless to have jarred Cheke's mind sufficiently free from such tradi-tional formulas to allow him to see the force of social mobility and individual enterprise for what it was, an ineluctable fact and, more-over, one that need not be considered wholly bad.

Interesting as he found the phenomenon of rebellion and the motives of those who took part in the Norfolk rising, Cheke devoted the bulk of his study to the impact of the rebellion on the national life. In the first place, it deranged the economy of the country to the extent that, by ruining a substantial portion of the year's food crop, it raised food prices and brought to the edge of starvation even those who thought to gain most by the rising. With famine and scarcity come disease, "a great decay of people," and the consequent "great diminish-ment of the strength of the realm." Rogues and vagabonds are left after the dissolution of the rebel camp to plague and intimidate the countryside, thus aggravating the already chronic diseases of idleness, vagrancy, and crime.[70] The reader is likely at this point to feel that Cheke is not so much drawing on immediate experience as general-izing from his very considerable knowledge of the history of wars and rebellions: it all sounds suspiciously familiar. But we must give him credit for recognizing the sequence of natural causes that any sudden derangement of the economy or of the social pattern is likely to set in motion.

One of the saddest things about the risings was, Cheke felt, that they not only failed to achieve their intended results but forestalled and delayed (presumably indefinitely) a specific program of reform at that very moment being brought to maturity in the king's council where that sort of thing should be done.[71] He appears to suggest that this is what happens when men not trained and appointed for the purpose try to diagnose their own ailments and prescribe for them. At best, to use his own metaphor, they fail to get to the bottom of the sore and merely let false skin grow over a still infected area.

Finally, Cheke traces the effects of rebellion on the national

70. *Ibid.*, pp. 999-1002.
71. *Ibid.*, 1003-1005; cf. p. 1010.

prestige and security. The spectacle of subjects so little regarding the commonwealth as to seek their own destruction could only serve to discredit England in the eyes of the world and to abate "the good opinion which was had of the just government and ruled order used heretofore in this noble realm. . . ."[72] Nor is this merely a question of patriotic sentiment. Referring no doubt to the Scots and the French, he indicates that the risings of 1549 had prevented England from proceeding with vigor against her enemies and, more than that, by demonstrating internal weakness and disunity, had actually invited invasion.[73]

ഗ ഗ ഗ

In his struggle to maintain some degree of equilibrium, some sense of direction in the wake of reform, the observant citizen found himself asking questions for which, even after the brisk discussion of the articulate thirties, he had little precedent. This is especially true of the religious reformers whose early enthusiasm had often carried them above and beyond the more worldly preoccupations of the humanists. Now, in the confused forties, the miscarriage of the policy of dissolution and the rebellions of 1549 forced reformers of all sorts, but especially those concerned primarily with religious reform, to face the facts of a revolutionary situation and to find, if they could, some answer to the question, what makes Englishmen act the way they do? If their answers were not always adequate or convincing, that is less important than the fact that they recognized the necessity for answers of some kind.

Meanwhile there were those who also recognized that the turbulent surface of life was itself conditioned by more profound processes of cause and effect, largely economic in character, processes that could not be explained satisfactorily in terms of individual conduct and must therefore be subjected to a special kind of investigation. To these, then, we must next turn our attention.

72. *Ibid*, p. 1007.
73. *Ibid.*, p. 1008.

CHAPTER X. THE SEARCH FOR CAUSE: THE ECONOMIC MECHANISM

UNSETTLING AS WERE THE RISINGS OF 1549 AND perspicacious as were some at least of the comments made upon them, it was not such events, nor even such particular problems as the distribution—or maldistribution—of the monastic properties, that elicited the most profound analysis of society during these critical years of the mid-sixteenth century. Rather, it was the economic conditions of which the rebellions were but passing manifestations and in which the monastic lands were but a single, complicating factor. To those conditions, in particular to the chronic but increasing "dearth," to the dislocation of agrarian life, to the problems of coinage and exchange, and to the relationship between national wealth and national power, a few humanistically inspired writers of the middle years turned the full power of their intelligence in an effort to understand the workings of their apparently so deranged society. And in this endeavor they were joined by practical men who made up in experience and in zeal for the commonwealth what they may have lacked in the historical perspective and intellectual discipline of a public-spirited humanism. The result was a literature, small in quantity but of the utmost historical significance, in which for the first time the groping search for underlying causes, for the impersonal factors operating within a society of persons, achieved a measure of success. After the *Discourse of the Common Weal* it remained only for later theorists to fill in the outlines therein drawn, not of an organism governed by the universal principles of justice accepted and analyzed with typical subtlety by the medieval schoolmen, but of an economic mechanism impelled by particular, often variable forces, natural in origin and observable, impersonal and amoral, yet subject to the intelligent direction of human agencies.

Throughout the preceding chapters we have frequently had reason to notice the power of economic issues to raise the public mind above the level of personal relationships and moral considerations and to accustom it to dwell in those areas of mechanistic cause and effect which have since become the normal province of policy. If, in the process, investigation was to stray at times dangerously far from the world of ordinary irrational men, and into the abstract world of "economic man," nevertheless it raised the exciting possibility that men could, by understanding the dynamics of their society, in some measure control them. In exploring this region of experience, Renaissance analysts were largely on their own. Far less than in the area of ethics or government were they able to call upon authority. As Heckscher once remarked, "there are few spheres in which the ancients contributed so little significant thought as the economic; and as for the Middle Ages, in the main they lay in the shadow of Aris-totle."[1] The early mercantilist theorists had to find their own bearings in a strange land. If their efforts to map new roads were therefore primitive, they were of necessity original. And, conversely, the fact that these men were forced during the mid-sixteenth century, in Eng-land as elsewhere, to grapple with increasingly baffling and dangerous economic problems did more than anything else to awaken them to the need for analysis and to kindle in their minds an appreciation of its potentialities.

It may be that Englishmen, though not in the mainstream of Renaissance influences, were in some respects more than ordinarily well situated to conduct such investigation. Perhaps their insular position freed them from the constant and acute distractions that must always have tended to divert Continental observers from such studies to those more immediately relevant to survival in a race for military and dynastic power. Some modern Continental scholars have, for instance, seen in Thomas More's handling of the external relations of his Utopians a projection of the islander's characteristic attitude toward the rest of the world.[2] In so far as the Utopians take part in power politics, it is economic power on which they depend, and their

1. E. F. Heckscher, *Mercantilism*, trans. Mendel Schapiro (2 vols.; London, 1935), II, 270. See also Etienne Antonelli, *Études d'économie humaniste* (Paris, 1958), Tome I, chap. ii; R. de Roover, "Scholastic Economics: Survival and Lasting Influence from the Six-teenth Century to Adam Smith," QJE, LXIX (May, 1955), 161-190.

2. See especially Gerhard Ritter, *The Corrupting Influence of Power*, trans. F. W. Pick (London, 1952), pp. 73-89. Cf. H. W. Donner, *Introduction to Utopia* (London, 1945), pp. 60-75. Note also that the author of the *Discourse of the Common Weal* also recognizes the importance of England's island position, but as a disadvantage in foreign trade rather than otherwise. Pp. 93-94.

objectives are such as bear—at least when observed from the point of view of such as Gerhard Ritter—a suspiciously close resemblance to those of more recent British imperialism.   Even more characteristic is their emphasis on welfare rather than on power in any form, a luxury only a people protected by geography from easy invasion could enjoy at all fully.   If there is anything to this interpretation at all, or if it is appli‑ cable also to those who followed More, it would help explain why English pamphleteers of the mid‑sixteenth century were so consistently preoccupied with economic issues, why they seemed to consider economic regulation the primary purpose of civil government, and why they preferred to think in terms of national economic power rather than of military strength or dynastic hegemony, and of welfare even more than of power.

Perhaps also the relative homogeneity of England's economy invited analysis.   The preponderance of wool and cloth in English trade, by presenting to the observer a limited and apparently simple pattern of relationships may have had the somewhat paradoxical effect of bringing him to an unusually clear understanding of those relationships in all their actual complexity, and so to a more mature understanding of the entire economic mechanism.   Perhaps also the English pamphleteer, especially the pamphleteer of humanist back‑ ground, in any case a man whose purposes were shaped by a strong bent toward the practical and by an equally marked sense of civic duty, found in economic life matter peculiarly suited to his interests and talents.   To this end he was aided for a brief while by the support and encouragement of his government.

Whatever the reason, English government in the forties and early fifties enjoyed—or suffered from—a plethora of economic counsel.   At first glance it seems a fugitive literature.   It does not result in the creation of a school of economic theory, nor is it dominated by any single intellect.   It was written in response to actual conditions and is intensely practical in its purpose.   Yet it is in the course of just such practical investigation, investigation undertaken in the interests of specific reform, that a few of these men managed to achieve insights into the causal relationships affecting economic life which were to become the groundwork of more consciously formulated theory.   And so, if England failed to produce in the sixteenth century a theorist of the stature of Bodin, she produced a whole generation accustomed as never before to the critical catechism of their economic experience, and, in the author of the *Discourse of the Common Weal*, a man who carried the analysis of economic affairs to a point beyond which it was to take subsequent investigators a long time to pass, and who arrived at basic theories which later writers were to develop.[3] The resulting literature could, it has been claimed, constitute a manual of economic policy quite comparable in quality to contemporaneous efforts on the Continent.[4]

What distinguishes Sir Thomas Smith (we are, it will be recalled, assuming that it was he who wrote the *Discourse*) and those several of his contemporaries who were thinking along similar lines is their unprecedented awareness of the impersonal, amoral causes operating within the economic system and of the necessity for a more or less systematic analysis of those forces. It is difficult, of course, to generalize without conveying a distorted picture of the English mind as it actually grappled with economic problems. As we have observed in previous chapters, men of intelligence had been forced for practical purposes to make up their mind about economic causes long before they felt called upon to set forth their conclusions in writing and in theoretical form or, still less, to pursue their investigations in a consciously systematic manner. Yet it is just this element of conscious purpose that is so characteristic of the Renaissance writers and becomes for that reason a matter of such fundamental importance in the present context.

To some extent the difference between these men and their predecessors of the thirties and, of course, the precocious More, is one of degree rather than of kind. Armstrong and Starkey, for example, the one from a practical, the other from an academic point of view, both recognized the need for causal analysis as a prerequisite to any understanding of the economic life of England. And More has been hailed as something of a pioneer in this respect. It must, however, be recognized that More and Armstrong and Starkey were all more concerned with the conditions themselves than with underlying causes, and so, though quite capable of seeing the relationship between poverty and idleness, crime and "dearth," and willing enough to look for particular causes (More's treatment of enclosures is a classic instance),

3. E. A. J. Johnson, *The Predecessors of Adam Smith* (New York, 1937), p. 37.
4. J. A. Schumpeter, *History of Economic Analysis* (New York, 1954), p. 166.

they did not feel impelled to study the economic mechanism in and for itself. Their analysis becomes in consequence somewhat fragmen-tary, their categories fixed too rigidly by the concept of a functional, hierarchical society. Armstrong, being less inhibited by academic habits than the other two, was perhaps for that reason more penetrat-ing in his economic analysis. Even so, he is only a partial exception.

Thus the tendency of these observers, realistic as they were, was to concentrate upon such things as enclosures, the misuse of monastic lands, idleness, poverty, and various mercantile sharp practices, all of which could rather readily be traced to the cupidity of men. This tend-ency, apparent in the most penetrating of comments, was not, to be sure, wholly unrealistic. These writers recognized that there was a spiritual force abroad in the land which, if not checked, would surely destroy society as they understood and valued it. We call it individual enter-prise. They, like their forebears, preferred to call it covetousness. To some extent the difference is one of terms, not meaning. Yet to trace economic disorders to covetousness was to relapse into the intellectual context of private morality, and of a static social ideal. Satisfying as it undoubtedly was to the ethical sensibilities of Christian humanists, this tendency led unavoidably away from the consideration of public policy and hence from the ultimate objective of economic analysis as it has come to be pursued in the modern world. (It also deflected the humanists from their own cherished objective of rational criticism.) To the modern mind the acquisitive instinct remains a force to be reckoned with, but only as one which acts in response to other, less personal forces, and one which may therefore be channeled or con-tained by intelligently conceived policy.

What has been said of the secular comment of the thirties applies also to the religiously oriented comment of the forties—only more so. The preachers and pamphleteers we have examined in the preceding chapter approached economic affairs by way of their preoccupation with religious reform. True, they shared the concern of their more secular contemporaries over the facts of economic maladjustment. But those facts they interpreted almost exclusively in terms, not only of social justice, but of private moral values. Now there was good precedent for their concern with economic matters as well as for their ethical treatment of them. Economic relationships had, after all, fallen tra-ditionally within the province of the church and of the ecclesiastical courts. And the Reformation had had the effect of nationalizing canonist principles rather than abrogating them. Preachers could still consider themselves as arbiters of economic life, not merely as moralists but as the custodians of all that was yet recognized as economic law. As such they fought a rear-guard action against the dynamic and, to them, disruptive, forces of an emerging capitalism. Indeed, on the question of usury, a matter of central importance both to the affairs of the mercantile community and to canonist economic doctrine, they continued to fight in the cause of conservatism throughout the latter half of the Tudor century.

It was thus no small accomplishment for a few men of Edwardian England to undertake the task of discovering the impersonal causes underlying the particular manifestations of economic change. Their task required that they see economic life as a whole and study it in the perspective of experience and within the context of secular values and public policy. That they succeeded only partially is less significant than that they made the attempt, for therein lies what in the realm of secular thought was the most significant contribution of that bedeviled generation.

Space will not permit us to follow in any detail all the questions raised in this literature. Nor would this be the place to do so. The reader must remember that we are here primarily concerned, not with the matter treated, but with the character of the treatment, with the assumptions and attitudes that conditioned the investigation and with the quality of insight achieved. We shall consequently have to be content to follow only a few of the more noteworthy arguments. This will mean that many examples of analytical thought will have to be passed over which at an earlier stage of this study we should have seized upon with eagerness. By the middle of the sixteenth century, however, the problem is no longer to discover the beginnings of analysis but to examine something that has become, if not a school of thought, at least a clearly recognizable tendency—indeed, among a few intel-lectuals an inveterate habit, consciously cultivated.

ᔕ ᔕ ᔕ

No student of the period, no one, especially, who is familiar with the early Tudor literature of criticism would forgive us if, among the economic problems canvassed in that literature, we did not address ourselves first of all to the agrarian.   Certainly agrarian troubles, and enclosures in particular, bulk larger in the critical comment than any other category.   It was, after all, still a predominantly agrarian society, and the men on whose minds the problems of the commonwealth weighed most heavily were likely to be those whose experience had, in one way or another, been with the land.   Most observers at the time would accordingly have agreed heartily with Lever when he main-tained that "the greatest grief that hath been unto the people in this realm hath been the enclosing of commons."[5]   Although such unequivocal statements represent an exaggeration of the facts—Lipson has rightly cautioned against accepting these emotionally charged expressions of contemporary opinion at their face value[6]—and although agrarian problems did not in fact give rise to the most mature essays in economic analysis, the agrarian problem can hardly be ignored, even for the highly selective purposes of this study.

Since the beginning of the century, changes in the use and hold-ing of land had been a constant source of concern for the socially conscious commentator.   For it was in that area of experience that the society of fixed hierarchical status was most obviously giving way before a new and apparently destructive force, and it was there that the principles of Christian justice traditionally linked with that social ideal were being most glaringly subverted.   We have had occasion in the preceding pages to see how persistently the subject obtruded itself into the discussion of even distantly related topics.   Now, in the reign of Edward VI, tendencies long apparent in the English economy had assumed the proportions of a social revolution.   Enclosures, the consolidation of farms, the displacement of peasants from their hold-ings, the raising of rents, the purchase of land by profit-conscious merchants could all with some justice be considered part of a vast and, to the conservative mind of the day, frightening cataclysm.   Little wonder, then, that agrarian conditions provoked such a quantity of comment[7] and, in a few instances, analysis of a significant order.

The immediate purposes of this study may perhaps be served sufficiently if we examine the way in which enclosures in particular became the center of analytical observation.   Enclosures consti-

5. *A Fruitful Sermon*, sig. Di.
6. E. Lipson, *The Economic History of England* (3 vols.; London, 1956), I, 179-180.
7. *Ibid.*, I, 161-173 contains a detailed survey of this comment.

tuted the most dramatic of all agrarian changes. They therefore lent themselves to colorful and epigrammatic statements, the extreme quotability of which has helped to perpetuate a distorted impression of the part actually played by them. When More speaks of sheep, naturally the gentlest of beasts, now devouring the very men themselves, or Becon tells us that whole townships have become "desolate and like unto a wilderness, no man dwelling there except it be the shepherd and his dog,"[8] it is hard not to go along with the speakers. Their indignation is infectious. Yet the very fact that enclosures entailed radical changes, even if only in limited areas, made it more than ordinarily easy to see them as the source of a whole complex of consequences, and hence made them an important object lesson in social dynamics.

The full title of an anonymous tract of the mid-century, characteristically summarizing its contents, epitomizes the popular approach to the problem: "Certain causes gathered together wherein is showed the decay of England, only by the great multitude of sheep, to the utter decay of household keeping, maintenance of men, dearth of corn, and other notable discommodities approved by six old proverbs."[9] Analysis by proverb may seem a far cry from the kind of analysis for which we are presumably looking. But the author manages with a certain crude ingenuity to trace just about all the ills of rural England to the spread of enclosures. Before he is finished he has found in sheep farming the source of poverty, vagrancy, and thievery,[10] and, in the proposition (left unexplored) that "shepherds be but ill archers," a threat even to England's military potential.[11] The tract fairly bristles with figures, and its naïve statistical analysis, proceeding from the most fanciful assumptions concerning the number of parishes in England and the most arbitrary estimate of the productivity of tillage, arrives at the astounding conclusion that sheep farming has thrown three hundred thousand persons out of work and turned them from a national asset into a public liability. Crude as this brief tract unquestionably is, it nevertheless summarizes most of the arguments advanced since the beginning of the century concerning the effect of enclosures for pasture on the national welfare.

8. *The Jewel of Joy*, pp. 417-477, 434.
9. Reprinted in Dunham and Pargellis, pp. 135-140 from *Four Supplications*.
10. Cf. Crowley, *An informacion and peticion*, p. 164.
11. Cf. *Vox Populi Vox Dei*, in excerpt in Tawney and Power, III, 29-30.

If, however, these arguments fairly represented all of which the minds of contemporary analysts were capable, we should be forced to conclude that the issue of enclosures had prompted little more than well-meaning, but superficial and grossly exaggerated propaganda. For-tunately we are able to see in the *Discourse of the Common Weal* a much more realistic and discriminating analysis of the subject. Sir Thomas Smith, the presumed author, specifically rejects the common opinion that enclosures are the only or even the major cause of the "dearth" that supposedly caused prices to rise. For, he maintained, "this enclosing and great grazing, if it were occasion of dearth of any thing, it must be of corn chiefly; and now these ii or iii years past, we have had corn good cheap enough; and the dearth that was then was most of cattle, as beeves and muttons; and the breed of these rather increase than diminish by pastures and closings."[12]   At the same time he recognizes that the problem is a real one, measured not only in terms of existing agrarian dislocation but in terms of the speed and momentum of the process itself. He warns that, if the rate of increase in the enclosing of land for pasture continues during the next twenty years as it has the preceding twenty, "it may come to the great dissolution and weakening of the king's strength of this realm, which is more to be feared than dearth." Men who are uprooted from their livings find it hard to compete for jobs among a growing population. And, since "hunger is a bitter thing to bear," they will be bound to "murmur against those who have plenty." Thus enclosures have become an important cause of "these wild and unhappy uproars amongst us"[13]— a reference to the risings of 1549.

He is, moreover, discriminating in his treatment of enclosures. It is, he recognizes, by no means a simple problem. For one thing, not all enclosures are bad, "but only . . . such as turneth commonly arable fields into pastures; and violent enclosures, without recompense of them that have right to common therein; for if land were severally enclosed, to the intent to continue husbandry thereon, and every man that had right to common, had for his portion a piece of the same to himself enclosed, I think no harm but rather good should come there-of."[14]   Smith is here ready to grant the force of the enclosers' argu-

12. *Discourse*, p. 52; see also p. 48.
13. *Ibid.*, pp. 48-49.
14. *Ibid.*, p. 49.

ments. From the modern point of view the advocates of the new agricultural methods naturally seem more realistic than those who would prohibit or restrict them.[15] Much as there is to be said against them on grounds of humanity—changes in the methods of production have always brought suffering with them—the future clearly lay in the enclosed farms of England, not in the open field village, a fact that had already been accepted cautiously by as humane an observer as Thomas Starkey.[16] Even when justifiable as contributing to more efficient tillage or to the production of a staple commodity like wool, Smith insists on evaluating enclosures in relation to a balanced national economy. Corn, meat, and wool are all essential to the common-wealth, and one must not be cultivated at the expense of the others.[17] Here is where the function of the policy-maker must begin. He believes it possible to maintain a balance by treating the profit motive as in itself a basic economic cause. He agrees with his fellow pam-phleteers that excessive or unjust enclosures result from covetousness. But he recognizes more clearly than almost any of his contemporaries that covetousness is more than a moral force. It is also an economic force, and as such it can be curbed or channeled by enlightened policy.[18]

Two things in particular tended to force the analytical mind of early Tudor England to pry still more deeply into the workings of the national economy. One was the price revolution. The other was the balance of foreign trade. Closely related, these problems were ideally fitted to serve as stimulants to analytical investigation, for they embodied in its most fundamental form the dynamism actually at work in Western society transforming it from its medieval to its modern configuration. They are especially significant because they called attention persistently to the impersonal, mechanical, and hence morally neutral factors shaping economic life and away from those elements more closely related to the individual will, and hence only too readily expressed in terms of a sometimes arbitrarily interpreted morality. Through their increasingly intensive study of prices and the flow of

15. E.g., Anthony Fitzherbert, *Surveying*, extract in Tawney and Power, III, 22-25; Thomas Tusser, *A Hundreth Good Points of Husbandrie* (London, 1557), STC 24372, also in extract in Tawney and Power, III, 63-68.

16. *Dialogue*, p. 96. See above, chap. viii.

17. *Discourse*, pp. 51-53. See also *Policies to Reduce this Realme*.

18. *Discourse*, pp. 53-60; cf. 120-122. The author of *Policies to Reduce this Realme* was also able to see this to a considerable extent.

trade a few shrewd observers were able to place the profit motive, itself a force of unquestioned power, in a more realistic perspective, to see it, that is, as a factor, human indeed, but one that must find expression within the impersonal mechanism of economic cause and effect.

The rise in prices was an enigma that confounded contemporaries prior to the publication of Jean Bodin's celebrated treatise.[19]   Of the fact itself there was, of course, no doubt.   It figures in almost every item of the profuse literature of social comment.   It was part of the personal experience of every man capable of remembering back more than a decade.   The Knight in the *Discourse of the Common Weal* ex-presses in classic form the predicament of even the reasonably pros-perous gentry when he declares that "albeit I may spend now more than I could xvi years ago, yet I am not able to keep the like house I did then."[20]   Inflation gave rise to situations that were hard enough for the experienced to understand but impossible for the unsophisti-cated.   In that same pamphlet, the Husbandman finds it hard to understand why he should pay rent at a higher rate despite the fact that he is able to charge higher prices for his produce.   "My bargain was but to pay for my taking vi pounds, xiii shillings, iiij pence yearly of rent, and I pay that truly; you cannot require more."   Nor is this discrepancy between the inflexibility of leases and the fluidity of prices any easier for the Knight to explain, for he replies, in honest confusion, "I cannot much say against that; but yet I perceive I shall be a loser still by this bargain, though I cannot tell the reason why."[21]   To the com-plaint of the Knight and the Husbandman, the other speakers, the Capper and the Merchant, yes even the learned Doctor, add their own testimony.   And the Doctor points out how the king himself suffers most seriously of all from inflated prices.[22]   The Knight expresses what was probably, even to the more informed observers, the most baffling aspect of this phenomenon: "I marvel much, master Doctor, what should be the cause of this dearth, seeing all things are (thanks be to God) so plentiful. . . . This is a marvellous dearth, that in such plenty cometh."[23]

19. Tawney, *Religion and the Rise of Capitalism*, p. 74
20. *Discourse*, p. 108.
21. *Ibid.*, p. 41.
22. *Ibid.*, First Dialogue, *passim.*
23. *Ibid.*, p. 37.

Modern scholarship has tended to link the precipitate rise in prices during the sixteenth century to the enormous increase in the precious metals available for minting.[24] Indeed, this relationship between prices and the quantity of money had by 1574 become apparent to Bodin and, not long thereafter, to the aging Sir Thomas Smith who appears to have altered the *Discourse of the Common Weal* so as to accommo‑ date that theory. During the preceding quarter‑century a few English‑ men were groping toward a similar explanation, but became pre‑ occupied and confused by local changes in the value of the coinage. The English monarchy, embarrassed by the extravagant policies of Henry VIII, had recourse between 1544 and 1551 to a policy of debasement which, though not unprecedented in English history, was so radical as to inflate prices with explosive rapidity.

Such considerations, even the effects of debasement, were not, how‑ ever, apparent to all observers. They involved the operation of forces too far below the surface of daily life and too far removed from the mo‑ tives of individual men. Most critics continued therefore to blame the sudden rise in prices on shortages of commodities. ("Dearth" and "dearness" naturally meant the same thing to men who believed prices, just prices that is, are normally stable and whose experience with in‑ flation had been hitherto confined to times of scarcity.) Englishmen were rightly concerned about the distribution of goods. Poverty, they knew, constituted a major social problem and one obviously aggravated by the increased cost of living. But, in the comparatively well‑fed England of the mid‑century, they found it hard to convince themselves that they were witnessing real shortage.[25] Why, then, the prevailing dearth? Surely it must be the result of the scheming of selfish men who seeek only their private wealth at the expense of the common wealth and who, deliberately or not, create scarcity amid plenty. Thus what a later generation was to recognize as the blandly amoral and highly

24. Much of the extensive scholarship on the price and monetary problem is reviewed in Raymon de Roover, *Gresham on Foreign Exchange* (Cambridge, Mass., 1949). See especially A. E. Feavearyear, *The Pound Sterling: A History of English Money* (2nd ed.; Oxford, 1963). See also Y. S. Brenner, "The Inflation of Prices in Early Sixteenth‑ Century England," *EcHR*, 2nd ser., XIV (Dec., 1961), 225‑239.

25. E.g., Lever, *Sermon, 14 December, 1550*, in *Three Fruitful Sermons*, sig. Mv; *Discourse*, pp. 36, 41‑42; Letter, William Lane to William Cecil, 18 January, 1551, in Tawney and Power, II, 182‑186. Cf. Brenner, who stresses, as a contributing factor, a relative shortage of victuals.

respectable figure of the enterprising individual, the economic man, following in all innocence the dictates of natural law as interpreted by enlightened self-interest, becomes at this point the villain of the piece, his role even more sinister than it had been customarily portrayed in the medieval literature of social comment.

Medieval social theory had, indeed, never been more vigorously enunciated nor more valiantly defended than in this period when it was being challenged as never before. And so we find the Tudor preachers in particular condemning the profit motive in language that recalls, yet at the same time outdoes, that of their medieval predecessors. They attacked more zealously partly because they knew far more about the nature and capabilities of the enemy. Lever, for example, is able with some insight to pin the blame for rising prices on the increasingly important part played by middlemen in the nation's economy. It is resale that leads to the inflated price of food. It is the "leasemonger," the dealer in land rentals, who drives up rents. These are the "merchants of mischief, coming betwixt the bark and the tree," flouting the natural order of things. "Take away all merchant men from any town or city, and ye shall leave almost the provision of things that be necessary. Take away leasemongers, regraters, and all such as by buying and selling made things more dear, and when they be gone, all things will be more plenty and better cheap."[26]

Harassed by an inflation for which he could find no real precedent and one which threatened the very existence of the social order as he understood it, each observer made use of whatever explanation he could find. Everyman became his own economist. Investigation in such circumstances tends to take the way of least resistance. For that reason it stopped more frequently than not at the door of the enclosing landlord. Similarly the rack-renter, the wool merchant, even the artisan and the husbandman—any person, in fact, who had something to sell —could be in some way linked with the rise in prices and held responsible.

But as investigation proceeded, and especially when to the force of ordinary curiosity was added the weight of experience, it tended to gain momentum. So it was that analysis tended occasionally to reach beyond the individual will and its moral conditioning into the mechanism of economic causation. Nor did it take the philosophically

26. *Sermon, 14 December, 1550,* in *Three Fruitful Sermons,* sig. Mv.

trained mind of the scholar to do so. In 1551, William Lane, a merchant of London, wrote to one of the king's secretaries, setting forth in crude, but forceful and concise terms a theory which was rapidly gaining ground among experienced and thoughtful observers. Prices of things which are not in scarce supply are, he says, set by the "exchange between our realm and other foreign realms." The exchange, in turn, is sensitive to the debasement of English coins. The fall of the exchange will in turn force up the price of cloth, thus starting a sort of chain reaction: "so that you may perceive that the exchange doth engender dear cloth, and dear cloth doth engender dear wool, and dear wool doth engender many sheep, and many sheep doth engender much pasture and dear, and much pasture is the decay of tillage, and out of the decay of tillage springeth in evils, scarcity of corn and the people unwrought [unemployed], and consequently dearth of all things."[27]

The relationship between prices, coinage, and foreign exchange constituted an area peculiarly equipped to foster the investigation of suprapersonal forces. It lay well beyond the will of private persons and even governments could influence what went on within it only indirectly. It lay therefore also well beyond moral criticism of the ordinary sort, of the kind, that is, which arose out of the assumption that the welfare of the community depended simply on the balance between virtue and vice in the people who composed it. It is consequently a matter of some significance that men like Lane should have been able and willing to follow the chain of causal connections they thought they observed from the superficial manifestations of inflation to the underlying factors involved in the mechanism of price and exchange. That Lane was apparently only one of the many who were similarly interested is even more significant.

The author of a much more elaborate and sophisticated treatise entitled *Policies to reduce this Realm of England unto a Prosperous Wealth and Estate* (1549) gives every evidence of contributing by means of his "little book" to just such a lively, not to say acrimonious discussion.[28] He has his own ideas, and they are not those held by certain others to whom he refers with respect as to a larger and more popular antagonist. Mistaking the symptom for the cause, he refuses to admit "as the most

27. Lane, William, to Robert Cecil, 18 Jan. 1551, in Tawney and Power, II, 182-186.
28. In Tawney and Power, III, 311-345. See pp. 312, 344-345.

men do affirm" that the debasement of the coinage in England was the major cause of high prices, but rather the "falling of the exchange between us and other nations."[29]   He finds, as a result of very detailed analysis, that "nothing hath brought the exchange so low but only the high price that the king's majesty giveth for gold and silver at his mints."[30]   And he is quite willing to accept as good a limited debasement.[31]

Though the falling of the exchange is a basic cause of trouble, it is not the only one.   Our author finds another in the tendency of merchants to buy up sheep-grazing land at the expense of individual tenants.   This makes food dear, and also wool, for these men have a semimonopoly on the wool trade. With food and wool prices high, cloth and all commodities rise proportionally in price, which, in turn, causes the landlord to raise his rents.   It is a complex situation, moving according to a series of interlocking circles of causation, vicious in their effects rather than in their origins, though the "covetous merchant man" still plays a large part.[32]

Whatever the value of the premises on which these men erected the shaky structure of their arguments, it is just this consciousness of investigating a phenomenon of great complexity that gives their work its significance.   That phenomenon was, moreover, one they no longer tried very hard to fit into the figurative language of medieval social discussion.   The mechanism of economic forces that determined the level of prices did not lend itself to the organic analogy of the the "body politic" any more than it did to criticism in terms of private morality.   Smith finally rejected it entirely.   In the *Discourse* he chose to illustrate the complexity of causal forces by the simple mechanical analogy of the clock: "To make this more plain to you; as in a clock there be many wheels, yet the first wheel being stirred it drives the next, and that the third, till the last moves the instruments that strikes the clock."[33]   It is merely a figure of speech, an illustration. It neither distorts his argument as the organic analogy distorted Starkey's in the *Dialogue*, nor does it tempt him, as the notion of the body politic seems to have tempted others, to confuse illustration with proof.

29. *Ibid.*, p. 315.
30. *Ibid.*, p. 317.
31. *Ibid.*, p. 344.
32. *Ibid.*, pp. 319-321.
33. *Discourse*, p. 98.

Among those who sought the key to the puzzle of prices, Smith stands, indeed, alone. Yet he differed from his contemporaries not so much in the direction of his investigation as in the distance he was able to travel along the same route, not so much in his understanding of the need for analysis as in the thoroughness with which he pursued the task, not so much in the questions he asked as in the quality of the insights he achieved in the process. The *Discourse* is a classic example of that combination of the theoretical and the practical which characterizes so much of the work of the Tudor humanists. Indeed, it reflects the fusion of scholarship and counsel, of philosophy and statesmanship, which Smith sought—with rather less success—to achieve in his own career.[34] One of the most respected scholars of his day, an authority on the language and customs of classical antiquity, he undertook to place his learning at the disposal of his prince and in fact served the Protector Somerset and Queen Elizabeth in a variety of advisory and diplomatic capacities. Had he been as sensitive to the human factor in politics as to the desiderata of economic policy, he might now rank with the great Tudor statesmen as well as with the leading minds of the English Renaissance. In the *Discourse* he attempted, not the dogmatic discussion of the ethical implications of economic activity in which the schoolmen were more interested and no doubt more adept, but rather a careful analysis of the economic mechanism as he saw it in actual operation and with particular reference to English national interests.

To the Doctor of the *Discourse*, as presumably to Smith himself, the study of economic matters is a branch of moral philosophy.[35] It is not necessarily or even primarily the study of those ethical principles that govern the actions of individuals. It is the study of society, and its end is the improvement of society. In order to improve society, however, it is necessary to understand it; that is the task of the philosopher, the most useful one he can perform within the world of affairs.

34. For data on Smith's career, see Mary Dewar, *Sir Thomas Smith: A Tudor Intellectual in Office* (London, 1964). Smith's interest in economic affairs was no passing phase. Mrs. Dewar is convinced that he wrote the penetrating *Memorandum for the Understanding of the Exchange*, once attributed to Gresham. (Her arguments will be developed in detail in a forthcoming critical edition of Smith's writings. Cf. de Roover, *Gresham*.) And he was also able to turn his scholarly attention to the economic conditions of ancient Rome, the result of his investigations being an essay in economic history entitled "The Wages of a Roman Footsoldier."

35. *Discourse*, pp. 22 ff.

Accordingly, Smith has the speakers in his *Discourse*, led by the human⁄
ist Doctor, address themselves, as a matter of overriding priority, to the
paradox of high prices in a time of plenty—"our dearth of all things,
though there be scarceness of nothing."[36] It is a complicated problem,
and perhaps the most significant thing about the author of this remark⁄
able document is that he recognizes the complexity, accepts it as a chal⁄
lenge, and refuses to accept the easy solutions. He will not, as we have
seen, grant that enclosures are, in themselves, a serious threat to the
price level, especially in a time when crops have been plentiful.
Neither will he blame the landlords who raise rents or the tenants who
raise the prices of their produce. Thus to all intents and purposes he
rules out of the argument those factors rooted in the moral nature of
man. Such explanations still exercised the fascination of a siren's
song on most of his contemporaries. They were superficially plausible.
They placed the blame where it seemed to belong, on people, or classes
of people, on those who might, if they listened to the exhortation of the
critic, conceivably amend their own fault. Smith would no doubt
also have agreed that men are individually responsible for their actions,
but he recognized more clearly than any of his English contemporaries
that men cannot be expected to act for long, or in any socially effective
way, contrary to their economic interests—especially since those interests
are in the long run directed by forces beyond their personal control.

Neither landlord nor tenant can alter the level of prices without
incurring more loss than they can afford. Nor can the encloser be
expected to cease enclosing so long as the profit to be had from enclosing
is greater than that from tillage. And even if both landlord and tenant
could be induced to sacrifice their private interests to the common
"wealth," it would do no good, for the prices they charge are deter⁄
mined ultimately by foreign trade. England cannot live by herself.
All Englishmen need imported goods, the prices of which are set
abroad more than in the retail market at home and as a result of factors
over which the English citizen has little control.[37]

To pass over a wealth of analysis too closely argued to be readily
summarized, Smith finds in the debasement of the English coinage
the "chief cause of all this dearth of things."[38] It is the goal toward

36. *Ibid.*, p. 36.
37. *Ibid.*, pp. 41⁄42.
38. *Ibid.*, p. 69. Note that the pamphlet entitled *Causes of Dearth*, printed by Lamond

which his notion of mechanical causation, expressed in the analogy of the clock, logically impels him. He must find the master wheel in the economic mechanism, the "original," the "principal," the "efficient" cause.

And thus, to conclude, I think this alteration of the coin to be the first original cause that strangers first sell their wares dearer to us; and that makes all farmers and tenants, that reareth any com/ modity, again to sell the same dearer; the dearth thereof makes the gentlemen to raise their rents, and to take farms into their hands for the better provision, and consequently to enclose more ground.[39]

And so, instead of enclosures being the cause of dearth, they become the result.

Unfortunately, the author's zeal for analysis outruns his under/ standing. His efforts to hold debasement solely responsible for the rise in prices becomes at times more ingenious than convincing, at least to the modern reader. It must be remembered, however, that he was something of a pioneer in this sort of investigation. As such, he must be pardoned for his occasional failure to see as far into the economic system as a man of Bodin's stature was able to do almost two decades later.

He was not, to be sure, alone in his feeling that in the alteration of the coinage lay a powerful causal force. The subject seems to have attracted considerable attention. Men as diverse in their character and background as Latimer, the churchman, Lane, the merchant, the ballad/writer who composed the latter day "song on the times" entitled *Vox Populi Vox Dei*, the humanist scholar, William Thomas and the anonymous, but astute author of *Policies to Reduce this Realm unto a Prosperous Wealth and Estate*, all writing within a year or so of the *Discourse*, bear witness to the currency of the theme.[40] If not the

---

with the *Discourse* and ascribed by her along with that tract to Hales, does not make this emphasis, but concentrates on scarcity of breeding stock, regrating of victuals, and the activities of the king's provisioners. *Discourse*, introd., pp. xlii/xlv.

39. *Ibid.*, p. 104.

40. For Latimer's comment on the subject, see *Works*, I, 137; "for the naughtiness of the silver was the occasion of dearth of all things in the realm." On William Thomas, see "To the King, touching the reformation of the Coin," in *Discourses*, printed in John Strype, *Ecclesiastical Memorials* (London, 1816), VI, 375/377. See also W. A. J,

discoverer of the relation between debasement and prices, Smith deserves credit for being the first to analyze the problem systematically before Bodin added another and more generally applicable explanation for the rise in European prices.[41]

Somewhat to oversimplify Smith's monetary theory,[42] he repudiated the notion that the value of money can be determined by proclamation. A prince may indeed be able to declare that adulterated coin retained the same weight of precious metal, and therefore the same value, as before the alteration. And for a time he can get away with his deception, because public confidence will allow the over-valued coins to pass at their face value. Soon, however, foreign merchants, detecting the difference, will accept the debased coins only at a discount.[43] Prices of imports will therefore rise and more money will leave the realm to pay for them. This has, indeed, already happened. Meanwhile good coins will also leave the realm, where they buy more than the new, and go where they will be "most esteemed." Now since foreign goods have risen in price, measured by the discounted English coinage, English merchants who have bought these high priced imports must in turn raise their prices. For, argues the Doctor, with non-canonist realism, "Must not they that buy dear, sell dear again their wares?"[44] Without explaining very clearly why this process takes place, Smith argues that the prices of domestic goods must then rise proportionally.[45] And so all prices rise as a result of the policy of debasement. *Quod erat demonstrandum.*

There most of Smith's contemporaries would have been content to stop. Prices were high and getting higher, and about all that remained for the social critic to do was to illustrate that fact. That, at any rate, is all most of them attempted to do. Smith, on the contrary, saw that inflation was in itself a protean factor in the economy, a causal force diverse in its effects and not always bad. In his analysis

---

Archbold, "A Manuscript Treatise on the Coinage by John Pryse, 1553," *EHR*, XIII (Oct., 1898), 709-710.

41. Johnson, p. 31; Tersen, *John Hales, économiste anglais du milieu du XVI*e *siècle* (Avallon, 1907), pp. 64-68.

42. *Discourse*, pp. 69 ff.

43. A much more detailed discussion of the exchange appears in the *Memorandum* (p. 76) dated by Mrs. Dewar in Mary's rather than Elizabeth's reign.

44. *Discourse*, p. 79.

45. De Roover considers the explanation here "an early and clear formulation of the terms-of-trade argument." *Gresham*, p. 242.

of those effects he is on a little sounder ground than in his search for the roots of inflation—which is natural enough since the latter were hidden and the former, though confusing enough in their ramifications, were more evident to the naked eye. Yet here again his discriminating analysis places him in a class by himself.

The price rise, he recognized, is not in itself, a disaster. Unlike most of the men of his day who adhered with more passion than under' standing to the medieval ideal of plenty and who therefore believed that commodities should always be "good cheap," Smith anticipated the mercantilist attitude of tolerance toward rising prices, if not of active sympathy.[46] Inflation clearly helped all those who live by buying and selling, for "as they buy dear, so they sell thereafter." So also it helps those who "have takings, or farms in their own main' tenance, at the old rent; for where they pay after the old rate, they sell after the new."[47]

Those, on the other hand, whose incomes are fixed by custom or contract, lose, in particular "all noble men, and gentlemen, and all other that live by a stinted rent or stipend."[48] Hence the landlords have to raise rents when they can or enclose their land in the interests of a higher return.[49] The same is true of laborers, serving men, and soldiers who, "having but their old stinted wages, can not find them selves therewith as they might afore time, without ravine and spoil."[50] Here the problem becomes a sore deeply seated in the social organism, threatening public order and, since the king must depend on a stalwart and plentiful body of "serving'men and yeomen," threatening also the safety of the realm in time of war.[51]

The king, indeed, is himself a loser, if not by the rise in prices, at least by the policy of debasement which obviously yields a temporary increase only, a profit similar to that of a man who "would take his wood up by the roots, to make the more profit thereof at one time, and ever after to lose the profit that might grow thereof yearly."[52] Worse than that, the debasement tends to cause coins, especially good coins, to flow

46. Heckscher, II, 227.
47. *Discourse*, pp. 80'81; cf. p. 33.
48. *Ibid.*, p. 81.
49. *Ibid.*, pp. 81'82.
50. *Ibid.*, p. 82; see also pp. 33'35.
51. *Ibid.*, p. 84.
52. *Ibid.*, p. 35; cf. p. 86.

out of the realm.[53]   The king is consequently left without sufficient means to buy the weapons and materials necessary in time of war.   For this reason "These coins and treasures be not without cause called of wise men *nervi bellorum*, that is to say, the sinews of war."[54]   Again it is the necessity of maintaining some foreign trade that makes the policy of debasement a delusion, otherwise the king might proclaim whatever coinage he saw fit.   As things stand, however, "We must frame our things, not after our fantasies, but to follow the common market of all the world; and we may not set the price of things at our pleasure, but follow the prices of the universal market of all the world."[55]   Englishmen in the sixteenth century, like their successors of the twentieth, seem to have needed reminding that they lived in an economic world not entirely subject to their own control.

It is interesting to notice in this connection that, although Smith rightly holds the king responsible for the policy of debasement, and hence, by implication, the architect of his own and his subjects' misfortunes, he refrains from criticizing the policy in terms of right and morality.   Earlier writers on coinage, Nicholas Oresmes for example, concentrated on the right of the community to determine changes in what they considered a property of that community.   To tamper with that property is to violate a right, and therefore to raise a moral issue. Smith refuses to become entangled in any such considerations.   He blames the king only because the debasement is likely to result in a loss of profit to him and is for that reason a potential danger to the country. His argument, in short, rests solely on considerations of national wealth and power.[56]

ΩΩΩ

It was, as we have had occasion to notice more than once in the preceding pages, the peculiar virtue (if that is the right word) of economic discussion that it tended to lead the articulate citizen toward just such considerations of national wealth and power.   As England moved from a town-centered to a nation-centered economy, as the political interests of the country became more clearly those of survival in a Europe of competing states, it became more and more apparent that national survival

53. *Ibid.*, pp. 32-33, 45, 78.
54. *Ibid.*, pp. 86-87.
55. *Ibid.*, p. 87.
56. Tersen, pp. 81-82.

depended on the ability of the government to have within its control the economic means without which political power could never be attained. The critic of society had accordingly to re-examine his ideal of "wealth." Down to the sixteenth century, and well into it, the word was customarily used in a sense synonymous with welfare. And welfare was thought of simply as the well-being of the body politic, the condition which allowed each part to live and function in its appointed place and in a manner befitting it. This was an ideal that was coming to bear less and less relation to the actual activities of the emerging society of private enterprise or to the legislation of a govern-ment since the fourteenth century increasingly preoccupied with foreign trade. But it continued nevertheless to direct the pen of the average com-mentator.

By the mid-sixteenth century, however, even the commentator, in-hibited as he still was likely to be by the verbal formulas of an earlier day, could no longer treat the nation's economy so exclusively in terms of welfare. For welfare itself had now to be justified, in part at least, as a prerequisite to national power. A plentiful population, suitably employed and prosperous, must now be interpreted not merely as a social desideratum but as a political necessity, the source of the money, the manpower, and the loyalty upon which the prince must be able to count as the means of maintaining his independence. Power and wealth thus interacted to create the ideal of the mercantilist rate. Power, it is true, tended in mercantilist thought to become an end in itself.[57] But the English pamphleteers of the mid-century were too humane—too medieval, if you will—to go quite that far. They assumed for the most part that power would be reflected in the ability of the government to maintain not only the independence of the state but also justice and and plenty for its citizens.

In order to achieve the objectives of wealth and power, the national economy had to be put on a profit-making basis. The mercantilist state was therefore a dynamic thing, depending on its ability to export more than it imported. But that implied the ability also of its produc-tive citizens to become still more productive. Thus the dynamism of private enterprise, which had in fact long since left behind the concept of a common welfare within a static social organism, became absorbed in the larger dynamism of the national state. The analytical observer

57. See Heckscher, II, 13-31.

who applied himself assiduously to the study of the economic system could therefore hardly fail to sense the inadequacy of the social and political ideal to which he gave lip service. The concept of the "commonwealth," with its emphasis on the welfare rather than the profit of the private citizens and its strong assertion of a static, hierarchical social ideal, thus becomes at times little more than a veneer thinly disguising a realistic appreciation of the forces actually shaping a new society.[58]

Not that these so-called "commonwealth men" were insincere. They were practical men first and theorists only secondarily. But their penchant for realistic observation and their willingness to follow their observations to tenable conclusions led them often beyond inherited theory. Economic issues thus served as the most powerful of solvents for clearing away attitudes no longer relevant to a society of capitalist enterprise and power politics.

For this reason it is important to notice how these pamphleteers followed the logic of their analysis from considerations of private welfare, which under their critical scrutiny became subtly extended to include those of private profit, toward considerations of national wealth, which in turn became subtly extended to include those of national power. In the process they were able for the first time to achieve a more or less clear view of the mercantilist state, and in the *Discourse* for the first time a reasonably comprehensive, if still somewhat primitive, explanation of it. In it, Smith was able to rationalize policies which had for two centuries been worked out for practical purposes and in piecemeal fashion and to do so in terms of an economic system, realistically observed and interpreted as a mechanism of natural but impersonal cause and effect.[59]

His primary concern was ostensibly, and no doubt quite sincerely, for the "common weal" as it had traditionally been envisioned. But we have seen that he was also quite ready to follow the logic of his analysis of prices and the monetary problem as it led into a consideration of those international factors over which even the English king had little direct control and which emphasized the peculiar interests of the nation. The problem of the coinage became inextricably entangled

58. See below, chap. xiii.

59. For the place of the author of the *Discourse* in mercantilist thought, see Johnson, chap. ii and Heckscher, II, *passim*. See also Tersen.

with other factors affecting the flow of international commerce, and it was a systematic examination of those factors which brought Smith to a consideration not merely of England's wealth but of her power as well.

Even if space permitted, it would be unnecessary to follow all the steps he took in this broader analysis. It should nevertheless prove enlightening to see the general direction in which he travelled. With the aid of a certain amount of oversimplification, he may be considered to have proceeded as follows. No people can live entirely to them/ selves. God has not endowed all regions equally and, although England has been plentifully endowed, she must depend on foreign trade for many things, necessary as well as desirable. But in the course of this unavoidable reciprocity, England must be careful not to come off second best. "We must always take heed," Smith warns his coun/ trymen, "that we buy no more of strangers than we sell them, for so we should empoverish ourselves and enrich them." England must be especially careful not to import luxury goods than "we might either clean spare or else make them in our own realm," for they cost the foreigner little but his labor. Even more serious is it to import luxuries that have been made abroad from raw materials produced in England. If such things must be bought, they should be exchanged for similar "trifles," not for staple raw materials or money. In short, England must be wary lest the balance of her foreign trade tip in favor of her competitors, with the result that England be drained of her treasure.[60] Treasure, in turn, though not in itself wealth, makes it possible for the king to command the means of maintaining his independence and hence the peace and security of his people. For, *"pecunia nervi bellorum"*; and the possibility of war must always be kept in mind by any responsible government.[61]

Indeed the object of national policy must be not merely to prevent other countries from profiting at England's expense, but to tip the balance of trade in her own favor. Accordingly the English people must be encouraged to be industrious and to make such articles as will command the most lucrative market abroad. England must, that is, export the labor of her artificers as well as the product of her fields and mines. No one industry should be allowed to develop at the expense of a balanced economy, for then the country would become dangerously

60. *Discourse*, pp. 62/68.
61. *Ibid.*, pp. 84/86; see also p. 35.

dependent on others for necessaries.[62]   Economic interests and political interests are, Smith implies, interrelated and reciprocal in their effects. The former must be evaluated in relation to the independence of the national state and to its ability to compete with other powers.   Diplomacy, on the other hand, must be directed toward the economic profit of the country.   Allies must be sought in order to insure a dependable source of essential commodities in time of war;[63] no league should be perpetuated longer than is profitable.[64]   Smith recognizes also the peculiar position of England as an island power, which, though isolated from embarrassing entanglements, is also to some degree isolated from easy access to Continental trade.[65]

Since money is the convenient measure of wealth and can be stored for the purpose of commanding wealth in the event of such future emergencies as war or crop failure, and since gold and silver are the accepted basis for coinage, the accumulation of treasure becomes a main object of national economic policy and any alteration in the value of money can have effects felt throughout the international market.[66]   Monetary problems, though not directly involving the wealth and power of a country, indirectly affect those primary objectives at every point and are therefore matters of central importance in any analysis of the economic system.

In this analysis, the whole is greater than the sum of its parts. Taken piece by piece, it is for the most part familiar.   The author's emphasis on industry, on the danger of importing luxuries, on the importance of a large and profitably employed population, on the need for increasing the amount of treasure in the country, and on the strategic significance of economic prosperity may be found scattered throughout the literature of economic comment for the preceding century and a half.[67]   Among his contemporaries they appear with greatly increased frequency and often in provocative juxtaposition: taken together, their

62. *Ibid.*, pp. 88-91.

63. *Ibid.*, p. 74.

64. *Ibid.*, p. 67.

65. *Ibid.*, p. 94.

66. *Ibid.*, pp. 69-79.   On the question of the degree of importance attached by Smith and other mercantilist pamphleteers to treasure, see Heckscher, II, 175-176, 211-212; cf. *Discourse*, p. 170.

67. See above, chap. iv.   Note also Starkey's comment, *Dialogue*, pp. 92-93.   See also Lipson, II, lxxviii.

work constitutes a primitive but practical system of political economy. But in the *Discourse* these parts are incorporated into a consciously articulated system.

ɷ　ɷ　ɷ

By now it should be clear that Smith, and to varying lesser degrees a few like-minded contemporaries, had come to see economic interests of all sorts, both public and private, as part of a vast complex of forces, suprapersonal and amoral in character, natural in origin, ponderable and capable to some extent of adjustment by human agencies. Yet Smith recognized that, impersonal as they were, these forces worked through persons and for persons. The self-interest of men remained the motive which kept the machine in motion, and self-interest fell within the province, still not formally disputed, of the moralist. Smith therefore had the choice of two alternatives: he could relapse into the habit of moral criticism and find the ultimate causal force in man's moral nature, or he could proceed on the assumption that the motivating desires in economic life are themselves part of the natural order of things and hence uniform, consistent, and predictable—and, considered collectively, amoral. To have chosen the former alternative would have been to abandon the search for cause before it started, and to place economic relationships therefore beyond the range of constructive policy. The latter alternative demanded a radically new approach to the problem of economic individualism, one which, if it did not necessarily collide head on with the traditional economic doctrines, tended inevitably to circumvent them and therefore to weaken them as values relevant to the formulation of public policy. Smith, as we have seen, chose this latter alternative.

By traveling in this direction rather than in the paths already well beaten by his more religiously oriented contemporaries, he was able to penetrate as yet unexplored regions of experience and in the process to travel far beyond still generally accepted theory. Spokesmen for the latter continued to treat the profit motive in terms of private morality, branding it simply as covetousness, and so disposing of it for good and all. Smith, observing it in the larger context of national, indeed of international society, considered it rather as a natural force, capable of being empirically evaluated and channeled in the interests of the community. By thinking along these lines, he had, I am sure, no intention of challenging the validity of moral judgments when applied to private life. And he was quite ready to accuse the English people generally of sloth and a decadent taste for luxury—though in these instances the moral weakness had a direct bearing on the national prosperity and was subject to discipline by the government. His attitude was rather that, like it or not, the profit motive is a fact which has to be reckoned with, and a force which cannot be contained simply by repressive legislation. But he became so accustomed to considering economic individualism in this broader context that he began to think it not simply a necessary evil, much as medieval moralists had considered sex, but as a potential' ly, perhaps even inevitably, beneficent force. "Is it not an old saying in latin, *honos alit artes*, that is to say, profit or advancement nourisheth every faculty; which saying is so true, that it is allowed by the common judgment of all men."[68]

Good or bad, however, there is no denying the uniform operation of economic self'interest, nor is there any point in arguing with it. Speaking of the vexing problem of enclosures, which drew more fire from the moral critics than any other problem of the time, Smith has this to say:

> For every man will seek where most advantage is, and they see there is more advantage in grazing and breeding than in husband' ry and tillage, by a great deal. And so long as it is so, the pasture shall encroach upon the tillage, for all the laws that ever can be made to the contrary.[69]

In dealing with this force of self'interest the government must proceed positively, by rewards rather than by penalties. It must be harnessed, not repressed. Men should be "provoked with lucre"[70] to do what is socially or nationally advantageous.

Nor was Smith alone in this tendency to treat self'interest as a natural and, in the long run, irresistible force. Two, at least, of his fellow commentators, prompted by something of the same distrust of restrictive legislation, bore equally vigorous testimony to the power of economic individualism. One of them, Sir John Mason, main' tained that experience with such ordinances proved that "nature will have her course, . . . and never shall you drive her to consent that a

68. *Discourse*, p. 57.
69. *Ibid.*, p. 53.
70. *Ibid.*, p. 60. See next chapter.

penny-worth of new shall be sold for a farthing." For who, he says, will "keep a cow that may not sell the milk for so much as the merchant and he can agree upon."[71] This comes about as close as it was possible to come in this period of fluid economic opinion to a clear statement of natural law as the presiding principle in the economic affairs of men.[72]

Smith himself even considered at one point in the *Discourse* whether there might possibly be a natural harmony of private interest within the economic life of the commonwealth. Speaking of the enclosure problem, the Knight offers the following:

> I have hear oftentimes much reasoning in this matter; and some, maintaining these enclosures, would make this reason. Every man is a member of the common weal, and that that is profitable to one may be profitable to another, if he would exercise the same feat. Therefore that is profitable to one, and so to another, may be profitable to all, and so to the common wealth. As a great mass of treasure consisteth in many pence, and one penny added to another, and so to the third and fourth, it maketh up the great sum; so each man, added to another, maketh up the whole body of the common weal."[73]

The Doctor is not quite ready to go so far toward a concept of natural harmony, nor is he quite ready to grant the ineluctable beneficence of self-interest. Not only is stealing an obvious example of an act which, while profiting the individual, is prejudicial to the community, even the problem of enclosures is by no means a clear instance to the contrary. And he concludes, cautiously, that "men may not abuse their own things to the damage of the common weal."[74]

Much as this conclusion seems to agree with the accepted social theory of the time as expressed, for example, by Crowley when he declared that a man cannot do "what he likes with his own,"[75] the significant fact is that the discussion took place, and, withal, so dis-

71. Sir John Mason to Cecil, 4 December, 1550, in Tawney and Power, II, 188. Notice similar argument advanced concerning usury by the Merchant in Thomas Wilson's *Discourse upon Usury*, ed. R. H. Tawney (London, 1925), pp. 249-251.

72. On this subject of the forerunners of a natural law concept as it developed in its modern form, see A. F. Chalk, "The Rise of Economic Individualism," *JPE*, LIX (Aug., 1951), 332-347. See also Heckscher, II, 293-294, 312-314; H. M. Robertson, *Aspects of the Rise of Economic Individualism* (Cambridge, 1933), pp. 65-66, 75.

73. *Discourse*, pp. 50-51.

74. *Ibid.*, pp. 51-52.

75. *Epigrammes*, pp. 47-50.

passionately.   It provides one more illustration of the kind of thinking toward which the English humanists moved in their effort to bring an' cient philosophy and contemporary life into the same working agree' ment.   Whereas the medieval schoolmen had ignored Aristotle's explanation of self'interest as something implanted by nature, the sixteenth'century humanists found that notion worth serious considera' tion despite its potential conflict with the still revered ideal of a society in which the "private weal" was habitually contrasted to the "common weal."[76]   Indeed it is worth noticing in passing that Aristotle, with his vigorous defense of private property and his willingness to see the practical life of man as an expression of a natural order, seems to have become the favorite philosopher of those humanists whenever they turned their attention most consistently toward the reform of the national community, whereas Plato served more suitably as patron when they concerned themselves primarily with intellectual prep' aration for citizenship.[77]

Thomas Starkey had also considered the possibility that private interests and public might tend to be identical.   Also quoting Aristotle, Starkey's *persona* Pole asserts that if you would know the common weal and wherein it consists, know the individual and his "wealth."   Lupset queries this, asking is not this the same as to say if every man seeks his own private weal he will be promoting the public weal—which is, by prior definition, wrong? Whereupon Pole replies it is only immoderate regard for private interests that is bad.   Enlightened self'interest will contribute to the common weal.[78]   Starkey handles the subject more gingerly than Smith, and insists on the moral implications of all wealth.[79]   And Smith himself is cautious enough.   Both men, however, were prepared to carry the question of economic individualism beyond the simpler criteria of private morality.   Both, indeed, went considerably farther in this direction than Thomas More who, while recognizing the force of self'interest, perhaps also the inevitability of its influence in human affairs as long as the institution of private property remained, could bring himself only to be resigned to it, never to see it

76. Chalk, pp. 336'337.

77. Smith himself refers to Aristotle as "the sharpest philosopher of wit that ever was." *Discourse*, p. 109.   Note, however, that he refers even more frequently to Plato, but on the level of education for and the duty of citizenship.

78. *Dialogue*, pp. 45'46.

79. *Ibid.*, p. 49.

as part of the natural order of things and hence capable of being treated outside the context of private morality. Indeed it is largely for this reason that More approached the problem of social reform much more pessimistically than did the "commonwealths" of the mid-century.[80]

A similar tendency to look for and to find natural causes is likewise discernible in these writers' treatment of the economic relations between one country and another. The idea of an international division of labor had, of course, been inherent in English economic discussion as soon as Englishmen recognized the significance of their own peculiar specialty in the wool and cloth trades. It is implied, though in crude form, in the realistic estimate made of England's position in European trade in the fifteenth-century *Libel of English Policy*. In the thirties, forties, and fifties of the century following, is becomes a more consciously recognized principle.

We have already seen how Clement Armstrong developed the idea.[81] God has established geographical differences between countries. England, for example, has been given the climate and soil needed to produce the finest of wools. Spain, on the other hand, is able to produce fruits and oils from plants that will not come to bearing in England.[82] Again, since God has not seen fit to endow England with gold and silver mines, she must depend on trade in the things she can produce for her supply of precious metals.[83] Nor can these facts of geography be challenged with impunity, as witness the futility of efforts to plant Spanish fruit trees in England.[84] To Armstrong these laws of nature retain the mystery of God's inscrutable decrees, yet they are observable and up to a point analyzable. And they provide a natural explanation for the flow of international trade. The Doctor in the *Discourse of the Common Weal* expresses a similar ideal of natural reciprocity. Since it is only reasonable for one region to help another when it lacks necessaries, "God hath ordained that no country should have all commodities, but that, that one lacketh, another bringeth forth and that, one country lacketh this year, another hath plenty thereof the same year, to the intent that one may know they have need

80. See above, chap. viii.
81. See above, chap. ix.
82. *A treatise concerninge the Staple*, in Tawney and Power, III, 98-100.
83. *Howe to Reforme*, in Tawney and Power, III, 117.
84. *A treatise concerninge the Staple*, in Tawney and Power, III, 99-100.

of another's help, and thereby Love and society to grow amongst all the more."[85]

The idealism of this passage stems naturally enough from the concern inherent in both the Christian and the humanist traditions for the welfare of all mankind. It finds expression again in William Cholmeley's *Request and Suite of a True-Hearted Englishman* (1553). Recognizing how, by "the unsearchable purpose of God" all nations lack certain necessaries, he sees them driven "to seek one upon another, and thereby to be knit together in amity and love, . . ."[86] It must not, however, be read out of context, the context of realism and economic nationalism that, in fact, pervades both the *Discourse* and the *Request*. In a later passage, Cholmeley puts the idea of natural reciprocity in a metaphor quite devoid of Christian idealism:

> The commodity of a country is like the water of a great river, and as they that stop the course of a river, and will suffer no man to fetch of the water from them, shall have more discommodity by the keeping of the water than others can have by the lack of it, and yet in short time it will break from them, maugre their heads, and so they that lacked it a while shall have the more plenty of it; even so, they that shall keep the commodity of their country from them that have the thing that it serveth for shall at the last (yea and that within short space) be glad to let it have the right course, and content themselves to be merchants to those places where the utterance of their commodities lieth most best.[87]

What rises to the surface of these turgid lines is not so much the beneficence of trade as its dynamism, not so much the ideal of peaceful co-operation among Christian peoples as stark national egoism. These English writers were willing to believe that, in so far as economic life revealed certain observable uniformities, certain natural tendencies, it revealed the purposes of God and must therefore be for the best. But they also recognized in both economic individualism and economic nationalism a dynamic force which cannot safely be left unregulated, which must indeed be channeled and at times restrained by human ingenuity. Despite a pronounced bias in favor of freedom from

85. *Discourse*, p. 61; see also pp. 67-68.
86. Ed. W. J. Thomas (Camden Society, 1853), reprinted in Tawney and Power, III, 130-148. See p. 130.
87. *Ibid.*, p. 142.

regulation, a bias that was to prevent English mercantilism from ever achieving complete realization, these men also assumed that it was the duty of the state to devise and implement whatever regulatory policy it considered necessary for the common welfare or for its own power. As things worked out, regulation tended to exert the stronger in/ fluence and, as in the *Discourse*, the search for cause became simply the diagnostic analysis that necessarily preceded the remedies to be provided by policy. Viewed, however, in the perspective of intel/ lectual history, it becomes a matter of real significance that these pamphleteers were also able to see arising out of the consistencies of human action, especially out of those predictable acts of enlightened self/interest, a system of morally neutral, impersonal cause and effect. Had they been less preoccupied with the practical problems of their day and more given to philosophical formulation, they would prob/ ably have evolved a concept of natural law which would have led more or less directly toward the ideas eventually expressed by men like Petty or Mandeville or Adam Smith himself. As it is, they seem to have been groping purposefully in that direction.

Perhaps it is even more important to notice that, just as they were beginning to accept the profit motive as natural to mankind, so they were becoming reconciled to the idea that the state has reasons of its own, and, at least in economic matters, those reasons are also grounded in the natural order of things. They were accordingly beginning to see the possibility of subjecting the interests of the state, like those of the individual, to objective analysis, free from the necessity of reference to moral values. As might be expected of people whose intellectual heritage disposed them still to think in terms of analogies, parallels, and corresponding planes of reality, they tended to consider these economic interests of the state analogous to those of the individual. In some instances the argument offered for one could be made to serve well enough for the other. The Doctor in the *Discourse*, for example, sets down as a basic principle of foreign trade that the country should import no more than it exports, for to do so would be to im/ poverish herself and enrich her competitors. Then he clinches the argument by pointing out that "he were no good husband [man] that hath no other yearly revenue but of husbandry to live on, that will buy more in the market than he selleth again."[88] Both the individual

88. *Discourse*, p. 63.

and the state are subject to the same market forces.   Both are dynamic, having as their objective the accumulation of wealth.

There were, to be sure, differences.   According to the prevailing assumption that the total wealth of the world was inelastic, the accumulation of wealth by any country meant competition of an absolute sort with other countries, despite the growing conviction that there existed a "natural" distribution of commodities throughout the world. Accordingly the national state had to be guided by considerations of power as well as by those of wealth.   And in the interests of power it could not allow its citizens the same freedom of action in foreign trade, or in strategic sectors of the home economy, that the mid-century writers thought it would ordinarily allow them in adjusting themselves to the forces of the market.   Enlightened self-interest, just barely tolerated in domestic affairs, could hardly be trusted beyond the coast-line.   There, however, the national state took up where the private citizen left off and, absorbing in itself the dynamism of capitalist enterprise, became in turn a causal force, reflecting in its own egoism the laws of the economic mechanism.

かか かか かか

In our enthusiasm—forgivable, I think—over the emergence of attitudes which were eventually to revolutionize Western thought, we must not forget that the opinions we have just been examining were still those of a minority, even of public-minded citizens. If to these few writers, impressed by the inveterate consistency of human nature and eager to explore the implications it presented, moral criticism seemed less relevant than objective analysis, there remained many articulate and public-spirited Englishmen who adhered to the exactly opposite position.   Enough has already been said of the attitude maintained by the Edwardian preachers to demonstrate that point without need of additional proof.   The burden of their message remained the dominant theme in the public thought of the period, rendering the voice of economic realism at times all but inaudible, and thereby lending a deceptively medieval air to the swelling chorus of comment upon the "very and true commonweal." Economic individualism remained to them a causal force of the first magnitude, but a moral force fundamentally.   It was simply the old enemy, covet-ousness, in a new, enlarged, and more alarming role.   If they recognized the dynamism inherent in it, they identified it not with in-evitable social change but with the vagaries of a presumably redeemable human nature.

The true character of their thought becomes perhaps clearest in the long drawn out controversy concerning usury.[89] On that issue the battle was not clearly joined until the controversial legislation of 1545 which gave qualified—and short-lived—legal support to the activities of the money lender.[90] Prior to that date, and, indeed for some years thereafter, usury tended to be overshadowed in the literature of comment by the more dramatic and more immediately pressing problems of agrarian and monetary dislocation. It was not until the restoration of some semblance of order in these areas and the return to a somewhat healthier economy in the reign of Elizabeth that the opponents of economic individualism were able to concentrate their attack on the problem of usury. And so, as Helen White has remarked, "it would be safe to say that usury is the burden of more sermons on social wrong of the time than any other single factor in contemporary life."[91] The full story of this intensive campaign thus lies outside the chronological scope of this study. It reveals, however, some things which may help to place in perspective the work of those more secular and objective analysts with whom we have been chiefly concerned in this chapter.

The usury controversy tended to focus attention on the factor of economic individualism in its purest, and, from the conservative point of view, its least defensible form. In the act of lending money at interest the profit motive, with all its dynamic implications, appeared naked and unadorned by any of the more readily appreciated social utilities that could be used to make respectable the acts of production and distribution. Any intensive examination of it was therefore likely to arrive at more penetrating insights into the psychological as well as the economic forces at work in a capitalist economy. The controversy consequently became for the conservative observer a last ditch stand against a force he could not readily understand but which he quite rightly believed was in the process of destroying society as he

89. On this general subject see Tawney's introduction to his edition of Wilson's *Discourse upon Usury*. See also Helen C. White, chap. vi. B. N. Nelson, *The Idea of Usury* (Princeton, 1949), provides valuable background.

90. Note Crowley's immediate reaction to this legislation. *Supplication of the Poor Commons*, pp. 82-84, *An informacion and peticion*, pp. 170-174.

91. Helen C. White, p. 198.

knew and valued it.   And for the economic realist, the quasi-scientific analyst, it became a siege operation against those ultimate positions toward which the conservative forces had retreated.

In a desperate effort to hold their ground, the spokesmen for the old order, though mostly men of humanist training and vigorously Protestant theology, had recourse to patristic cand canonist authority and to the scholastic argument based on abstract justice rather than on social reality.   Of this tendency, Thomas Wilson's *Discourse upon Usury* is the classic example.[92]   Nor were they seriously weakened in their defense by Calvin's relaxation of the traditional strictures against usury.   English Protestantism took a long time to absorb the implications of the Calvinist ethic.   Not, indeed, until the seventeenth century were English puritans able to assume that the forces of the market were divinely established and profit, in particular the profit to be had from purely financial transactions, morally justifiable.

It soon became clear, however, that the defenders of the old order were fighting in a lost cause.   The fight in Parliament was over by 1571.   In that year a compromise measure, among other things reviving the legislation of 1545 with its approval of interest at ten percent, met with little opposition.   Thomas Wilson, the humanist scholar and trained civilian, spoke vehemently and at great length against the bill, marshalling "in a single phalanx Solon, Ezekial, Augustine, the Council of Nicea, and the English law books."[93]   But he spoke almost alone.   Only one member saw fit to speak in his support.   The day was carried by men of lesser eloquence and greater realism who welcomed a compromise which would give statutory comfort to their consciences.   Taking a firm stand against excessive interest, they spoke with equal resolution in favor of a realistic acceptance of the economic mechanism as it existed in fact.   As Tawney summarized their position: "Business was business; to denounce men for pursuing their own economic self-interest was frivolous; to prohibit interest would ruin the country."[94]

92. For biographical treatment of Wilson, see A. J. Schmidt, "Thomas Wilson, Tudor Scholar-Statesman," *HLQ*, XX (May, 1957), 205-218, and "Thomas Wilson and the Tudor Commonwealth: An Essay in Civic Humanism," *ibid.*, XXIII (Nov., 1959), pp. 49-60.

93. Tawney, ed., *Discourse upon Usury*, p. 159.

94. *Ibid.*, p. 160.   See also extracts from D'Ewes Journals in Tawney and Power, II 154-160.

This was a very different position from that which the members had taken when, in 1552, they had repealed the act of 1545. At that time the land-owning gentry had shown a distinct tendency to "compound for sins they were inclined to by damning those they had no mind to," and to side piously with the idealists against the money-lenders. Now, if not entirely amoral in their attitude, the members seem to have been willing to talk the language of expediency rather than of abstract justice. What had brought about the change? I suggest that it was in considerable part the work of the pamphleteers who, in the middle decades of the century, acting as informal, largely self-appointed consultants, brought a more or less objective analysis of the economic mechanism to the aid of the policy-makers, and, as publicists, brought new insights and critical methods to the attention of the governing class. Ideas would undoubtedly have caught up sooner or later with practice. The attempt of conservative idealists to hold back the tide of economic individualism by moral exhortation and an appeal to authority is, however, an example of the stubborn reluctance of formal concepts and traditional values to change with the changing circumstances of actual life. In this instance, the change was almost certainly made more rapidly as a result of the prior exploration of social cause undertaken by the commentators of the mid-century. So it was that, despite a continued guerrilla action by the spokesmen for the old order, it became ever easier for men both in and out of government to discuss economic policy in a secular context and in terms of ponderable forces.

CHAPTER XI. REMEDY AND POL-ICY: THE HUMANIST APPROACH

DIAGNOSIS, TO THE TUDOR PAMPHLETEER MORE THAN to his medieval prototype, was but the first step toward remedy, and analysis of social forces the prerequisite to policy. Although he himself made no distinction between the kind of remedial action his self-appointed role as physician to the body politic necessitated and the more inventive use of causal analysis he sometimes made in the course of his labors as a volunteer consultant, there remains a distinction to be made. Remedy could still be contemplated within the context of a static social ideal; it shared the conservative implications of the organic analogy. It was meant to restore the social organism to health. Policy, on the other hand, tended in the circumstances of sixteenth-century life to be constructive. It was meant to counter the demands of new situations with new expedients, to recognize, tacitly if not explicitly, the fact and nature of social change. This appeal to constructive intelligence on the part of the articulate citizen remained a tendency only, yet it was one that affected every assumption and preconception the Tudor citizen brought with him from the still rich heritage of medieval culture.

The reader will recall that the medieval commentator, as far as we are able to trace his thought, seems to have been willing to let any question of remedy lie implicit in his criticism of society. He found the cause of social dislocation in the failure of men, trapped by the inordinate propensities of their congenitally sinful nature, to perform their divinely appointed duties. Such being the case, only moral regeneration could effect any complete or lasting cure. Meanwhile the role of government was simply that of a coercive, restraining agency, dedicated to the preservation of that combination of peace and justice which was accepted as the criterion of health in the political body. Specific measures tended therefore to be ignored as either too obvious to need mention or beyond the province of the critic.

Occasionally, the reader will also remember, the political literature of the late medieval period reveals flashes of a practicality that would seem to have been to an increasing extent characteristic of English thought. In *Mum and the Sothsegger*, that anonymous bit of political realism in the sheep's clothing of dream allegory, still more in the economic advice proffered in the *Libel of English Policy*, in the proposals for administrative reform advanced by George Ashby in his *Active Policy of a Prince* and, especially, by Fortescue in his *Governance of England*, it is possible to see the mind of the pamphleteer approaching that of the policy-maker. Those responsible for the actual business of governing, like those who built the economic and technological ve-hicle for medieval life, had always been faced with the problem of devising means for coping with situations never before encountered in exactly similar form. But, like the other practical men of the day, they exercised their ingenuity unselfconsciously. They would have been surprised indeed if they had been told that the situations they met and in their way coped with were new at all. What lends significance to the works mentioned above is the willingness of the authors to bring matters of policy under discussion, to proceed beyond negative criticism. If they still were not quite able to envisage the function of the commen-tator clearly as that of a seeker after constructive policy, they were none-theless ready to act on the assumption that criticism is useless unless it points the way at least toward remedial action.

Realism of this sort, intuitive rather than consciously nourished, continued to be an essential element in the attitude of Renaissance Englishmen toward public life and affairs. But it remained for the men of early Tudor England, their purpose shaped by the force of increasingly pressing circumstance, their minds quickened in varying degrees by the example of a reinterpreted classical antiquity, to bring governmental policy as well as social causation under conscious scrutiny. Let us therefore see to what extent these men turned their minds to the solution of those problems which we have in preceding chapters observed them in their effort to understand.

It would be unnecessary as well as boring to follow them as closely in their search for remedy as in their pursuit of cause. For the most part the former tended to be determined by the latter anyway. If poverty could, as More asserted, be traced in part to enclosures,[1] then the thing to do was to limit enclosures. If, as Morison maintained,

1. See above, chap. viii.

sedition could be traced to poverty and poverty to unemployment,[2] then by all means train those who are idle in some useful trade. If, as Armstrong argued, England's economic problems could be traced in large part to the inordinate number of staplers and to the drain of bullion from her coffers,[3] then the answer was obvious—reduce the number of staplers and prohibit the export of precious metals. If, according to Starkey, English law was confused and the process of justice as a result "without end and infinite,"[4] then codify the law, perhaps even adopt Roman law. If the prevailing high prices of commodities could be traced, as in the *Discourse of the Common Weal*, to a debased currency,[5] then the coinage must clearly be restored. If, as an anonymous critic of enclosures pointed out, sheep farming increased because it was so profitable to the landowners, then simply tax sheep to the point where a too attractive profit will disappear.[6]

Yet the problem of remedy is not quite so simple as these random instances, thus baldly stated, would indicate. The last two demonstrate, for example, that remedial action must go well beyond mere restrictive or prohibitory legislation and, by adjusting the conditions of economic activity, shape in a positive way the fortunes of the country. We are here at the point where remedy attains maturity in constructive policy. As the analysis of cause proceeded and reached more and more deeply into the social fabric, even the formula *sublata causa, tollitur effectus*, simple enough on its face, implies an increasingly complex process.

These more significant implications will, I believe, become clear enough if we follow two closely related lines of investigation: first, the humanist approach to constructive policy, and, second, the development of constructive thought in the particular context of national economic life. For, as we have seen in the preceding chapters, it was the humanist pamphleteers who were able to achieve, from the vantage point of their new learning, a new perspective on the life of their day and a new inspiration for the exercise of intelligent citizenship. And, as we have also seen, it was in the complex mechanism of economic life that the citizen-counselor, whether or not he was influenced by human-

2. See above, chap. viii.
3. See above, chap. ix.
4. *Dialogue*, pp. 174-175.
5. See above, chap. x.
6. *Policies*, Tawney and Power, III, 327-330.

istic habits of thought, found the most challenging opportunity to exercise his practical ingenuity as well as his analytical ability.

თ   თ   თ

In this, as in other aspects of early Tudor humanism, it is im/ possible to proceed safely without first making our peace with the protean and illusive genius of Thomas More. Again it is the younger More with whom we have principally to deal, the More of the *Utopia*, still raking the English scene with the critical eye of an uncommitted intellectual and from the lofty standpoint of Erasmian reform. In his treatment of public affairs, he stood at this early date alone among his English contemporaries. Nor did his subsequent career in the service of the monarchy give him either leisure or opportunity to show to what extent he might have been able to anticipate the purposeful search for remedy and the exploration of constructive policy that became more and more characteristic of secular pamphlet/writing during the middle decades of the century. His keen analytical insight reappears in his controversy with Simon Fish. But by that time he was im/ mersed in the task of defending the existing order; ironically, it was the egregious Fish who undertook, however irresponsibly, to explore new and ostensibly practical alternatives.[7]

Yet the *Utopia* fails to give the historical wayfarer the unequivocal direction he hopes will guide him through an otherwise confusing terrain. Some scholars have concluded that More deliberately avoided proposing remedies, and that such reforms as he does suggest in passing seem calculated only to mitigate evils that can never be wholly cured in a society based on private property and moved by a com/ petitive search for material wealth.[8] Since this brings us again face to face with the ancient foes, pride and covetousness, we may well get the feeling that More has limited the range of policy as absolutely within the bounds of human nature as had the medieval moralist.

Even if this were true, it would leave a great deal more room for practical policy than John Gower, for example, would have thought

7. *Supplication*, reprinted in Dunham and Pargellis, p. 96.

8. Pierre Mesnard, *L'essor de la philosophie politique au XVIᵉ siècle* (Paris, 1936), pp. 156/ 157; J. W. Allen, *A History of Political thought in the Sixteenth Century* (London, 1928), pp. 153/154; H. W. Donner, *Introduction to Utopia* (London, 1945), pp. 74/75; Russell Ames, *Citizen Thomas More and his Utopia* (Princeton, 1948), p. 13. See above, chap. viii, for a fuller discussion of More's premises.

possible. Pessimistic as he may have been concerning the possibility of sweeping changes, certainly if those changes involved the habits of men, particularly pessimistic as was Hythloday's prognosis for the success of enlightened counsel in the courts of princes, a stubborn belief in the possibility of specific, limited reform underlies the whole dialogue of counsel and gives it point. True, the discussion of remedy in Book I is brief and baldly stated—More for the most part let remedy remain implicit in his analysis. But it is enough to show how the chain reaction of social cause and effect might be at least interrupted by legislation. It shows, in particular, how the economic roots of poverty, vagrancy, and crime could be removed.

> Cast out these pernicious abominations, make a law, that they, which plucked down farms, and towns of husbandry shall re-edify them, or else yield and uprender the possession thereof to such as will go to the cost of building them anew. Suffer not these rich men to buy up all, to engross, and forestall, and with their monopoly to keep the market alone as please them. Let not so many be brought up in idleness, let husbandry and tillage be restored, let cloth working be renewed, that there may be honest labors for this idle sort to pass their time in profitably, which hitherto either poverty hath caused to be thieves, or else now be either vagabonds, or idle serving men, and shortly will be thieves.[9]

More was too much of a realist to expect great creativity to emanate from the councils of actual states; he himself was too deeply committed to the fundamental values of the old order to accept without protest the radical changes taking place in his own day or to rationalize them in governmental policy. Yet his thought was also perceptibly tinctured by the idealistic and optimistic appraisal of man's intellectual capabilities characteristic of the humanist tradition. More's own creative bent finds expression in the ostensibly fanciful second book of *Utopia* rather than in the obviously practical first book. The society of the Utopians, so different from More's own England, was nevertheless related to it in the many indirect ways in which satire is related to reality. Although it should not be necessary for us to warp our wits trying to discover hidden in that tissue of serious fancy the substance of a legislative program for Henrician England, the point of the satire would, I

9. *Utopia*, Everyman Ed., pp. 25-26.

believe, be lost if we were to assume that More had no more purpose in writing it than to say some devastatingly witty things about the society of his own day.[10]

In his second book, More created a society in which the factor of human nature ultimately limiting all of man's efforts—the innate propensity to pride, greed, envy, and sloth—were either neutralized or curbed by an economic system ingeniously contrived by a wise law-giver.[11] It is an elaborate system, cleverly articulated. Nothing like it could have been conceived by a mind which did not believe such construction at least possible. That any such system could be put into effect in England More was realistic enough not to hope, and he admits that some aspects of Utopian society were not such as he would even wish for.[12] Yet the Utopian state remains a masterpiece of constructive thought.

᷒ ᷒ ᷒

Of the next generation of Tudor humanists, Thomas Starkey provides the most comprehensive and in many respects the most brilliant example. This, it will be recalled, was the generation that reached influential maturity in the decade of the revolutionary thirties, the decade of Cromwellian patronage. It was the generation of Elyot and Morison and Marshall, all of whom nourished a touchingly confident faith in the ability of experienced and learned men to provide the counsel upon which good government depended and who laid a solemn obligation upon such men to provide that counsel. It was also the generation of that astoundingly articulate businessman, Clement Armstrong, who, though not very learned, certainly without pretensions to humanistic learning, nevertheless shared with the scholars their faith in the efficacy of counsel informed by learning and experience. To these men, and especially to Starkey, it was becoming ever more apparent that such counsel must be positive as well as negative, con-

10. An extreme example of this interpretation is contained in C. S. Lewis, *English Literature in the Sixteenth Century* (Oxford, 1954), p. 169. For the opposite interpretation see, for example, P. Coles, "The Interpretation of More's 'Utopia,'" *Hibbert Journal*, LIV (July, 1958), 364-370.

11. See Hexter, *More's Utopia*, especially pp. 172-176. In his paper, "Thomas More: On the Margins of Modernity," *JBS*, I (Nov., 1961), 20-37, Hexter points to the novelty of More's looking to public law rather than merely to exhortation of the individual conscience.

12. *Utopia*, Everyman Ed., p. 115.

structive as well as critical or analytical, that the informed citizen could and must contribute not merely to the information available to the government concerning the ills of the body politic, but to the policies essential to its health and strength.

As More had so shrewdly recognized, this more constructive task of the citizen-counselor was a difficult one, both frustrating and dangerous. The men of the thirties also approached it with appropriate hesitation and offered their suggestions concerning policy with a timidity that was more than conventional form. Yet, like More, they felt compelled to offer them, and did so with considerably greater confidence than More, the man of affairs, was ever able to muster up. They were, in a sense, like More's wise man finally persuaded to action, like Hythloday stripped of his skepticism and of his cynical disenchantment with the ways of rulers. Starkey, in particular, seems almost deliberately to take up in his *Dialogue* where More left off in his own discussion of counsel in the first book of *Utopia.*[13]

"Much easier is it to spy a hundred faults in a common weal than to amend one, even like as it is in man's body of corporal diseases, they which of every man may well be perceived, but of every man they cannot be cured."[14] With these words Starkey's Reginald Pole introduces the last and most difficult stage in his dialogue with Thomas Lupset. Difficult as it is, this, they agree, is also the essential stage, for "the process of our communication hitherto is but of little or no value, except we find out convenient remedies prudently to be applied to such sores and diseases in our body politic before noted in yesterday's communication."[15] To this end they call upon "Him who . . . governeth and ruleth all things," not, as we might perhaps expect, to effect the desired remedies by the workings of His inscrutable Providence, but "to illuminate and light our hearts and minds (which without Him can no truth perceive) that we may see the convenient mean of restoring to this politic body his perfit state and common wealth. . . ." Thus it is in a spirit less of humble piety than of

13. It is apparent that Starkey knew the *Utopia* and may have been directly influenced by it, Burton (ed.), p. 15.
14. *Dialogue*, p. 135.
15. *Ibid.*, cf. pp. 143 and 151.

confidence in the capacity of the informed and inspired mind that they proceed to devise remedies.

The resulting proposals are clearly meant to be practical. They are, it is true, sketched in outline rather than developed in detail. This is partly because the dialogue does not permit any more lengthy discussion. It is also, however, because Starkey draws a line, shadowy but effective, between the counsel of the citizen and that of the king's appointed council. Pole, accordingly, refuses to go into detail in the remedial policies he proposes, declaring it his intention to touch only "the most general points and the rest leave to the cure of them which in every cause have order and rule, whose prudence and policy shall ever see, according to the time and place of everything pertaining to their office, the particular remedy."[16] But the proposed remedies are shrewd and constructive just the same, and follow logically from the analysis that precedes them. As in that analysis, Starkey's realism is to some extent obscured by the elaborate absurdities of the organic analogy. The modern reader finds it fully as hard to believe in the cure of "dropsy" in the body politic or "frenzy" in its mind as he did in the initial diagnosis. He must, however, remember that the Renaissance Englishman was still quite able to see in such arguments by analogy a force that somehow transcended mere illustration.

Starkey's interlocutors proceed systematically. In each instance of disorder in the body politic they seek to remove the cause. England, for example, lacks the population required for a healthy society, and the reason is a lagging birth rate. The solution must therefore be found in measures calculated to increase marriages. Relax the law of clerical celibacy. Require nobles and gentlemen to provide livings for retainers that will permit them to raise a family. Tax bachelors, give exemption to fathers, and see to it that poor girls are provided with dowries.[17] Idleness is a blight on the economy, so require every man to set his children to letters or to a craft, and reduce the number of serving men. In addition, reward craftsmanship and penalize wilful idleness.[18] What Starkey calls "ill-occupation" is just as serious as idleness, and the remedy follows from that already pre- scribed for idleness. Good education for the young is the basic

16. *Ibid.*, p. 143.
17. *Ibid.*, pp. 137-141.
18. *Ibid.*, p. 142.

remedy. But the government can also do a great deal by limiting the importation of luxuries and the proliferation of "vain crafts" at home.[19] There is an "ill proportion of parts" in the English body politic. By this Starkey means that men do not stay in their vocation but "fly to the most easy craft and to such whereof is most hope specially of gain." This, Pole suggests, can be remedied only by having inspectors insure that only those fitted for a craft be admitted to it.[20] The country is inadequately defended because the population is not trained in military exercises. Require each class, therefore, to cultivate such exercises as are appropriate to its status.[21] The economy suffers from lack of tillage, so enforce existing statutes limiting enclosures.[22] There is also a shortage of necessary commodities. This can be cured partly by requiring every man to labor in his craft, but a more fruitful policy would be to control foreign trade in the interests of domestic industry, especially the cloth trade, and of English shipping. Rents and food prices are too high, so reduce them by regulation.[23] Poverty, to Starkey as to most of his contemporaries the primary social problem, can be relieved by most of the above measures, but, more specifically, should be met on principles adopted by the city of Ypres.[24] Theft is caused by idleness and ill-education. Therefore set the idle to work and improve education. Starkey also recommends in this regard some such reform of the penal system as More had advocated.[25] The Common Law is confused and complicated and, as in matters of in-heritance and wardship, not even just. So why not codify it, or, better still, adopt the civil law of Rome with its principles already reduced to essentials and based on considerations of equity.[26] Finally, treason and sedition stem from tyranny and the failure of the government to provide justice. Here the remedy is radical: reform the government itself in such a way that, if a wise and just prince cannot be insured by election (which would be preferable in theory) he may be kept from

19. *Ibid.*, pp. 143-145.
20. *Ibid.*, pp. 147-148.
21. *Ibid.*, p. 148.
22. *Ibid.*, p. 156.
23. *Ibid.*, pp. 157-159.
24. *Ibid.*, p. 160.
25. *Ibid.*, pp. 177-178.
26. *Ibid.*, pp. 174-175.

folly and evil by the service of wise men operating through reformed institutions.[27]

The above summary, though by no means exhaustive, should give some idea of the scope of the discussion engaged in by the hypo‚ thetical Pole and Lupset. But it conveys little of the subtlety of Starkey's thought, nor does it reveal the most significant implications that arise from his proposals for reform. Far from being a piecemeal treatment of England's problems or an application of simple remedies to evils superficially diagnosed, this section of the dialogue can, on closer examination, be seen to imply a keen awareness of the close relationship between one policy and another. Just as in his analysis of cause Starkey was able to see how more immediate causal factors could be traced to ones of more fundamental significance, so in the section devoted to remedy he recognized that certain policies, calculated to remove such underlying causes, became for that reason matters of primary importance. "For even like as one disease cometh of another in the politic body, so the cure of one also followeth another."[28] In‚ deed, it is in this section that Starkey's analysis of English society, hitherto somewhat fragmented and more than necessarily distorted by the analogy of the political body, achieves a certain unity and clarity.

Starkey makes it quite clear that reform of the central government is a prerequisite to all other reforms. Since the head of the body politic governs all other parts, any disease involving the head will affect the rest of the body. If tyranny arises in the brain and injustice spreads throughout the nervous system (after reading Starkey for a while one is tempted to embroider his analogy), nothing can be right in the limbs. And, conversely, "the which disease if we could find the mean to cure, all the misorders in the rest of the party should easily be healed: for all hang upon this."[29] It is upon a good prince that the welfare of the realm to an overwhelming degree depends. To have a good prince "is the ground of all felicity in civil life." For the prince "instituteth and maketh almost all under‚officers; he hath authority and rule of all. Therefore, if we could find a mean to have a good prince commonly, this should be a common remedy almost, as I said, for all the rest of the misorders in the polity."[30]

27. *Ibid.*, pp. 153‚166.
28. *Ibid.*, p. 157; see also pp. 146‚147, 150, 154, 168.
29. *Ibid.*, p. 150.
30. *Ibid.*, p. 151.

Except for the emphasis placed on causal relationships, this sounds only too much like the truisms that passed for political wisdom in much of the medieval political writing. Good government depends upon a good governor. Hence the *raison d'être* of the whole dreary family of the "mirror of princes." It is also a main theme of early Tudor pulpit comment. And when Starkey goes on to demonstrate that a good prince needs good counsel, we seem to be on territory no less familiar. We are prepared once more to be told, as Lever and Hooper and Latimer *et al.* so frequently told their hearers at Paul's Cross, that repentance on the part of those responsible for counsel and policy is the only practical remedy since it is the only one good in the sight of Him who controls man's earthy fortunes as well as his spiritual destiny.

But this is not Starkey's approach at all. Government is to him essentially secular, natural in origin, subject to the dictates of human reason, and under God only in the larger sense that all creation is part of the divine plan.[31] God gave man the power to govern his life well or badly. He gave him "a sparkle of his own divinity—that is to say, right reason—whereby he should govern himself in civil life and good policy according to his excellent nature and dignity." But, lest man too nearly approximate the perfection of the angels, God also embedded in his nature so many "affects and vicious desires, by reason of this earthly body" that man must constantly strive against them with all the resources of his rational faculty.[32] So it is up to man himself to make his life on earth good, by which Starkey means according to right reason, or bad, governed, that is, by the antisocial passions. Government will accordingly be just, in the common interest, and in accord with the law of nature (to Starkey the embodiment of reason), or unjust, contrary to reason and the law of nature, perverted to the selfish and appetitive ends of the governor, in short, tyrannical. Government is thus the agency through which, at its best, reason can be applied to the civil life of the community.

Translated into more practical terms, as Starkey meant it to be, this

31. For Starkey's political theory, see *ibid.*, pp. 60´61, 99´103, 150´156. See also F. L. Baumer, "Thomas Starkey and Marsilius of Padua," *Politica*, II (Nov., 1936), 188´205, and *The Early Tudor Theory of Kingship*, 116, 135, 148, 160´162, 209´210; Allen, 142´156; R. W. and A. J. Carlyle, *A History of Medieval Political Theory in the West* (8 vols.; Cambridge, 1936), VI, 261´263.

32. *Dialogue*, p. 152.

all means that the political institutions of England should be so ordered as to guard against any such perversion of power. While careful to point out that England enjoyed in Henry VIII a prince devoted to the welfare of his people,[33] Starkey, like Fortescue before him, knew that there had been those on and around the throne who had held the king's will to be law; he was painfully aware of the slender safeguards existing in the English system of government to prevent such despo- tism from degenerating into tyranny.[34]

The responsibility lies ultimately with the people. Despite a veneration for Roman law far exceeding Fortescue's distant respect, Starkey refused to agree that power once delegated by the community to the governor could never be resumed. Nor was he willing to accept the still widely held commonplace that tyrants are, like just rulers, the creatures of God, but set over a people for their sins.[35] Starkey is here referring, of course, not to the people as a whole. There are times, indeed, when he seems to share some of Machiavelli's low opinion of the masses.[36] Moreover, some men are by nature more capable of rational action than others;[37] the degree to which wisdom can be brought to bear on the affairs of the commonwealth depends largely on the quality of education given to the governing classes.[38] It is, at any rate, to the governing classes, specifically those represented in Parliament,[39] that he looks for the political wisdom needed to protect England from tyranny and the injustice that stems from it. And he is optimistic enough to believe that there are among them enough wise men to insure success.[40]

The ideal safeguard against tyranny would therefore be an elective monarchy, the electors being presumably men of wisdom and respon- sibility. In a curious blend of realism and idealism, Starkey points out that so vital a matter as government ought not to be left to the accidents of hereditary succession. "It is not man that can make a wise prince of him that lacketh wit by nature, nor make him just that

33. Ibid., pp. 102, 154.
34. Ibid., pp. 99, 164-165.
35. Ibid., p. 154.
36. Ibid., pp. 150-168.
37. Ibid., pp. 152-153.
38. See below.
39. E.g., Dialogue, p. 154.
40. Ibid., p. 151.

is a tyrant for pleasure. But this is in man's power; to elect and choose him that is both wise and just, and make him a prince; and him that is a tyrant, so to depose."[41] Starkey's interlocutors agree, however, that it is impossible to change the custom of the national community so radically without running serious risk of confusion and even of civil strife.[42] There is a point at which reason must make some compromise with historical fact and with habit, however irrational it may be. The only practicable alternative is therefore to hedge the hereditary monarch in with institutions through which the wisdom of the community can be brought constantly to bear on public policy.

The normal place for the will of the "whole body of the people" to find expression is Parliament. That institution, however, should not be convened frequently, nor for other than very special purposes. In the interim, that is to say normally, its authority should be vested in a council which would represent its interests and, therefore, the interests of the realm as a whole. This council, chosen initially by Parliament,[43] and composed of "four of the greatest and ancient lords of the temporality; two bishops, as of London and Canterbury; four of the chief judges; and four of the most wise citizens of London," would "see that the king and his proper counsel should do nothing again the ordinance of his laws and good policy."[44] As such they would embody the negative, restraining aspect of the medieval con, stitution as described by Fortescue. It would guarantee a monarchy limited by law—ultimately by the law of nature, and more immediately by the positive laws of the realm wherever they were in agreement with the higher law.[45]

But this council would do much more than this. It would also call Parliament whenever it deemed it necessary. It would "pass all acts of leagues, confederation, peace and war"—matters generally ad, mitted to be under the king's own jurisdiction.[46] More than that, it would appoint the members of the king's own council without whose

41. *Ibid.*, p. 153.
42. *Ibid.*, pp. 103, 154/155, 168.
43. *Ibid.*, p. 167.
44. *Ibid.*, p. 155.
45. On the relation of natural and positive law in Starkey's thought, see *ibid.*, pp. 30/36, 164/166; Baumer, *Early Tudor Theory of Kingship*, p. 160.
46. See, for example, Sir Thomas Smith, *De Republica*, Book II, chap. iii.

authority he should "do nothing pertaining to the state of this realm."[47] This council also would supervise the distribution of the "common offices of authority and dignity" so as to insure the promotion of virtuous men rather than political adventurers.[48] And it would call to account "all other inferior lords, knights and gentlemen which did not their office and duty in administration of justice with equity toward all their subjects in such things as they had jurisdiction of."[49]

In thus reducing the problem of government once more to that of good counsel, Starkey, like Fortescue, was thinking in consonance with a tradition deeply embedded in medieval thought. But both Starkey and Fortescue recognized what the medieval commentator failed to see, namely that good counsel could not be left simply to the integrity of those concerned, to the willingness of good men to tell the truth and of the prince to pay attention to it. Both saw that there had to be institutional machinery which would at once permit good counsel to reach the prince with some regularity and compensate for the vice or weakness of individual men. Starkey, however, goes considerably further in this direction than Fortescue, whose principal concern seems to have been to reform the royal administration, the strictly regal side of the balanced *dominium politicum et regale*, in such a way that the king would have little temptation to transgress the boundaries separating his legitimate prerogative from the personal and property rights of his subjects and a minimum of opportunity for so doing. Starkey is similarly interested in preventing tyranny and in reaffirming the traditional principle that the king must rule according to law. But Starkey seems anxious to go further than this and subject the king not only to negative limitation but also to some positive control. In matters of major policy as well as in legislation he leaves ultimate authority in the hands of Parliament and the council to which it delegates its authority. And although he gives the king and his own council wide latitude in administration, he will not allow the king to choose his own council, "for that were . . . to commit all to his affects, liberty and rule."[50] Indeed he comes curiously near to the formula which in later controversies vested sovereignty in the "king in parliament" when he speaks

47. *Dialogue*, pp. 155-156; see also pp. 166-167.
48. *Ibid.*, pp. 156, 166-167.
49. *Ibid.*, p. 156.
50. *Ibid.*, p. 166.

of the authority of the prince resting not "in him alone, but in him as the head joined to his counsel as to the body."[51]   In any case he is committed to the concept of a mixed constitution.

This approach to constitutional reform, suspended as it is some-where between Marsilius of Padua and the seventeenth-century rev-olutionaries, seems oddly out of place in the England of Starkey's own day.   At a time when most of his contemporaries were thankful enough to have a strong monarchy, and when most political writers, in-cluding those of Protestant persuasion who had no choice but to court the royal power, were preaching a doctrine of absolute obedience, Starkey's idea must have seemed vaguely heretical.   It has been suggest-ed that this may in fact account for his failure to secure publication for his pamphlet.[52]   However close many of his suggested reforms may have been to the desires of Henry and Cromwell—his support of the secular government against the papacy in the matter of first fruits and appeals to Rome,[53] for example, or his suggestions for reform of legal procedure[54]—Starkey's constitutional ideas could hardly have fallen on receptive ears.   Yet he presented them in all seriousness, apparently quite unconscious of the hopelessly academic figure they cut in their temporal setting.

Much as Starkey feared tyranny in the rule of a prince unlimited by such constitutional checks, he seems to have had no fear at all of government as such.   Here, at least, he was at one with his con-temporaries.   To a generation still not far removed from the disorders of the preceding century and faced with the ever present threat of renewed confusion in their own day, strong government, when in-formed by wise counsel, was the unquestioned alternative; to a gen-eration still accustomed to the corporate character of medieval society, regulation was the natural and inevitable instrument of social organ-ization.   This was especially true of such commentators as Starkey, whose outlook was conditioned by the secular example of ancient society and who recognized in governmental institutions the only means by which right reason could be applied at all directly to the national life.   Whereas critics whose concern was primarily with

51. *Ibid.*, p. 165.
52. Baumer, "Thomas Starkey and Marsilius of Padua."
53. *Dialogue*, pp. 119-120, 178-179.
54. *Ibid.*, pp. 171-173.

religious reforms, pamphleteers like Crowley or preachers like Latimer, Hooper, or Lever, could see little hope for reform except through the moral regeneration of all those responsible for social evils, Starkey and the humanists put their faith in governmental action and social organ- ization—though even the religious reformers found it necessary to look to a presumably godly prince for the godly reformation they de- sired.   Despite the value placed by the humanists on the individual, despite their belief in man's natural dignity and his ability to choose between good and bad, between the example of the angels or that of the beasts, the generation of the 1530's was very far from advocating a libertarian society.   Unable to see any natural harmony in the habits and desires of men, they would have found the notion that that government is best which governs least totally incomprehensible.   The freedom they valued was that of the mind and will.   Freedom from social control meant little to those whose ideal society was hierarchical, functional, and, ostensibly at least, static.   Indeed, the England that Starkey would create is almost as regimented as that of More's Utopians.

Once the institutions of government have been reformed so as to make them sensitive to the will and wisdom of the leaders of the community, all other needed reforms would follow.   From this paternalistic government would emanate legislation and policies cal- culated to contribute to the health of the body politic in all its members. A major proportion of this governmental action would be devoted to economic regulation.   Although such other matters as the judicial system, defense, religious practices, and education are also subject to regulation of this sort, it is in economic relationships and those social problems that are economic in origin that the government will find its greatest challenge.   Like most other observers of sixteenth-century society, Starkey recognized that the old social order, the society as traditionally defined in terms of ordained status and function, was being undermined by the force of private enterprise.   Much of the regulatory legislation he proposes would therefore curb this tendency in the interests of social stability.   In order to keep the social organism "knit together in unity, provision would be made by common law and authority that every part may exercise his office and duty—that is to say, every man in his craft and faculty to meddle with such thing as pertaineth thereto, and intermeddle not with other."[55]   Like the more

55. *Ibid.*, p. 146.

analytical of his contemporaries, he also believed that inadequately regulated economic activity, especially of merchants and landlords, but also of those who chose "ill occupation" or idleness, was sapping the wealth of the country and contributing to social injustice. The government becomes accordingly the source of more or less ingeniously contrived policies, based on more or less realistic analysis of the economic mechanism in its larger aspects, and developed on more or less familiar mercantilist lines.[56]

Starkey recognized that it was not enough to have good laws if they were not enforced. So he was careful to equip his reformed government with adequate supervisory and coercive power. Not only would he make all lower officials accountable to that council which was to act as the trustee of Parliament, but in addition he would create new officers, modelled after the censors of ancient Rome who were "judges of the manners of all other," to be called "Conservators of the Common Weal." These officers, not unlike More's Syphogrants,[57] would be charged with the duty of checking up on all other officers "to the intent that they might with more diligence do their duty,"[58] of rooting out idleness and such crafts as are "vain and unprofitable to the commonweal," and of overseeing the training of the young in crafts and trades.[59] Here the medieval social ideal with its emphasis on the duty of every man to perform the service appropriate to his estate is brought up to date, such sanctions as it needed beyond the traditional agencies of local government now secular, vested in formally appointed monitors, rather than moral and exercised by the self-appointed Jonahs of the community.

Starkey's emphasis on governmental action arose in part from his faith in the ability of man to order his own affairs in the light of reason and, somewhat paradoxically, in part also from a sober awareness of the frailty of human nature and its stubborn resistance to any form of persuasion other than that of enforced law. If man would really follow reason he would need few laws, and "it should be nothing hard to remedy all such faults as we have before found in our commonalty." But the experience of "thousands of years" has proved

56. E.g., *ibid.*, pp. 158 ff.
57. *Utopia*, p. 56. Cf. Marshall's [?] draft of a bill for relief of the poor, discussed below in this same chapter.
58. *Dialogue*, p. 183.
59. *Ibid.*, pp. 144-145.

that man by instruction and gentle exhortation cannot be brought to his perfection. Wherefore it was necessary to descend to the constitution of laws civil and politic, that whereas man, blinded by affects and vanities thereof, would not follow the trade of right reason, he should at the least by fear of punishment be constrained to occupy and apply his mind to such things as were convenient to his excellent nature and dignity, and so at the last, by long custom, be induced to follow and do that thing for the love of virtue which before he did only for fear of the punishment prescribed by the law.[60]

Law, then, serves as a means by which man may be brought to the perfection of which he is by nature potentially capable. And it is not to be despised. But it is only one means. For, since "the perfection of man standeth in reason and virtue," he needs also the help of Christian doctrine[61] and humane education.

Although Starkey pays formal and doubtless sincere respect to the former, it is to the latter that for his practical and essentially secular purposes he looks with the greater confidence. Reform of education becomes, indeed, along with a reformed government, a prerequisite for all other reforms.[62] In presentation, he subordinates it to the problem of constitutional reform; but it is readily apparent that his hopeful willingness to trust a paternalistic government with the welfare of the national community depends upon his belief in the ability of educated counselors and all citizens of learning and experience to bring the light of reason to bear on the affairs of the commonwealth. That light, that "sparkle" of divinity in man, is not given equally to all men. The degree to which it is communicated to any man depends partly on the "nature of his body," but also "according to his education and good instruction in the commonwealth where he is brought forth of nature." This, then, is why "one man is more wise than another; yea, and one nation more prudent and politic than another."[63] Reason cannot function without knowledge, and its effectiveness will depend on the quality of the knowledge it is permitted to transmute into the precious metal of wisdom.

Starkey therefore proposed establishing colleges in the universities

60. *Ibid.*, p. 138.
61. *Ibid.*, pp. 184-185.
62. *Ibid.*, p. 171.
63. *Ibid.*, pp. 152-153.

to be devoted especially to the training of the governing class, and run by "certain of the most virtuous and wise men of the realm." Here the youth of the aristocracy would be trained "in virtue and learning," and, more specifically, "in the administration of justice, both public and private, and in the arts of war."[64]   Starkey refuses to go into any more detail—Pole maintains quite sensibly that to do so would require a whole book—but it is fair to say that in its intellectual aspects, it is basically a humanistic curriculum.   The men who have charge of the institution have undoubtedly derived their own virtue and wisdom from just the kind of studies in which Pole and Lupset (and of course Starkey himself) had been trained and which, according to the central theme of the *Dialogue*, it is the duty of such learned men to turn to the uses of the national community.[65]   At any rate "this [the above mentioned college] should be the most noble institution that ever was devised in any common weal; of this, surely, should spring the fountain of all civility and politic rule."[66]

∽ ∽ ∽

Despite the utilitarian bent of their thought and their strong sense of duty to promote practical reform, the writings of the early Tudor humanists are bound to have an academic ring to modern ears.   More seems visionary, Starkey the typical intellectual.   It is particularly easy to forget the potentially practical role of the scholar, Starkey, who hoped to place his learning and experience in a very real form at the service of his prince, yet who did not, in fact, hold any important post in the councils of state.   More redeemed the dialogue of counsel in the first book of *Utopia* from mere academic argument by his own subsequent entry into the royal service.   To appreciate the degree to which Starkey meant the *Dialogue* to be a book of practical counsel, it is useful to read what he wrote after that date.   The pamphlets he wrote for Cromwell had, of course, the kind of practicality that necessarily goes with propaganda, and, in the *Exhortation*, he gave form to, if he did not actually formulate, the Henrician *via media*.[67] But it is in his letters that we can see the citizen-counselor transcend the publicist.

64. *Ibid.*, pp. 169-170.
65. See above, chap. vii.
66. *Dialogue*, p. 169.
67. See above, chap. viii.

One long letter, in particular, addressed to the king about 1537 when the final defection of Pole from the royal cause had somewhat weakened Starkey's position at court, reveals the constructive character of his mind.[68] The lesser monasteries had just been suppressed. Although Starkey approved of the policy in itself, he was greatly disturbed about the effect such a wholesale redistribution of property would have on English society. Accordingly he made a number of statesmanlike suggestions, chiefly that the sequestered properties be employed for the advancement of learning and that they be distributed not among those already wealthy but made available at reasonable rents to poorer people, especially to "younger brethren," a peculiarly English type to which he had given considerable attention in the *Dialogue*.[69] If he was here trying to regain preferment, he was doing a poor job of it, for he was speaking the language of the statesman, critical of the government's policies, not that of the courtier. In a later day he might well have thrived as the editorial mind of an opposition journal. In the England of Henry VIII he was apparently not even able to publish the kind of counsels he believed a man like himself able and in duty bound to offer.

ഗ ഗ ഗ

The constructive and utilitarian bent of the Henrician com-mentators, especially those of humanist background, can perhaps best be illustrated by their efforts to cope with the problem of poor relief. The reader will recall how large a place poverty had in the critical literature of this and even earlier periods. More than any single prob-lem (if it can rightly be called a single problem, so deeply embedded was it in the social fabric) it offended the humanist's sense of justice and challenged his ability to do something constructive to solve it, or, at worst, to mitigate the evils that stemmed from it. By the 1530's it may or may not have become more pressing than ever. Observers, at any rate, believed that the poor had increased in numbers, that the unemployed poor constituted not only a reproach to a Christian society but a menace to the whole community, and that such measures as had hitherto been used to relieve them had broken down. What made the problem all the more challenging was its complexity. Not all

68. Herrtage, pp. xlix-lxi.
69. *Ibid.*, p. lviii.

indigent persons were helpless: some could work, but were unable to find employment. Nor were all the victims of circumstance: some found a life of vagrancy a career wide open to their special talents. The problem of vagabondage, with its very real threat to the security of communites still largely innocent of police protection, always complicated that of the deserving poor. The two were, of course, closely related. If, as More pointed out, men can find no work, they will soon take to the road out of sheer necessity.

The kind of remedy the critical observer was likely to propose depended on which aspect of the larger problem—unemployment, vagrancy, mere idleness, or helpless indigence—appeared to him most urgent and on how far back in the social process he was willing to go in treating the causes of poverty. And his answer to either question depended to a large extent on his point of view. From the pulpit, poverty still appeared much as it had to the medieval canonist, a moral rather than a social problem, one involving not only the duty of the well-to-do to exercise the stewardship inherent in the holding of property, but also the duty of the poor to seek employment. Yet the preaching prelates of Henrician and Edwardian England influenced to a great, though varying, degree by the utilitarian emphasis of Northern humanism could see much farther into the social system than had their predecessors and were therefore capable of treating poverty more realistically.[70] Those, on the other hand, who bore the responsibility of actual government tended naturally to strike at the fact of poverty rather than its causes and to do so largely through a policy of coercive legislation. Reflecting the concern of local administrators for the safety of property, and especially their obsessive fear of vagrancy, the men who framed the earliest Tudor poor laws set their faith for the most part in police measures of the utmost severity.[71] To the humanists, poverty appeared as a primarily social problem, secular in its immediate context. They believed that its causes could be discovered by analysis of observable conditions and that remedies could be devised on that basis.

70. See, for example, Ridley's plan for the city of London, E. M. Leonard, *The Early History of English Poor Relief* (Cambridge, 1900), pp. 32-33. See also W. K. Jordan, *Philanthropy in England, 1480-1660* (New York, 1959), chap. v. On canonist attitudes, see Brian Tierney, *Medieval Poor Law* (Berkeley and Los Angeles, 1959).

71. 22 Henry VIII, c. 12 and 27 Henry VIII, c. 25. See also Salter, chap. vi and Jordan, pp. 83-86.

The problem seems, indeed, to have interested some of their num⁄ber greatly. The humanists of northern Europe found in the relief and cure of poverty an outlet for their reforming zeal rivaled only by reform of the church. Moreover, as intellectuals capable of viewing society from a new and revealing point of view and bringing to bear on its problems a kind of understanding to which their contemporaries could seldom aspire, they were on occasion listened to with respect by secular policy⁄makers. In 1526, for example, the peripatetic Spanish humanist, Juan Louis Vives, published a detailed and constructive plan drawn up for, and no doubt requested by, the city governors of Bruges.[72] Though apparently never translated into English, this treatise was begun while Vives was living in England, and it became the "theoretical foundation on which rested, directly or indirectly, nearly all later practical work,"[73] in England as well as on the Conti⁄nent. A similar scheme, worked out in 1531 for the city fathers of Ypres, was translated by the English humanist and printer, William Marshall, and published in 1535.[74] In that same year someone drew up a draft for a new poor law to replace the largely ineffective act of 1531. It is anonymous and clearly not a government draft, but it appears to have been prepared for actual consideration by Cromwell, probably, indeed, at his request, and it is obviously the work of a humanist, very probably William Marshall.[75] Although it was never enacted, it apparently became the basis for the much less radical poor law of 1536 which, in turn, marks the real beginning of poor relief legislation in England.

Few documents reveal as clearly as this the capacity of the humanist mentality for constructive thought. The scope of his ingenuity is, to be sure, limited by the immediacy of the situation and the presumably practical purpose to be served by his bill. He does not therefore, attempt to get at the deeper social, economic, and moral roots of pauperism as More had done. He addresses himself rather to the fact of poverty, to the actual relief of the poor, and to the more long⁄term

72. *De Subventione Pauperum,* in Salter.

73. Salter, p. xv.

74. William Marshall (trans.), *The Forme and Maner of Subvention or Helping for Pore People* (London, 1535), in Salter. Cf. a "discourse" addressed to the king in 1532, referring apparently to a plan already worked out. *LP,* V, no. 1501.

75. G. R. Elton, "An Early Tudor Poor Law," pp. 55⁄67. The following analysis is based on the substantial excerpts from this document printed by Elton.

matter of seeing "that other shall not hereafter fall into like misery."[76] Yet the originality of his positive proposals and their remarkably constructive character reflect not only an inventive mind but one already thoroughly accustomed to social analysis. Diagnosis thus becomes a mere starting point for him.

The author accordingly devotes the bulk of his lengthy draft to a series of detailed proposals for administrative machinery which, in their general character, go far beyond anything actually adopted in Tudor England. To begin with, he proposes to solve unemployment, the most immediate, and the largest root of pauperism, by an elaborate, though short-term plan of public works. A body called the "council to avoid vagabonds" is to be created which will superintend "certain common works, as well for making of the Haven of Dover, renovation and reparation of other havens and harbors for ships, as for making of the common high ways and fortresses, scouring and cleansing of water-courses through the Realm."[77] This scheme, which G. R. Elton quite rightly describes as "astonishing," is to be administered through local officers responsible to the central board.[78] Nothing like this had ever been proposed in England, nor does the author appear to owe anything directly to Continental influences.[79] The whole thing, moreover, is to be paid for by means of a graduated income tax. Even more astonishing is the future provision that the poor should be given free medical care (whatever that might mean to a Tudor Englishman) at public expense. In this instance the money is to be provided by charity; but it is to be organized charity, systematically administered by local authorities, not the largely indiscriminate alms-giving of the medieval community.[80]

At this point the author has recourse to moral sanctions. Compulsory collections are to be made only for public works. For the relief of the local needy no compulsory alms are to be levied. (That principle only became law in 1552.) And it is interesting to see how

76. *Ibid.*, p. 57.
77. *Ibid.*, p. 58.
78. *Ibid.*; it is interesting to notice the similarity between these officers and More's Syphogrants and, to some extent also Starkey's "Conservators of the Public Weal." See discussion above in this chapter.
79. *Ibid.*, pp. 58-59.
80. Canonist authorities were in this respect often ahead of general practice. Tierney, chap. iii, *passim*, and pp. 125-128.

this man, who for the most part places his faith in administrative machinery rather than in the willingness of men to perform their moral duty and who shows little of the tendency, still usual, to preach against idleness,[81] resorts to the pulpit for moral support in the collection of alms. The bishops of every diocese are to supply every parson

> a compendious sermon or collation wherein the manifold virtues of charity, and how meritorious it is in the sight of God, and what guerdon or reward is prepared for such as use the same; and also the manifold virtues of labor and occupation, and how highly it is commended by scripture, and how wholesome it is for the body, and on the other side how odious the vice of sloth and idleness is in the sight of God, and how pernicious it is to the carnal body [are set out].[82]

Clearly the church still had its place and responsibility in the system of poor relief, regardless of how far the administrative machinery had been secularized.

Much of this draft bill went beyond the will as well as the grasp of the contemporary ruling class. To that extent it was not practicable. And so the act of 1536, while accepting the general principles of the draft—the necessity of finding work for the unemployed, for the organization of voluntary charity by local authorities—omitted the machinery by which these principles were to be put into effect.[83] Although successive acts to some extent supplied this deficiency, it was not until the end of the century that England developed the administrative techniques which put her ahead of all other nations in this matter of poor relief. And even then some of the proposals that emanated from the fertile brain of the early Tudor humanist remained too radical for the policy-makers. Though Cromwell himself no doubt had too much else to do to listen with the necessary imagination to so startling a scheme—his interest in poor relief may itself have been related to the extensive and complicated plan already taking form in his mind for dissolving the customary monastic sources of charity—it remains a matter of the utmost significance that, as Elton says, "a scheme of such magnitude and precise detail, so much practical humanitarianism and sound common sense, so much immediate and so much more ultimate

---

81. See preamble.
82. Elton, "Early Tudor Poor Law," p. 61.
83. *Ibid.*, p. 64.

effect, grew up in 1535 in a circle of advisers and thinkers who sur-
rounded the government of Thomas Cromwell."[84]

If, however, Marshall's approach to the problem of poverty is set
side by side with the more general treatments of Starkey and Morison,
it will appear, if no less significant, perhaps less surprising. In the
Dialogue, Starkey was in a position to go more deeply into the causes
of poverty than Marshall and to find his remedy, as was his custom,
in policies aimed at removing the cause. Unlike most of the humanists
who wrote on the subject, Starkey could not get very worked up over
the plight of the "impotent poor." If a society was functioning as it
should, there should be few of them. And they could be dealt with
quite adequately "after a manner lately devised by the wisdom of the
citizens of Ypres, a city in Flanders"[85]—the same scheme that Marshall
translated and published in 1535. The trick was, then, to get the
economy working properly. If, in a series of regulatory measures, the
government could only remedy the scarcity of goods and reduce the
correspondingly high prices, there would be little left of the problem
of poor relief except to see to the very few really helpless people.
Abundance and the right kind of employment for all would take away
"this miserable poverty" and reduce the number of sturdy beggars, and
even of thieves, to negligible proportions.[86] Proper employment would
entail limiting the number of idle servingmen, people engaged in luxury
trades or in vice, and providing a supervised system of education in
useful crafts and the assignment of the right man to the right trade.[87]
It was at this last point that Starkey and Morison saw eye to eye.
Tracing sedition to poverty, Morison proposed a system of education
in craft skills not unlike that which Starkey had in mind.[88] For the
wisdom necessary for so comprehensive a system of economic and
vocational control, both men put their faith in government—presumably, of course, when informed by the counsel of such as themselves.

က္ခ က္ခ က္ခ

The most striking example of the humanist's capacity for constructive thought, the *Discourse of the Common Weal,* will have to wait

84. *Ibid.,* p. 67.
85. *Dialogue,* p. 160.
86. *Ibid.,* pp. 156-160.
87. *Ibid.,* pp. 142-145.
88. *Remedy,* pp. 35 ff. See also Zeeveld, pp. 119-121.

until the next chapter. In it the second line of inquiry mentioned at the beginning of this chapter—the search for economic policy—becomes of primary importance. The *Discourse*, in other words, is more valuable as an example of how closely constructive thought, as well as causal analysis, arose out of the investigation of economic problems than as an example of humanist thought. More, Starkey, and Marshall should be quite capable by themselves of bearing witness to the latter.

CHAPTER XII. REMEDY AND POL-ICY: THE MERCANTILIST ANSWER

JUST AS THE ANALYSIS OF ECONOMIC PROBLEMS, MORE than any of the others that troubled the national community, led the citizen-counselor to a more mature appreciation of the complex forces at work in his society, so the search for solutions to those problems, more than anything else, led him to explore the positive, the constructive potential of government. And, just as the degree of success he achieved in discovering the causal factors moving the economic mechanism depended on his ability to recognize the dynamism inherent in economic life, so his ability to assign a positive role to government depended on his success in recognizing in government a potentially constructive agent, even up to a point the director of social change. Thus, despite his more or less explicit commitment to the ideal of stability within a social system based on status rather than on contract, on fixed vocation rather than individual enterprise, on devotion to the common welfare rather than to private profit, contemplation of economic problems led him, at times it would seem against his will, toward a view of society and of government's place in it that was more nearly modern than medieval. More particularly, such contemplation seems to have been uniquely instrumental in preparing him and his successors to accept the idea of government as a sovereign power capable of making whatever changes it saw fit and bound in its own interests to do so.

Early Tudor commentators were, as we have seen, remarkably sensitive to economic considerations. Except when engaged in some particular piece of propaganda, and sometimes even then, they tended to interpret society in terms of its economic relationships and government as an agency whose principal duty it was to adjust those relationships in the common interest—which, it was generally implied, meant also its own interest, since government must, like the head in the natural body, identify its own good with the good of the entire organism. So it was that More and Starkey, though comprehensive in the range of their criticism, found themselves dealing to a surprisingly large extent, for men whose personal interests were not those of the marketplace, with economic problems.

But both were concerned rather with economic considerations in relation to the broader problem of the good life than as matters worth investigation in themselves. And in the case of Starkey, who did undertake to survey the economic scene after a fashion systematically, his search for a master policy drew toward constitutional reform rather than toward any integrated economic policy. He appreciated the inter' action of economic forces in the England of his day. But the legislation he proposed remained largely piecemeal and depended more on administrative machinery capable of enforcing a broad social ideal by regulatory and coercive measures rather than on the devising of policies calculated to harness the forces observable in the economic process. It was not until the reign of Edward VI that the quest for constructive policy, like the search for cause, reached a peak of maturity which placed it within clear sight of modern thought. That era of disillu' sionment, false hope, and confusion was also, as we have seen in previous chapters, one in which the economic problems were as thought' provoking as they were distressing and the atmosphere of public life for a short while unusually conducive to the discussion of policy. Scholars, preachers, and men of affairs all contributed to a spirited discussion of England's "wealth."

Our attention must, however, be directed primarily to the relatively small group of writers whose analysis of the economic system in terms of non'moral, impersonal cause and effect we have examined at an earlier point in this study.[1] These were the men who proceeded from analysis of this sort to a more or less realistic discussion of policy expressed in terms of secular society and in the confident faith that it could be put into actual effect by the national government.[2] We must again remember, of course, that much of the economic discussion of the period, no doubt the bulk of it, remained traditional in tone. Indeed, as in the sermons of the great preaching prelates, the moral and religious emphasis which linked them with the tradition of medi'

1. See above, chap. x.
2. On the relationship between projects for reform and actual policy, see G. R. Elton, 'State Planning in Early Tudor England," *EcHR*, 2nd ser., XIII (April, 1961), 433' 439. See also F. J. Fisher, "Commercial Trends and Policy in Sixteenth'Century England," *EcHR*, 1st ser., X (Nov., 1946), 95'117.

eval criticism was intensified by the theocentric tendencies of Protestant thought.[3]

Both groups shared in some degree the ideal of a Christian common‑wealth, ethical in its purposes, and dependent upon the willingness of all of its members to direct their special interests in such a way as to make them coincide with the common good. But those who in‑terpreted this ideal primarily in religious terms had little faith in policy and legislation. In so far as laws were needed to enforce right action, they believed there were already enough on the statute book to deal with the most flagrant instances of social injustice, provided only that those in charge of their administration did their duty conscientiously. And, in so far as acts of Parliament or proclamations, such as the act of 1545 legalizing "usury," gave expression to special or evil interests, they were futile: for, as Crowley warned, "If you let these things pass and regard them not, be ye sure the Lord will confound your wisdom. Invent, decree, establish and authorize what you can: all shall come to naught."[4] Those, on the other hand, who interpreted the common‑wealth idea in a more secular light considered its ends attainable by intelligently contrived policy.

Preaching could, of course, be considered useful as an auxiliary to policy. Convinced, apparently, that compulsory alms‑giving was either unfeasible or morally indefensible, the author of the draft bill for a poor relief law discussed in the preceding chapter found it necessary to look to the pulpit for support of his proposed system. And the pulpit was an effective medium for propaganda of all sorts. But the prevailing tendency among the more secular commentators was to consider exhortation too far removed from the immediate concerns of statecraft to be worth more than respectful reference. It was essential to the moral life of the community, yes; and no nation could prosper that was built on weak moral foundations. The practical counselor had, however, to deal with what was tangible. He had to consider the moral life of the community to a large extent as a given circum‑stance, a limitation to be accepted, perhaps even utilized by the policy‑

3. E.g., Cranmer, *Sermon on Rebellion*, p. 191; Hooper, *Early Writings*, pp. 435, 449, 496; Lever, *A Fruitful Sermon*, sig. Aiiii ff., and Cv ff., *Sermon, 14 December 1550*, in *Three Fruitful Sermons*, sig. Nii, and also epistle to 1572 edition, *A Sermon . . . thyrd Sondaye in Lente, 1550*, sig. Fiii; Crowley, *Way to Wealth*, p. 148; *Supplication to . . . Henry the Eyght*, pp. 37‑38.
4. *Way to Wealth*, p. 175.

maker. Starkey, for example, paid only formal and belated respect to the value of preaching to the commonweal in the very last pages of the *Dialogue,*[5] and even then he appears to be referring to strictly religious teaching rather than to the social gospel. One of the most perceptive writers of the reign of Edward VI gives vent with rare candor to a feeling of utter disillusionment with preaching as a means for the solution of the nation's immediate problems: "Is there not exclamation made almost in every sermon against the insatiable sheep pasturers? But neither can the fear of God nor the shame of the world drive them to distribute their grounds again into husbandmen's hands and occu-pancy."[6]

∽ ∽ ∽

Here we begin to see what makes the economic literature of the mid-century appear so much more familiar—and cogent—to the modern mind than the larger body of social comment still expressed in the language of traditional moral complaint. Much as we may sympathize with the appeal to the moral sense, much as some may deplore the impersonal, amoral character of modern economic thought, the unavoidable fact remains that investigation did lead away from judg-ments of what is right or wrong, just or unjust, and toward an under-standing of what does or does not create wealth and power, from con-siderations of personal duty within a corporate society toward a more frank acceptance of the acquisitive instinct as the motive power in an in-creasingly complex and dynamic system. The pamphlet-writers of the mid-century were poised between the medieval and modern worlds, able still to appreciate the moral foundations of medieval thought and to believe in the possibility of at least approximating the traditional ideal of social stability, yet no longer able to live in innocence of the morally neutral forces operating within a constantly moving social mechanism. It is this not always comfortable position that at times imparts to their work a baffling ambivalence. It allowed them, per-haps required them, to appeal to constructive policy in the interests of

5. *Dialogue,* pp. 185-190. Cf. Herrtage, p. lxi. Notice also how the author of *Piers Plowman's Exhortation* turns what seems to be an expression of the social gospel so familiar to contemporary pulpit audiences into a thoroughly practical discussion of economic problems.

6. *Policies to Reduce this Realme of England vnto a Prosperous Wealthe and Estate,* in Tawney and Power, III, p. 327.

stability and to consider the "very and true common weal," so redolent of medieval social theory, not as an organism enfeebled only by the failure of its parts to perform their appointed function, but as an ideal which requires the constant application of creative intelligence for its realization, something that exists in the mind as a goal to be striven for rather than as an historical fact. But more of this later.[7]

Essential to this change in attitude and assumption is the realistic recognition of the limits imposed on policy by human nature, considered as a given condition rather than as, in itself, the object of reform. Essential also is at least the dawning recognition that there are limits to the power even of regulatory legislation to do what moral exhortation has failed to do. Such understanding of the conditions ineluctably established for economic activity, conditions now for practical purposes if not in theory recognized as natural laws, I have tried to analyze in an earlier chapter.[8] Now it becomes equally relevant to the question of constructive policy. It permitted the commentator to see that government action must be more than merely regulatory. To be effective, economic policy must accept self-interest as a fact, in itself an economic force which cannot be entirely or safely thwarted, which in reality makes the economic system work either well or badly and which, wisely channeled, can be made to contribute essentially to the wealth and power of the national community.

These tendencies can be illustrated in the most advanced stage of maturity reached during this early Tudor period by the two most remarkable of the several pamphlets on economic matters to appear in the reign of Edward VI, namely, the anonymous tract entitled *Policies to Reduce this Realm of England unto a Prosperous Wealth and Estate*, and, inevitably, the *Discourse of the Common Weal of this Realm of England* which we are assuming was written by Sir Thomas Smith. It might, however, be helpful to start with the most perceptive comment on economic affairs in the preceding reign, namely, the writings attributed to Clement Armstrong.

໙ ໙ ໙

As we have seen in a previous chapter,[9] Armstrong had examined the economic life of England from the vantage point of his ex-

7. See below, chap. xiii.
8. See above, chap. x.
9. See above, chap. viii.

perience as a London merchant rather than, like his contemporary, Starkey, from the more academic point of view of the humanist. He was worried about much the same things: high prices, idleness, the imbalance between tillage and pasturage and between agriculture and industry, with the failure of English artisans to compete with imported manufactured goods, and with the consequent drain of precious metals from the realm to pay for what Englishmen could either make them-selves if they put their minds to it or perfectly well do without. These, indeed, were commonplaces of contemporary criticism. Armstrong was unusual only in his ability to seek out what he believed to be the most fruitful cause of trouble, the key to the economic log jam. Wool, he said, was England's natural endowment. If Englishmen could not exploit their advantage in this respect to the full they were bound to lose out in the competitive European market. What is more, since wool is at the very heart of the economy, what affects it affects in one way or another the entire community. Not that this, either, was new to men of Armstrong's generation—or to John Gower's for that matter. But he goes further and demonstrates with some plausibility and a wealth of data that the trouble lies in the organization of the wool trade itself. Accordingly he finds his master policy in a reform of the Staple, more specifically in establishing a staple in London, reducing the number of staplers, and placing them all under close governmental supervision.

The details of his proposals need not detain us.[10] The important point is that he was able to show to his own satisfaction at least that here, at the hub of mercantile activity, was where constructive policy should begin. Once the staplers were reformed and their activities curtailed, many of the other difficulties would solve themselves. Pastur-ers, for example, those sheepmasters and enclosers of arable land for wool production who were the favorite whipping-boy of the early Tudor social critic, would find it less profitable to raise wool and would restore land to cultivation, which in turn would remedy the dearth of meats and grains, thereby reducing poverty. Moreover, since lands of marginal utility for wool growing would then be returned to tillage, only those most suited to produce good wool would be retained and the quality of English wool, upon which the foreign trade of the

10. The following summary is a conflation of ideas expressed throughout the three tracts attributed to him.

country depended, would be raised and the threat of Spanish competition reduced. Meanwhile English wool would, with additional
encouragement by the king, be manufactured more profitably at home
and English cloth made more capable of competing effectively with
Continental products. This, together with a general policy of fostering
all "artificiality" (including even the printing industry)[11] and restricting
the importation of goods from abroad to those which England was
not able to produce herself, would ensure a constant flow of gold and
silver into the realm, a matter of the utmost importance to the estate of
the king and the national wealth, according to Armstrong's rigorously
bullionist turn of mind.

To accomplish all of this requires the immediate, direct, and constant activity of the king's government. But what of that government?
How should it operate? Armstong express himself on this point only in
passing, but what he says he says with his accustomed vigor. His
attitude toward government is strictly pragmatic. He has little of that
faith in institutional reform which characterizes the work of Fortescue
and Starkey. Nor, on the other hand, does he depend, like the
moralists of his own and earlier generations, on the virtue or godliness
of governors. True, the king, he says, rules by God's law as "lord of
all within his dominion."[12] And he admits that no legislation can be
passed without the advice and consent of the "common house" of
Parliament.[13] So far he is in perfect agreement with Fortescue. But
therein lies a difficulty. This lower house is full of just the kind of
men, merchants, staplers, enclosers, who are pursuing their "singular
weal" at the expense of the "common weal." Complaints registered,
as he tells us is customary, before "the king and his lords in the head
house" may be then drafted into needed legislation, but the resulting
bills will not pass the lower house.

Armstrong therefore advises the king and the lords to take direct,
extra-parliamentary action. In particular he would have the king
"ordain that the common weal of the whole realm may by his ministers
be ministered in all market towns, wherein all woolen cloths are
wrought and made, for therein the common weal resteth." In this
way, again to quote Armstrong's inimitable prose, "the king and his

11. *How the Comen People*, p. 60.
12. *Ibid.*, pp. 51-52.
13. *Howe to Reforme*, in Tawney and Power, III, 121.

lords shall never more be troubled with no works of acts of parliament for the common weal," but depend directly on "the governors and rulers of his rich towns" through which the foreigners' gold and silver must pass.[14] He seems to have had in mind the kind of informal government by council (he probably drew no clear line between the lords as they met in the upper house and as they functioned in the Privy Council) that had been tried in practice since the days of Edward IV, though seldom so frankly proposed in theory.[15]

Perhaps the key to his idea of government may be found in his reference to anyone who "plaineth of the destruction of the wealth of the common people" and is for that purpose "brought afore the king and his lords in the head house."[16] This is the principle of counsel in its essential form. It is Truthteller engaged in providing the king and his lords with the facts upon which policy depends and which Mum, entrenched in the Parliament house, refuses to give.[17] Despite the somewhat primitive picture these words conjure up, Armstrong was no doubt thinking of such counsel as men of experience and, presumably, wisdom, had to offer—of counsel, that is, in the broader sense. For he had little confidence in the ability of the lords, no matter how well disposed they might be—and it is odd how he seems to trust these men whose economic interests differed little from those of the burgesses and gentry of the lower house—to do more than "harken always to mischiefs done in the realm daily for lack of a right order of life in the whole commonalty."[18] He insists, as we have seen, that they are dependent on the analysis of cause performed by men like himself; the whole drift of his writing implies that they would do well to listen also to the remedies such citizen-counselors might propose.

It is thus a highly paternalistic government to which Armstrong proffers his counsel. Its policy must be constructive, based on a searching analysis of cause. But it is also policy aimed at controlling private enterprise in the common interest directly by restraint and surveillance rather than indirectly by inducement. Although a merchant himself, and something of an entrepreneur, he retained a virtually canonist distrust of economic self-interest. Or rather, he believed that self-interest,

14. *Ibid.*, p. 122.
15. See above, chap. v.
16. *Howe to Reforme*, p. 121.
17. See above, chap. iii.
18. *A treatise concerninge the Staple*, in Tawney and Power, III, p. 94.

to be legitimate, must coincide with the common interest. That, however, he seems to have considered unlikely, men being the acquisitive creatures they are. So it must be made to coincide, and that becomes the duty of the national government.

Although less given than more sophisticated writers to the use of the organic analogy in explaining the nature of society, Armstrong's mind was still very much governed by the traditional concept of society as an organism, ideally stable, if not static, depending for its health on the proper functioning of all its parts for the good of the whole body. In one notable exception to his otherwise factual and bald style, he described the "mystical body" of the commonwealth in almost as elaborate detail as Starkey had done in his *Dialogue*.[19] The trouble with the England of his day was that everyone seemed bent on his own wealth even at the expense of the common wealth. "In England is no right order, where all and every man seeketh the policy against the order of God, one to rob another in destroying the whole wealth of the realm."[20] Armstrong was quite aware of the dynamism inherent in the economy of his day. It was a fact to be analyzed and reckoned with. And it could be turned to the common good, but only by rigid governmental control.

He also recognized the dynamic character of national economic policy, and was much more willing to accept it as inevitable and, within limits, good. He was shrewd enough to see that England was in fact engaged in deadly competition with her European neighbors for economic advantage, especially for that favorable balance of trade which can be measured in an actual influx of gold and silver. In a sense, he granted the legitimacy of the profit motive as a national policy while holding it under extreme suspicion in private relationships. Yet even on the level of international trade he deplored that perversion of self-interest which he criticized in individual men, which indeed concerned him more than the acquisitive instinct itself. He believed that all nations have natural endowments,[21] and it is their right and duty to exploit them to the full. But there are limits to the ruthlessness of this national egoism, just as there are to individual self-interest, the only difference being that there exists an agency capable of restraining

19. *How the Comen People*, pp. 52-54.
20. *A treatise concerninge the Staple*, pp. 100-101.
21. See above, chap. viii.

the latter, whereas there is none to curb the former. At one point he suggests, as something rather to be wished for than hoped after, that there should be "a right ordinary Emperor" to administer the natural gifts and the wisdom of God to all realms impartially."[22]

The fact remains, however, that foreign competition and the need for constantly applied intelligence in meeting it direct Armstrong's approach to economic policy even more than his interest in domestic welfare. If the latter alone had been his concern, he would probably have been content merely to prescribe rigid regulation, calculated to maintain the body of the commonwealth in its ordained form by preventing any sort of social mobility as well as by frustrating that illegitimate expression of the profit motive which he considered the origin of social disorder. As it was, the exigencies of foreign trade required him to consider policies aimed at promoting rather than merely maintaining the national wealth and to explore the effects of these policies on domestic conditions. Like so many of his generation, Armstrong is poised intellectually between the new and the old, his realistic appreciation of social forces leading him often far afield from those ideological positions into which he had been born, yet not so far as to require him to abandon them entirely.

ᶜᵖ ᶜᵖ ᶜᵖ

The author of *Policies to Reduce this Realm of England unto a Pros-perous Wealth and Estate* (the reader will surely not mind if this tract is referred to hereafter simply as *Policies*) was able in most respects to make a more sophisticated approach to economic problems than Armstrong. He was, indeed, a more sophisticated man. Apparently educated in the humanistic tradition,[23] no doubt one of the group of humanist pamphleteers who turned their learning to the discussion of current issues under the encouraging auspices of the Protector Somer-set,[24] his lucid style contrasts sharply with the crude vigor and syntactical confusion of Armstrong's prose. He was also able to see further into the intricacies of the economic system.

Since he believed, and undertook to demonstrate in a spate of facts

22. *A treatise concerninge the Staple*, pp. 92-93.
23. He makes frequent references to classical authors, rather for illustration than authority, and, moreover, not always those familiar to readers of the commonplace books.
24. His pamphlet is addressed to the Lord Protector.

and figures, that the basic cause of high prices lay in the "falling of the exchange between us and Flanders and between us and other nations,"[25] his basic remedy became the deceptively plausible one of lowering the price paid by the king's mint for bullion.[26]   If those rich enough to do so prefer not to take their fine gold and silver to be minted at this rate but to keep it in plate, then the king can, in case of national emergency, with safety and convenience put a tax on every pound of plate as long as the emergency lasts.[27]   The big problem is to ensure a constant flow of bullion into the country.   That can be assured if the country merely exports more in value than it imports, which in turn can be assured if steps are taken to see that all citizens are not only employed but employed to the best advantage—that is, with special emphasis on the manufacture of wares for export.[28]   Of such wares, cloth is England's specialty.   The cloth industry must therefore be freed from extraordinary imposts, the burden of taxes being thrown farther back in the economy to landlords and the wealthy merchants.[29] In order to employ agricultural labor most effectively, waste land must be put into cultivation and the large sheep farms engrossed by "covetous merchant men" redistributed "unto husbandmen's occupying."   Here the answer is to tax sheep in such a way as to put a premium on the small holding and to discourage the engrossing of pasturage in the hands of wool merchants.   Also, if the export of grain is encouraged it will become profitable to bring marshy and wild land under the plough.[30] Meanwhile home industries of all sorts should be protected from foreign competition by import duties.   These can be imposed safely enough because, our author assures us, English goods will be in as much demand abroad as foreign products are in England.[31]

This program, typical of the nascent mercantilism of early Tudor policy, differs from Armstrong's mainly in its comprehensiveness and in the greater range of its vision.   Where Armstrong, for example, found it hard (though not quite impossible) to see beyond the immediate exchange of goods for money, the author of *Policies* was able

---

25. *Policies to Reduce this Realme*, p. 315.   See above, chap. x.
26. *Ibid.*, pp. 315-318.
27. *Ibid.*, p. 324.
28. *Ibid.*, pp. 321-324.
29. *Ibid.*, pp. 324-325, 327.
30. *Ibid.*, pp. 319-320, 326-331, 338.
31. *Ibid.*, pp. 331-334.

to think readily in terms of a balance of trade which would result indirectly in the desired influx of treasure.[32]   And, in accounting for the rise in prices, he went beyond the machination of merchants— though they also played their part—to those arcane and impersonal forces operating through the monetary system and the foreign exchanges. He was, it is true, more capable of discerning those forces than in understanding them.   He was ready enough, for instance, to recommend as safe and good a policy of limited debasement of the currency,[33] and this at a time when the national economy was already in precarious equilibrium as a result of the crumbling of its monetary foundations. But, sound or not, it was for its day a remarkably integrated program, based on a keen awareness of the highly complex factors involved.

If we examine it closely we can see emerging from it a fairly clear picture of what this author considered to be the chief objectives of economic planning and the kind of role government should play in such matters.   Like Armstrong, he sought higher revenue for the king and lower prices for consumer goods and a plentiful supply of them. Both men sought the wealth of the national community.   And both saw that external trade, over which the king had only indirect control, was to a large extent the governing consideration.   But the author of *Policies* was much more willing than Armstrong to accept the fact of international competition, with all the implications of a struggle for power as well as for the wealth that necessarily went with it.   Armstrong saw in external trade the means of increasing the wealth of the English people: "The whole wealth of the realm is for all our rich commodities to get out of all other realms therefor ready money, so shall all people in the realm be made rich thereby."[34]   In *Policies* a favorable balance of trade, while obviously contributing to private wealth, has as a major purpose to increase the king's revenue so that he can wage war more effectively.   The possibility of war is a recurrent theme in the pamphlet, reflecting a consistent undercurrent of thought.[35]   Even the welfare of English farm laborers should be a factor in the king's military calculations.[36]   The author also tended to look more sharply than Armstrong for the political implications of policies aimed at low

32. *Ibid.*, p. 321; see also p. 318.   On Armstrong, see above, chap. viii.
33. *Ibid.*, pp. 318, 344.
34. *A treatise concerninge the Staple*, p. 105.
35. *Policies to Reduce this Realme*, e.g., pp. 313-315, 318, 324, 329, 331, 342.
36. *Ibid.*, p. 329.   Fortescue expresses somewhat the same opinion in the *Governance*.

prices and plenty. A flourishing realm, he asserts, consists not only in being "strong against the invasion of enemies," but also being "not molested with civil wars, the people being wealthy."[37] The author shared the conviction of Morison and Starkey, and doubtless many others in that disturbed period, that sedition arose out of poverty and social injustice.[38] But it remained in its effects a political problem, and one especially pressing in that year of 1549.

Perhaps this element of political sophistication permitted this author to adopt a more mature attitude than his predecessor toward the role of governmental policy in controlling the economic system. Although the policies advocated by Armstrong were, for his generation, remarkably ingenious, designed to get at the cause of trouble, they depended for the most part on the direct action of the king's govern- ment—by statute if possible, but, where Parliament proved inhibited by vested interest, by administrative decree, enforced by supervisory commissions. His proposed measures were in the final analysis meant to prevent people from doing something they very much wanted to do. Profoundly attached to the divinely appointed social system as he had been taught to define it, he felt it necessary to thwart what he considered the inordinate ambitions of private persons, merchants, landlords, or even "poor men's sons" who aspire to a life above their station.[39] The Edwardian author, in contrast, placed small confidence in such nega- tive, restraining action. He was not so worried as Armstrong over the difficulty of getting disciplinary legislation passed in Parliament. Rather, he doubted its efficacy once passed. Laws or administrative decreees were useful only if they could be enforced; experience told him they could not be enforced against prevailing interests, especially in a country like England where the means of enforcement lay in the hands of the economically important citizens.

"And surely there cannot be a more pernicious thing to bring the people from a due obedience than to make such laws as shall not be kept."[40] This principle, supported in theory by Aristotle, our author saw borne out time and again in English experience. Take, for example, the case of laws passed to prevent eating of meat on fish days,

37. *Policies to Reduce this Realme*, p. 313. These last words are underlined in the original text.
38. *Ibid.*, e.g., pp. 323, 325.
39. E.g., *A treatise concerninge the Staple*, p. 106; *Howe to Reforme*, p. 117.
40. *Policies to Reduce this Realme*, p. 335.

or those meant to limit excess in apparel. Neither had worked. Neither "the king nor all his council" could enforce them—to the manifest derogation of their own authority.[41]   Or, again, in the matter of price fixing as a means of controlling the cost of food, attempts by the lord mayor of London to do so had failed utterly. Consequently he writes, "I marvel . . . at those men which have not only already seen the success of price setting, but also the success of the most part of proclamations and penal statutes, and yet will hold opinion this present dearth of victual may be redressed by setting of prices upon victual."[42]

Then he comes to a phrase of key importance: "surely it is not the setting of low prices that will any thing amend the matter. But it must be the taking away of the occasion of the high prices." Policy, in other words, must remove the cause of the disorder rather than try, against a whole complex of private interests, merely to suppress the symptoms.   More than that, it must accept those interests as given conditions for the policy-maker and seek accordingly to channel them as far as possible toward the common good. Instead of limiting enclosures by statutes which were not enforceable, he would tax sheep, a measure he seems to have considered more likely to be enforced, thereby making it more profitable for landlords to restore some sheep pastures to tillage. Instead of prohibiting the eating of flesh on fish days under penalty of law, he would sell licenses to do so, and use the proceeds to subsidize fishermen, thereby ensuring a larger supply of fish and lowering its price. This, in turn, would tend to bring down all food prices, and, since food prices are connected with all prices, affect ultimately the entire price level.[43]   Again, the import duty he proposed on all luxury goods would, he maintained, do more to moderate excess in apparel "than ever any statutes have done or can do in that be half."[44]   Finally, he believed that prices would adjust themselves more safely and effectively if everyone is allowed "quietly to sell all kind of victual in the market at what price he can."   The legitimate province of economic regulation lay farther back in the economy, in the area of monetary policy and international trade, territory in which

41. Ibid., pp. 334-335; see also p. 331.
42. Ibid., p. 340.
43. Ibid., pp. 334-347.
44. Ibid., p. 331.

the individual could register a less clearly defined claim than in the marketplace.

∽ ∽ ∽

Sir Thomas Smith wrote the *Discourse of the Common Weal* at about the same time as the author of *Policies* was proffering his counsel to Protector Somerset. And in their approach to the issues of public life both men were traveling in roughly the same direction. But where the latter picked his way with some hesitancy, not always sure of his bearings,[45] Smith moved with ease and assurance. There is a philosophical depth to the *Discourse* which is lacking in even so sophisticated a work as *Policies*; nor is the latter any more impressive in its presentation of fact, or in its catechism of experience. Moreover, attitudes that are merely implied in *Policies* become explicit in the *Discourse*. For our purpose therefore it is a considerably more important document, its treatment of remedy comparable in quality to its analysis of cause.[46] In both respects it deserves to stand as the culminating product of early Tudor discussion. And it deserves special attention as the most advanced example of the humanist's ability to adapt his training to the utilitarian ends of government.

Smith had apparently thought a great deal about the methodology of both the making and discussing of policy. In their intellectual aspects he saw no difference between the two. The work of the statesman and of the citizen-counselor both involved the most rigorous application of mind to the solution of the country's problems. The only difference was that the statesman, ultimately the prince himself, being human in the range of his mind, must depend on the more intensive examination and more leisurely deliberation of the informed citizen. Now there are, the Doctor points out, two ways to "amend any thing that is amiss." One is by "precedent," the other by "art." If the first way is followed "we may take either our common wealth, when it was well, for a precedent, or an other common wealth that we see well ordered, to whose examples we might conform our things."[47]

45. His disclaimer of absolute wisdom in the last pages is, of course, standard operating procedure for Renaissance pamphlet-writing. But in this case his challenge to other writers to engage in further discussion seems genuine, and may indicate that he felt himself to be, in fact, on debatable ground.

46. See above, chap. x.

47. *Discourse*, p. 105.

This emphasis on precedent and example no doubt still reflects something of the medieval reliance on custom and authority. But it must be read in the context of Renaissance humanism.[48] The humanists had given new meaning to the study of the past. Still unduly respectful, especially toward classical example, their search for precedent still a search for authority more often than an exam‑ ination of experience, the humanists were more nearly able than their predecessors to see the present in historical perspective, and they tended to identify history with experience. So it is to the study of other times and other places that Smith refers here, to the kind of com‑ parative and historical analysis in which Fortescue had pioneered, to which Hythloday rallied his hearers in *Utopia*, and to that especially which Smith himself was to undertake in his later treatise, *De Republica Anglorum*.

It is the second method, however, that he is prepared to follow in the ensuing discussion of economic policy. To proceed "by art" means to search out and remove the causes of trouble, since, *sublata causa, tollitur effectus*. That seems obvious enough, and it is a method the author of *Policies*[49] and, for that matter, most of the more analytically inclined writers of the period also followed. Smith, however, goes about it more systematically, more conscious of the fact that he is following a particular method. Since, as we have seen,[50] he insisted in his analysis of causes on their complexity and on the consequent necessity of establishing the priority of causes from those most immedi‑ ate to the underlying, the "efficient" cause, remedial policy must, in removing the causes of economic maladjustments, be so devised as to deal with the underlying cause no matter how far back in the economy it might lie. His approach may therefore be considered positivistic rather than either authoritarian or strictly historical.

As his application of policy to causes proceeds, however, it becomes apparent that he is doing more than merely removing them. Whether he is now acting in as deliberate accord with a methodological principle as before, there is no doubt that by the time he has said his say he has projected his policy discussion into the dynamic area of economic

48. Johnson, pp. 34‑35.
49. *Policies to Reduce the Realme*, p. 341.
50. See above, chap. x.

nationalism. The removal of causes becomes, therefore, something more than the mere remedying of that which is amiss.

His prior analysis of the English economy had reduced its many and complex ailments to four primary categories: first, and "chiefest," the "universal dearth," which modern historians call the price revolution; second, the "exhausting of the treasure of this realm," the *bête noire* of all early mercantilist thought; third, that hardy perennial of social criticism, "enclosures and turning arable ground into pastures"; and finally, the "decaying of towns, townships, and villages."[51]   In the last section of the *Discourse* he proceeds to prescribe remedies for these ills.   Having found the "efficient" cause of high prices to be debasement of the coinage, he seeks his remedy in a radical policy of restoration.[52]   Debased coins must be called in and new ones issued at full weight.   No gradual increase of bullion content will do, for then all the heavier coins will be withdrawn from circulation.   The necessary bullion can be had partly by converting plate into coin and partly by placing such restrictions on trade with other countries as will bring in a steady flow of precious metals.   For a while payments may have to be made in kind.   In the long run, however, any shortage of treasure must and can be made up by the improvement in foreign trade likely to follow an intelligent tariff policy and, especially, the reform of the coinage itself.   In any case it is necessary to secure such an influx of treasure because the ability of the country to maintain its military posture and hedge against bad times depends on an adequate store of money which is, "as it were, a storehouse of any commodity ye would have."[53]

This will not be a simple process.   It will, Smith admits, work hardship on some, especially those who incurred debts during the period of inflation.   Even if the worst of the resulting inequities are adjusted by law, as they must be, some people will be bound to suffer. The government will, however, be doing all it can reasonably be expected to do if it tries to make its policy "profitable to the most number, and do hurt [but] to the fewest."[54]   This formula, though presented on the authority of Cicero, has in the context of Smith's

51. *Discourse*, p. 98.
52. *Ibid.*, pp. 105120.
53. *Ibid.*, p. 114.
54. *Ibid.*, pp. 119120.

argument a curiously modern, utilitarian ring."[55] The end of policy is not absolute justice but the nearest approximation compatible with the greatest happiness of the greatest number.

Since inflated prices are, according to Smith's analysis, the chief economic problem in England, causing or exacerbating dislocations throughout the whole economy, the solution to it will in a sense be also the solution to other economic problems as well. A restored coinage would help to turn the balance of foreign trade in England's favor and a readjustment of prices would reduce many of the forces impelling individuals toward the unprofitable use of their labor or the irresponsible exploitation of their land. But there are special causes which must be dealt with in order to remedy particular maladjustments. Both the decay of towns and the shortage of treasure must be remedied by regulation of foreign trade. Towns like Coventry have declined because of the vanity of Englishmen in seeking foreign-made goods rather than contenting themselves with those made at home. Here the government must step in and prevent the importation of such foreign goods as can be made in England. Why, he argues, should Englishmen pay the wages of artificers now working beyond the sea? The answer, then, is to restrict imports by heavy duties, encourage skilled craftsmen to settle in England, and disregard the complaint of native guild masters that is bound to ensue. The prosperity of the country is more important than that of any craft.[56]

The old and thorny problem of enclosures also requires special treatment. Enclosures—or rather the irresponsible exploitation of the practice, for Smith was at pains to point out that not all enclosures were bad[57]—can be traced ultimately to avarice. But, since avarice is no more likely to be taken away from men than anger, say, or fear, policy must proceed indirectly in such a way as to remove the "occasion" of covetousness,[58] namely, "the exceeding lucre that . . . [men] see grow by these enclosures, more than by husbandry."[59] The thing to do, then, is "to make the profit of the plow to be as good, rate for rate, as the profit of the graziers and sheepmasters."[60] This can be done

55. Johnson, p. 35.
56. *Discourse*, pp. 125-131.
57. *Ibid.*, pp. 49-53.
58. *Ibid.*, pp. 121-122.
59. *Ibid.*, p. 122.
60. *Ibid.*, p. 53; see also pp. 122-124.

by adjusting the overseas trade in wool and grain in such a way as to encourage the export of grain and discourage that of wool.[61]

Having accepted with a frankness uncommon even in his generation the basic and ineradicable character of economic self-interest, Smith proceeds to build his remedial policies around it and to do so quite without tears. Like the author of *Policies*, he saw that it was a force too strong to be held effectively in check by restraining legislation. If a law were passed limiting enclosures, he says, "yet men studying still their most profit, would defraud the law by one means or other." Like his anonymous contemporary, he saw that policy must be positive as well as negative: "all things that should be done in a common wealth be not to be forced, or to be constrained by the straight penalties of the law; but some so, and some other by allurement, and rewards rather."[62] The carrot must supplement the stick. Although the author of *Policies* was groping his way to the same idea, Smith recognized more clearly the possibility of a sort of natural harmony of interests, public and private, and of the impersonal market forces. "For every man, as Plato sayeth, is naturally covetous of lucre, and that where in they see most lucre they will most gladly excercise."[63] And at an earlier point in the *Discourse* the Doctor agrees somewhat cautiously with the Knight's suggestion that what is profitable to each man must be profitable to the commonwealth as a whole, merely stipulating that it must not, like some enclosures, work also to the disadvantage of others.[64] Neither writer was as yet willing to argue that private and public interests will necessarily coincide. But both, especially Smith, had already gone beyond the point of believing that they could be forced to coincide. State regulation remained to them the normal tool of the policy-maker, but it must take into account both the ineluctable force of self-interest and the substantial area in which it did coincide, or could by inducement be made to coincide, with that of the national community.[65]

This idea that the government should exploit the cupidity of land-

61. *Ibid.*, pp. 122-124; cf. pp. 54-55.
62. *Ibid.*, pp. 57-58.
63. *Ibid.*, p. 122; cf. p. 53.
64. *Ibid.*, pp. 50-51.
65. On this subject, also discussed in chap. x, above, see Chalk; Heckscher, II, 293-294, 296, 312; Robertson, pp. 65-66.

lords rather than try to suppress it is as fresh and original as the proposal, for which the *Discourse* is more famous, that inflation can be cured by reforming the coinage. The ancients knew the power of money but refused to consider it a means of government. The medieval prince, following patristic teaching, was content either to order what is good or forbid what is bad.[66] And if governors were sometimes ready for practical purposes to recognize the force of covetousness and use it, commentators remained strictly orthodox. Even Starkey, while willing enough to accept self-interest as a natural force, to be taken into account by makers of policy, could see little alternative but to curb it in the common interest by restrictive legislation. Only in the *Discourse*, and to a more limited degree in *Policies*, is a new note audible.

Smith knew as well as the medieval moralist or the Levers and Hoopers of his own day that men are moved in their economic rela- tionships more by cupidity and vanity than by any sense of respon- sibility to the community. But he refused to be depressed by the knowledge. He relied not on moral regeneration as a means toward the actual improvement of conditions but on intelligent policy. For that reason he was more optimistic than the medieval commentator who knew human nature too well to trust it, yet could see no alter- native but to hope that through the counsel of good men government might be made good. He was also more optimistic regarding the possibility of ameliorating things by policy than Thomas More who recognized in theory the immense potential existing in the mind of man for constructive statecraft, yet shared too much of the traditional outlook on human nature to expect much improvement in practice. More's few suggested remedies for actual conditions remain therefore such as to restrain, for example, the covetousness of landlords rather than to use it and turn it somehow to the common good. And when he dealt in fancy and created the complex society of *Utopia*, he designed its entire mechanism so as to inhibit man's innate tendency toward self-aggrandizement.[67]

Smith, on the contrary, though doubtless no more ready than any- one else to condone pride and avarice as moral qualities, remained quite prepared for the purposes of constructive statecraft to separate

66. Tersen, p. 74.
67. See above, chap. xi.

their economic expression from their religious implications. There are times, indeed, when he seems to consider them less as deadly sins than as mere natural impulses. Can we, the Doctor asks at one point "devise that all covetousness be taken from men?" and answers, "No, no more than we can make men to be without ire, without gladness, without fear, and without all affections."[68] This is man viewed as he is rather than in the shadow of his Fall. Though neither irreligious nor even especially anticlerical (he leaves the spiritual life of the church strictly to the clergy, while placing its temporal concerns equally strictly in the hands of the secular authorities),[69] his attitude toward civil society is profoundly secular.[70]

∽ ∽ ∽

Perhaps what separates Smith's approach toward government most sharply from that of his medieval predecessors and, in varying degrees, from those of his own generation who retained characteristically medieval habits of thought, was his ability to see in intelligent policy the possibility of improving man's material condition, if not of altering the structure of his society. More effectively even than those likeminded commentators of the mid-sixteenth century to whose work we have had reason to refer, Smith was able to move from analysis to constructive policy. Even more than they he saw government not merely as the nerve center of the community reacting defensively through the innate conscience of its members to whatever appeared to be disturbing the community, but the brain, capable of controlling or diverting those moving forces. And the counselor, whether acting as a public-spirited citizen or as a member of the duly appointed governing circle, became one whose task it was not merely to point out wrongs to be redressed as in a court of law, but to understand the inner workings of society and to devise policy accordingly.

To these men especially who contemplated with such singleness of purpose the mechanism of economic life, government could no longer be considered essentially protective, as it had been during the centuries

68. *Discourse*, p. 121.
69. *Ibid.*, p. 142.
70. This is also true of the *De Republica Anglorum*, which seems more than likely to have been by the same author. In the original portions of that tract, Smith makes virtually no reference to the traditional biblical sources of authority, and he appears to consider civil authority as of natural origin.

preceding. Where the medieval commentator assumed that the purpose of government was primarily to maintain peace and justice, to preserve, that is, the political body *in statu quo*, the Renaissance humanist assigned to government a more active function. He saw that, in the face of increasingly uninhibited private enterprise and of correspondingly competitive interstate relationships, the government of England had to be prepared to shape its policies, ultimately also its laws, to cope with these forces and if possible to turn them to the benefit of the people and of the state.

CHAPTER XIII. THE COMMON, WEAL AND THE SENSE OF CHANGE: SOME IMPLICATIONS

IF THE ECONOMIC COMMENT OF THE MID-SIXTEENTH century is read with the ear as well as the eye, with an ear attuned to the overtones of thought still for the most part expressed in conventional forms, it becomes apparent that the ideal of the commonwealth has become subtly transformed. It has, to be sure, changed more for some writers than for others. Few commentators of the period had the insight of the two just studied. But the trend is unmistakable—and important, for the commonwealth formula underlay virtually all early Tudor social and political thought. This study would therefore remain incomplete if the idea were not subjected to a more systematic examination than has been possible in the preceding chapters.

It should, I believe, be examined primarily in relation to the increasing sensitivity to change also apparent in the early Tudor literature of diagnosis and remedy, of analysis and policy. The persevering reader will by now have noticed that these writers were curiously ambivalent in their treatment of their own society. Apparently more and more aware of the processes of social change, especially as they affected the economic life of the national community, they explored those processes ostensibly with reference to a static social theory. They discuss positive policies, sometimes of a startlingly progressive sort, but in the interests of stability. In general they seem bent on reconciling the facts of a revolutionary situation with the conservative, in a very real sense reactionary, ideal of the "very and true common weal." If we take them strictly at their word, if, that is, we accept their more formal definition of what a commonwealth is or should be, we find them not only conservative in purpose, but linked far more closely with medieval thought than with anything approaching modernity. If, on the other hand, we follow them in the course of their analysis of actual conditions, and, even more, in their efforts to devise remedial policy, we see that they have somehow achieved a new perspective. They are able, as few of their predecessors had been, to see English conditions in their unique relation to time and place. Without greatly disturbing their basically traditional idea of what society should be and of what is the ultimate purpose of civil government, certainly without developing a theory of progress, they were able to recognize the dynamic element in society, and in government the potentiality for constructive action, for hedging against and in a measure controlling those moving forces.

What, then, is one to make of this paradox presented by con-structive realism deployed in the cause of a reactionary social ideal, exploration of change conducted within an ostensibly static framework? Perhaps, as with so many aspects of early Renaissance thought, the difficulty is more apparent than real. Perhaps the commonwealth idea was not so nearly static as it appeared. Perhaps, indeed, the traditional formulas in which it ordinarily found expression simply mask a new sense of change, a dawning awareness of social process.

Failure to understand the true nature of the ambivalence that seems at times to be built into the thought of the period, failure in particular to allow for the divergence between traditional theory, part of the rich legacy of medieval thought, and fresh attitudes prompted by actual experience in a time of revolutionary change, has too often resulted in failure also to appreciate the significance of the early Tudor pamphleteers and commentators of various sorts who examined their society with an eye both critical and constructive. It has even obscured the degree to which they did, in fact, move toward a new theory of society and government. Men of different generations and diverse backgrounds, from More of pre-Reformation days to Smith of the mid-century, from humanists like Starkey and Elyot to reforming divines like Latimer, Lever, and Hooper, from Armstrong, the business man, to Crowley, the social gospeler, these men were all deeply troubled by the problems affecting the welfare of the English community. They accordingly explored with anxious concern the processes of change they saw going on around them: the rise in prices and the prevailing "dearth," en-closures and the vagaries of foreign trade, social unrest and the problem of the abbey lands, poverty that seemed only to increase in the face of plenty and crime that followed close on the heels of poverty. Even though they did so ostensibly with reference to a static social theory, they were able to achieve attitudes that allowed them to see well beyond the formal boundaries of their inherited intellectual estate, and especially to gain a new sense of time and place, and a new feeling for the relativity of human institutions. They were in addition able to appreciate to a greater extent than their predecessors the positive role of government among the forces of change. It is here that a few at least of the early Tudor writers reveal most clearly their position as forerunners of modern thought.

ᔕ ᔕ ᔕ

On the face of it, the ideal of the commonwealth was little more than a vigorous and impassioned restatement of orthodox medieval theory.[1] At its center is the political body, divinely ordained in a form analogous to the natural body, each part having its appointed function to perform for the good of the whole organism. From it radiate a number of important implications. Private interests must be subordinated to those of the community. Indeed, if the moral attitude of the individual man is what it should be, if, that is, he is moved by Christian charity and a true sense of duty, his interests will never conflict with those of the community. Only if he is moved by pride, avarice, or any other of the vicious drives inherent in his corrupted nature will he pursue his private interest to the detriment of the common "wealth." The ultimate purpose of a well-ordered commonweal is to provide the conditions necessary for a life of virtue, led by the individual in diligent, contented, unambitious devotion to his temporal calling and, of course, in the confident and not unrelated hope of salvation hereafter.

To this ideal, social and ethical rather than political, the Tudor pamphleteers added little in a formal way except to recognize more clearly than most medieval writers the complexity of the political body. The latter had, it is true, accepted the fact that their society had actually outgrown the traditional, tripartite division of estates.[2] But in their doctrine of "vocation" the Tudor commentators recognized the facts of a vastly more complex society. Yet the doctrine of vocation

1. The best treatment of the commonwealth ideal is still to be found in J. W. Allen, *A History of Political Thought in the Sixteenth Century*, Part II, chap. iii. For related ideas and general background, see A. O. Lovejoy, *The Great Chain of Being* (Cambridge, Mass, 1936).

2. John Gower, for example, finds it impossible to hold the survey of society he undertakes in the *Mirour de l'Omme* and in *Vox Clamantis* within the traditional framework and instead recognizes a wide variety of vocations and interests.

or calling remained in intent simply a fuller statement of the traditional social theory.

Like its prototype, the Tudor commonwealth was a profoundly conservative ideal. The analogy of the body politic was itself con-servative enough: with full confidence that it will block further argu-ment, Richard Morison asks the rhetorical question, what will happen if the foot says "I will wear a cap like the head"?[3] But in the context of early Tudor life the commonwealth ideal was stated in deliberately, explicitly, at times passionately conservative terms. It was fundamental-ly a protest against the spirit of private enterprise which was in fact undermining the traditional social relationships and a warning of the dangers of sedition arising out of the resulting social mobility as well as from the political unrest of the period. In the name of the common-wealth, Thomas More made the classic indictment of the new cap-italism. To his indictment the so-called "commonwealth men" of the mid-century added little more than documentation and reiteration. In their writings, however, the commonwealth tended more and more to merge with the social gospel that generally accompanied radical religious reform. Crowley, especially, saw in the idea that a man can do what he will with his own a dangerous doctrine; his notion that property carried with it the duty of stewardship in the common interest led him to state the commonwealth ideal in terms of extreme protest and reaction.[4]

Morison and Cheke, responding to the risings of 1536 and 1549 respectively,[5] invoked the commonwealth ideal in support of the government in its fight against sedition. Though aware of the eco-nomic distress that underlay the rebellions, they found it necessary to appeal, not to the social conscience of entrepreneurs, but to the duty incumbent upon all members of the commonwealth to submit to authority and to preserve due order and degree. Alarmed less by the self-seeking landlords and merchants than by the social radicalism that lurked always just beneath the surface of sixteenth-century agrarian life, they stressed the hierarchical aspect of the commonwealth ideal,

3. *A Remedy for Sedition*, ed. E. M. Cox (London, 1933), p. 20. On Morison and his authorship of this tract see Zeeveld.

4. See expecially, *An informacion and peticion agaynst the oppressours of the pore Commons* in *Select Works*, ed. Cowper, p. 157, and *One and Thyrtie Epigrammes*, in *ibid.*, pp. 47 and 50. See also above, chap. ix.

5. See above, chaps. viii and ix.

with its emphasis on obedience to constituted authority, be it that of prince, landlord, or *pater familias*, rather than the aspect of social justice, with its emphasis on Christian charity and selfless co-operation in the common interest. The two aspects were not, however, easily separated. As in the sermons of Lever and Hooper, the covetousness of the propertied classes and the inordinate ambition of those who were not content with their inferior status were both open to censure as detrimental to the common interest.[6] The commonwealth thus became the rallying slogan for both social and political conservatism in an era of social and political change, the apparent radicalism in its expression a reaction against the real radicalism inherent in a dynamic economy.

In a way it is odd that this ideal, which during half a century of revolution in church and state succeeded in capturing the minds and imaginations of public-spirited Englishmen, should have remained so nearly exclusively a social and ethical ideal and involved so little in the way of political thought. Except for the recurring reference to the standard Tudor doctrine of obedience, which by itself meant little more than that sedition was a danger to the whole country and, more narrowly, that the Protestant minority had perforce to assume that ecclesiastical reform would come at the hand of a presumably godly prince, few of the writers who sought the "very and true common-weal" felt called upon to debate strictly political questions. Indeed, but for the Henrician propagandists who were charged with the task of explaining the Royal Supremacy at home and abroad, most of the Tudor "political" literature prior to 1550 was concerned with social and economic analysis and the discussion of ways to remove the causes of the maladjustments thus uncovered. Among these writers, only Thomas Starkey and Sir Thomas Smith raised fundamental questions concerning the forms of government. Even to Starkey's philosophical mind the problem was to provide the best agency for economic and legal reform rather than to investigate the theoretical bases of political power. And when, in his treatise *De Republica Anglorum*, Smith came to deal with the commonwealth of England as it "standeth and is governed at this day the xxviii of March *Anno* 1565," he eschewed speculation, stuck to the facts, and refused to separate the more strictly political and constitutional aspects of the subject from the social.

6. E.g., Lever, *Sermon, 14 December 1550*, in *Three Frutiful Sermons*; Hooper, *Early Writings*, pp. 452, 505-506.

As J. W. Allen has pointed out, the commonwealth ideal was peculiarly English. Even Bodin's conception of the *"république bien ordonnée"* carried with it "no vision of a people united in love and amity as members of one body, ever having the commonweal before their eyes, without regard for their own vain pleasures,"[7] such as emerges alike from the writings of Starkey, the humanist, and Crowley, the evangelical reformer. The answer lies, no doubt, partially in the fact that the Tudor monarchs did not find it necessary to challenge the conveniently vague constitutional theory to which they had fallen heir. Both Henrys were able to, indeed had to, make common cause with the more influential elements among their subjects; the resulting appearance of co-operation between king and people in the national interest was able to survive, after a fashion, even the confusion of the Edwardian period. Encouraged by Cromwell in the reign of Henry VIII and, for a brief but critical period, by Somerset in that of Edward VI,[8] the articulate citizen found it possible to discuss the ills of English society in the comfortable, if illusory, hope that he spoke to a wise and conscientious government and that he would be given respectful attention. Perhaps also the commonwealth ideal could only have enjoyed so vigorous a revival in an island kingdom, relatively free from more immediate pressures of Continental politics. The English were, like the similarly insular Utopians, able to turn their attention to a large extent inward toward considerations of welfare rather than outward toward the typical objectives of power politics. And, insofar as they were forced to face the facts of power, they were able to set the discussion in economic rather than political terms, to turn it, in other words, toward considerations of foreign policy which would be reflected as much in domestic prosperity as in the enhanced diplomatic position of the monarchy.

ഗ ഗ ഗ

The Tudor pamphleteers were more interested in analyzing the specific problems facing the commonwealth than in defining it—and they were better at it, too.[9] Like some of the slogan words we use

---

7. Allen, p. 151. It is, of course, a concept totally lacking in Machiavelli's idea of *lo stato*: J. H. Hexter, "*Il Principe* and *Lo Stato*," *Studies in the Renaissance*, IV (1957), 113-138.

8. See above, chap. vi.

9. A few representative definitions may be found in the following works: Brinkelow,

today, it became a formula everyone thought he understood and felt free to adapt to whatever situation he found himself in. It could, and usually did, mean something like the state, an English equivalent of the latin *respublica*—sometimes interpreted narrowly in the sense simply of government, sometimes more broadly to denote the national community considered in its social as well as in its political or constitutional aspects. This latter is the sense in which Sir Thomas Smith most frequently used the term in his *De Republica Anglorum*.[10] "A common wealth," Richard Morison wrote, "is, as I think, nothing else, but a certain number of cities, towns, shires, that all agree upon one law, and one head, united and knit together by the observation of the laws."[11]

It usually also carried overtones implying something rather like the more literal sense of "common weal," that is, the general welfare, considered in sharp contrast to private interests. Morison qualified the somewhat neutral definition quoted above as follows: "A common wealth is like a body, and so like that it can be resembled to nothing so convenient as unto that." Again: "A common wealth is then wealthy and worthy his name, when every one is content with his degree glad to do that, that he may lawfully do, gladder to do that, which he seeth shall be for the quietness of the realm, all be it his private profit biddeth him do the contrary."[12]

Some radical agitators, appealing to the age-old communal spirit of the country village and to the related tradition of Christian communism, seem to have interpreted the term even more literally as meaning that wealth should be held in common.[13] Apparently alarmed by agitation of this kind, Elyot preferred to abandon the word entirely in favor of the "public weal," adapted more literally from its Latin prototype, and suitably equipped with aristocratic implications.[14]

Complaynt, pp. 51-52; Crowely, *Informacion*, pp. 168-169; [Clement Armstrong] *How the Comen People*, p. 52, see also n. 57 below; Elyot, *Governor*, I, 1 ff.; Cheke, *Hurt of Sedicion*, Sig. Eiiii; Morison, *Remedy*, pp. 19-20; Edmund Dudley, *The Tree of Commonwealth*, ed. D. M. Brodie (Cambridge, 1948), pp. 9 and 15; Starkey, *Dialogue*, pp. 62-63; Hales, *Defence*, p. lx; Smith, *De Republica*, p. 20.

10. See especially Book I, chap. x.

11. *Remedy*, p. 19.

12. *Ibid.*, p. 12.

13. There is a reference to this sort of thing in *ibid.*, p. 12.

14. *Governor*, I, 1 ff. Cf. S. E. Lehmberg, *Thomas Elyot, Tudor Humanist* (Austin, 1960), pp. 40 ff.; Caspari, p. 104.

Elyot was more sensitive than most of his humanist contemporaries to such implications. To him the "public weal" is primarily hierar^chical, "compact or made of sundry estates, and degrees of men."[15] His elaboration of this principle of order and degree is well known, partly as a classic in itself, and partly because it so clearly foreshadowed the much more famous speech of Shakespeare's Ulysses: "Take away order from all things, what should then remain? Certes nothing finally, except some man would imagine Chaos."[16]

Chameleon^like the idea took on the color of the background against which it was set. In the published sermons and in the pam^phlets of the evangelical reformers, the commonwealth assumed the tones of a theocracy, its governing agencies responsible immediately to God, its motive power the moral character of its people, its ultimate law the Scriptures, and its forum the pulpit. In the writings of the humanists it was described in more secular terms, its government natural in origin, accountable immediately to no one, its active element reason, and its spokesman the man of humane learning and practical experience. One group held the purpose of the common^wealth to be that of providing the conditions necessary for a life of virtue led in accordance with religious teachings. The other looked rather to the conditions that would allow man to lead a life of virtue in accordance with what they believed to be his natural dignity and inherent perfection. Yet these were divergent tendencies rather than mutually exclusive positions. Whether they emphasized the moral nature of man or his rational faculty, exponents of both positions could no doubt converse intelligently. Usually, in fact, both had similar educational backgrounds. They both accepted the ideal of a co^operative society, based on the good will of its components and their sense of civic duty, and they both believed the end of civil government to be that of providing the conditions necessary for a life of virtue.

ഗ   ഗ   ഗ

We can come nearer to resolving the paradox of the Tudor com^monwealth in Starkey's *Dialogue* than in any other document of the

15. *Governor*, I, 1.

16. *Ibid.*, I, 4^8. On the problem of order see E. M. W. Tillyard, *The Elizabethan World Picture* (New York, 1944). Cf. E. W. Talbert, *The Problem of Order* (Chapel Hill, 1962), which undertakes to readjust Tillyard with special reference to Shakespeare's plays.

period. In it Starkey, the most reflective among his generation of English humanists, set the discussion of diagnosis and remedy concerning the ailments of English life within an unusually broad intellectual framework. At first glance, however, the riddle seems merely to be restated, not answered, the paradox of constructive policy stirring within a static organism left unresolved. Any number of quotations might be selected which, stripped of their larger context, embody the essentially static ideal of the divinely ordained, corporate, hierarchical, functional society in which each class or group performs its appointed duty in the common interest.

The organic analogy employed in the idea of the body politic, with all its conservative overtones, provides the structure for most of the *Dialogue*[17] and gives to the concept of the commonwealth an appearance of unimpeachable orthodoxy.

> And so thus when every part, after this manner, doth his office and duty required thereto with perfect love and amity one to another, one glad to succor and aid another as members and parts of one body, to the intent that after this worldly and civil life here peaceably passed and virtuously spent they may at the last all together attain such end and felicity as by the goodness of God and ordinance of nature is determed to the excellent dignity and nature of man, then shall there be stablished and set in such a multitude of people so governed, so ruled, with such policy, that thing which we so long have sought: that is to say, a very and true commonweal, which is nothing else but the prosperous and most perfect state of a multitude assembled together in any country, city or town, governed virtuously in civil life, according to the nature and dignity of man.[18]

In this common weal the explicit duty of the governors is apparently purely remedial: "to see the administration of justice to the whole community."[19] And "all labours business and travail, of wise men handled, in matters of the commonweal, are ever referred to this end and purpose: that the whole body of the commonalty may live in quietness and tranquility, every part doing his office and duty, and so

17. See especially pp. 55, 57-58, 62-64.
18. *Ibid.*, pp. 62-63.
19. *Ibid.*

(as much as the nature of man will suffer) all to attain to their natural perfection."[20]

Nor are these statements mere verbal convention. There is no doubt whatever but that Starkey hoped by governmental action to curb some at least of the disruptive forces he observed—especially in English economic life. Good government to him is one which controls private enterprise in the interests of the community and shapes national policy in the direction of welfare and stability rather than of power. But it is a disciplined society he has in mind rather than a static one. He is less concerned with the profit motive than with those activities of men, arising out of their irrational "affects," that do not contribute to the general welfare and cause an imbalance in the political organism. There is little talk in the *Dialogue* of avarice, but much of idleness and "ill employment." He insists, like most writers of the day, on men laboring in their vocation, and would have officers, modeled after the Roman censors, appointed to curb their "natural" tendency to "fly to the most easy craft, and to such whereof is most hope specially of gain, by the which they may ever their pleasure sustain."[21] It is wasteful pleasure, however, that is here the villain rather than profit, and it is to the profit of all that men be prevented from applying themselves, "without respect . . . to every craft and faculty."[22]

Starkey here justifies the social order on grounds of utility rather than of providential ordinance. And it is in the power of government to make whatever adjustments within it that will enhance the "wealth" of the country. Indeed, if all parts of the political body "exercise with diligence their office and duty," then the economy will actually expand. At this point Starkey appears to inject the not entirely incompatible idea of growth into the organic analogy. "For there [wherever] you shall see riches and convenient abundance of all things necessary; there you shall see cities and towns so garnished with people that it shall be necessary in places desert to build more cities, castles and towns for the minishing of such a multitude, which is a sure argument and certain token of the flourishing of this politic body."[23]

20. *Ibid.*, p. 24.
21. *Ibid.*, p. 147.
22. *Ibid.*
23. *Ibid.*, pp. 64-65.

This social system, disciplined by a paternalistic government in the interests of organic health and growth, may still not seem significantly far removed from the traditional ideal of a society in which wealth meant welfare and welfare was linked strictly to status, its level deter-mined by the standard of life appropriate to each order. But the orthodoxy still clinging to Starkey's formal definitions is further belied by the implications arising from the context in which it is placed. For the surrounding argument is shot through with a sense of change—not the sort that is clearly inherent in the providential plan (that he did not question) but such as arises from man's "natural" situation and is to some degree the product of his own God-given faculties.

What, more than anything else, shaped Starkey's attitude toward society and government was his almost painful awareness of the need to reconcile the absolute with the contingent, the changeable condition of man with the eternal verities as embodied in natural law and the Christian revelation. If he paid more attention to the former, it was because Christian teaching was vouchsafed only to a part of mankind at a particular time, whereas the law of nature had always been apparent to the rational mind of men.[24] And Starkey was trying very hard to see the human race as a whole, both in time and place. He nourished a profound faith in the ability of men to interpret the law of nature by means of that "sparkle" of the divine reason God had chosen to allot to mankind and to adapt its immutable principles to the variable contingencies of history and geography. It is through just such a process of constant adaptation that man can attain that approximation to perfection Starkey believed inherent in his "excellent nature."[25]

In the *Dialogue*, the interlocutors find that before they can get down to cases concerning the nature of commonwealths in general and the English commonwealth in particular they must reconcile the varying laws and customs of various peoples, of Turks, Saracens, Jews, as well as Christians, with the basic principles governing the life of all man-kind.[26] Man has implanted in him a sense of virtue which "inclines him ever to the civil life, according to the excellent dignity of his

24. *Ibid.*, pp. 184 ff.
25. *Ibid.*, pp. 23 and 26.
26. *Ibid.*, pp. 28-29.

nature. And this inclination and rule of living, by these virtues stabled and confirmed, is called, as I said, the law of nature, which though all men follow not, yet all men approve."[27] These "natural seeds and plants of virtue" must be nourished by laws and customs devised by man and called civil law. Now this civil law "is diverse and variable." It "taketh effect of the opinion of man; it resteth wholly in his consent and varieth according to place and time, inso- much that in diverse time and place contrary laws are both good and convenient to the politic life." Such laws and customs spring none the less from the law of nature "as brooks out of fountains and wells."[28] But they provide a wide and fertile field for the ingenuity of govern- ments.

"Laws are made for the people and for the order of them, and not the people for the laws, the which, therefore, must be applied some- what to the nature of them."[29] This relativistic principle is deeply ingrained in Starkey's thought. It is basic especially to the penetrating discussion of legal reform in the *Dialogue*. Like most of the Italian- trained humanists, those in particular who had followed Reginald Pole to Padua and studied there under his patronage, Starkey had familiarized himself with Roman law. These studies provided him with an outside vantage point from which he could view the laws and institutions of England in a fresh and realistic perspective. This, he wrote at one point, had been his main purpose in studying abroad.[30] He tended, like most of his humanist contemporaries, to idealize the civil law of Rome. In it he saw exemplified that which was both reasonable and natural.[31] (It had the added advantage, of course, of being Roman.) But he also found in its simplicity and flexibility certain particular advantages over England's Common Law, the "crudities" of which, "given to us by such a barbarous nation as the Normans be,"[32] brought out all the scorn of the humanist for his medieval predecessors.

Yet the English Common Law enjoyed the sanction of custom, and it was the somewhat paradoxical virtue of civilian studies that they

27. *Ibid.*, p. 31.
28. *Ibid.*, p. 33.
29. *Ibid.*, p. 106.
30. Herrtage, p. x; cf. p. lxxiv.
31. *Dialogue*, pp. 22, 108, 175.
32. *Ibid.*, p. 175.

fostered a more tolerant, because a more historical, attitude toward custom. The more the civilians knew of Roman history and thought, the more they realized that Roman law was the expression of a peculiar society, historically unique, worthy of imitation, but in all but the most general sense inimitable. They consequently developed a certain regard for the likewise unique character of their own society and for its cumulative wisdom.[33]

The stage was thus set for a debate on fundamental principles. It was much the same debate that is implicit in Fortescue's writings, only now it is explicit and accompanies a more immediate crisis in English legal thought.[34] The *Dialogue* reflects both the civilian's readiness to subject custom to criticism on rational grounds and also his dawning sense of the relativity of law and of the necessity of adapting pure reason to the facts of time and place. It is not always certain which of his *personae* represents Starkey's own views. Pole is given the task of showing how English law fails to achieve the purposes of the ideal commonwealth, which is to say the rule of reason. Lupset speaks for the force of custom and the contingency of history, and he occasionally gives historical explanations for the failure of the Common Law in certain instances to square with the dictates of "equity and conscience." More than likely their argument, taken as a whole, reflects the dialectical process by which Starkey was refining his own thinking.

Take for example the law of inheritance. Pole attacks the custom of primogeniture on grounds of reason and nature. He also appeals to the example of the ancient Romans whose laws "be drawn out of nature."[35] Surely this combination of reason, nature, and ancient example should have persuaded Lupset, the humanist. But we are here dealing with a generation of humanists who have fallen heir to the learning of a century and a half of classical scholarship and are able to go well beyond mere imitation of the ancients and to adapt classical precept and precedent to the realities of divergent cultures.

33. On this subject, see J. G. A. Pocock, *The Ancient Constitution and the Feudal Law* (Cambridge, 1957). For similar developments in sixteenth-century French legal theory, see Julian H. Franklin, *Jean Bodin and the Sixteenth-Century Revolution in the Methodology of Law and History* (New York, 1963), pp. 37 ff.

34. See above, chap. v.

35. *Dialogue*, p. 108. See also pp. 105-108. In pp. 109-111 Starkey deals similarly with the authority of a lord over a minor who has inherited land held from him by knight's service.

Lupset accordingly presents another side of the argument. This, he says, is all very well in the abstract, but laws must conform to the character and conditions peculiar to any given people. Laws must, moreover, be judged to some extent pragmatically: the proof of their validity is that they work. What is good for ancient Romans or contemporary Frenchmen or Italians is not necessarily good for English-men. This, he maintains, was taken into account by the men who instituted the law of primogeniture.

> They well considered the nature of our people, which by nature
> be somewhat rude and sturdy of mind, insomuch that if they had
> not in every place some heads of governors to temper their affects
> rude and unruly, there would among them be no order at all.
> And therefore it was not without cause, as it appeareth, ordained
> and stablished that in every great family the eldest should succeed,
> to maintain a head which by authority, dignity and power should
> better contain the rudeness of the people.[36]

There are, it would appear, nevertheless strict limits to any such appeal to custom and to the contingencies of time and place. Pole refuses to accept Lupset's contention that English law must be crit-icized in the light of its origins in the days when "William the Con-queror subdued our country and stablished our laws" and made them conform to the then reasonable principles of feudal tenure. To say that a custom was reasonable in origin is not to say that it must remain so in an enlightened society. "We must," he declares, "consider the time of nature to the which we would form our common weal."[37] Yet it remains significant that Starkey allowed the latitude he did to such appeals. It is important to see how consistently he places law in its social and historical setting. Considered in the light of reason alone, it were better if England had an elective monarchy, but the facts of English life and English history are such as to require the retention of hereditary succession.[38] The entailing of estates may violate principles of abstract justice, but can be justified as a means of pre-serving the authority of a governing class which depends on the integrity of its estates for its power and efficiency.[39] There are times

36. *Ibid.*, p. 106.
37. *Ibid.*, pp. 110-111.
38. *Ibid.*, pp. 102-103.
39. *Ibid.*, p. 108.

when Starkey stains the white radiance of pure reason with an almost Burkean sense of historical relativity.

The necessity of adapting the laws of nature, as interpreted by reason, to the variable conditions of human society implies the possibility of making new law in a sense more real than was common in medieval thought. "For this is the nature of all man's ordinance and civil law, that according to the time, person and place they be variable, and ever require prudent correction and due reformation."[40] It also justifies a more radical and constructive criticism of the existing order than was usual in the preceding period.[41] For legislative change must be preceded by constant adjustments of policy, which in turn arise from a constant review of existing conditions—the kind of review Starkey and the early Tudor humanist pamphleteers felt it their duty to undertake, either officially or as volunteer counselors.

This application of intelligence to the ordering of society Starkey apparently considered a constant process. It implied an awareness of development that is as familiar to modern thought as it would have been foreign to medieval.[42] Starkey interpreted the nature of man himself in terms of potentiality rather than of what he is or has been in some golden age. He has in him the makings of a perfection only a little lower than the angels and of a depravity only slightly removed from the beast. It is up to him by reason and diligence to realize the higher potentiality inherent in his nature and to avoid those propensities, also natural, which would draw him in the opposite direction. He made use of the Aristotelian notion that the mind of man, "first of itself a clean and pure table, wherein is nothing painted or carved," is shaped by sense perception; and, as he uses the idea, it takes on just a hint of that pregnant proposition of later philosophers that, since man is the product of his environment, he can achieve the perfection inherent in his nature by the rational reform of that environment.[43] Applied reason, reason which reaches beyond the exercise of the discursive intellect and embraces the principles of right behavior, thus becomes the active agent in human society, and history becomes for Starkey the

40. *Ibid.*, p. 140.
41. *Ibid.*, pp. 65-69.
42. F. L. Baumer, "Thomas Starkey and Marsilius of Padua," pp. 188-205; C. W. Previté-Orton, "Marsilius of Padua," *PBA*, XXI (1935), 137-183.
43. *Dialogue*, pp. 23-31, 42.

story of man's struggle to achieve the perfection to which his nature inclines him.

For the most part it has been a successful struggle. Starkey's view of man's past is far from sophisticated according to modern standards, nor is it always consistent. But some sort of primitivism provides for him, as for many a thinker in subsequent generations, an essential starting point.[44] Following classical sources rather than Christian, he believed that man initially lived in the wild forest without civil policy. What this presocial existence was like depended to some extent on which authors Starkey had in mind at the moment. Although at one point he toys with the romantic view that it was more virtuous than the later life in cities,[45] he clearly prefers the version more flattering to human intelligence—and, incidentally, more adaptable to the modern notion of progress. The following passage deserves to be quoted *in extenso*:

> A time there was, Master Lupset, as we find in stories many and diverse, when man, without city or town, law or religion, wandered abroad in the wild fields and woods none other wise than you see now brute beasts to do. At the which time he was led and drawn without reason and rule by frail fantasy and inordinate affects, and so long continued and many years, till at the last certain men of great wit and policy, with perfit eloquence and high philosophy, considering the excellent nature and dignity of man, and perceiving right well that he was born and of nature brought forth to higher perfection than he applied himself unto, began to persuade the rest of the people to forsake that rudeness and uncomely life, and so to follow some order and civility. And first of all to build them certain cities and towns whereto they might assemble to their common aid, succour and commodity . . . . Then, after, they devised certain ordinance and laws whereby they might be somewhat induced to follow a life convenient to their nature and dignity. These laws and ordinance, at the first beginning, also were unperfit and somewhat rude, according to the time and nature of the people; for it was not possible suddenly to enact law and policy to bring such a rude multitude to perfit civility, but ever as the people by process of time in virtue increased, so particular laws by politic men

44. *Ibid.*, pp. 143-144. See also Zeeveld, pp. 250 ff.
45. *Dialogue*, pp. 27-28.

were devised. And thus in long time, by perfit eloquence and high philosophy, men were brought by little and little from the rude life in fields and woods to this civility which you now see stablished and set in all well-ruled cities and towns.[46]

Some such anthropology, derived from Greek philosophy, probably as interpreted by Cicero,[47] seems naturally enough to have been widespread among the classically educated Englishmen of the period. They could have found a developmental interpretation in Erasmus' diatribe against war, but, since Erasmus used it to explain the rise of warfare among otherwise civilized peoples, his view is more pessimistic than Starkey's. Closer to Starkey is a passage in Elyot's *Governor*. And both are foreshadowed in Stephen Hawes's part humanist, part chivalric *Pastime of Pleasure*.[48] These more optimistic views of man's distant past present a picture of his struggle from a primitive to a more or less sophisticated civil life in which the emphasis is clearly placed on the constructive mind working to devise laws that would permit man to fulfil his natural potentialities. Once established, civil life continues to involve the element of diligent planning,[49] of "conspiring together in virtue and honesty" for the "maintenance and setting forward of the common weal."[50]

From then on, as mankind moves into the more revealing light of history, it becomes apparent that the road is not always straight. Indeed, since the classical ages of Greece and Rome, man's paths have fallen in strange places. The early history of England itself is for Starkey a record of barbarism only partially relieved by a sensible compromise between reason and history, utility and the sacredness of custom. Englishmen presumably now live in an age of relative enlightenment, else no such dialogue as that between public-spirited intellectuals like Pole and Lupset would be imaginable. But policy-

46. *Ibid.*, p. 60; cf. p. 22.
47. On Cicero's interpretation of the Aristotelian tradition see A. O. Lovejoy and George Boas, *Primitivism and Related Ideas in Antiquity* (Baltimore, 1935), chap. ix.
48. *Erasmus Against War*, ed. J. W. Mackail (Boston, 1907), pp. 18-23; *Governor*, I, 117; cf. 83; Stephen Hawes, *The Pastime of Pleasure*, ed. W. E. Mead, E.E.T.S., O.S., No. 173 (1928), ll. 876-891. See also Thomas Wilson, *Arte of Rhetorique* (London, 1553), *STC* 25799, preface; Forrest, *Pleasaunt Poesye*, p. lxxxv. Somewhat the same idea emerges in More's *Utopia*, pp. 49, 81-82, and also in Fortescue's prehumanist *Governance of England*, chap. ii.
49. *Dialogue*, pp. 29-31.
50. *Ibid.*, pp. 34-39.

makers must still consider the contingencies of time and place. Even Plato, Cicero, and Seneca would have done less or differently if their historical situation had been different.[51] Thus it is that governments have developed different forms in different places, depending on the "wisdom and policy" of their founders and the "nature of the people."[52]

If it were possible to reduce Starkey's concept of civil society to a simple formula it would be something like this. The ideal commonwealth derives its essential characteristics from the law of nature, but its particular manifestations vary according to time and place. Man is capable of finding out by reason and precept what the essentials are and by wisdom and constructive thought of adapting those essentials to the variable circumstances of his life. The ideal commonwealth is something which man must constantly strive to realize. It lies in the future, not in a past golden age. Could it be realized, it would be static, disciplined, hierarchical, organic—in short, much like the body politic that John of Salisbury described in the twelfth century, which provided the framework of John Gower's social commentary in the fourteenth and Fortescue's political in the fifteenth. But between the actual and the ideal lies the long road of constantly shifting relationships. And it is the task of all wise men to seek the ideal in the particular, the unique, and the changing.

 so so so

The thought of early Tudor English writers is often most revealing when it is least philosophical. The profound work of Starkey or of More tells us much—even more when we read between the lines, but it remains unusual in its intellectual dimensions. What intelligent Englishmen thought regarding the commonwealth is perhaps more accurately revealed in those writings meant for the more immediate and practical purpose of uncovering the ills of the body politic and discovering remedies. It is in this literature that we see the commonwealth, as it were, in action rather than as an ideal to be sought. It is here that the emphasis of the humanists on applied intelligence and the native realism of contemporary Englishmen combine in a powerful working alliance. And it is in the resulting discussion of actuality

51. *Ibid.*, pp. 36-37; cf. p. 40.
52. *Ibid.*, pp. 60-61.

that the concept of the commonweal loses some of the rigidity that marks its more formal definitions.

Answering the complaint made by the rebels of 1536 against Henry VIII's employment in high office of men of low degree, Richard Morison raised the issue of careers open to talent.[53] If, in thus supporting the position of a man like Thomas Cromwell, he went further than most of his readers were willing to go, possibly even further than he himself realized, Morison challenged by implication the very ideal of social stasis to which he paid verbal tribute in the name of the commonwealth. While advocating a society of degree, he left room for the dynamism of individual men. Content to guard the commonweal of England against sedition, he seems not to have been worried about personal ambition. And when, in 1549, the commonwealth was again in danger from rebellion, Sir John Cheke countered the equalitarian sentiments attributed to the Norfolk rebels by pointing out to them that equality of goods would simply freeze the social structure and prevent any poor man from improving his lot and would take from his children the opportunity of advancement.[54] Again, in defending the existing social order, and in the traditional terms, a man of insight and experience was forced to recognize the dynamism operating within that social order.

The impact of actuality on traditional forms of thought becomes especially apparent, as we have had cause to note previously, in the literature devoted to economic problems. Those problems called attention with peculiar insistence to the dynamic character of sixteenth-century society. The spectacle of landlords and merchants seeking their private profit no less than their economic survival and overturning customary relationships in the process, of prices rising with the impersonal force of the tides, of nations competing for the trade and treasure of the entire world, could hardly fail to impress upon the public-spirited observer the fact of change. Nor need change of this sort be considered entirely as deterioration within the organism of the commonwealth, as sickness within the political body. Indeed, social critics found it increasingly difficult to blame these changes on men and their failure to do what they were supposed to do. Some, it is

53. *Remedy*, pp. 16-22. Cf. Elyot, *Governor*, I, 6; II, 376, 378 ff. See above, chap. viii.

54. *Hurt of Sedicion*, pp. 989-990. See above, chap. ix.

true—Crowley is a good example—persisted in reducing the whole complex problem to its moral elements. But the more realistic were driven, at times it would seem almost against their will, toward the analysis of economic forces.

Crude as it generally was, such analysis, involving a more or less consistent effort to uncover the causes of prevailing conditions, became at the same time an enlightening study of the phenomena of change. From Sir Thomas More to Sir Thomas Smith, from the *Utopia* to the *Discourse of the Common Weal of this Realm of England*, English commen-tators turned their attention with surprising consistency toward the factors that were so obviously changing their society. Only a few, however—Smith is the best example if we grant him authorship of the *Discourse*[55]—contemplated the processes of change at all dispassionately. Most persisted in looking backward. Yet, even when, like the preposterous animals, their eyes were set in the back of their heads, they could hardly miss the meaning of social change, nor could they ever again be entirely successful in their effort to reconcile observed facts with the essentially static ideal of the commonwealth. Smith came close to ignoring it entirely, just as he abandoned the organic analogy in favor of the mechanical one of the clock.[56] The rest, in varying degrees, subordinated formal definition to a treatment of the commonwealth as it actually worked.

Some were able to strike a rather interesting compromise between a realistic recognition of the dynamism inherent in economic life and the conservative ideal of a static social organism. Clement Arm-strong, the most economically oriented of the Henrician pamphleteers— and the most experienced in the world of business—is a case in point. No man of his day accepted with more righteous enthusiasm the traditional social ideal. On the other hand, none of his contemp-oraries had a keener insight into the economic system nor a better under-standing of the powerful forces at work in it. But he managed after a fashion to make the most of both worlds by transferring the area in which the dynamic force of self-interest might legitimately operate from the individual to the state. No man, he maintained, should be "suffered to live out of right order," by which he meant "the mystical body" of the whole commonwealth, but must labor "in the degree and

55. See above, chap. vi, for discussion of the question of authorship.
56. *Discourse*, p. 98.

order that they are called to."[57] Much of the trouble in England had, he felt, come about as a result of poor men's sons, "natural born to labor for their living," apprenticing to merchants and becoming nothing but buyers and sellers seeking their singular weal at the expense of the common weal.[58] Like most protomercantilists, he had little patience with the enterprise of middlemen and valued only such activity as was in a direct way productive. For that reason he greatly favored "artificiality" over more merchandising. Even here, however, the profit from industry is to the king and the commonweal rather than to the individual. God has given to kings each his special commodity—in England, wool—and they should see that their people work up this gift to the advantage of the realm as well as for their own living. To kings, then, should accrue "all profit or increase within their realms, the which is over and above that all their subjects hath no need."[59] Accordingly, no man must be allowed "to do any thing, but only that, which might be to the wealth of the whole body and its members."[60]

A paternalistic government capable of curbing and channeling the economic enterprise of its subjects in the common interest became, therefore, Armstrong's answer (and a characteristic one in his day) to the economic forces that threatened the social order as he understood it. Moreover, the world being what it is, the government has to conceive of its "wealth" not merely in terms of domestic welfare, the more usual interpretation, but in those of a naked struggle for economic advantage and survival among competing nations. This he deplored, and wished there could be some international agency, "a right ordinary Emperor," who could moderate such cut-throat competition in the interest of all Christendom.[61] But he accepted it as a fact, and one which no existing human power could alter. Armstrong merely stated in rather more explicit form what most of the "commonwealth men" believed and what underlay both their social conservatism and their almost unbounded faith in the efficacy of paternalistic regulation in the interests of a higher "wealth." It was a commonplace of their idealism that in all respects the object of the individual's effort in

57. *How the Comen People*, pp. 52-53.
58. *Howe to Reforme*, pp. 115-129, 126-127.
59. *How the Comen People*, pp. 51-52.
60. *Ibid.*, p. 53.
61. *A treatise concerninge the Staple*, pp. 90-114, 91-93.

secular life should be the profit of the national community. John
Hales stated in the context of practical discussion a position Robert
Crowley expressed in that of Christian idealism: "It may not be lawful
for every man to use his own as him listeth, but every man must use
that he hath to the most benefit of his country."[62] But, whereas
Crowley interpreted such benefit to mean maintaining the community,
as God meant it to be, *in statu quo*,[63] those writers more sophisticated in
the ways of the economic world were quite capable of seeing that the
profit of the country was to the political body as the ordinary profit of
business was to the body natural. The latter, of course, depended upon
the former. Armstrong wrote that the "whole wealth of the realm is
for all our rich commodities to get out of all other realms there for
ready money," then added that "after money is brought in to the whole
realm, so shall all people in the realm be made rich therewith."[64]
Even he, with all his lip service to the traditional notion of the commonweal, was never quite able to keep the dynamism of economic activity
within bounds, not even the bounds of logic.

Here again it is possible to see a major crack beginning to appear
in the monument erected by these early Tudor exponents of the
commonwealth to the ideal of stability. It could be patched over for
the time being with a judicious mixture of individual responsibility
and paternalistic regulation, but the repair was not likely to last. In
the *Discourse of the Common Weal*, and to a lesser extent in a few other
pamphlets of the mid-century,[65] the idealism of the commonweal,
though still present in spirit, no longer conceals, nor is it meant to
conceal, the dynamism inherent alike in private and state enterprise.

In a metaphor quite devoid of Christian idealism, William
Cholmeley declared that "the commodity of a country is like the
water of a great river," which men and governments cannot, even if
they would, keep dammed up.[66] The *Discourse of the Common Weal*
contains a systematic analysis of foreign trade in terms of a constantly
moving mechanism of impersonal cause and effect which the govern-

62. *Defence*, p. liv; Cf. Crowley, *Informacion*, p. 157 and *Epigrammes*, pp. 47 and 50.
See also Allen, p. 139.

63. *The Voyce of the Laste Trumpet*, ll. 1021-1032.

64. *A treatise concerninge the Staple*, p. 105.

65. See especially *Policies* and Cholmeley, *The Request and Suite of a True-Hearted
Englishman*.

66. *Request*, p. 142.

ment of England must harness in order to maintain its wealth and power. And in this same treatise the author finds in individual self-interest a force which, no matter what its moral implications, must be accepted by the analyst and the maker of policy as a natural fact of human life, to be channeled by constructive policy rather than thwarted by repressive legislation. He even seems to find in the profit motive a potentially, perhaps even a necessarily, beneficent force.

In its economic aspects at least, the commonwealth has become for Smith a mechanism of forces, impersonal and amoral in character, subject to analysis and manipulation by intelligent policy. It was still not a developing thing. We must still not look for the idea of progress in the work of the sixteenth-century humanist, even though he may have helped prepare the way for it. But Smith is beginning to see economic life as a machine functioning according to laws of its own, natural laws that propel society toward ends of wealth and power rather than of stability.

ﾝ ﾝ ﾝ

At this point there emerges from the idea of the commonwealth an appreciation of the role of government in society that is more nearly modern than medieval, one indeed that renders obsolete the idea itself. Paternalistic regulation in an age of rapid change called for policy decisions that reached beyond the province traditionally assigned to government. To the medieval mind, government was primarily protective in its function. The duty of the king and, in varying degrees, of the entire ruling class was to serve as the dispensers and enforcers of a justice usually assumed to be pre-existent and subject merely to declaration in the form of positive law. It mattered little that the central government of the realm was in fact always engaged to some extent in devising policies to enhance the wealth and improve the diplomatic posture of the country. (This is especially observable in the period from the reign of Edward III.) The king continued to be considered primarily as a judge and a soldier and his government the agency through which rights were defined and wrongs redressed, all in the interests of justice and peace. Early Tudor writers continued to stress this protective, judicial-military capacity of government.[67] Even

67. E.g., Dudley, *Tree of Commonwealth*, p. 62; More, *Utopia*, p. 40; Brinkelow, *Complaynt*, pp. 42-43; Forrest, *Pleasaunt Poesye*, p. xcix; Crowley, *Last Trumpet*, pp.

Starkey, despite his faith in the ability of intelligent policy to bring about a true commonweal, falls back on the notion that the immediate end of government is peace and justice, or, to use his words, the "quietness" and "tranquility" of the realm.

In the economic pamphlets of the mid-century decades this emphasis fades, and in the *Discourse* even the wording changes. If, then, the *Discourse* is set side by side with the treatise that most nearly parallels it in the area of political thought, namely the *De Republica Anglorum*, if, especially, we grant Sir Thomas Smith authorship of both documents, it becomes apparent that we are witnessing an approach to the problem of government that has gone beyond the transitional formula of the commonwealth and is well on its way to the more characteristically modern notion of sovereignty. In the *Discourse*, the emphasis of the interlocutors is on policy, the product of the inventive mind operating on the conclusions arrived at by realistic analysis. In the *De Republica*, Smith describes a government still much the same in structure as that which Fortescue had described almost a century earlier, but one in which the spirit has changed. Seen in conjunction with the constructive role assigned to government in the *Discourse*, Smith's interpretation of Parliament—or, more accurately, the king in Parliament—as the "most high and absolute power of the realm of England" becomes more meaningful. It becomes apparent that he had in mind a power capable of making law in a more frankly original sense than Fortescue, preoccupied with making the limited monarchy he envisioned fulfil its essentially protective function, and concerned mainly with the protection of property rights, would have understood. For there, in Parliament, the prince confers with representatives of the estates of the realm who "consult and show what is good and necessary for the common wealth" and between them take action in the form of bills which are "the Prince's and whole realm's deed." Furthermore, "that which is done by this consent is called firm, stable, and *sanctum*, and is taken for law." And it

95-99; Hooper, *Early Writings*, p. 558; Hugh Latimer, *Works*, I, pp. 67 and 193; Elyot, *Governor*, II, 186-187; Christopher St. German, *The Doctor and Student*, ed. W. Muchall (Cincinnati, 1874); Starkey, *Dialogue*, I, chap. xi. On the medieval concepts of sovereignty, see Wilks, *The Problem of Sovereignty in the Later Middle Ages* (Cambridge, 1963). See also chap. ii, above.

encompasses just about everything that touches the interests of the subject, including his property.[68]

ဢ   ဢ   ဢ

The exact distance traveled by Smith beyond the point Fortescue accepted as the limit of his speculation has been the subject of some debate.[69] Although this is not the place to reopen the subject in its complex totality, neither can it be ignored in the context of this study. Some have found in Smith's words a clear statement of legislative sovereignty. In his realistic, unspeculative way, so the argument goes, he arrived at pretty much the same position as Bodin did in the more formal area of political philosophy.[70] On the other hand, it has been argued that Smith did not separate the legislative aspect of government at all clearly from its judicial, that Parliament remained to him largely a court which declared or established what was law rather than made law in any original sense. Even if his comments on the powers of Parliament are taken at their face value, it is worth noticing that those powers do not extend beyond domestic affairs. Foreign affairs, questions of war and peace and the negotiation of treaties, remain under the prince's personal jurisdiction, as does the coinage, a matter of peculiar significance in relation to external trade.[71]

The difficulty here stems, I believe, less from any vagueness or ambivalence in Smith's thought than from the tendency of historians to examine it only in the context of legal and constitutional theory. To be treated within such formal limits would have surprised Smith himself. Like most of the Tudor humanists he preferred to hew to the line of factual analysis and let the implications fall where they might.

68. *De Republica*, Book II, chap. i, pp. 48-49.

69. The reader may find the rather extensive literature on this subject reviewed in the recent article by R. W. K. Hinton, "English Constitutional Theories from Sir John Fortescue to Sir John Eliot," *EHR*, LXXV (July, 1960), 410-425.

70. Alston, in *De Republica* p. 142. Indeed, since he had nothing to say about the law of nature, which Bodin still held to be superior to all positive law and hence a limitation on the law-making capacity of any government, Smith had already taken one significant step beyond Bodin's position. G. L. Mosse, "Change and Continuity in the Tudor Constitution," *Speculum*, XXII (Jan., 1947), 18-28. See also Mosse, *The Struggle for Sovereignty in England* (East Lansing, 1950), chap. i. It must, however, be remembered that Smith was not undertaking to deal with the larger philosophical problems in the *De Republica*, but rather to comment on what he took to be fact.

71. *De Republica*, II, chap. iii.

He must accordingly be treated primarily in relation to his assessment of fact, and, more especially, in relation to the sense of change and of the relativity of institutions.

He shared with Fortescue a keen appreciation of the relation of government and law to the society they serve. But his experience in an age of rapid economic change and his obvious interest in such matters[72] gave him a far deeper insight into the workings of society. In his conviction that a commonwealth "must be according to the nature of the people,"[73] and in his ability to contemplate the culture of antiquity in its historical setting, he was much closer to Starkey. To an even greater degree than Starkey he was able to apply both his analysis of contemporary reality and his historical scholarship to the problems of the commonwealth.[74] He saw the latter not as a static organism but as the constantly changing object of man's inventive genius, something wherein "the mutability of men's wits doth invent and assay new ways and amend that wherein they do find fault."[75]

The *De Republica Anglorum* belongs rather to the pamphlet literature of the mid-century in which the English humanists applied their learning and their ingenuity to the solution of the problems actually facing the national community than to the literature of political philosophy. In it he looks upon government primarily as the agency through which wisdom may be translated into policy. If we set it side by side with the *Discourse of the Common Weal* this emphasis becomes stereoscopically clear. There is a consistency of approach in these two documents which, regardless of authorship, links them in the same pattern of thought. In that enlarged context government becomes a positive thing, concerned primarily with regulating the economic life of the nation in the interests of the common "wealth" and of national power.[76] It is capable of establishing policy (as in matters of coinage) by royal proclamation,[77] and, when necessary, of translating policy into law by statute.

Seen from this point of view the distance separating Smith and

72. *Ibid.*, p. 60. See also above; chap. x.

73. *Ibid.*, p. 28.

74. See above, chaps. viii and xi for discussions of Starkey. Smith's use of history will be discussed at a later point in this chapter.

75. *De Republica*, p. 33.

76. See above, chap. xii.

77. *De Republica*, p. 60.

Fortescue becomes more nearly measurable. On their face, Fortescue's words seem to mean much the same as Smith's.[78] He grants to Parliament unique authority over any changes in the laws of the land, and his concept of the *dominum politicum et regale* rests solidly on the principle of consent. But there are differences, and they involve the assumptions made by the two men concerning the nature of the social mechanism. Government remained for Fortescue essentially pro-tective, its function that of preserving peace and doing justice. At its best, English government was ideally suited to accomplish this. But as things stood in the era of the Wars of the Roses, there was, so Fortescue seems to have felt, a very good chance that, in order to maintain his power, the king might lay his hand on the property of his subjects without their consent, and that the entire system would there-fore become like the arbitrary government of the French king—un-limited by law and hence readily subject to deterioration into tyranny. Fortescue's concern was accordingly to restore to working order the traditional machinery of English government. That meant making it possible for the ideal balance to be maintained between the pre-rogatives and powers of the crown and the rights of the subjects, a balance inherent rather in the feudal concept of dominion than in anything like the modern and quite incompatible idea of sovereignty. To do so, the king's own council had to be made efficient, for from it flowed the current that kept the whole mechanism in operation. This, as we have seen, is why Fortescue has so little to say about Parliament and so much about a reformed council. Parliament's authority in matters of taxation and legislation he takes largely for granted, and apparently for the very good reason that he considered it basically negative, an essential limitation on the will of the prince, but not the source of new law. Such constructive measures as the situation required could be worked out satisfactorily in council.

Fortescue appears to have made a clear distinction between policy, which he identifies with the administrative side of government, and the amending of the laws, which must be done in Parliament. A reformed council could deliberate on "the policy of the realm; as how the going out of money can be restrained, how bullion may be brought into the land, . . . how the prices of merchandise grown in this land may be held up and increased, and the prices of merchandise

78. For a fuller discussion of Fortescue, see above, chap. v.

brought into this land abated."[79]   And so on.   Then, and separately, "how also the laws may be amended in such things as they need reformation in; whereby parliaments shall be able to do more good in a month to the mending of the law than they shall be able to do in a year, if the amending thereof be not debated and by such council ripened to their hands." Fortescue did not see in constructive policy the kind of force that would ordinarily require change in the laws, nor did he envision any controversy concerning the location of sovereign power.   The idea just did not enter his mind.   Despite a sense of history more mature than any of his English contemporaries, despite, indeed, an equally unusual ability to recognize the relation of institutions to the society they serve, he seems never to have shaken off the assumption that society was created in a prescribed mold and that the national community was an essentially static organism.

Smith, writing almost a century later, was no longer able to proceed on that assumption.   Between his generation and Fortescue's lay the volcanic upheavals of the price revolution and the Reformation; between their thought, so similar in its purposes and verbal formulas, lies the literature of social analysis and constructive policy with its deepening appreciation of the nature of social process.   Smith was therefore no longer able to separate policy from legislation.   They both had perforce to deal with obviously changing conditions.   And, if the question of sovereignty had not yet been raised in its modern guise, it was already becoming quite clear to a man of Smith's insight that unlimited authority to meet change with change had for practical purposes to reside somewhere.

Meanwhile, if Tudor political writers continued to speak the language of Fortescue and to leave the relation of crown, council, and Parliament unexplored,[80] they tended nevertheless to stress the place of Parliament and to see it as the agency through which the intelligence of the community must ultimately be brought to bear on the problems of a changing society.   The Tudor pamphleteers were more con- cerned to adapt the old idea of good counsel to the realities of a rev- olutionary age than to argue about the structure of government.

Smith was unique in that he, alone of the men who reached intellectual maturity in the pre-Elizabethan era, followed realistic

79. *Governance*, chap. xv.
80. See Baumer, *Early Tudor Theory of Kingship*, especially chap. v.

analysis to the conclusion that there was, in fact, a law-making power in the English commonwealth which could do about anything it wanted to do and from which there was, in actuality, no appeal to a higher law. More than any man of his generation, he was able to see the "very and true commonweal" for what it was, a shell of traditional thought which, like the crystalline sphere of Ptolemaic cosmology, encased an intricate mechanism of moving parts. And it is my contention that his approximation to the idea of legislative sovereignty stemmed from his unusually mature awareness of the simple fact that this mechanism to some extent can, and to that extent must, be subject to the unfettered direction of government.

ഗ   ഗ   ഗ

It will, I hope, have become apparent from what has gone before that the Tudor ideal of the commonwealth derives its meaning as much from a maturing sense of time and place as from any inherited theory of society. The time and space world of the Tudor Englishman was expanding rapidly—more rapidly, indeed, than the stock of words and images needed to describe it. New worlds were being discovered —More may well have had actual voyages in mind when he wrote *Utopia*.[81] English scholars were coming to appreciate the virtues of a comparative study of laws and institutions. Not necessarily dependent on humanism—Fortescue's comparison of English and French laws owes nothing to the newer classicism—comparative study nevertheless flourished under humanist influences. It was a consciousness of the need for placing English society in perspective that, so he tells us, made Starkey turn his primarily classical scholarship more and more toward the contemporary world and in particular to the laws and institutions of Italy. Similarly, William Thomas intended his *History of Italy* to acquaint Englishmen with the good and bad examples afforded by Italian governments.[82]

For the purposes of such analytical investigation the data of history necessarily complemented the data of more first-hand experience. And so the sense of the relativity of institutions in the present was inseparable from a sense of their unique development in the past.

81. For this theory, see A. E. Morgan, *Nowhere was Somewhere* (Chapel Hill, 1946).
82. *The Historie of Italie* (London, 1549), *STC* 24018. For Starkey's comment, see Herrtage, p. x.

Roger Ascham, for example, undertook to analyze the plight of contemporary Germany from an historical point of view and with an awareness of historical cause not unworthy of comparison with Machi/avelli's *Florentine History*.[83]   And Sir Thomas Smith found in Roman history a source not so much of imitable example as of comparative data for his study of the English commonwealth.

Smith, in fact, reveals in the *De Republica*—and the *Discourse* bears a more than family resemblance—a sense of history more acute than was common among writers of his own day.   He exemplifies in an unusually high degree the tendency of early Tudor historical thought to be employed for the light it might shed on contemporary life rather than expressed in formal, literary historiography.[84]   It is in the practical application of their historical learning, especially in the in/creased understanding it gave them of the processes of change, that the English humanists become significant.   Smith brought to his study of English political and economic life a mind well stocked with knowl/edge of ancient Rome.   But—and here is where Renaissance historical thought achieves its characteristic perspective—the more he knew of the Romans the more clearly he was able to distinguish them from Tudor Englishmen and the more meaningful became the comparisons he was accordingly able to make between them.   It was no doubt his interest in English monetary problems that led him to study Roman coinage.[85]   And his equally profound interest in law and the institu/tions of government led him to compare not only English and Roman

83. *A Report and Discourse . . . of the affairs and state of Germany . . .* , in *English Works*, ed. W. A. Wright (Cambridge, 1904).   For his statement of purpose, see p. 126. On his place in historical scholarship, see Ryan, *Roger Ascham*, chap. viii, and W. F. Staton, Jr., "Roger Ascham's Theory of History Writing," *SP*, LVI (April, 1959), 125/137.

84. With the possible exception of Polydore Vergil's *Anglica Historia* and More's *Richard III*, early Tudor formal history was at best a more or less sophisticated chronicle. Not until Thomas Blundeville published his *True Order and Method of Writing and Reading Histories* (1574), an abridgment and adaptation of two Italian treatises (ed. H. G. Dick, *HLQ*, III [Jan., 1940], 149/170), did any Englishman interested primarily in history as a discipline rationalize in theory what a few commentators had for some time been doing for practical purposes, namely, extend the investigation of cause beyond the range of the immediately observable into that area of experience which can only be explored by historical research.

85. *Discourse*, pp. 76/77.   See also the pamphlet attributed to him entitled *A Discourse for Demonstrating the Reduction of Roman Coins to Our Money*, in John Strype, *The Life of the learned Sir Thomas Smith* (Oxford, 1820), pp. 130/134.   This latter work was no doubt related to his investigation of the wages of a Roman footsoldier.

law, the constant theme of the second and third books of the *De Republica*, but also the social structures of ancient Rome and Tudor England.[86] But the comparison is one in which the differences prove, and are meant to prove, as enlightening as the similarities.

This sense of change, of history, of the relativity of institutions and customs, readily apparent as it is and important, must not be exaggerated. We should not expect to find in it the already germinating seeds of a new historical philosophy, still less of the modern idea of progress which regards men as advancing in a definite and desirable direction in their temporal existence and which infers that this process will continue indefinitely.[87] The work of the pamphleteers of the mid-sixteenth century unquestionably contributed to both by cultivating among their readers a state of mind conducive to such speculation. Yet, here as in the area of political thought, they remained for the most part content to live within the boundaries of traditional theory and to restrict their field of vision to those things that lay within the reach of man's analytical and constructive intellect. Their Christian inheritance predisposed them to see in history a sequence of unique events following a purposeful, providential pattern. Their classical learning disposed them to look for some cyclical recurrence of advancement and decay.[88] But those at least who share the optimistic regard of the humanists for man's mind, for his "natural dignity and perfection," and who had not succumbed to the savage melancholy with which the preachers viewed the course of man's pilgrimage through a world of sin, could find plenty of room within the limits of either tradition for the factor of human creativity. Indeed, the more they knew of the actual workings of society the larger that area appeared to them and the more convinced they seem to have become that it was the natural province of policy. So busy were they in explaining it that they seem not to have been very much concerned with the more abstract philosophical problems.

When, like Starkey in the *Dialogue*, they did undertake to contemplate the course of man's earthly life, they tended to concentrate on the fact, observable in history and to some extent in contemporary life,

86. *De Republica*, Book I, see for example, chap. xviii in which the *equites Romani* are seen to be basically different from the English knights. These passages were apparently taken from Harrison, but represent Smith's point of view nonetheless.

87. J. B. Bury, *The Idea of Progress* (New York, 1932), p. 5.

88. E.g., Smith, *De Republica*, pp. 12-13.

of the progressive and generally successful application of mind to the solution of practical problems and to have been cautiously optimistic about the future. Instead of being oppressed by the sinful propensities of human nature, which they recognized all too clearly, they preferred to consider man at least equally inclined to virtue and infinitely edu/cable.[89] Conversely, they appear not to have bothered much with cyclical theories, with the vagaries of fortune, with millenary specula/tions, nor with such morbid ruminations on the subject of mutability and decay as troubled their Elizabethan and Jacobean successors.[90]

They do reveal in their writings a rather consistent tendency to reconcile in some manner the changing condition of man with the absolutes of nature, reason, and Christian revelation. In the latter they found the stability they craved, and in the former the legitimate, the necessary province of constructive policy. Both More's *Utopia* and Starkey's *Dialogue*, the two most philosophically oriented commentaries on society written in early Tudor England, are shaped in large part by this willingness to look for the permanent values of an ideal common/wealth as embodied in the varying forms of actual society. Between the eternal values and the contingent facts of actual life lay, for both More and Starkey, that vast area subject to the creative mind of man. It was a wider area than most of their medieval predecessors would

89. See above, chap. vii.

90. But cf. Smith, *De Republica*, pp. 12/13 and Starkey, *Dialogue*, pp. 65/69. Light on sixteenth/ and seventeenth/century concepts of mutability and their relation to the idea of progress has been shed from a number of directions. The following, though by no means exhaustive list, includes some representative interpretations. E. L. Tuveson, *Millenium and Utopia: A Study in the Background of the Idea of Progress* (Berkeley and Los Angeles, 1949); R. F. Jones, *Ancients and Moderns* (St. Louis, 1936), chap. i; E. A. Strathmann, "The Idea of Progress: Some Elizabethan Considerations," *RN*, II (Spring, 1949), 23/25; E. Zilsel, "The Genesis of the Concept of Scientific Progress," *JHI*, VI (June, 1945), 325/349; A. C. Keller, "Zilsel, the Artisans, and the Idea of Progress in the Renaissance," *ibid.*, XI (April, 1950), 235/240; H. B. White, "Bacon, Bruno, and the Eternal Re/currence," *Social Research*, XXV (Winter, 1958), 449/468; H. Weisinger, "Ideas of History during the Renaissance," *JHI*, VI (Oct., 1945), 415/435; V. Harris, *All Coherence Gone* (Chicago, 1949), especially, chaps. i and iv; L. Bradner, *Edmund Spenser and the Faerie Queene* (Chicago, 1948), chap. vii; T. E. Mommsen, "St. Augustine and the Idea of Progress," *JHI*, XII (June, 1951), 346/374; W. L. Gundersheimer, "Louis Le Roy's Humanistic Optimism," *ibid.*, XXIII (July/Sept., 1962), 324/339; K. Koller, "Two Elizabethan Expressions of the Idea of Mutability," *SP*, XXXV (1938), 228/237; Hans Baron, "The Querelle of the Ancients and the Moderns as Problem for Ren/aissance Scholarship," *JHI*, XX (Jan., 1959), 3/22.

have allowed or could have imagined. And it becomes, for good or ill, the increasingly characteristic habitat of the modern mind.

It is important, however, to recognize that for More, as for Starkey, the "very and true common weal" remained ideally static, something to be striven for, a goal located in the future—though More seems less sure of the progressive potentiality of man than Starkey—yet, once realized not necessarily subject to further organic development. The society of the Utopians represents one of many theoretically possible answers to the initial question debated by Starkey's *personae*, namely, what constitutes a true commonweal? To this extent it was impossible for these Englishmen of the early Renaissance to achieve or understand the modern idea of progress. But we might remember that so modern a mind as that of Karl Marx also came to a Utopian state of stable equilibrium at the end of its dialectical journey through history.

Only when they leave the ideal and concentrate upon the actual, only in a document like the *Discourse of the Common Weal*, in which policy arises out of the analysis of fact, or the *De Republica Anglorum*, in which the commonwealth of England is placed in the relativistic context of comparative study, are we able to entertain the illusion that we are in the presence of modern minds. Smith has moved consciously away from the notion of a static social order: "for never in all points one common wealth doth agree with an other, no nor long time any one common wealth with it self."[91]

The context of historical philosophy or of progress is in any event too artificial, too indirectly related to the actual concerns of these men to be of much help in interpreting their thought or even in establishing their place in the history of thought. What they achieved was not a new idea nor any new system but rather a fresh point of view. It was one that affected all aspects of Renaissance thought and separates it more surely than any other characteristic from medieval. It involved a sense of the uniqueness of time and place and of the infinitely varying relationships of actual society—within, of course, the limits prescribed by the eternal values and the divine plan—to those temporal and geographical contingencies. It may be considered part of that basic change in vision which Erwin Panofsky has recognized as the essential

91. *De Republica*, p. 33.

characteristic of Renaissance art,[92] but which was by no means confined to the eye of the artist. It involved a change in temporal as well as spacial perception, a sense of history, of anachronism, to use Panofsky's phrase, as well as of the distance between the eye and the object. It is what made Sir Thomas Smith appreciate the difference between the English knights and the *equites* of ancient Rome, and, conversely, it was the lack of it that permitted writers of the Middle Ages to treat the worthies of classical antiquity as "chivalrous paynim knights," differing in no essential from their medieval counterparts. It moved John Colet to interpret the Gospels in relation to the culture of their own time, and Erasmus to attack the efforts of those purists who thought they could revive in its pristine form the language of Cicero.[93]

The medieval thinkers knew and used the past, including that of classical antiquity, but they were never able to view the ancient cultures in their totality or to see them as more than the sum of readily borrow‑able parts. Nor did they recognize them as different in quality from their own, or separated by more than the efflux of time. The Renais‑sance mind found it necessary to explain both past and present in relation to time and place. Renaissance writers had come to under‑stand that the universal truths, the laws of nature which they saw no reason to question, must be sought in circumstances that vary from time to time and from country to country, circumstances which, more‑over, must be examined in conjunction. And it is in this latter con‑text of the historically conditioned moment, of the moving and to a degree controllable mechanism of social forces, that the early Tudor humanists were coming to interpret the commonwealth idea rather than in the context of medieval thought.

ဟ ဟ ဟ

The "very and true commonweal" was thus a peculiarly Janus‑headed ideal. It served English social and political thought as a

92. Erwin Panofsky, *Renaissance and Renascences in Western Art* (Stockholm, 1960) p. 113.

93. See M. P. Gilmore's stimulating paper, "*Fides et Eruditio*: Erasmus and the Study of History," in *Teachers of History, Essays in Honor of Lawrence Bradford Packard* (Ithaca, 1953), pp. 9‑27, reprinted in his *Humanists and Jurists: Six Studies in the Renaissance* (Cam‑bridge, Mass., 1963), pp. 87‑114. On the historical attitude of the Erasmian humanists, see also Harbison, *The Christian Scholar in the Age of the Reformation*, pp. 35‑36 and 92 ff.

useful, perhaps a necessary, vehicle during its transition from a medieval to a modern form. And it disappeared when its work was done, merging quietly with a more modern concept of the state. In the course of its brief career it gave a deceptively traditional color to much of early Tudor thought—deceptive, that is, because it masked an increasingly keen awareness of social process. Not that the Englishmen of the period were happy about the changes they saw taking place all around them. On the contrary, the conservative color of the commonwealth ideal was certainly meant to serve a protective purpose, and it often gave expression to wishful thinking. But as time went on it came, among the shrewder minds of the mid-century, to serve simply as the loose shell of conventional discourse within which a new understanding of society was to germinate.

CONCLUSION

CONCLUSION

ONE IS TEMPTED TO FIND FOR THESE ARTICULATE CITIZENS OF early Renaissance England a special place among the makers of modern thought. That their writings do in fact document an important phase in the transition from medieval to modern public discussion is unquestionable. It is also true that a few of the more reflective among them reveal particular tendencies we recognize as modern. We may, for example, detect a more or less consistent preference for the data of experience over the precepts of traditionally accepted authority, more particularly an eagerness to examine experience in search of those natural causes in the affairs of men with which the social scientist no less than the policymaker must work. In their ability to treat the observable world as an area capable of being explored and understood in and for itself, and for practical purposes distinguishable from that of religion, and in the tendency of at least their economic comment toward the quantitative, they reveal an affinity with late nominalism and with early scientific thought. Again, their observations are at times ordered by a sense of perspective which allowed them to study the problems of the national community in a relation to the coordinates of time and place which is as familiar to the modern mind as it would have been strange to the medieval.

In yielding too readily to this, the characteristic temptation of the historian, there lies, however, the danger of giving a quite false impression of the Tudor commentator. Even at his thoughtful best he was practical rather than systematic, realistic rather than consciously empirical. Despite occasional forays into the territory of theory, especially in regard to the workings of the economic mechanism, he did not look upon himself as a theorist. He reflected the utilitarian bias of Northern humanism rather than the speculative discipline of the schools; nor, insofar as he shared the humanists' optimistic faith in the ability of the human mind to analyze and solve the problems of temporal existence did he show any of the skepticism and pessimism increasingly apparent in the thought of the later century. It has been said, and rightly, that Tudor Englishmen had really no political theory but rather social theory, no theory of the state but only of society.[1] The "very and true commonweal" is hardly a substitute for the state as it was beginning to take shape in Continental thinking, nor is it without ambiguity as a theory of society. It was in the approach they made to the problems of society and in the kind of questions they asked and in the areas in which they sought for answers, rather than in the shaping of new formulas, that the Tudor pamphleteers reflect the changing atmospheres of Renaissance culture; and, insofar as they also contributed to that climatic change, they may, indeed, be considered to have prepared the way for modern thought.

The Tudor commentator—and this he had in common with some at least of his medieval precursors—was concerned less with government in the abstract than with English government, and less with the nature of any government than with its utility. It was to the conditions of English life that he turned his attention, almost instinctively, rather than to English institutions. And he recognized that it was his primary duty as a citizen-counselor to diagnose the ailments of the political body and to prescribe remedy.

The English were no doubt fortunate in being able to devote themselves so wholeheartedly to the examination of government in its functional relation to the national community rather than in and for itself. Though just emerging from a long period of political unrest and still faced with the constant threat of rebellion, the Tudor monarchy was, by the fourth decade of the century, relatively firmly established, its interests roughly congruent with those of the English people, its representatives intelligent enough not to raise theoretical issues regarding the locus of power in the state. The attention of critical observers tended consequently to be diverted from such issues, and especially from a Machiavellian preoccupation with the means by which a government can maintain its power. The sources of discontent in Tudor England tended to be social and economic rather than political. Thus, for example, the king's own propagandists, grappling with the problem of sedition, tended to find its cause in social injustice or maladjustment rather than in political machination. And it was possible for even those publicists not engaged in propagating the doctrine of obedience to accept it without much discussion

1. Christopher Morris, *Political Thought in England: Tyndale to Hooker* (London, 1953), introduction.

and to proceed forthwith to the labor of social and economic reform. It was, after all, a period of crisis in all the major categories of national life, economic and social as well as religious and political; it was very natural that these public-spirited Englishmen should concentrate on what their government could and should do rather than on what it was or should have been. Perhaps, also, it was easier for them than for their Continental neighbors to turn their attention toward the source of "wealth" (in the contemporary sense of "welfare") rather than toward those of political power because they were protected by their island position from the grosser sort of external pressure; possibly for that same reason they interpreted the problems of foreign policy in terms rather of economic than of political power.

Concerned primarily with government-in-action, the Tudor pamphleteers were able to achieve points of view and to adopt attitudes which allowed them to see far beyond their generally traditional system of thought. It was possible for at least a few of them to discuss government as though legislative sovereignty were a fact without raising the theoretical issue of sovereignty. They were able to analyze the causal forces in society and explore the possibility of amelioration by means of constructive policy, to acquire a practical understanding of the processes of social change, without concerning themselves with the problem of change in the abstract, much less with the typically modern question of progress. Through such analysis, empirical in a crude, unself-conscious way, they could also acquire a grasp of economic principle—the balance of trade, for example, or the monetary basis of prices—without pausing for the kind of theoretical formulation Bodin was soon to provide. Apparently conservative—intentionally so, indeed, for they were constantly in search of some rock of stability in the stream of change—they strove to chart, after a fashion, the very currents they distrusted, at times even to plot a course so as to make the best of their unavoidable force.

This practical citizenship, this sense of contributing to the counsel upon which they, like their predecessors, believed all government to depend, was not, of course, the discovery of these early Tudor commentators. Characteristic as it is, its roots reach well back into the preceding age. From the mid-fourteenth century on, a few dedicated citizens, some situated near the center of government, some relatively remote, conceived it their duty to offer the fruits of their critical obser-

vation to the king and his official council—and in written form.   Nat'
urally enough, these self'appointed counselors, these volunteer con'
sultants, became most articulate in periods of chronic crisis.   The late
fourteenth century was one of those periods.   Though much smaller
in scale, its problems were not unlike those that made the early Tudor
period one of still more profound disturbance.   They provoked, at
any rate, the first considerable literature of public discussion in English
history, a literature at times truly remarkable for the realism of its
comment.   At rare and irregular intervals during the succeeding
century, writings of even greater insight appeared, bearing witness to
the paradoxical capacity of that apparently decadent culture to produce
remarkable individuals.

   Yet the late medieval literature of public discussion reveals, with a
few notable exceptions, an approach quite different from that of the
more realistic of the Tudor pamphleteers.   The problem of counsel,
as seen from the fourteenth'century citizen's point of view, was es'
sentially one of fearless complaint and honest criticism.   It was there'
fore primarily a moral problem.   If the king received good counsel
and if he and the lords who were his official and natural counselors were
virtuous enough to listen to it and act upon it, all would be well.   If
not, evil would spread unchecked throughout the realm.   Parliament
and the king's own council provided the institutional channels through
which the complaints of the people, considered the primary element of
all good counsel, should reach the administrative center of government.
But the literate citizen felt encumbent upon him the duty of sup'
plementing these more formal sources of counsel.   It was ordinarily a
self'imposed duty, a duty of conscience.   Preachers and poets, clerics
and the occasional literate layman felt alike obliged to serve as the voice
of the people, which was also the voice of God.   In them became
articulate not so much the public mind as the public conscience.
Yet, dedicated as they were to the welfare of the community, these
medieval critics seldom felt it necessary to look for remedy beyond
moral exhortation or to meddle with matters of policy.   Such matters
they considered the responsibility of the king and his lords.   It should,
they seem to have reasoned, take little ingenuity to redress a wrong once
it is truthfully and boldly reported.   For theirs was a simple, direct,
and limited view of government.   Its function they held to be pri'

marily that of maintaining peace and justice, of protecting the national community from aggressors without and transgressors within.

With the advent of the Tudor age, especially with the vast increase in public discussion provoked by the upheavals of the 1530's and 1540's, new and positive elements were added to this sturdy, but limited, tradition of complaint. By that time the learning of the humanist scholars had become widely diffused among English intellectuals, and its lessons were being applied to the problems of the commonwealth. Within the context of this "applied humanism" there emerged what was for England a new ideal of intelligent and articulate citizenship. Like the "civic humanists" of the preceding century in Italy, the citizen-counselors of Tudor England drew heavily upon the rational, utilitarian, and secular example of classical antiquity, and, in accordance with the Erasmian tradition, to which they owed even more, they sought to realize their vision of a society remade in both body and soul. The humanist of the reign of Henry VIII and Edward VI believed it the duty of the wise man to apply his wisdom to the benefit of the commonweal in all its aspects. His wisdom was not the product of an abstract learning, nor of a cloistered virtue, nor was its object exclusively the contemplation of things divine. It was also a practical, applicable wisdom, informed by learning, both classical and Christian, inspired by the virtue such learning encouraged, and conditioned by experience in the world of affairs. It might, indeed, be argued that it is here, in the "commonwealth" literature of the 1530's and 1540's that English humanism enjoyed its most characteristic and perhaps its most fruitful application. Be that as it may, only misunderstanding will ensue if the new learning of Renaissance England is considered primarily a pre-Reformation phenomenon, or if it is studied in terms of linguistic scholarship alone, or of a particular style, or of any specific set of ideas— or, *pace* C. S. Lewis, of a "new ignorance." Its true significance can only be appreciated if it is recognized as a new approach to contemporaneous life in all its aspects, involving in particular a willingness on the part of its devotees to apply the fruits of their studies to the diagnosis and remedy of the ills, both spiritual and material, that beset the body of the commonwealth.

These practitioners of an applied humanism did not, of course, have the public forum entirely to themselves. The medieval moralist lived on and flourished and accounted for perhaps more than his share of the rapidly increasing volume of published comment. He returned, his characteristic features newly emphasized in the light of confessional controversy, in the person of the Protestant pamphleteer or of the preacher at Paul's Cross who took upon him the mantle of the prophets and spoke in the accents of Jonah admonishing the Ninevites to repent or perish. Nor were the humanists easily distinguishable from the religious reformers. They shared for the most part both the traditions of medieval Christendom and the reinterpreted legacy of classical culture. Yet they could be, and often were, radically divergent in their outlook on the practical issues of their society. And it was the more secular-minded humanists who were coming to speak the recognizable language of modern discussion.

In their writings, counsel becomes something more than complaint and negative criticism. They believed, with a touching and optimistic faith, in the educability of men for the duties of active citizenship, and in the efficacy of reason—not merely the discursive intellect, but "right" reason, moved by a sense of what should be and informed by learning and experience—as a means toward the attainment of good government. Their scholarship meant little to them (so they said) unless it could be applied to the betterment of the commonweal. Accordingly they undertook to examine their society systematically in order not merely to find out what was wrong with it but to devise remedies. Nor was the remedy they sought merely the amending of "that which is amiss"—for which purpose, as one medieval author wrote, "a parliament assembled is." It was, among the more advanced minds at least, remedy that took the form of constructive policy, calculated not only to curb wrongdoing but to promote the kind of action most likely to benefit the national community.

This meant getting at the causes of trouble—the underlying causes rather than those immediate ones that were more symptoms than causes. It meant pursuing the train of cause and effect well back into the social system. On the other hand, it meant staying within the limits of what is tangible, and therefore within the area in which government had jurisdiction and could exercise some positive control. More and more they left to preachers and moralists what they believed to be the constant and ineluctable factors inherent in man's nature and in the will of Providence, and concentrated upon those that came within the ever-broadening province of policy. Virtue became for them more the end of civil polity than its means.

Social analysis of an increasingly penetrating character thus becomes one of the most characteristic and significant contributions of the early Tudor commentators. Where the medieval critic of society had been content to trace illness in the body politic to the failure of each member to perform its appointed function, and that in turn to the moral delinquency of the persons who composed each part, a few at least of the Tudor pamphleteers were beginning to turn their attention to such impersonal and morally neutral forces as those of the marketplace which, though not evil in themselves, provided the occasion of evil in a commonwealth. Although their humanistic interests and their consequently increasing awareness of the diversity of cultures no doubt predisposed these writers to causal analysis, events forced their pace. From the revolutionary decade of the thirties to the years of illusory hope and very real confusion that followed the accession of Edward VI, crisis after crisis demanded the attention of these amateur analysts and forced them to probe more and more deeply into the mechanism of the national community.

Economic problems seem to have been especially thought-provoking. Clearly pressing, revolutionary in their effects, safely removed from the more sensitive issues of political life and for that reason less subject to inhibiting pressures, these problems fascinated the Tudor commentator. Whether he viewed English society from the more or less secular point of view of the humanist or from the standpoint of the Protestant reformer, he found himself examining the same kind of phenomena—high prices and poverty, idleness and "ill-employment," vagrancy and crime, enclosures and depopulation, even the mysterious dislocations in overseas trade and the vagaries of the exchanges. These were all profoundly disturbing to the thoughtful observer, accustomed as he still was to the ideal of a stable society of fixed order and degree. And it was still very easy for him to see in their baneful effects the collective wages of collective sin, for which the only remedy was collective repentance. Yet it was also possible for a few, more realistic in their approach and secular in their orientation, to regard them as malfunctions within a highly complex mechanism, one that could be studied in and for itself. Ethical in its implications—the most secular of the Tudor writers was as ready as his evangelical contemporaries to recognize the moral underpinning and purpose of society—its dynamics could be considered morally neutral, subject to intelligent manipulation, even capable of being harnessed in such a way as to enhance the wealth of the country and improve its position among competing powers.

Viewed in this context, the prince becomes rather the head of a policy-making council than the political artist of the Machiavellian tradition; the materials he and his advisers must work with are the data of social analysis rather than the lessons to be derived from the political decisions of historical personages. And, in his increasing awareness of social process, with its concomitant demand for constructive policy, the Tudor commentator was, in fact if not by intent, drifting toward a concept of sovereignty more nearly modern than that which it had been possible for medieval theorists to envisage: the difference between medieval and modern concepts of sovereignty depends, after all, on differences in social as well as in political consciousness, in particular upon the degree to which it was possible to recognize in society a mecha-nism of moving forces.

What we can see taking shape in the minds of these articulate Tudor Englishmen as they sought to understand the workings of their society is a new perspective, a new way of looking at the social scene, a new sense of direction in their approach to social problems, a change not so much in the content of their thought or in its formal frame of reference as in its character, in the nature of the questions asked and the areas in which the answers are sought. Fundamental to this re-orientation is a more mature appreciation of the phenomena of change. The more or less consistent refusal of the medieval commentator to discuss positive remedial measures can be explained only in part by his conviction that moral causes were the only ones with which such critics as himself need be concerned. It must also be explained in relation to his view of society as a static organism, analogous to the human body and subject to similar oscillations between health and disease, but impelled by no inner dynamism toward objectives of worldly improvement. The purpose of society was, he believed, to make possible such a life on earth as would prepare its individual members for the life beyond; its government had, as its primary duty, the maintenance of peace and justice, not the increase of its wealth and power. It had, to be sure, a life history like all organisms, but it was a history providentially moved, leaving little place for man's creative capacity. In its structure, it remained a static organism, and for practical purposes it must be treated as such.

Now it is in just this area of practical purposes that the Tudor view of society begins to change. At first glance the Tudor "commonweal" seems little different from the "body politic" of medieval tradition— indeed in the language of its exponents the two terms are pretty much synonymous. But for practical purposes the commonweal was soon made to serve as the focal point for realistic and sometimes very penetrating analysis of those social forces of which the sixteenth-century observer was becoming increasingly aware. Even its conservatism, the apparent concern for stability expressed by its spokesmen, implies a profound consciousness of change. And in the most original of the "commonwealth" pamphlets, its conservative character all but disappears, its traditional phrases quite belied by a new spirit of inquiry and a willingness to accept the facts of change for what they are, even to make constructive use of them. It came increasingly to be examined in relation to the changing actualities of time and place and the diversity of cultures. In the minds of its exponents the "very and true commonweal" becomes less an ideal to be recaptured than one to be sought in the future and worked for by intelligent policy.

BIBLIOGRAPHY

LIST OF ABBREVIATIONS

CR	*Contemporary Review*
E.E.T.S.	Early English Text Society
O.S.	Old Series
E.S.	Extra Series
EcHR	*Economic History Review*
EHR	*English Historical Review*
HLQ	*Huntington Library Quarterly*
HTR	*Harvard Theological Review*
JBS	*Journal of British Studies*
JEGP	*Journal of English and Germanic Philology*
JHI	*Journal of the History of Ideas*
JMH	*Journal of Modern History*
JPE	*Journal of Political Economy*
LP	*Letters and Papers, Foreign and Domestic, of the Reign of Henry VIII*, ed. Brewer and Gardiner
PBA	*Proceedings of the British Academy*
PMLA	*Publications of the Modern Language Association*
QJE	*Quarterly Journal of Economics*
RN	*Renaissance News*
SP	*Studies in Philology*
STC	Pollard and Redgrave, *Short Title Catalogue*
TRHS	*Transactions of the Royal Historical Society*
UTQ	*University of Toronto Quarterly*

CHECK LIST OF WORKS CITED

Adam Davy's Five Dreams about Edward II, ed. F. J. Furnivall. (E.E.T.S., O.S., No. 69), 1878.

Adams, R. P. *The Better Part of Valor.* Seattle, 1962.

Allen, J. W. *A History of Political Thought in the Sixteenth Century.* London, 1928.

Ames, Russell. *Citizen Thomas More and his Utopia.* Princeton, 1948.

Antonelli, Etienne. *Études d'économie humaniste.* Paris, 1958.

Archbold, W. A. J. "A Manuscript Treatise on the Coinage by John Pryse, 1553," *EHR*, XIII (October, 1898), 709-710.

[Armstrong, Clement.] *How the Comen People may be set to worke an Order of a Comen Welth*, in Pauli, *Drei volkswirthschaftliche Denkshriften* (q.v.).

——. *Howe to Reforme the Realme in settying them to worke to restore Tillage*, in Tawney and Power, *Tudor Economic Documents.* III (q.v.).

——. *A treatise concerning the Staple*, in ibid.

Ascham, Roger. *A Report and Discourse . . . of the affaires and state of Germany*, etc., in *English Works*, ed. W. A. Wright. Cambridge, 1904.

——. *The Scholemaster*, in ibid.

Ashby, George. *The Active Policy of a Prince*, in *The Poems of George Ashby*, ed. Mary Bateson. (E.E.T.S., E.S., No. 76) 1899.

Aspin, Isabel S. T. (ed.). *Anglo-Norman Political Songs.* (Anglo-Norman Texts Society, XI) Oxford, 1953.

Aston, M. E. "Lollardy and Sedition, 1381-1431," *Past and Present*, No. 17 (April, 1960), 1-44.

Aurner, Nellie. *Caxton, Mirror of Fifteenth-Century Letters.* Boston, 1926.

Bailey, D. S. *Thomas Becon and the Reformation of the Church in England.* London, 1952.

Bale, John. *The Dramatic Writings of John Bale*, ed. J. S. Farmer. London, 1907.

Baron, Hans. *The Crisis of the Early Italian Renaissance.* Princeton, 1955.

——. "Fifteenth-Century Civilization and the Renaissance," in *The New Cambridge Modern History.* Cambridge, 1957.

——. "Moot Problems of Renaissance Interpretation: An Answer to Wallace K. Ferguson," *JHI*, XIX (January, 1958), 26-34.

——. "The Querelle of the Ancients and the Moderns as a Problem for Renaissance Scholarship," *ibid.*, XX (January, 1959), 3-22.

——. "Secularization of Widsom and Political Humanism in the Renaissance," *ibid.*, XXI (January-March, 1960), 131-150.

Baskerville, C. R. "Sir Richard Morison as the Author of two Anonymous Tracts on Sedition," *Library*, 4th ser. (1936), No. 1, 83-87.

Baumer, F. L. *The Early Tudor Theory of Kingship.* New Haven, 1940.

——. "Thomas Starkey and Marsilius of Padua," *Politica*, II (November, 1936), 188-205.

Becon, Thomas. *The Fortress of the Faithful*, in *The Catechism of Thomas Becon*, ed. J. Ayre. (Parker Society.) 1844.

——. *The Jewel of Joy*, in ibid.

——. *The Policy of War*, in *Early Works*, ed J. Ayre. (Parker Society.) 1843.

Bennett, H. S. *English Books and their Readers, 1475-1557.* Cambridge, 1952.

Bennett, J. A. W. "The Date of the B-text of *Piers Plowman*," *Medium Aevum*, XII (1943), 55-64.

Berges, W. *Die Furstenspiegel des hohen und späten Mittelalters.* Leipzig, 1938.

Bindoff, S. T. "Clement Armstrong and his Treatises of the Commonweal," *EcHR*, XIV (1944), 64-83.

Bland, A. E., P. A. Brown and R. H. Tawney. *English Economic History, Select Documents.* London, 1915. *Speculum*

Bloomfield, M. W. "Present State of *Piers Plowman* Studies," *Journal of Medieval Studies*, XIV (April, 1939), 215-232.

———. *Piers Plowman as a Fourteenth-century Apocalypse.* New Brunswick, 1962.

Blundeville, Thomas. *The True Order and Method of Writing and Reading Histories*, ed. H. G. Dick, *HLQ*, III (January, 1940), 149-170.

The Boke of Noblesse, ed. J. G. Nichols. London, 1860.

Bouwsma, W. J. "The Politics of Commynes," *JMH*, XXIII (December, 1951), 315-328.

Bradner, L. *Edmund Spenser and the Faerie Queene.* Chicago, 1948.

Brenner, Y. S. "The Inflation of Prices in Early Sixteenth-Century England," *EcHR*, 2nd ser., XIV (December, 1961), 225-239.

Bright, A. H. *New Light on Piers Plowman.* Oxford, 1928.

Brinkelow, Henry. *The Complaynt of Roderyck Mors*, ed. J. M. Cowper. (E.E.T.S., E.S., No. 22) 1874.

Bühler, C. F. " 'Wirk alle thyng by conseil,' " *Speculum*, XXIV (July, 1949), 410-412.

Bury, J. B. *The Idea of Progress.* New York, 1932.

Bush, Douglas. *The Renaissance and English Humanism.* Toronto, 1939.

———. "Tudor Humanism and Henry VIII," *UTQ*, VII (1938), 162-177.

Cam, Helen. "The Legislators of Medieval England," *PBA*, XXXI (1945), 127-150.

———. "The Relation of English Members of Parliament to their Constituencies in the Fourteenth Century: A Neglected Text," in *L'organization corporative du Moyen Roman Age à la fin de l'Ancien Régime.* Louvain, 1939. III. Reprinted in *Liberties and Communities in Medieval England.* Cambridge, 1944.

Carlyle, R. W. and A. J. *A History of Medieval Political Theory in the West.* 8 vols. Cambridge, 1936.

Carré, M. H. *Phases of Thought in England.* Oxford, 1949.

Cary, George. *The Medieval Alexander.* Cambridge, 1956.

Caspari, Fritz. *Humanism and the Social Order in Tudor England.* Chicago, 1954.

Cecil, William. *Considerations Delivered to the Parliament*, reprinted in Tawney and Power, *Tudor Economic Documents.* I (q.v.).

Certain Causes Gathered Together Wherein is Showed the Decay of England, ed. J. M. Cowper, in *Four Supplications.* (E.E.T.S., E.S., No. 13) 1871. Reprinted in Dunham and Pargellis, *Complaint and Reform in England* (q.v.).

Chadwick, D. *Social Life in the Days of Piers Plowman.* Cambridge, 1922.

Chalk, A. F. "The Rise of Economic Individualism," *JPE*, LIX (August, 1951), 332-347.

Chambers, R. W. *Thomas More.* New York, 1935.

Cheke, John. *The Hurt of Sedicion Howe Greuous it is to a Communewelth.* London, 1549. Reprinted in *Holinshed's Chronicles*, ed. H. Ellis. 6 vols. London, 1807-1808. III, 987-1011.

Chester, A. G. *Hugh Latimer: Apostle to the English.* Philadelphia, 1954.

Cholmeley, William. *Request and Suite of a True-Hearted Englishman*, ed. W. J. Thomas. (Camden Society.) 1853. Reprinted in Tawney and Power, *Tudor Economic Documents*. III (q.v.).

Chrimes, S. B. *An Introduction to the Administrative History of Medieval England*. New York, 1952.

——. *English Constitutional Ideas of the Fifteenth Century*. Cambridge, 1936.

——. "Sir John Fortescue and his Theory of Dominion," *TRHS*, 4th Ser., XVII (1934), 117-147.

Clarke, M. V. *Medieval Representation and Consent*. London, 1936.

Coffman, G. R. "John Gower in His Most Significant Role," in *Elizabethan Studies and other Essays in Honor of George F. Reynolds*. ("University of Colorado Studies," Ser. B. Vol. II, No. 4.) 1945.

——. "John Gower, Mentor for Royalty: Richard II," *PMLA*, LXIX (September, 1954), 954-964.

Coghill, N. H. K. "The Pardon of Piers Plowman," *PBA*, XXX (1944), 303-357.

Coles, P. "The Interpretation of More's 'Utopia,'" *Hibbert Journal*, LVI (July, 1958), 365-370.

Cranmer, Thomas. *Miscellaneous Writings*, ed. J. E. Cox. (Parker Society.) Cambridge, 1846.

Crotch, W. J. B. *The Prologues and Epilogues of William Caxton*. (E.E.T.S., O.S., No. 176) London, 1928.

Crowley, Robert. *An informacion and peticion agaynst the oppressours of the pore Commons*, in *Select Works of Robert Crowley*, ed. J. M. Cowper. (E.E.T.S., E.S., No. 15) 1872.

——. *One and Thyrtie Epigrammes*, etc., in *ibid*.

——. *The Voyce of the Laste Trumpet*, in *ibid*.

——. *The Way to Wealth*, in *ibid*.

Cuttino, G. P. "King's Clerks and the Community of the Realm," *Medieval Representation in Theory and Practice, Speculum*, XXIX, No. 2, Part 2 (April, 1954), 395-409.

Darby, H. S. *Hugh Latimer*. London, 1953.

The Decaye of England by the great multitude of shepe, in *Four Supplications* (q.v.).

The Declamacion of Noblesse, ed. R. J. Mitchell, in *John Tiptoft*. London, 1928.

De Roover, Raymond. *Gresham on Foreign Exchange*. Cambridge, Mass., 1949.

——. "Scholastic Economics: Survival and Lasting Influence from the Sixteenth Century to Adam Smith," *QJE*, LXIX (May, 1955), 161-190.

Dewar, Mary. *Sir Thomas Smith: A Tudor Intellectual in Office*. London, 1964.

Discourse of the Common Weal of this Realm of England. See Smith, Sir Thomas.

Donaldson, E. Talbot. *Piers Plowman, The C-Text and its Poet*. New Haven, 1949.

Donner, H. W. *Introduction to Utopia*. London, 1945.

Dudley, Edmund. *The Tree of Commonwealth*, ed. D. M. Brodie. Cambridge, 1948.

Dunham, W. H., and S. Pargellis. *Complaint and Reform in England*. New York, 1938.

Elton, G. R. "An Early Tudor Poor Law," *EcHR*, 2nd ser., VI (August, 1953), 55-67.

——. "State Planning in Early Tudor England," *ibid.*, 2nd ser., XIII (April, 1961), 433-439.

——. *The Tudor Revolution in Government: Administrative Changes in the Reign of Henry VIII*. New York, 1953.

Elyot, Sir Thomas. *A Preservative agaynste Deth*. London, 1545.

——. *The Boke named the Governour*, ed. H. H. S. Croft. 2 vols. London, 1883.

——. *Of the Knowledge which Maketh a Wise Man*, ed. E. J. Howard. Oxford, Ohio, 1946.

Emerson, E. H. "Reginald Pecock: Christian Rationalist," *Speculum*, XXI (April, 1956), 235⁄242.

Erasmus, Desiderius. *Erasmus Against War*, ed. J. W. Mackail. Boston, 1907.

Feavearyear, A. E. *The Pound Sterling: A History of English Money*. 2nd ed. Oxford, 1963.

Ferguson, Arthur B. *The Indian Summer of English Chivalry*. Durham, N. C., 1960.

Ferguson, W. K. *Europe in transition, 1300⁄1520*. Boston, 1962.

Fish, Simon. *A Supplicacyon for the Beggars*, ed. F. J. Furnivall, in *Four Supplications* (q.v.). Reprinted in Dunham and Pargellis (q.v.).

Fisher, F. J. "Commercial Trends and Policy in Sixteenth⁄Century England," *EcHR*, 1st ser., X (November, 1946), 95⁄117.

Fisher, John H. *John Gower, Moral Philosopher and Friend of Chaucer*. New York, 1964.

Forrest, William. *Pleasaunt Poesye of Princelie Practise*, ed. (in extract) S. J. Herrtage. (E.E.T.S., E.S., No. 32) 1878.

Fortescue, Sir John. *De Laudibus Legum Angliae*, ed. and trans. S. B. Chrimes. Cam⁄bridge, 1942.

——. *De Natura Legis Naturae*, in *The Works of Sir John Fortescue*, ed. Lord Clairmont. London, 1869.

——. *The Governance of England*, ed. C. Plummer. Oxford, 1885. Reprinted in W. H. Dunham and S. Pargellis, *Complaint and Reform in England* (q.v.).

Four Supplications, 1529⁄1553 A.D., ed. T. J. Furnivall and J. M. Cowper. (E.E.T.S., E.S., No. 13) 1871.

Fowler, D. C. *Piers the Plowman: Literary Relations of the A and B Texts*. Seattle, 1961.

Fox, Edward. *Opus eximium, de vera differentia regiae potestatis et ecclesiasticae*. London, 1534.

Frank, R. W. *Piers Plowman and the Scheme of Salvation*. New Haven, 1957.

Franklin, Julian H. *Jean Bodin and the Sixteenth⁄Century Revolution in the Methodology of Law and History*. New York, 1963.

Fulgens and Lucres. A Fifteenth⁄Century Secular Play, ed. F. S. Boas and A. W. Reed Oxford, 1926.

Fuller, Thomas. *History of the Worthies of England*. London, 1652.

Galbraith, V. H. "Nationalism and Language in Medieval England," *TRHS*, 4th ser., XXIII (1941), 113⁄129.

Gardiner, Stephen. *De Vera Obedientia Oratio*, ed. P. Janelle, in *Obedience in Church and State*. Cambridge, 1930.

Gee, J. A. *The Life and Works of Thomas Lupset*. New Haven, 1928.

Gilbert, A. H. *Machiavelli's Prince and its Forerunners*. Durham, N. C., 1938.

——. "Notes on the Influence of the *Secretum Secretorum*," *Speculum*, III (January, 1928), 84⁄98.

Gilbert, Felix. "The Humanist Concept of the Prince and the *Prince* of Machiavelli," *JMH*, XI (December, 1939), 449⁄483.

——. "Sir John Fortescue's *Dominium Regale et Politicum*," *Medievalia et Humanistica*, II (January, 1944), 88⁄97.

Gilbert, Sir Humphrey. *Queene Elizabethes Achademy*, ed. F. J. Furnivall. (E.E.T.S., E.S., No. 8) 1869.

Gilmore, M. P. "*Fides et Eruditio*: Erasmus and the Study of History," in *Teachers of*

History, Essays in Honor of Lawrence Bradford Packard. Ithaca, 1953. Reprinted in his *Humanists and Jurists: Six Studies in the Renaissance.* Cambridge, Mass., 1963.

Gower, John. *The Complete Works of John Gower,* ed. G. C. Macaulay. 4 vols. Oxford, 1899-1902.

———. *The Major Latin Works of John Gower,* ed. and trans. E. W. Stockton. Seattle, 1962.

Gundersheimer, W. L. "Louis Le Roy's Humanistic Optimism," *JHI,* XXIII (July-September, 1962), 324-339.

[Hales, John.] *Causes of Dearth,* in E. Lamond (ed.), *A Discourse of the Common Weal,* introd.

Hales, John. *The defence of John Hales ayenst certeyn sclaundres* etc., in *ibid.*

Harbison, E. H. *The Christian Scholar in the Age of the Reformation.* New York, 1956.

Harris, V. *All Coherence Gone.* Chicago, 1949.

Hawes, Stephen. *The Pastime of Pleasure,* ed. W. E. Mead. (E.E.T.S., O.S., No. 173) 1928.

Hay, Denys. *The Italian Renaissance in its Historical Background.* Cambridge, 1961.

Heckscher, E. F. *Mercantilism.* Trans. Mendel Schapiro. 2 vols. London, 1935.

Herrtage, S. J. (ed.). *England in the Reign of Henry VIII: Starkey's Life and Letters.* (E.E.T.S., E.S., No. 32) 1878.

Hexter, J. H. "The Education of the Aristocracy in the Renaissance," *JMH,* XXII (March, 1950), 1-20.

———. "*Il Principe* and *Lo Stato,*" *Studies in the Renaissance,* IV (1957), 113-138.

———. *More's Utopia: The Biography of an Idea.* London, 1952.

———. "Thomas More: On the Margins of Modernity," *JBS,* I (November, 1961), 20-37.

Hinton, R. W. K. "English Constitutional Theories from Sir John Fortescue to Sir John Eliot," *EHR,* LXXV (July, 1960), 410-425.

Hoccleve, Thomas. *The Regiment of Princes,* in *Hoccleve's Works,* ed. F. J. Furnivall. (E.E.T.S., E.S., No. 72) 1897.

Holinshed, Raphael. *Chronicles of England, Scotland, and Ireland,* ed. H. Ellis. 6 vols. London, 1807-8.

Holmes, G. A. "The 'Libel of English Policy,'" *EHR,* LXXVI (April, 1961), 193-216.

Hooper, John. *Early Writings,* ed. S. Carr. (Parker Society.) Cambridge, 1852.

Hoopes, Robert. *Right Reason in the English Renaissance.* Cambridge, Mass., 1962.

Hughes, E. "The Authorship of the *Discourse of the Common Weal,*" *Bulletin of the John Rylands Library,* XXI (1937), 167-175.

Huppé, B. F. "The A-text of Piers Plowman and the Norman Wars," *PMLA,* LIV (March, 1939), 37-64.

———. "The Authorship of the A and B texts of *Piers Plowman,*" *Speculum,* XXII (October, 1947), 578-620.

———. "The Date of the B-text of *Piers Plowman,*" *Studies in Philosophy,* XXXVIII (January, 1941), 34-44.

Jacob, E. F. *Essays in the Conciliar Epoch.* Manchester, 1943.

———. *The Fifteenth Century, 1399-1485.* Oxford, 1961.

———. *Studies in the Period of Baronial Reform and Rebellion, 1258-1267.* Oxford, 1925.

Janelle, Pierre. *L'Angleterre Catholique à la veille du Schisme.* Paris, 1935.

Johnson, E. A. J. *The Predecessors of Adam Smith.* New York, 1937.

Joliffe, J. E. A. *The Constitutional History of Medieval England.* London, 1937.

Jones, R. F. *Ancients and Moderns.* St. Louis, 1936.

Jordan, W. K. *Philanthropy in England, 1480-1660.* New York, 1959.

Jusserand, J. J. *Piers Plowman, a Contribution to the History of English Mysticism.* New York, 1894.

Kail, J., ed. *Twenty-six Political and other Poems.* (E.E.T.S., O.S., No. 124) 1904.

Kantorowicz, E. H. *The King's Two Bodies.* Princeton, 1957.

Keeney, Barnaby C. "Military Service and the Development of Nationalism in England, 1271-1327,"*Speculum*, XXII (October, 1947), 534-549.

Keller, A. C. "Zilsel, the Artisans, and the Idea of Progress in the Renaissance," *JHI*, XI (April, 1950), 235-240.

Kingsford, C. L. *English Historical Literature in the 15th Century.* Oxford, 1913.

———. *Prejudice and Promise in Fifteenth Century England.* Oxford, 1925.

Kleineke, W. *Englishe Fürstenspiegel vom Policraticus Johanns von Salisbury bis zum Basilikon Doron König Jacobs I.* Halle, 1937.

Knappen, M. M. *Tudor Puritanism.* Chicago, 1939.

Koller, K. "Two Elizabethan Expressions of the Idea of Mutability," *SP*, XXXV (1938), 228-237.

Kristeller, P. O. *The Classics and Renaissance Thought.* Cambridge, Mass., 1955.

———. "Studies on Renaissance Humanism during the Last Twenty Years," *Studies in the Renaissance*, IX (1962) 7-30.

Ladner, G. B. *The Idea of Reform.* Cambridge, Mass., 1959.

The Lamentacion of England. London, 1558.

Lapsley, G. T. *Crown, Community and Parliament in the Later Middle Ages.* Oxford, 1951.

Latimer, Hugh. *The Works of Hugh Latimer*, ed. S. E. Corrie. 2 vols. (Parker Society.) 1844, 1845.

———. *Seven Sermons Before Edward VI*, ed. E. Arber. London, 1895.

Levisse, E. *Histoire de France.* Paris, 1911.

Le Branchu, Jean-Yves. *Écrits notables sur la monnaie.* Paris, 1934.

Lehmberg, S. E. *Thomas Elyot, Tudor Humanist.* Austin, 1960.

Leonard, E. M. *The Early History of English Poor Relief.* Cambridge, 1900.

Letters and Papers, Foreign and Domestic, of the Reign of Henry VIII, ed. J. S. Brewer and James Gardiner. 21 vols. London, 1862-1910.

Lever, Thomas. *A Fruitful Sermon made in Paules Churche . . . 1550.* London, 1550.

———. *A Sermon preached the thyrd Sondaye in Lente . . . 1550.* London, 1550.

———. *Three fruitful Sermons made by Thomas Lever . . . 1550.* London, 1572.

Lewis, C. S. *English Literature in the Sixteenth Century.* Oxford, 1954.

Lewis, P. S. "The Failure of the French Medieval Estates," *Past and Present*, No. 23 (November, 1962), 3-24.

The Libelle of Englishe Polycye, ed. Sir George Warner. Oxford, 1926.

Lipson, E. *The Economic History of England.* 3 vols. London, 1956.

Lovejoy, A. O. *The Great Chain of Being.* Cambridge, Mass., 1936.

——— and George Boas. *Primitivism and Related Ideas in Antiquity.* Baltimore, 1935.

Lydgate, John. *The Minor Poems of John Lydgate*, ed. H. N. MacCracken. (E.E.T.S., O.S., No. 192.) 1934.

McFarlane, K. B. "Bastard Feudalism," *Bulletin of the Institute of Historical Research*, XX (May and November, 1945), 161-180.

McIlwain, C. H. *Constitutionalism, Ancient and Modern.* Ithaca, 1947.

———. *The Growth of Political Thought in the West.* New York, 1932.

McLaughlin, T. P. "The Teaching of the Canonists on Usury," *Medieval Studies*, I (1939), 81-147, II (1940), 1-22.

Major, J. M. *Sir Thomas Elyot and Renaissance Humanism*. Lincoln, 1964.

Major, J. Russell. *Representative Institutions in Renaissance France, 1421-1559*. Madison, 1960.

Marshall, William (trans.). *The Forme and Maner of Subvention or Helping for Pore People, Devysed and Practysed i the Cytie of Hypres in Flanders*, in *Some Early Tracts on Poor Relief*, ed. F. R. Salter (q.v.). London, 1936.

Mason, A. R. "Rebellion in Norfolk, 1549," *CR* (March, 1959), pp. 164-167.

Mason, H. A. *Humanism and Poetry in the Early Tudor Period*. New York, 1959.

Mesnard, Pierre. *L'essor de la philosophie politique au XVIᵉ siècle*. Paris, 1936.

The Mirror of Justices, ed. and trans. W. J. Whittaker. (Seldon Society, VII.) 1895.

Mohl, Ruth. "Theories of Monarchy in *Mum and the Sothsegger*," *PMLA*, LXV (March, 1944), 26-44.

——. *The Three Estates in Medieval and Renaissance Literature*. New York, 1933.

Moisant, J. *De Speculo Regis Edwardi III . . . quem . . . conscripsit Simon Islip*. Paris, 1891.

Mommsen, T. E. "St. Augustine and the Idea of Progress," *JHI*, XII (June, 1951), 346-374.

More, Sir Thomas. *The Dialogue Concerning Tyndale by Sir Thomas More*, ed. W. E. Campbell. London, 1927.

——. *Supplication of the Poor Souls in Purgatory*, ed. Sister Mary Thecla. Westminster, Md., 1950.

——. *Utopia*. (Everyman Edition.) London, 1937.

Morgan, A. E. *Nowhere was Somewhere*. Chapel Hill, 1946.

Morison, Sir Richard. *An Exhortation to Styrre all Englyshmen to the Defence of theyr Countrye*. London, 1539.

[——.] *A lamentation in whiche is shewed what Ruyne and destruction cometh of seditious rebellyon*. London, 1536.

[——.] *A Remedy for Sedition*, ed. E. M. Cox. London, 1933.

Morris, Christopher. *Political Thought in England: Tyndale to Hooker*. London, 1953.

Morton, A. L. *The English Utopia*. London, 1952.

Mosse, G. L. "Change and Continuity in the Tudor Constitution," *Speculum*, XXII (January, 1947), 18-28.

——. "Sir John Fortescue and the Problem of Papal Power," *Medievalia et Humanistica*, VII (1952), 89-94.

——. *The Struggle for Sovereignty in England*. East Lansing, 1950.

Mum and the Sothsegger, ed. M. Day and R. Steele. (E.E.T.S., O.S., No. 199.) London, 1936.

Nelson, B. N. *The Idea of Usury*. Princeton, 1949.

Oberman, H. A. "Some Notes on the Theology of Nominalism: With Attention to its Relation to the Renaissance," *Harvard Theological Review*, LIII (January, 1960), 47-79.

Owst, G. R. *Literature and Pulpit in Medieval England*. Cambridge, 1923.

Panofsky, Erwin. *Renaissance and Renascences in Western Art*. Stockholm, 1960.

Pauli, R. *Drei volkswirthschaftliche Denkschriften aus der Zeit Heinrichs VIII von England*. Göttingen, 1878.

Pecock, Reginald. *The Repressor of Over Much Blaming of the Clergy*, ed. C. Babington. (Rolls Series.) 1860.

————. *Reule of Crysten Religioun*, ed. W. C. Greet. (E.E.T.S., O.S., No. 171) 1926.

Peter, John. *Complaint and Satire in Early English Literature.* Oxford, 1956.

Phillimore, J. S. "The Arrest of Humanism in England," *Dublin Review*, CLIII (1913), 1-26.

Piers the Plowman, ed. W. W. Skeat. 2 vols. London, 1924.

Pocock, J. G. A. *The Ancient Constitution and the Feudal Law.* Cambridge, 1957.

Policies to Reduce this Realme of Englande vnto a Prosperous Wealthe and Estate, in Tawney and Power (q.v.). III, 311-345.

Pollard, A. F. *England under Protector Somerset.* London, 1900.

————. *The Evolution of Parliament.* London, 1934.

Porter, H. C. *Reformation and Reaction in Tudor Cambridge.* Cambridge, 1958.

Postan, M. M. "The Fifteenth Century," *EcHR*, IX (1939), 160-167.

————. "Some Social Consequences of the Hundred Years War," *EcHR*, XII (1942), 1-12.

Power, Eileen. *The Wool Trade in English Medieval History.* Oxford, 1941.

Power, Eileen and M. M. Postan (eds.). *Studies in English Trade in the Fifteenth Century.* London, 1953.

Powicke, F. M. *Henry III and the Lord Edward, the Community of the Realm in the Thirteenth Century.* 2 vols. Oxford, 1947.

————. *Ways of Medieval Life and Thought.* London, 1949.

Previté-Orton, C. W. "Marsilius of Padua," *PBA*, XXI (1935), 137-183.

————. *Political Satire in English Poetry.* Cambridge, 1910.

Pyers Plowmans Exhortation unto the Lordes, Knights and Burgoysses of the Parlyamenthouse. London, 1550.

Quirk, R. "Langland's Use of Kind Wit and Inwit," *JEGP*, LII (April, 1553), 182-188.

Rice, E. F., Jr. *The Renaissance Idea of Wisdom.* Cambridge, Mass., 1958.

Richardson, H. G. "The Commons in Medieval Politics," *TRHS*, 4th ser., XXVIII (1946), 21-45.

Ritter, Gerhard. *The Corrupting Influence of Power.* Trans. F. W. Pick. London, 1952.

Robbins, Rossell Hope. *Historical Poems of the XIVth and XVth Centuries.* New York, 1959.

Robertson, D. W. and B. F. Huppé. *Piers Plowman and Scriptural Interpretation.* Princeton, 1951.

Robertson, H. M. *Aspects of the Rise of Economic Individualism.* Cambridge, 1933.

Rose-Troup, Frances. *The Western Rebellion of 1549.* London, 1913.

Rotuli Parliamentorum. 6 vols. London, 1767-1777.

Roy, W. and J. Barlow. *Rede me and be nott wrothe*, ed. E. Arber. London, 1871.

Ryan, L. V. *Roger Ascham.* Palo Alto, 1963.

St. German, Christopher. *The Doctor and Student*, ed. W. Muchall. Cincinnati, 1874.

Salter, F. R. (ed.). *Some Early Tracts on Poor Relief.* London, 1926.

Sampson, Richard. *Oratio quae docet hortatur admonet omnes potissimum Anglos regiae dignitati cum primis ut obediant*, etc. London, 1533.

Sandys, Edwin. *Sermons*, ed. J. Ayre. (Parker Society.) 1841.

Schenk, Wilhelm. *Reginald Pole: Cardinal of England.* London, 1950.

Schmidt, A. J. "Thomas Wilson, Tudor Scholar-Statesman," *HLQ*, XX (May, 1957), 205-218.

———. "Thomas Wilson and the Tudor Commonwealth: An Essay in Civic Humanism," *ibid.*, XXIII (November, 1959), 49-60.

Schumpeter, J. A. *History of Economic Analysis.* New York, 1954.

Secrees of Old Philosoffres, ed. R. Steele. (E.E.T.S., E.S., No. 66.) 1894.

Shephard, M. A. "The Political and Constitutional Theory of Sir John Fortescue," in *Essays in History and Political Theory in Honor of Charles Howard McIlwain.* Cambridge, Mass., 1936.

Siebert, F. S. *Freedom of the Press in England, 1476-1776.* Urbana, 1952.

Skeel, C. A. J. "The Influence of the Writings of Sir John Fortescue," *TRHS*, 3rd ser., X (1916), 77-114.

Skelton, John. *The Poetical Works of John Skelton,* ed. A. Dyce. London, 1843.

Smith, L. B. "English Treason Trials and Confessions in the Sixteenth Century," *JHI*, XV (October, 1954), 471-498.

———. *Tudor Prelates and Politics, 1536-1558.* Princeton, 1953.

Smith, Sir Thomas. *De Republica Anglorum,* ed. L. Alston. Cambridge, 1906.

———. *A Discourse for Demonstrating the Reduction of Roman Coins to Our Money,* in John Strype, *The Life of the Learned Sir Thomas Smith* (q.v.).

[———.] *A Discourse of the Common Weal of this Realm of England,* ed. Elizabeth Lamond. Cambridge, 1893.

[———.] *Memorandum for the Understanding of the Exchange,* in R. de Roover, *Gresham on Foreign Exchange* (q.v.).

The Song of Lewes, ed. C. L. Kingsford. Oxford, 1890.

Spiers, J. *Medieval English Poetry.* London, 1957.

Starkey, Thomas. *A Dialogue between Cardinal Pole and Thomas Lupset,* ed. J. W. Cowper. (E.E.T.S., E.S., No. 12) 1871. In modern spelling, ed. K. M. Burton. London, 1948.

Staton, W. F., Jr. "Roger Ascham's Theory of History Writing," *SP*, LVI (April, 1959), 125-137.

Stillwell, Gardiner. "John Gower and the Last Years of Edward III," *SP*, XLV (July, 1948) 454-471.

Strathmann, E. A. "The Idea of Progress: Some Elizabethan Considerations," *RN*, II (Spring, 1949), 23-25.

Strype, John. *Ecclesiastical Memorials.* 7 vols. London, 1816.

———. *The Life of the Learned Sir Thomas Smith.* Oxford, 1820.

Suggett, Helen. "The Use of French in England in the Later Middle Ages," *TRHS*, 4th ser., XXVIII (1946), 61-83.

A Supplication of the Poore Commons, in *Four Supplications* (q.v.).

A Supplycation to our most Soveraigne Lorde Kynge Henry the Eyght, in *Four Supplications* (q.v.).

Tait, J. "On the date and authorship of the 'Speculum Regis Edwardi,'" *EHR*, LXI (January, 1901), 110-115.

Talbert, E. W. *The Problem of Order.* Chapel Hill, N. C., 1962.

Tawney, R. H. *The Agrarian Problem in the Sixteenth Century.* London, 1912.

———. *Religion and the Rise of Capitalism.* (Penguin edition.) 1947.

Tawney, R. H. and Eileen Power (eds.). *Tudor Economic Documents.* 3 vols. London, 1924.

Taylor, F. "Some Manuscripts of the *Lybelle of Englyshe Polycye,*" *Bulletin of the John Rylands Library*, XXIV (1940), 376-418.

Tersen, A. *John Hales, Économiste Anglais de milieu de XVIᵉ Siècle.* Avallon, 1907.

Thomas, William. *Discourses,* in John Strype, *Ecclesiatical Memorials* (q.v.), VI.

——. *The Historie of Italie.* London, 1549.

Thornley, Isabel. "The Treason Legislation of Henry VIII, 1531-1534," *TRHS*, 3rd ser., XI (1917), 87-123.

Three Prose Versions of the Secreta Secretorum, ed. R. Steele. (E.E.T.S., E.S., No. 74.) 1898.

Tierney, Brian. *Medieval Poor Law.* Berkeley and Los Angeles, 1959.

Tillyard, E. M. W. *The Elizabethan World Picture.* New York, 1944.

——. *The English Renaissance: Fact or Fiction.* Baltimore, 1952.

Tiptoft, John. *The Declamation of Noblesse,* in R. J. Mitchell, *John Tiptoft.* London, 1938.

Tout, T. F. *France and England: Their Relations in the Middle Ages and Now.* London, 1922.

Tract on the Office of Steward, in L. W. V. Harcourt, *His Grace the Steward and Trial of Peers.* London, 1907.

Tusser, Thomas. *A Hundreth Good Points of Husbandrie.* London, 1557.

Tuveson, E. L. *Millenium and Utopia: A Study in the Background of the Idea of Progress.* Berkeley and Los Angeles, 1949.

Unwin, G., (ed.). *Finance and Trade under Edward III.* Manchester, 1918.

Vox Populi Vox Dei, in *Ballads from Manuscripts,* ed. F. J. Furnivall. 2 vols. (Ballad Society.) 1868-1872, I, 124-146.

Walsingham, Thomas. *Historica Anglicana,* ed. H. T. Riley. 2 vols. (Rolls Series.) 1863, 1864.

Weisinger, H. "Ideas of History during the Renaissance," *JHI,* VI (October, 1945), 415-435.

Weiss, Roberto. *Humanism in England during the Fifteenth Century.* Oxford, 1941.

——. "Learning and Education in Western Europe from 1470 to 1520," in *The New Cambridge Modern History.* Cambridge, 1957.

White, H. B. "Bacon, Bruno, and the Eternal Recurrence," *Social Research,* XXV (Winter, 1958), 449-468.

White, Helen C. *Social Criticism in the Popular Religious Literature of the Sixteenth Century.* New York, 1944.

Whiting, B. J. "The Vows of the Heron," *Speculum,* XX (July, 1945), 261-278.

Wickert, Maria. *Studien zu John Gower.* Koln, 1953.

Wilkinson, B. *Constitutional History of Medieval England.* 3 vols. London, 1958.

——. "English Politics and Politicians of the Thirteenth and Fourteenth Centuries," *Speculum,* XXX (January, 1955), 37-48.

——. "The Political Revolution of the Thirteenth and Fourteenth Centuries," *Speculum,* XXIV (October, 1949), 502-509.

Wilks, Michael. *The Problem of Sovereignty in the Later Middle Ages.* Cambridge, 1963.

Williams, G. H. *The Radical Reformation.* Philadelphia, 1962.

Williams, Penry, and G. L. Harriss. "A Revolution in Tudor History," *Past and Present,* No. 25 (July, 1963), pp. 3-58.

Wilson, Thomas. *Arte of Rhetorique.* London, 1553.

——. *Discourse upon Usury,* ed. R. H. Tawney. London, 1925.

Workman, H. B. *John Wyclif.* 2 vols. Oxford, 1926.

Wright, Thomas (ed.). *Political Poems and Songs Relating to English History . . . from the Accession of Edward III to that of Richard III.* (Rolls Series.) 1861.

—— (ed.). *The Political Songs of England from the Reign of John to that of Edward III* (Camden Society.) 1839.

Wyclif, John. *De Blasphemia*, ed. M. H. Dziewicki. London, 1893.

————. *De Civili Dominio*, ed. R. L. Poole and J. Loserth. 4 vols. London, 1885-1904.

————. *De Officio Regis*, ed. A. W. Pollard and C. Sayle. London, 1887.

————. *De Simonia*, ed. Dr. Herzberg-Fränkel and M. H. Dziewicki. London, 1898.

————. *The English Works of Wyclif Hitherto Unprinted*, ed. F. D. Matthew. (E.E.T.S., O.S., No. 74.) 1880.

————. *Opera Minora*, ed. J. Loserth. London, 1913.

————. *Select English Works of John Wyclif*, ed. T. Arnold. 3 vols. Oxford, 1869-1871.

————. *Trialogus*, ed. G. V. Lechler. Oxford, 1869.

Zeeveld, W. G. *Foundations of Tudor Policy*. London, 1948.

Zilsel, E. "The Genesis of the Concept of Scientific Progress," *JHI*, VI (June, 1945), 325-349.

INDEX